SAP® Smart Forms

 **PRESS**

SAP PRESS is issued by
Bernhard Hochlehnert, SAP AG

SAP PRESS is a joint initiative of SAP and Galileo Press. The know-how offered by SAP specialists combined with the expertise of the publishing house Galileo Press offers the reader expert books in the field. SAP PRESS features first-hand information and expert advice, and provides useful skills for professional decision-making.

SAP PRESS offers a variety of books on technical and business related topics for the SAP user. For further information, please visit our website: *www.sap-press.com*.

Horst Keller, Joachim Jacobitz
ABAP Objects – The Official Reference
A comprehensive guide to all ABAP-language elements
2003, approx. 1100 pp., ISBN 1-59229-011-6

Frédéric Heinemann, Christian Rau
The Complete Guide for ABAP and Web developers
SAP Web Application Server
2003, approx. 600 pp., ISBN 1-59229-013-2

Sigrid Hagemann, Liane Will
SAP R/3 System Administration
2003, approx. 450 pp., ISBN 1-59229-014-4

A. Rickayzen, J. Dart, C. Brennecke, M. Schneider
Practical Workflow for SAP
2002, 504 pp., ISBN 1-59229-006-X

Helmut Stefani
Archiving Your SAP Data
A comprehensive guide to plan and execute archiving projects
2003, approx. 360 pp., ISBN 1-59229-008-6

Werner Hertleif, Christoph Wachter

SAP® Smart Forms

Creating forms quickly and easily—
no programming required!

04/21/2008

SAP PRESS

© 2003 by Galileo Press GmbH
SAP PRESS is an imprint of Galileo Press,
Boston (MA), USA
Bonn, Germany

German Edition first published 2002 by Galileo
Press.

Translation: Jeffrey S. Zalkind, Lemoine Inter-
national, Inc., Salt Lake City, UT
Proofreading: J.J. Andrews
Cover Design: department, Cologne,
Germany
Printed and bound in Germany

ISBN 978-1-59229-010-9
1st edition 2003, 4th reprint 2007

Contents

1 Introduction

1.1 Create Forms with Style

Documents that have a uniform, consistent design (forms) play an important role at every company:

▶ In relationships between business partners (for example, the entire sales order process, from purchase order to invoice to dunning notice)

▶ In internal business processes (in payroll accounting, for example, or in quality reports)

Thanks to their reproducible structure, forms help to organize the information contained within them, providing a stable foundation for functional communication. Although any given form (such as an invoice) will remain fairly constant over time, many different types of forms are required for day-to-day business. These forms can be output, and therefore distributed, on a printer or via electronic media such as fax, e-mail, and the Internet.

An effective ERP (enterprise resource planning) system has to support all these requirements. For the SAP system, the solution for Basis Release 4.6C and later is called **SAP Smart Forms**.

With its new graphical user interface, Smart Forms can help even occasional users to quickly get started with forms in the SAP system. Smart Forms not only reduces the time required to create and maintain forms; thanks to its intuitive graphical user interface, you can also implement many types of change to the form, without needing any programming skills whatsoever.

Smart Forms enables end users (or at least key users) to create and modify forms themselves. The direction of future forms development is clear: away from the specialists and towards everyday SAP end users. Smart Forms features the following functions:

▶ High performance, even during mass printing

▶ Integrated connection to the SAP Transport Organizer

▶ Support for various hardware platforms

▶ Multilingual capability

▶ Web publishing via XML output

In the medium term, forms created with Smart Forms will replace those designed using the former tool, SAPscript. Forms created with the new technology are already available for the primary applications, such as the Sales and Distribution

(SD), Financial Accounting (FI) and Human Resources Management (HR) modules, as well as in Customer Relationship Management (CRM) and Supply Relationship Management (SRM) within the mySAP.com solutions.

The conversion of the SAP system to Smart Forms is an ongoing process. New forms developed by SAP are designed exclusively in Smart Forms. Migration tools are available for migrating customer-designed SAPscript forms, although some manual postprocessing is required.

1.2 Using This Book

1.2.1 Book Structure

Smart Forms empowers SAP end users to create and modify forms themselves, which means that this task is no longer the exclusive domain of specialists. This book is dedicated particularly to end users like you, who are probably designing your own forms for the first time.

We assume that you, the reader, have not had much experience with form design to date. Accordingly, we want to help make your start in Smart Forms as easy as possible.

Despite the simplification provided by Smart Forms, designing and maintaining complex forms are still activities that require detailed skills, both in Smart Forms itself and in related areas. At a minimum, basic ABAP programming skills are required to include calculation routines in a form or to create a customer-specific main program.

This book provides the knowledge you need to carry out all these activities. Of course, you cannot learn everything at the same time. Accordingly, this book is divided into a series of steps that are intended to expand your knowledge successively for specific areas.

The book has the following structure:

▶ **Chapter 2:** Getting Started
If you are dealing with forms and their creation with Smart Forms for the first time, you should read this chapter, which provides a general, summarized introduction to the topic. If you do not have any experience with forms to date, you will benefit especially from the summary description of form layout theory provided in this chapter. You will work on exercises based on short, practical examples to learn the basic functions for developing forms with Smart Forms. The chapter concludes with an overview of all the basic elements that make up a form in Smart Forms.

► **Chapter 3:** Tools
Before you start developing forms, you might want to learn about the tools you will be using. Because Smart Forms is highly intuitive, however, you might also decide to skip this chapter at first and refer back to it only when necessary.

► **Chapter 4:** Form Layout
In this first detailed chapter on form design, you will learn how to define the layout of the form, using output areas to describe the pages of the form.

► **Chapter 5:** Elementary Node Types
This chapter introduces the elementary node types (texts, graphics) that are components of nearly every form. It concentrates mainly on the modules that require little experience with database queries—or at least no ABAP skills—as both this book and Smart Forms are aimed at users with a corresponding skill level.

► **Chapter 6:** Form Data
Nearly every form is used to output variable data, the contents of which are not known until the form is executed. In Smart Forms, this data is supplied through a main program. To design the form and correctly define and output the relevant data, however, you have to understand its structure. This chapter will help even users without database experience to understand the necessary connections.

► **Chapter 7:** Form Flow Logic
A form initially consists of individual text elements, data fields, and so on. In this chapter, you learn how to make sure that both the form pages and the data contained therein are output in the proper sequence (invoice items before invoice total, for example).

► **Chapter 8:** ABAP Programs in Forms
Despite all the features offered by the basic modules in Smart Forms, the modules you have seen so far cannot cover all the specific requirements of a form. In specific cases, you can write program code to meet a specific requirement directly in the form. This is the first time you will be confronted with ABAP programming. We do our best to give you a "soft landing" here as well. However, even experienced ABAP developers may find a useful tip or two on the special features that apply to the Smart Forms environment.

► **Chapter 9:** Main Program
No matter how much experience you have in designing forms, at some point, you will also have to create an individual main program for data retrieval and (print) output. In this chapter, you will see that this activity isn't as difficult as it seems: you can create a customized main program even if you have only rudimentary ABAP programming skills.

► **Chapter 10:** Special Output Processes

Smart Forms features a wide variety of output options. Each output device (printer, fax machine, e-mail, XML, and so on) has its own control parameters that the form and/or main program can use for output.

► **Chapter 11:** Migrating SAPscript Forms

Up to and including Release 4.6B of the SAP system, SAPscript was the standard tool for developing forms. This tool is still supported, particularly in light of the large number of SAPscript forms still in use. The advantages of Smart Forms over SAPscript have already been mentioned. Therefore, the migration of SAPscript forms to Smart Forms is an important issue. Although an integrated migration tool enables you to automate many aspects of migration, so many additional activities are required that it makes sense to describe them here.

► **Chapter 12:** New Features in Basis Release 6.1

SAP shipped Smart Forms for the first time with Basis Release 4.6C. The information contained in this book is based on Release 4.6C. The next Basis release, *Web Application Server 6.10*, features a variety of useful enhancements. Among other things, it now supports interactive processes that go far beyond the passive form output processes of the past. This chapter describes the enhancement in summary form. Changes to the specific functions in Release 6.1 are described in the appropriate places in the text.

► **Chapter 13:** Form Development Environment

During form development, every user will encounter related SAP functions that do not directly involve form development, such as Customizing output determination and troubleshooting with the debugger in the ABAP development environment. You will find it advantageous to have some basic knowledge in these areas as well, in order to better develop and check your forms. You will find this basic knowledge in this chapter. It is structured as a compendium with many sections that you can refer to as necessary.

► **Chapter 14:** Appendix

The Appendix contains sample printouts from the described forms and programs, as well as a brief introduction to the flight data model upon which all the examples are based. You will also find the selection of notes from SAPNet useful.

1.2.2 Where to Start

Here are a few tips to help you find the best place to start reading, depending on your current knowledge and skills:

▶ Beginners should start with *Getting Started* in Chapter 2. You should give yourself a good half-day for this chapter.

▶ If you have already had some experience with the tools in Smart Forms, you will probably want to start designing forms right away. The information you need starts in Chapter 4, *Form Layout*.

▶ If you are a program developer who has been asked to write a main program, Chapter 9, *Main Program*, will give you the information you need to integrate a new form in the system.

▶ Users experienced with SAPscript will probably be most interested in the differences between SAPscript and Smart Forms, and especially in the migration of existing forms. If this description applies to you, Chapter 11, *Migrating SAPscript Forms*, is the place to start.

1.2.3 General Information

When using this book, please remember the following:

▶ The name of the solution introduced in this book is *SAP Smart Forms*, or simply *Smart Forms*. This term refers to the full solution for creating forms in the SAP system. You use Smart Forms to create forms and styles, among other things. Therefore, the term "Smart Forms" always refers to the solution, *not* to individual forms. The full solution features various tools—such as the *Form Builder* and the *Style Builder*—that are introduced and described in this book.

▶ You use Smart Forms to create *forms* and *styles* (among other objects). Of course, these are general terms that have different meanings in other contexts. To distinguish the Smart Forms objects from such alternative definitions, you will see the long forms of the terminology when necessary, such as *SAPscript forms* or *form templates*.

▶ There are several ways to access the functions within Smart Forms: through the menu path, using the function keys, and clicking on the corresponding buttons or icons with the mouse:

  ▶ In most cases, only the specific menu path is named. This menu path is often related to the function key settings. You will usually be able to find the corresponding icon intuitively.

  ▶ When the described activity can also be reached by calling a main transaction, both the SAP menu path and the transaction code are listed.

▶ Menu paths that refer to the Implementation Guide, and not to the SAP *Easy Access* menu, are flagged with the prefix "IMG:".

▶ Smart Forms is a graphics-based solution for creating forms. As such, the mouse is an especially effective input instrument. When activities with the mouse are described, we refer to the *left* and *right mouse buttons*, and assume the standard mouse button settings. While we are aware that left-handed users often change these settings, we assume the default settings for simplicity's sake.

2 Getting Started

End users who are dealing with forms and their creation with Smart Forms for the first time should read this chapter, which provides a general introduction to the topic. If you do not have any experience with forms to date, you will benefit from the summarized description of form layout theory provided in this chapter. You will work on exercises based on short, practical examples to learn the basic functions for developing forms with Smart Forms. The chapter concludes with an overview of all the basic elements that make up a form in Smart Forms.

2.1 General Information on Form Development

2.1.1 Overview

Form processing with Smart Forms involves three basic elements:

▶ A form with the actual information on page breaks, texts, data, and so on

▶ A style (*Smart Style*) with information on formatting, such as font sizes, margins, line spacing, and so on

▶ An ABAP main program that supplies the data required in the form and initiates the output of the graphically formatted form

When you develop a form in Smart Forms, you have to coordinate these three elements. Usually, most of the work involved in developing forms entails adapting existing forms and styles to meet your company's specific requirements.

This task is simplified by the fact that a single main program can address several forms, as long as they largely involve the same data. In the medium term, data retrieval routines of this sort will be available for all SAP system modules that output data in forms (for example, divided by application to retrieve all the data required for invoicing).

Therefore, you can concentrate primarily on designing the form. In the process, you have to deal with two basic issues:

▶ The layout of the form (see Section 2.1.2)

▶ The flow logic in the form (see Section 2.1.3)

After this brief overview, you will work through an example that illustrates the specific procedures (Section 2.2). You will learn the most important functions for designing a form in Smart Forms. The chapter concludes with a tabular overview of all basic elements of a form (Section 2.3).

2.1.2   Form Layout

The blanket term *layout* encompasses all the possible settings that involve the arrangement of elements in a form.

When you use typical forms, you will discover that the same areas occur again and again. Take the invoice form, for example. It usually has output areas for the header and footer, as well as an address window for mailing the form to a business partner. In addition, many forms contain an area for outputting one or more items (the invoice items, in this case).

These output areas in the form are called *windows* in the SAP terminology. Figure 2.1 shows the invoice form that you will be using in the following exercises.

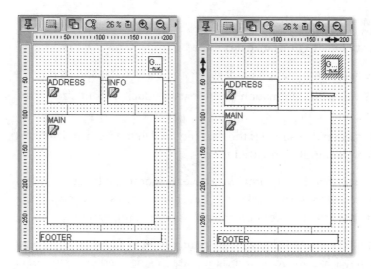

Figure 2.1 Page layout of the sample form

The figure is a screen shot from the *Form Painter*, a graphics-based tool in Smart Forms. It contains two different page layouts, which are explained further below.

First look at the rectangles that you see on each page. These are the output areas (windows). You can output information (as text, data, or graphics) only within one of these windows. You have to format this information so that it does not exceed the window size. This ensures, for example, that the information output on a pre-printed form, such as your company letterhead, remains within the specified areas.

Drawing this rough layout may seem a bit strange at first, as the actual contents are still missing. If you need further familiarization, you will find an identical invoice, filled with sample contents, in the Appendix. The purpose of this form is to output a customer's flight bookings and corresponding prices as invoice items in a table, using the large MAIN window in the center. The other windows will contain the information for your company logo, the customer's address, and other data (such as the person responsible, customer number, reference, date, and so on).

The screen shot from the Form Painter contains two pages, usually called the *first page* and *next page*. This is the regular practice, at least for forms involving correspondence between business partners: the first page is output on the specified letterhead, while the next pages contain a continuation of the items that did not fit in the first page.

The windows differ only slightly between the two pages. The next page, on the right, does not have an INFO window. Instead, only the page number is output in the margin, as you will see later.

2.1.3 Form Flow Logic

Figure 2.2 illustrates the flow of form output in graphical form. The graphic illustrates the most important difference between *draft pages* and *print pages*. The first page created with Smart Forms usually has only one print page. In contrast, the next page can have any number of print pages. Therefore, whenever this book mentions *pages* that were created with Smart Forms, it always refers to *draft pages*.

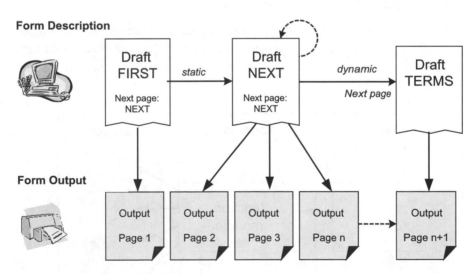

Figure 2.2 Form output with multiple pages

When the form is output, the windows defined in the layout are filled with real data from the application. When processing first/next pages, the output control in Smart Forms has to determine independently when to start a new print page with the layout of the next page.

In the case of your invoice, this determination is clear: if the invoice items (including the corresponding subtotals and totals lines) do not fit in the current print page, another print page has to be created. As a result, the invoice items play a special role in your form. To define this special status, the invoice items are output in a special window with type *main window* (in the example, MAIN is selected as the main window).

If the main window fills up during output and data is still outstanding, Smart Forms automatically opens a new (*static*) print page. In contrast to all other windows with type *secondary window*, a main window may occur only once in the entire form.

This sequence, with first page and next page, is the most common case of form logic. Please note, however, that a form in Smart Forms can contain any number of draft pages, such as your company's general terms and conditions as an attachment. In this case, additional criteria have to be determined in order to allocate the correct draft page to a print page (*dynamic page break*).

2.1.4 Form Data

Thus far, you have simply assumed that the required data was available when the form is output. The assigned main program supplies this data using a procedure that is completely separate from the form.

This separation of data retrieval and form is typical of Smart Forms, and is a decisive strength of its architecture: when you change the logic or the output format, you have to modify only the form, not the underlying main program and its ABAP coding.

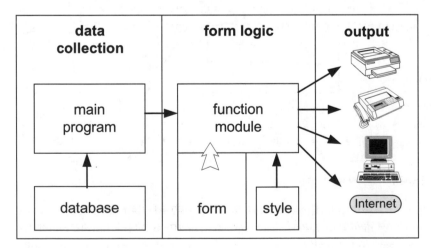

Figure 2.3 Separation of data and form

As a result of this fundamental separation between the main program and the form, there must be a defined interface between the two in order to transfer the data. To achieve this, a *function module* is generated automatically in the background when the form is activated. This function module contains all the settings that the main program needs to transfer the data and output the form.

Background: If you have never come into contact with the ABAP development in the SAP system before: ABAP is SAP's own programming language, and was also used to create most of the applications in the SAP system. An ABAP function module encapsulates program coding as an independent unit that can then be called by different applications. During the activation process, the form is transformed completely into a function module, which can then be called by an ABAP program just like any other function module.

Even though the benefits of separating data retrieval and the form are emphasized repeatedly throughout this book, you can also define options for retrieving and outputting specific data within the form itself. This feature can be very useful: thanks to the custom data retrieval routine, you do not have to revise the main program each time you add another piece of information. You can continue to use an existing main program in this case. This feature helps to standardize the system and prevents the main programs from multiplying uncontrollably.

2.1.5 Output

The last step in form development is usually its integration into the overall SAP system. In most cases, this requires configuration activities in Customizing (for output control, for example). In particular, these settings control the type of form used and its output time within a given business process. Fax and e-mail are available as output media in addition to conventional printer output.

XML for Smart Forms (*XSF*) is a new, certified interface to Smart Forms that enables data interchange using the open XML standard. Output in XML format enables you to display any form in a Web browser, and in the future will support active data interchange with the end user via Internet.

2.1.6 Tools

To design a form, you use graphics-based tools such as the *Form Builder*, *Form Painter*, and *Table Painter*. Figure 2.4 shows where form editing functions in Smart Forms are located in the SAP menu.

In the Form Builder, the entire form logic is modeled in a hierarchy tree, whose branches consists of individual *nodes*—for global settings, windows, texts, or graphics, for example. You can make changes by selecting the corresponding attributes or by dragging and dropping with the mouse.

In the graphics-based Form Painter, you can even create and resize form windows directly with the mouse—simply by tracing a blank form, where applicable.

You can check and test individual nodes or the entire form. In the process, Smart Forms provides information about possible causes of the errors.

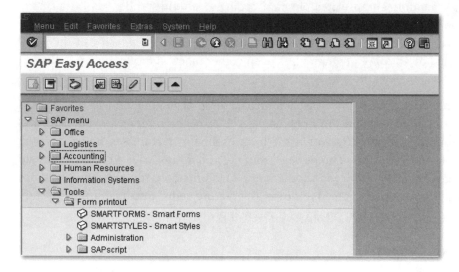

Figure 2.4 Call via SAP menu

In the next section, you will process a specific example to familiarize yourself with form development in Smart Forms.

2.2 Sample Exercise

2.2.1 Requirements

You will first learn how to create and output a new form in Smart Forms, based on a brief tutorial. This form is based on a course example that is used in the relevant SAP course, albeit with slightly modified contents. This example is contained in all SAP systems with Release 4.6C and later (IDES and the standard delivery system).

The example form does not use data from an actual SAP module, but instead is based on the *SAP flight data model*, a module that is also used only for demonstration and training purposes. Its corresponding tables describe the flight operations of various airlines, with customers, timetables, bookings, and so on. As far as the sample applications are concerned, the relevant information from the flight data model is summarized in the Appendix.

The form in the example corresponds to an invoice for all flights that a customer has booked with various airlines. In the following, it is referred to as the *flight invoice*. Like any form in Smart Forms, you need two primary components for the flight invoice:

▶ A form created in Smart Forms (SF_EXAMPLE_01)
▶ A main program that supplies the appropriate data and triggers form output (also called SF_EXAMPLE_01 in this case)

To output the flight invoice, proceed as follows:

▶ Start the main program.
▶ Choose the appropriate data (the customer, for example).
▶ Output the data as a print preview or view directly via printer, fax machine, and so on.

Steps in the Sample Exercise

As simple as the steps for outputting the flight invoice seem, you first have to overcome a minor obstacle if you are working in a client other than *000* (which is usually the case) or with a language other than *DE*. In this case, instead of the requested printout of the flight invoice, you will see an error message from the system due to missing text modules.

This is the problem you have to solve first. Getting started involves the following steps:

1. First, create or copy the required text module (*standard text*). This lets you avoid the error message described above, and the form contains all the necessary run attributes.
2. You can then view the sample form SF_EXAMPLE_01 for the flight invoice and conduct tests with it.
3. Before you make any changes to the sample form, create a copy. You then have your own custom form for the flight invoice that you can revise over time as necessary.
4. To learn the basic functions for designing forms in Smart Forms, you will make several proposed changes to your new form.
5. At the end of this introduction, you will create an independent main program, which forms the basis for the exercises in the subsequent chapters.

You should give yourself a good half-day for this exercise. When you are finished, you will be familiar with many of the components for maintaining forms in Smart Forms.

> **Note:** In order to carry out the exercises in the system, your user ID must have the necessary authorizations in your test system:
>
> ▶ First of all, you need access to form editing (menu path **Tools · Form printout**, for example, transaction SMARTFORMS).
>
> ▶ Even though you will not be changing any original SAP forms or programs during the exercises in this book, you have to be registered as a developer at SAP in order to create the main program for the form.
>
> ▶ For the same reason, you also need access to the ABAP development environment (*ABAP Workbench*).

2.2.2 Preparation: Creating the Standard Text

To output the sample form for the flight invoice, SF_EXAMPLE_01, a specific text module has to exist in the system, but is not present in all installations. It exists only in client 000 and language DE. Check this module and create it if necessary.

> **Background:** Text modules are standardized texts that are saved in a central location in the SAP system. These texts can be integrated in several different forms. If you have to change the contents of the text module, you do this in the central location. The changes are then made automatically in all the affected forms. Typical examples of such text modules are seasonal advertising texts, for example, and standardized company headers and footers.

You could also use text modules to create forms in SAPscript, where they are referred to as *standard texts*. To ensure compatibility with existing texts in the system, Smart Forms can read these SAPscript texts and include them in a form. This is exactly what happens in your sample form.

Start the maintenance transaction for standard texts from the SAP menu, using path **Tools · Form printout · SAPscript · Standard text (SO10)**.

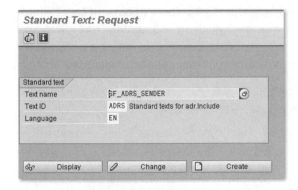

Figure 2.5 Standard text in SAPscript (initial screen)

The required standard text is shown in Figure 2.5. It is essential that you enter the text name exactly as shown in Figure 2.5. When you enter the text, change the text ID to ADRS, since it is probably set to ST initially.

Then choose menu path **Standard text · Display** or the corresponding pushbutton to see whether the text exists. If not, you have two possible alternatives:

▶ Choose **Utilities · Copy from Client** to copy the text from source client 000, which is the fastest method for language DE.

▶ Choose **Standard text · Create** to enter a new text directly.

Both alternatives are explained in brief below.

Copying a Text from Client 000

When you call the menu path to copy from another client, a dialog box like the one in Figure 2.6 appears. Enter the information as shown in the diagram. If you happen to be working in language DE, you are already finished. Because the text is defined only in language DE, it is also copied only with this language attribute.

Copy Texts Between Clients	
Text name	SF_ADRS_SENDER
Object name	TEXT
Text ID	*
Language	*
Source client	000
Target name	SF_ADRS_SENDER
✔ Action log	
✔ Overwrite after confirmation	

Figure 2.6 Copying a standard text between clients

If you are logged on in a different language, first call the generated text for processing through the initial screen, as shown in Figure 2.5, and then use **Standard text · Save as**… to save it with the appropriate target language. You can also take this opportunity to change the contents of the text module, if necessary.

Repeat these steps for standard text ADRS_FOOTER, which is also required in the form. You can then output the form (see Section 2.2.3).

Creating a New Text

To create a new text directly, choose **Standard text · Create** or use the corresponding pushbutton, as shown in Figure 2.5. Set the language to the logon language you will use to output the sample form. A window for processing the SAPscript texts appears. The text is the sender line in the address window. Figure 2.7 shows one proposal for the text. You can use it or enter a text of your choice.

If your text editor looks slightly different, then the *line editor* mode is probably active in your system. If necessary, choose menu path **Goto · Change Editor** to switch to the graphics mode shown in Figure 2.7.

Figure 2.7 Processing a standard text in SAPscript

Formatting

Before you save your entries, you have to reformat them, since the sender line is usually printed in a small font (to fit in a window envelope, for example). This is not the case so far.

In Smart Forms, as in SAPscript, the possible format statements are contained in different *styles*. A suitable style for output in an address window is defined in the system. The style belongs to the header information of the text. To check the current settings, choose menu path **Goto · Header**.

You can configure the correct formatting with two steps:

1. Choose menu path **Format · Change Style** and select entry **SAPADRS** in the list of styles

2. In the format list, change the paragraph format from **standard format** to **SD window ADDRESS Brief sender**.

The text should now be so small that you can hardly read it on the screen.

Completion

Save the new standard text and exit the word processing screen. Repeat the above steps for standard text ADRS_FOOTER, which is required in the footer area of the form.

2.2.3 Outputting the Sample Form

Once you have completed these minor tasks, you are finally ready to get started with the world of Smart Forms. To begin, choose SAP menu path **Tools · Form printout · Smart Forms (SMARTFORMS)**.

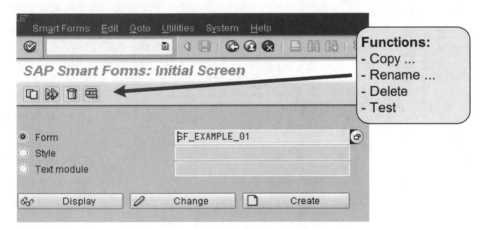

Figure 2.8 Initial screen for Smart Forms

The initial screen for Smart Forms (Figure 2.8) provides three options:

The first and most important option lets you edit the forms in Smart Forms. You have already entered the name of the sample form; you can also use the input help to display a list of all the forms defined in the system.

▶ You have already used **styles** once before, when you formatted the sender line. They contain paragraph and line formats. Use this option to maintain the styles for the forms in Smart Forms.

▶ The last option, **Text Module,** is similar to the function you just used for SAPscript. Use this option to maintain text modules that are used specifically for Smart Forms (this has several advantages, which are described further below).

Before you call the form for the first time, choose menu path **Smart Forms · Generate**. This is just in case no one has ever viewed the form in your system before. During this activity, the appropriate function module, which you will need for the tests later, is generated in the background.

Because the flight invoice is part of the standard SAP system, you can make only limited changes to the original form. Therefore, you will create your own copy of the form in a later step. Press the **Display** button to gain a first impression of the form. The editing screen for the form is displayed in the *Form Builder*.

Now open the *Form Painter*, a graphical tool for designing forms. To do this, choose menu path **Utilities · Form Painter On/Off** or press the equivalent pushbutton in the toolbar. Your screen should then look something like Figure 2.9.

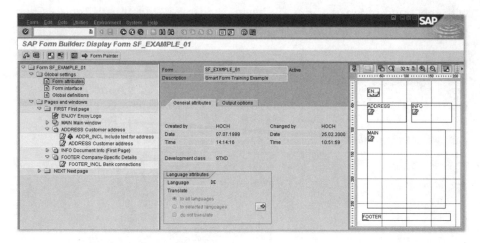

Figure 2.9 Overview of Form Builder and Form Painter

The display consists of three areas:

▶ On the right-hand side of the form is Form Painter with its graphical overview of the current page. Note the separate areas (the *windows*). The page sections already illustrate the major divisions, as in typical business correspondence: windows for the address and the footer, and a window for outputting the items in the body. In this case, the items are the flight bookings. If you look at the sample printout in the Appendix, you will immediately recognize the windows, which contain real data there.

▶ On the left-hand side, the Form Builder shows the hierarchy of all the elements in the form (including the windows that you see in the Form Painter on the right) in a *navigation tree*. Each element in the form is represented by a single node in the navigation tree. The nodes of the navigation tree are your guideline to processing the form. You can use them to control all the functions in the form. Individual nodes can each have subnodes. This creates *subtrees* or *branches*, which you can expand and collapse by clicking the mouse.

▶ In the center of the screen, the Form Builder displays the attributes of the selected node. The corresponding user inputs will usually take place here. These *node attributes* are distributed among several tab pages, grouped by topic. Almost all nodes have the tab pages **Output options** and **Conditions**.

If you have ever used the new *SAP Easy Access* menu, you will already be familiar with the basic functions in the navigation tree. You can select any node in the navigation tree by double-clicking it, or you can select a window node directly in the Form Painter.

A Brief Tour of the Navigation Tree

The **Pages and windows** branch contains two page nodes named FIRST and NEXT. Of course, you can also create and output forms that contain more than two pages. In this example, the layout of the NEXT page is used for all print pages from page 2 onward. Double-click to select each of the two pages in turn. The corresponding node attributes are updated automatically, along with the graphical layout display of the respective page in the Form Painter.

Open the subordinate branches for the FIRST page in the navigation tree. In the next level, the page is divided into individual sections, which are referred to above as *windows*. These windows, with their sizes and locations, are also displayed in the Form Painter. Click on one of the windows in the navigation tree to select it. The corresponding window in the Form Painter is selected automatically (this selection works in the opposite direction as well).

Address Information

Now open window node ADDRESS, which is designed for output in the address window. It has two subnodes: ADDR_INCL is responsible for outputting the sender line, and ADDRESS is responsible for outputting the customer address.

Choose tab page **General attributes** under the attributes for node ADDR_INCL (sender line). The selection list for input field **Text type** shows that several different options are available for integrating a text into the form. In this case, **Include text** is the default setting. You use it to include an SAPscript text. The **Text key** area contains a direct reference to the standard text that you entered in the previous step.

> **Note:** You will also see the attribute **No error if no text exists**. It is *not* set. Therefore, if you try to output the form and the standard text does not exist, an error message will appear and the form will not be output.

Settings for the Entire Form

You should now be familiar with the form layout. To finish your initial tour of the form, take a look at the top node in the navigation tree, **Global settings**. This node contains settings that apply to the entire form. The **Form interface** node, for example, contains all the parameters for exchanging data with the corresponding main program.

If you choose subnode **Form attributes**, for example, the name of the form appears, followed by the status—**active** or **inactive**. Only active forms have the necessary function module that reflects all the form settings and enables output via the main program.

Testing the Function Module for the Form

When you activate the form, a function module is automatically generated in the background. The main program will use this function module to output the form. You will now subject this function module to a brief test, in which no data is output yet.

To do so, perform the following steps:

▶ Choose menu path **Form · Test** or press **F8** in the Form Builder. The name of the generated function module appears. This is also the initial screen for the *Function Builder*, which is normally used to maintain function modules in the SAP development system (therefore, the test function you use here is merely "borrowed" from there).

> **Note:** If the system reports "No function module has been generated yet", you forgot to generate the function module as described at the start of Section 2.2.3. Please do so now, if necessary.

▶ Now choose menu path **Function Module · Test · Individual test** or press **F8**. A list of all the interface parameters that the function module expects from the main program appears. Theoretically, you can also enter data here; however, the method using the real main program is preferred in most cases.

▶ Now choose menu path **FModules · Execute** or press **F8**. A dialog box for the printer appears. You have to specify a printer here, even if you only want to display the **print preview**. Choose your local printer or simply LOCL.

▶ Then press the **Print preview** button or press **F8** again.

You now see a flight invoice with minimized form contents. Because you outputted the form without any data, it does not contain an address and the list of flight bookings is blank (you can easily tell where the data would appear, however). Only the contents of the INFO window (in the upper right) are completely visible—with all the corresponding data—because they are fixed in the form definition.

You have just learned how to access the test function via the menu in great detail. However, the fastest way to start the test is simply to press the **F8** key four times in a row. Icons are also available for this purpose in the toolbar of the Form Builder and the other tools.

Outputting the Form via the Main Program

In order to output the flight invoice correctly, you have to call a suitable main program. The main program is just like any other ABAP program, which means that you can execute it using transaction SA38 or via the application menu at **System · Services · Reporting**. The name of the appropriate program for the flight invoice is SF_EXAMPLE_01.

Start the program as usual, with the Execute icon, the **F8** key, or the menu.

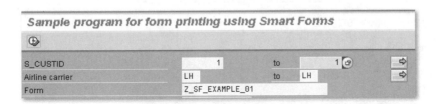

Figure 2.10 Sample program for form printing

A selection screen for the flight data appears, like the one shown in Figure 2.10.

▶ Choose the customer number and airline as proposed (the corresponding data should be contained in your tables).

▶ The selection screen also enables you to specify the appropriate form. SF_EXAMPLE_01 is the default value, which means that you can start the output immediately.

The standard spool dialog box appears. Choose your local printer or simply LOCL. The latter will print the form on your local (Windows) printer. If you want to save paper, use the print preview.

You have now gained a first impression of what the basic version of the flight invoice offers. You will find a printout of the form in the Appendix, to compare with the one from your system.

Now that you have successfully printed your first form, you will next make several changes in order to get to know more functions in Smart Forms. To do this, you first have to create a working copy of the sample form.

2.2.4 Creating Your Own Form as a Working Copy

In order to make changes to the flight invoice, you first have to create a copy of the sample form. You can then experiment freely with your new form.

First return to the initial screen in Smart Forms in the SAP menu, via **Tools · Form printout · Smart Forms (SMARTFORMS)**. Enter the sample form again, SF_ EXAMPLE_01.

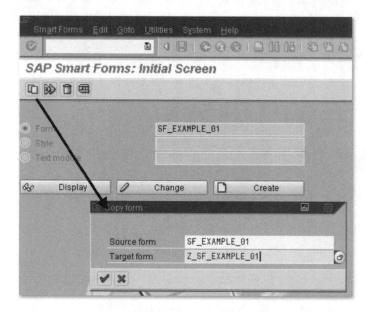

Figure 2.11 Copying a form in the Smart Forms initial screen

Then, in the initial screen, choose menu path **Smart Forms · Copy** or use the corresponding icon in the toolbar.

The system prompts you to enter the name of the new form as shown in Figure 2.11. Choose a name from the customer namespace (that is, one starting with Z or Y). We recommend naming your form Z_SF_EXAMPLE_01, as shown in the picture. Please be sure to use this name, as this new sample form is referred to frequently throughout the course of the book.

Once you confirm the name, the system prompts you to enter several attributes of the new form. These attributes ensure that the form is properly integrated in the SAP development environment (see Figure 2.12).

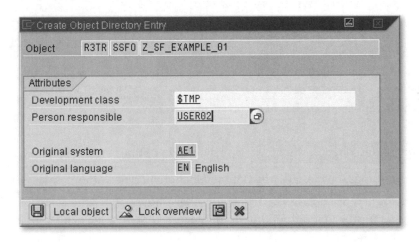

Figure 2.12 Object directory entry for form

Your user ID is proposed automatically as the administrator (person responsible) for the new form.

It is even more important to assign a development class. The development class defines such things as how your form is saved in the system, and determines whether it will be transported to a production system later. The transport is not the goal of this exercise, however. Keep your experiments private for now. Development class $TMP is defined in all SAP installations for this purpose. It makes the new form a *local object* that cannot be transported into other SAP installations, but does not otherwise restrict what you can do with the form.

You can enter development class $TMP manually or press the **Local Object** button. In the latter case, the input screen is also closed, placing you back in the initial screen. The new form name is now proposed directly in the initial screen for further processing.

Activating the Form

Although you have now created a new form as a copy of an existing one, you cannot really use it (that is, output it) until you activate it. Therefore, press the **Change** button to switch to change mode for the form.

First check the status of the form in the **Form attributes** node in the navigation tree of the Form Builder. The form's **inactive** status appears after the form name.

Activate your form with menu path **Form · Activate** or using the corresponding icon in the toolbar. During this process, the entire form is subjected to a check and then set to **active**. The corresponding function module is also generated automatically.

> **Note:** When you activate the form, you will probably see several warning messages for your flight invoices, which you see in an additional window below the node attributes. You will deal with these messages later. Right now, the only important thing is that you see "Form Z_SF_EXAMPLE_01 activated" in the status bar. This means the form has been saved and can now be output.

Test the form as described in the previous section. Two options are available:

▶ Press **F8** four times for the quick test of the function module without data.

▶ Via main program SF_EXAMPLE_01 in reporting: Choose the same selection parameters as for the first output, but do not forget to change the name of the form (Z_…).

2.2.5   Changing Your Form

You will now make the following changes to your copied form, Z_SF_EXAMPLE_01:

▶ Eliminate the warnings that appear when you activate the form.

▶ Change and move the contained graphic.

▶ Change texts in the invoice form.

You should test the form again and output it after each change.

Eliminating the Warnings

When you open the form in the Form Builder, the warnings you saw the last time you activated it are no longer displayed. To see them, you can activate the form again. Alternatively, you can use the function **Form · Check.**

The same checks are performed as during **activation**. As long as at least one error message is displayed, this **check** is the preferred method, since the last activated version of the form is still available for execution in this case. Individual checks exist for each node in addition to the overall check. They are described in detail later in this book.

After the overall check, you will probably see three warning messages for the flight invoice, as shown in Figure 2.13.

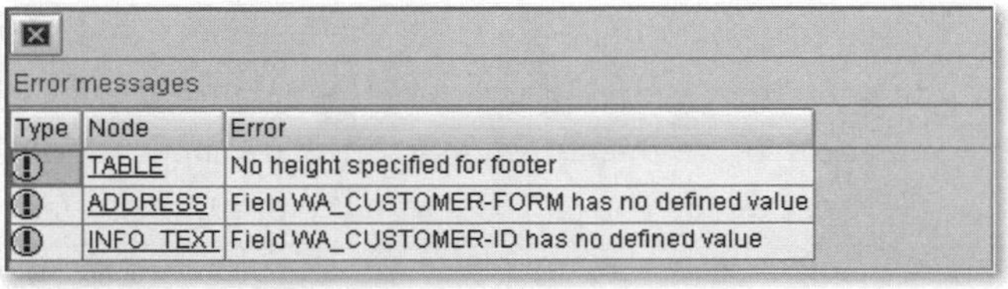

Type	Node	Error
☉	TABLE	No height specified for footer
☉	ADDRESS	Field WA_CUSTOMER-FORM has no defined value
☉	INFO TEXT	Field WA_CUSTOMER-ID has no defined value

Error messages

Figure 2.13 Error messages after overall check

Smart Forms distinguishes between two categories of messages: *error messages* and *warning messages*. If error messages appear, the form is not activated and cannot be output. This type of message is indicated by an icon in the first column (only warning messages occur in your example).

To simplify things, however, only *error messages* are mentioned in the following, and refer to both warning and error messages.

Adjusting the footer

An error message always contains the name of the corresponding node and a description of the contents. Because the system cannot always differentiate between the cause and the effect of an error, however, we recommend a somewhat loose interpretation of the reported messages in order to determine the actual cause.

When you double-click on the information for a node, that node is selected and highlighted accordingly in the navigation tree and the Form Painter. In the node attributes, the tab page where the error is suspected appears. Try this with the first message for node TABLE: the corresponding tab page, **Events**, is displayed. It contains an input field for the height of a footer area (which is described in more detail further below). Choose "1 cm" as the entry (the amount and unit of measure are located in separate input fields).

Now repeat the overall check. The first warning message should no longer appear.

Field has no defined value

The two remaining warning messages refer to problems with *fields*. This usually involves data that the main program passes on to the form. Obviously, the system performs a check of the field contents.

Navigate to one of the nodes that has an error message. One of these nodes contains the output of the customer address to which the invoice will be sent. You cannot change anything in the data retrieval here, however. Therefore, the note in the error message does not help you here.

> **Background:** As you already know from your initial tests, the data for the customer is specified by the selection in the main program. This data is passed on to the form correctly during execution, as you can see from the printouts so far. Therefore, the message itself does not make any sense. You could almost say that Smart Forms does not perform the check properly in this case, and the check routine itself is the problem. This issue is discussed in more detail further below.

A trick can help you suppress the warning messages and satisfy the check routine: the fields have to be mentioned as active variables somewhere else in the form. Therefore, proceed as follows:

▶ Open the **Global definitions** node in the **global settings**, and then the **Initialization** tab page. You will see a blank list of output parameters in the upper right. Enter WA_CUSTOMER here. The system now responds as if values have already been assigned to the corresponding field.

▶ Now repeat the overall check. It should end without any error messages.

Activate the changed form. We suggest another output test via the main program. Remember to use the correct form name starting with Z_…

Changing and Moving a Graphic

In the previous printout, as well as in the graphical display of the Form Painter, you can see that the flight invoice contains a graphic in the upper left-hand corner. You will now choose a different graphic and change its position in the form at the same time.

Assigning a new graphic

First select the node for a graphic. You will find it in node ENJOY on the FIRST page or by selecting the corresponding window with the mouse in the Form Painter. The node attributes in the center screen area are updated automatically.

The name of the graphic appears in the **General attributes** tab page and can be changed accordingly. An **F4** value help function is available for this field, and displays all the graphics defined in the system.

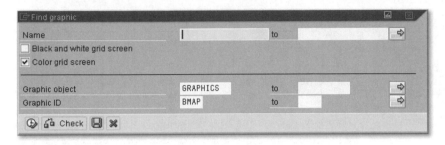

Figure 2.14 Selecting a graphic

Choose the default settings in the selection screen as shown in Figure 2.14. Make certain to also choose **Black and white grid screen**. All the suitable graphics defined in the system are displayed.

For example, select the graphic SAPSCRIPT_SMALL_DOG. Although it is defined only in black and white, you will use it frequently in the later chapters. Once you have added the graphic to the form, press **Return**. The new contents and format are then copied to the Form Painter.

Resizing the graphic

Obviously, this graphic is quite small. You can change the node attribute **Resolution** in the **General attributes** to change the size later. Experiment a bit with the defined resolutions or simply choose "75". This is a suitable size for your sample form.

Note: The resolution of the graphic is specified in *dpi* (*dots per inch*). If you increase the space between the dots, the graphic occupies a larger area. It is output with a larger size, but the display is rougher due to the lower resolution.

If you subsequently change the resolution subsequently to a smaller value, clarity is always lost in the printout. Therefore, you should only use only graphics that already have a suitable original size in a production form. If you do not specify a resolution in the node attributes, the system automatically uses the size from the original graphic data.

Changing the position of the graphic

Now change the location of the graphic as shown in Figure 2.15.

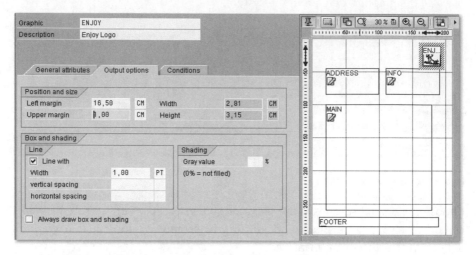

Figure 2.15 Output options for the graphic

Choose the **Output options** tab page in the node attributes. You can configure the location using the coordinates for the left and top boxes. But be careful: if you specify values that are too large, you may push the graphic completely off the page. A corresponding warning message indicates such situations in the later over-all check. Change the left margin to "17.0 cm" and the upper margin to "0.5 cm" and press **Return** to confirm.

You will also see the size and height of the graphic in the node attributes. The system calculates these values from the original size of the graphic, based on the selected resolution. Therefore, you cannot change the values here.

The new position of the graphic is immediately visible in the Form Painter. Even better, you can move the graphic directly with the mouse. To do this, position the cursor in the graphics window and drag it to the desired location. The entries in the node attribute fields change accordingly.

Node name

Each node has an ID and a name. Because you have changed the graphic, these terms no longer fit the node. Change the entries to GRAPHIC and LOGO; you are now independent of the actual name of the graphic. Activate the form, which saves it automatically.

> **Exercise:** The form also has a NEXT page, which is used to output the form from page two onwards if the flight bookings do not all fit on the first page. Select the graphics node in this page as well and move it to the right. Did you wonder why the graphic still appeared on the left in this form, even though the contents of the graphic and the node name have been changed, like as in the FIRST page? This is not an error—it is a feature in Smart Forms that you will use to your advantage in later chapters.

Changing the Invoice Text

In this step, you will see how to change the texts in the invoice that appear before and after the list of flight bookings to meet your needs.

These texts are located in the MAIN window, together with the table of booked flights, which is the most important window in the form. If the customer's invoice contains a large number of flights, there may not be enough space on the first page to print them all. Smart Forms detects this situation automatically and opens another print page. However, this check is performed only for one (special) window in the form, the *main window* (aptly named MAIN in the example). This special status is indicated by the corresponding node attribute **Main window** in the **General attributes** tab page.

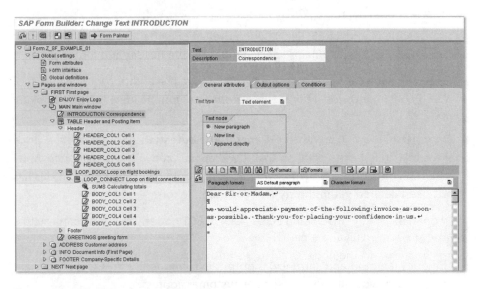

Figure 2.16 Editing texts in the main window

Open the INTRODUCTION node below MAIN, as shown in Figure 2.16 above, and then open the **General attributes** tab page in the node attributes. You can use the mini text editor here to change the introductory text in the invoice as necessary.

Paragraph and character formats are available for formatting the texts in a text node (see Figure 2.16). If you want to print only a single word or character with *bold* type, select the corresponding part of the text and then choose the desired character format. The inline editor provides word processing functions that should be familiar from most standard programs, and are therefore not explained in any detail here.

> **Note:** The configured paragraph/character formats have to be defined in a style (as a *Smart Style*). To see which style is currently assigned to a form, choose the **Form attributes** node and then the **Output options** tab page under the global settings in the navigation tree.

You can use the same procedure to edit the GREETINGS node at the end of the invoice.

Outputting the Items

Obviously, the flight bookings have to be output between the two text nodes INTRODUCTION and GREETINGS. Open the TABLE node. In addition to another node, LOOP_BOOK, it contains special nodes for the header and footer areas.

▶ Open the node for the **header area**. You will see five additional nodes, each of which contain individual texts; these are the column headers for your booking table.

▶ Open HEADER_COL5 with the **General attributes** tab page. Move the **price** three tab stops to the right, so that it will appear above the actual price information in the output. A right-aligned format would be useful here, but this has not been defined yet in the style of your sample form.

Now open the LOOP_BOOK and LOOP_CONNECT nodes. They control the actual output of the bookings.

▶ The price (amount and currency) is output in subnode BODY_COL5. Fields are used here, as you already saw for the customer address.

▶ You also see that all the text elements together represent one output line for the flight bookings. The higher-level node LOOP_CONNECT (with repeated processing of the lines, depending on the number of flight bookings) lets you output the multiple, consecutive lines for each respective booking. The versatile options for controlling such output are described in detail in Chapter 7.

Completion

Activate the form, which saves it automatically. Use program SF_EXAMPLE_01 to output the new version of the flight invoice again, making sure that you specify the correct form with Z_...

Before you exit the form, take a bit of time to explore the other functions for maintaining nodes, which are the real "meat and potatoes" that you will use nearly every day during form development.

Addendum: Managing Nodes

So far, you have learned about the important node types for the **page**, **window**, **graphic**, and **text**. However, you have not learned how to manage these nodes yet (create, change, delete, and so on). Both the navigation tree and the Form Painter contain a comprehensive context menu, which you should be familiar with from the SAP system.

Position the mouse on any node in the Form Builder navigation tree and press the right mouse button. A context menu with all the administration functions that are possible for the current node appears, like the one shown in Figure 2.17 below.

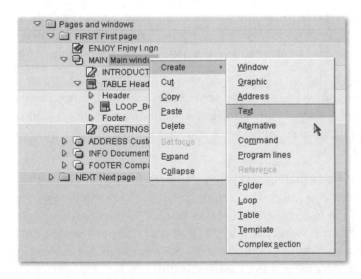

Figure 2.17 Functions for a node in the context menu

You now see a list of all the node types that are available in Smart Forms. These nodes are described in detail in the later chapters. The context menu contains only the node types that can be used as subnodes for the currently selected node. Figure 2.17 shows the selection for the MAIN node. Try calling the context menu for one of the page nodes in the list, such as FIRST.

When you create a form, you frequently have to move and copy nodes, such as text nodes. Instead of using the corresponding functions in the context menu, you can often work faster with the mouse (*Drag&Drop*). To do so, position the cursor on the appropriate node, click and hold the left mouse button, and drag the node to another position. You just moved the node. Hold down the **Control key** when you drag the object to create a copy of the object in the target location. If you are not already familiar with this technique from other applications, you will learn how to use it quickly.

> **Note:**
>
> ▶ Not all nodes are logical in every location. If you move the mouse over an "illegal" zone of the navigation tree, the cursor changes accordingly.
>
> ▶ In some cases, the Form Builder cannot automatically determine the desired target location of a node (below or after an existing node, for example). An additional prompt appears in this case.

2.2.6 Creating a Custom Main Program

Until now, you have been able to use the standard main program, SF_EXAMPLE_ 01, for all your outputs. Because the name of the form is queried as a parameter in the selection screen, you can also retrieve the new, copied sample form from there.

This procedure shows that you can use the same main program to output many different forms. The only condition is that the forms in question have to use similar data, which the main program supplies. Since you have merely copied a form so far, this condition is fulfilled.

You may have found it a bit irritating that you had to overwrite the default setting for the form name each time you tested the output, since the definition of the form name is fixed in the main program. Because you will be making changes to the main program later on anyway, you might as well start now, and create a custom main program for form output—initially with a different form name. Here, as well, you usually start with a copy of an existing main program, which you can then change as necessary.

Steps to Create a Custom Main Program

You use the *ABAP Editor* in the development environment to create programs. The tool is located in the SAP menu under **Tools · ABAP Workbench · Development · ABAP Editor (SE38)**.

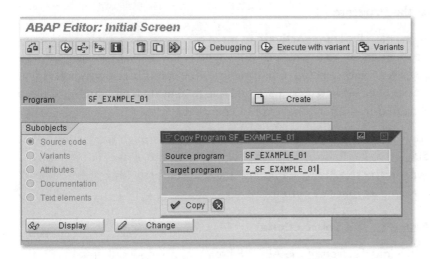

Figure 2.18 Copying programs via the ABAP Editor

In the initial screen, select the name of the sample program and then choose **Program · Copy**. We suggest naming the program Z_SF_EXAMPLE_01 (see Figure 2.18).

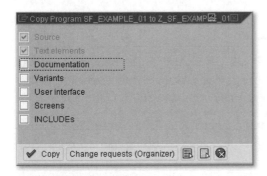

Figure 2.19 Options for copying a program

An additional prompt, like the one in Figure 2.19, appears. So far, your program does not contain any independent objects. Therefore, press the **Copy** button to continue. The prompt for the object directory entry, which you also saw when you copied the form (see Figure 2.12), appears. You should use this new program only as a *local object* (development class $TMP).

The copy is now created; see the message in the status bar at the bottom of the screen. The new program immediately appears in the initial screen of the transaction. Check the program using the same icon 🔓 as under Smart Forms. You should not see any error messages.

Starting the Program

Choose menu path **Program · Activate** to make the program executable. Depending on the situation, an additional prompt window may appear, in which the current program is already selected. Confirm again. The status bar now indicates that the object has been activated. You always have to activate a program—just like a form in Smart Forms—after you create or change it.

You can now execute the program directly, instead of through transaction SA38, which you used so far. To do so, choose **Program · Execute**. Make sure you use the correct form in the selection parameters (the one starting with Z_...). The result will be the same as your last output test.

First Change to the Source Code

Return to the initial screen of the ABAP Editor. You will now call up and edit the source text for the first time. Which, of course, gives you the perfect opportunity to specify your copied form correctly in the main program.

Open the source text in change mode as shown in Figure 2.20. As you can see, the default setting for the form name appears in program line 13. The current line number of the cursor item appears as a navigation aid in the status bar at the bottom of the editor window. The exact structure of the corresponding ABAP statement will be dealt with in a later chapter.

Write the name of the new form (such as Z_SF_EXAMPLE_01) between the single quotation marks. Activate the program again and execute it as a test. The correct form name should now appear automatically in the selection screen.

You're done! You have now created and changed your first program. You can now execute your new program from within the regular reporting transaction, SA38.

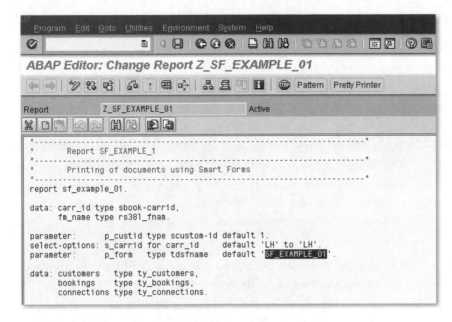

Figure 2.20 Changing the form name in the main program

2.3 Overview of Node Types

In the previous sections, a practical example showed you the basic functions in Smart Forms. You have seen how a form is modeled in a navigation tree in the *Form Builder*. Each branch of this tree consists of a certain number of individual nodes whose attributes completely describe the form. Each node has to have a certain type, depending on what you want it to do in the form.

The navigation tree of each form has two root nodes that are created automatically when you create a new form:

▶ The **Global settings** branch, which always contains the subnodes **Form attributes**, **Form interface** and **Global definitions**, which you use to maintain the form-wide attributes and settings.

▶ The **Pages and windows** branch, in which you create the pages in the form—with all necessary elements—as subnodes. Smart Forms determines the sequence in which the nodes are processed during output, based on their arrangement in the overall structure. You can only create page nodes on the first level, and only windows or other node types that define the attributes of a window (graphic, address, and so on) in the subordinate levels.

Note:

▶ The subnodes **Form attributes**, **Form interface**, and **Global definitions** are referred to frequently in the coming chapters. You will always find these nodes in the **Global settings** branch..

▶ As you gain more experience in working with Smart Forms, you will quickly realize that references to **Form attributes** or similar on terms always refer to the identically named node in the navigation tree. Therefore, the addition "node" is often omitted in such references in the following chapters.

▶ All the nodes that you insert when designing a form are located under the **Pages and windows** branch. This is not always mentioned explicitly in the definition of subordinate nodes in the coming chapters.

From the information in this brief introduction, you can see that the position of the node in the navigation tree has a decisive influence on the form output, in addition to the node type. Because the nodes in a branch can influence one another, you cannot define every node as a subnode of every other node. Accordingly, the overview of node types below lists not only their respective meanings, but also the types of possible subnodes for each node type.

Node type	Meaning	Possible subnodes
Node types with layout attributes (layout nodes)		
Page	Draft page of the form	Window, graphic, address
Window	Output area in a page, differentiated between main window and secondary window	All types except window and page nodes
Template	Output of a static table	All types except window and page nodes
Table	Output of a dynamic table with any amount of application data	All types except window and page nodes
Elementary nodes (without subnodes)		
Text	Used to output all texts and data except addresses	None
Graphic	Places graphics in a form (in addition to one background image as a direct attribute of each page node)	None

Table 2.1 Overview of node types

Node type	Meaning	Possible subnodes
Address	Includes an address; the address data is read directly from database tables and formatted for print output	None
Flow control		
Command	Special functions such as start new page, reset paragraph numbering, and output special commands for printer control	None
Loop	Enables the repeated processing of all subnodes; depends on the number of data records in an internal table	All types except window and page nodes
Table	Dynamic data output like in the loop, with the addition of format specifications via output tables	All types except window and page nodes
Alternative	Branch dependent on a condition	Direct subnodes are automatically the event nodes TRUE and FALSE. Its subnodes: all but window and page nodes
Other nodes		
Folder	Set of subnodes grouped together for organizational purposes	All types except window and page nodes
Complex section	Can simulate one of the following node types: template, table, loop, and folder (no longer used)	Depends on the simulation mode
Program liens	ABAP program code, for example, as a conversion routine	None

Table 2.1 Overview of node types (continued)

The attributes of the defined nodes are described using at least three tab pages, which are nearly always identical and differ only in the contents of the queried attributes:

▶ **General attributes**
The first tab page describes the individual content or meaning of the node. The structure of the tab page varies widely depending on the node type. Some node types have a different name than **General attributes** for this tab page.

▶ **Output options**
This tab page describes attributes such as **position**, **style**, **box**, and **shading**.

For example, you can define a box and shading for the corresponding node (exceptions: page and program nodes). Node types that are used for text out-

put also have the **Style** attribute (text nodes, as well as templates). If you specify this attribute, it overrides the default style defined for the form in the
respective branch.

A node may have additional output options, depending on where it is
inserted—for example, when you output the cells of a template or an output
table.

▶ **Conditions**

This tab page enables you to execute nodes only when certain conditions
apply. This is the fastest way to generate a custom flow control, and can be
used for all node types except the page node.

3 Tools

3.1 Overview

To reach the basic tools in form editing, use the SAP menu path **Tools · Form print-out**. Figure 3.1 shows the entries for the corresponding transactions and area menus.

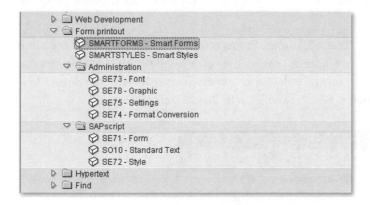

Figure 3.1 Area menu for form printout

You will always use the main transaction SMARTFORMS to access all the forms, styles, and text modules described in this book. Starting transaction SMARTSTYLES gives you separate access to the styles in Smart Forms, but otherwise there is no difference between the two transactions.

The items in the **Administration** area menu provide access to the following:

▶ **Font**
You use the font management function for SAP print output to include soft fonts and print bar codes, for example, which you can then address in the form using print controls. You should have some printer skills if you intend to configure the print environment. This subject is discussed in detail in Section 13.6.

▶ **Graphics**
You can include bitmap graphics (images) in a form. These graphics have to be available in the database system, however. Because the SAP system does not have a separate transaction for editing bitmap graphics, you need to import them from your local work center. This procedure is described in detail in Section 13.4.

▶ **Settings**
All graphics and SAPscript texts are classified by attributes (object number, ID) when saved in the SAP database tables; you first have to define these attributes

in the system. This activity is more a part of Basis administration than of Smart Forms development.

► **Format conversion**
Relevant only within the framework of SAPscript form development.

The **SAPscript** area menu contains the former transactions for creating forms under SAPscript. You also use them to maintain SAPscript standard texts, which are similar to text modules in Smart Forms and which you can also include in the forms in Smart Forms.

The usual path to working with Smart Forms is to call the transaction of the same name (SMARTFORMS). Figure 3.2 shows the corresponding initial screen. You use this transaction to edit forms, styles, and text modules. Each component is identified by a unique name, which can be up to 30 characters long.

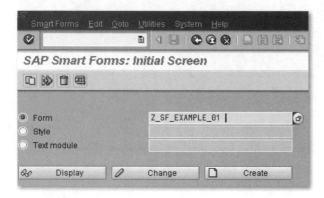

Figure 3.2 Smart Forms initial screen

In addition to the standard functions for **display**, **change**, and **create**, the initial screen also contains the special functions **copy**, **rename**, **delete**, and **test**. Remember that when you rename a form or style, you have to activate it again before you can use it.

You can define a transport request to transport an active form to other SAP systems. Please note that the corresponding function module is not transported with the form. You have to generate it again in the target system. To do so, choose menu path **Smart Forms · Generate**. The new function module then has a different name than it has in the source system as well.

Note: The form is generated automatically the first time it is called by the corresponding main program.

You have to define certain attributes in order to include a form in a transport request. These attributes are located under menu path **Goto · Object directory entry**. From here, you can change such attributes as the development class.

Before you start dealing with the *Form Builder*, the main form editing tool, in any detail, you should first familiarize yourself with the basic functions of the *Style Builder*. The proper format templates are a key prerequisite for creating your own forms with style.

3.2   Style Builder

3.2.1   Overview

In a style (*Smart Style*), you define paragraph and character formats that you can then use to format texts and fields in a form in Smart Forms. The tool for maintaining styles is called the *Style Builder*.

The formats contained in a style can be used in different individual forms. When you change a style, all the forms that use the respective style are updated automatically the next time they are output. Therefore, you do not have to revise the forms. The use of a centralized style simplifies form design, while helping you adhere to your company's corporate identity at the same time.

The reference to a style used within a form can be defined in various nodes (but always in the **Output options** tab page):

▶ The general definition for the entire form is made in the form attributes.

▶ You can define an alternate style for an entire branch in the navigation tree by assigning it to a node type with layout information (such as a template).

▶ The node of an output element itself (such as an address or text node) can be assigned its own style.

A style consists of the following data:

▶ Header data with the default values of the style

▶ Paragraph formats, including indents and spacing, font attributes such as *Bold* and *Underscored*, tabs, and numbering and outline

▶ Character formats, including effects (*superscript*, *subscript*, *colors*), bar code, and font attributes

Instructions in paragraph formats always refer to the entire text paragraph; if you want to format individual characters differently within a paragraph, you use the character formats. Because this procedure is a standard feature of word processing programs, it is not explained in any detail here.

You can include only styles with **active** status in a form. So you have to activate the style before you can use it. During activation the system checks the style for errors and, if necessary, displays an error list.

You can convert an existing SAPscript style to Smart Forms. This process is described in detail in Chapter 10.

3.2.2 Functions of the Style Builder

You can start the *Style Builder* either from within the Smart Forms initial screen or directly via transaction SMARTSTYLES in SAP menu path **Tools · Form printout**. You are already familiar with style SF_STYLE_01 from the previous chapter. Choose this style and press the **Display** button.

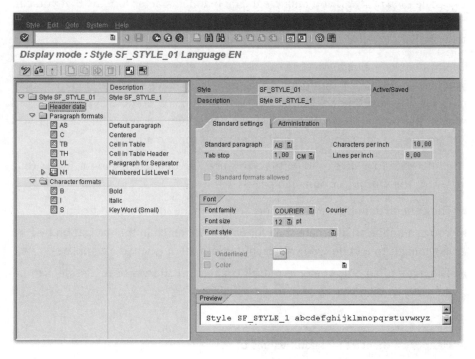

Figure 3.3 Style Builder: Editing screen

Figure 3.3. shows the editing screen of the Style Builder, with the following elements:

▶ On the left-hand side, a navigation tree as a navigation aid (the *style tree*); it always contains the three fixed nodes **Header Data**, **Paragraph Formats**, and **Character Formats** at the top level. The contents of the individual node types are discussed in detail further below.

▶ To the right, in the respective tab pages, the attributes for the selected node (Figure 3.3 shows the default settings for node **Header Data**).

▶ In the lower right, a preview of the formatting (font, for example) configured in the current style.

All processing functions for a node (create, copy, delete, etc.) can be accessed via the context menu for that node (right mouse button).

The diagram above shows the selected style, but only in display mode. The reason for this is simple: the active style was designed and distributed by SAP. As a result, you should not make any changes here. Instead, you should make a copy of the style in the customer namespace and then expand the style to meet your needs.

3.2.3 Creating Your Own Style as a Copy

To create your own style as a copy of an existing style, return to the Smart Forms initial screen.

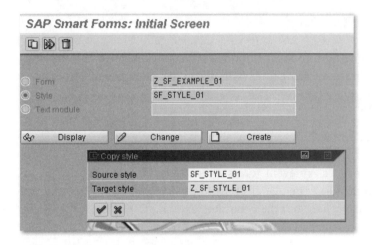

Figure 3.4 Copying a style

Select the existing style as the source. Select the input field for styles and choose the name as shown in Figure 3.4. To access the copy function, choose menu path **Smart Styles • Copy** or use the toolbar. Choose a target in the customer namespace once again (starting with Y or Z). We suggest using the name in the example above, since you will use it often later on.

The familiar prompt for entering the development class appears. choose $TMP again or press the **Local Object** button. The copy is generated and you go back to the initial screen.

You cannot use the new style immediately. As with forms, you have to activate it first. Open the style with menu path **Smart Styles · Change** or press the corresponding button. Then, in the Style Builder screen, choose **Style · Activate**.

> **Note:** The Goto menu in the Style Builder also contains an item for style variants. This is a planned functionality that has not been implemented yet.

Including the Style in the Form

To use the new style in your flight invoice, you have to change the assignment.Open the sample form for the flight invoice, Z_SF_EXAMPLE_01. Choose the **Output Options** tab page in the form attributes and change the style to your new name. Then activate the form and test it as described in Chapter 1 (by pressing **F8** four times, for example).

> **Tip:** If you have created a new style but you cannot enter it in the input field of the form, you probably forgot to activate it.

If you have also assigned the style to subnodes, which makes sense only for alternate styles, you will have to change the style individually in those nodes.

Renaming a Style

You can also rename a style. However, you should do so only when you are absolutely sure that the style is not used in any forms, or at least when you plan to change the references in all relevant forms after the change. If a form contains entries for nonexistent styles, the overall check in the form cannot detect this. The form output will be cancelled, but the generated error messages will not give you any indication of the true cause of the error.

> **Note:** Changes to the IDs of paragraph and character formats (which you will read about in the next section,) are detected during the form check. Therefore, output is still possible even if you do not modify the form afterwards. Please note, however, that the corresponding formats are then somewhat random.

You will now learn about the most important characteristics of a style, using the new style that you just created. As a closing exercise, you can also create new formats, which you will need later for formatting the text node.

3.2.4 Header Data of a Style

Under the **Header Data** node type, you will see the general default values for the respective style (see Figure 3.3). Open the **Standard Settings** tab page. The system will always use the corresponding attributes if you do not specify any custom values in the actual paragraph and character formats.

You can define the following default values here:

▶ **Standard paragraph**
When you create a text node in the form, the node is assigned a standard paragraph automatically; the corresponding entry in the text node is **Default paragraph**. Smart Forms uses the assignment of the standard format in the header data of the defined style to determine which paragraph format should be used.

The entry for the standard paragraph is a reference to a different paragraph format in the style. Accordingly, you cannot assign it unless this true paragraph format is already present in the style.

▶ **Tab stop**
Smart Forms uses this tab spacing when no tabs have been defined in the paragraph format.

▶ **Font attributes**
These include the font family, font size (height), font style (*Bold/Italic*), and the attributes *Underscored* and *Color*.

▶ **Characters per inch and lines per inch**
This information is necessary if you want to use measurement information in the units of measure CH (characters) or LN (lines)—for margins or indents, for example. The definitions of the units of measurement apply only to the style, not to the entire form. You can define separate values in the form attributes.

> **Note:** If you want to use CH and LN, use the same definitions in both areas; otherwise the units of measurement may become confusing (also see section 4.2). You should not change the default values if you do not have a good reason, because they are already configured for the standard printer settings.

3.2.5 Maintaining Paragraph Formats

A paragraph format contains information on indents, spacing, font settings, text color, and tabs. You can use a paragraph format as often as you like within a form to format texts and fields (see Section 5.1).

Much of the information in the paragraph format (see Figure 3.5) is identical or similar to the settings familiar from most word processing programs. Therefore, this section is limited to a brief summary. You can also use paragraph formats to create structured texts (numbering and outlines). Because this case is slightly more complex, it is described in detail below.

A style can contain any number of paragraph formats. Use the copy function again to create a new one. To do so, position the cursor on a paragraph format with similar attributes and choose **Copy** from the context menu. Then enter a new two-character name identifier. When you confirm your entries, the new paragraph format is added to the list of existing paragraph formats.

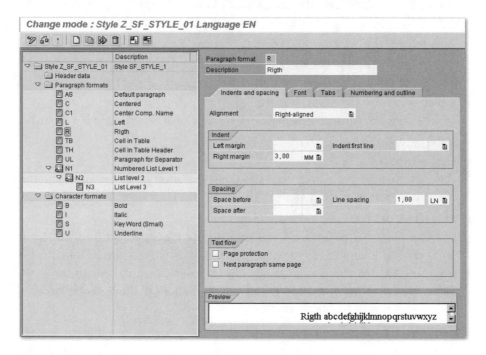

Figure 3.5 Paragraph format in the Style Builder

Margins and Spacing

The graphic in Figure 3.6 shows the margin settings for two sample paragraph formats (A1 and A2).

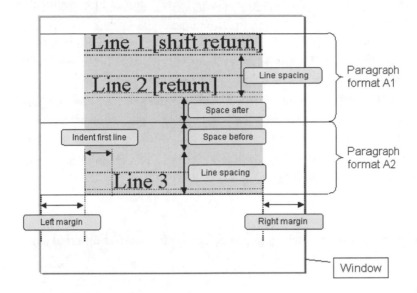

Figure 3.6 Attributes in the paragraph format

Meanings of the attributes for the paragraph format:

▶ **Alignment**
Text alignment in the paragraph (*Left*, *Centered*, *Right*, or *Justified*).

▶ **Left/right margin**
Spacing to the margins of the output area to which the corresponding text node is assigned (window, possibly also a cell of a template/output table).

▶ **Indent (first line)**
Distance of the text to the left/right margin. The first line can have a different indent, if desired. Negative values are also possible; the first line starts to the left of the rest of the paragraph in this case.

▶ **Spacing**
Height of the gap to the previous/next paragraph (space before/space after), as well as specification of the line spacing for the current paragraph. See also the note on line spacing below.

▶ **Text flow**
The **Page Protection** attribute in the main window controls whether or not a paragraph should always be kept together on one page. If you set it, the paragraph will not be separated by a page break. If you set the **Next Paragraph on Same Page** attribute, the paragraph following the current paragraph will also appear on the same print page—that is, the paragraphs remain together.

The settings for the font (font family, size) apply within a paragraph until overridden by information in the character format.

Tabs

You can define any number of tabs for each paragraph format; five different alignments are defined (see Figure 3.7):

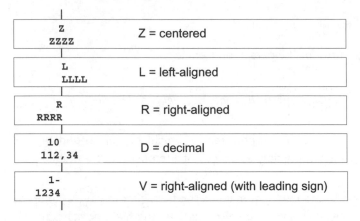

Figure 3.7 Tabs in the paragraph format

You can define any number of differently aligned tabs within a line. Once the last tab defined in the paragraph format is reached (counting from the right), the system automatically uses the tab spacing defined in the header data of the style. In practice, you frequently use templates and output tables to define table formats in a form as well.

Numbering and Outline

You can define multiple paragraph formats with references to one another to create multilevel outlines in the subsequent output. To do so, you have to define one paragraph format for each outline level.

Smart Forms supports two different cases:

▶ **Bullet lists**
In this case, the same list character is used repeatedly within a level.

▶ **Numbering**
In this case, the outline character is increased automatically by the system.

This and all other information for list paragraphs is defined in tab page **Numbering and Outline**. Figure 3.8 shows a structure consisting of three paragraph formats, along with the corresponding print result.

Definition:		List	Left delimiter	Right delimiter	Number chaining	Position
🖼 N3	List le	1, 2, 3, ...				
		1, 2, 3, ...	.		ok	5 mm
		a, b, c, ...	.	)	ok	10 mm
Result :	1 1.1 1.1.a) 1.1.b) 1.2 2	List level N1 List level N2 List level N3 List level N3 List level N2 List level N1			In our example all list levels have a left margin of 25 mm (input on tab page "Indents and spacing")	

Figure 3.8 Outline in the paragraph format

Each outline level has a separate paragraph format. By assigning a *Top paragraph format*, you define the levels of the individual paragraph formats, as well as the counting style for the outline characters.

3.2.6 Sample Exercise: Outlines

Start with the paragraph format for the top level. First, use the context menu to create a new paragraph format for the top outline level (with code N1, for example). The new paragraph format is always added to the end of the list of existing paragraph formats. Or choose an existing paragraph format that you no longer need. The style used here, which is based on SF_STYLE_01, already has an N1 paragraph format, which you can continue to use.

Now create a paragraph format for the next inferior level (with code N2, for example). Once again, the new paragraph format is added to the bottom of the list. Now change the setting for **Top Outline Paragraph** for this paragraph format in tab page **Numbering and Outline**. Enter the paragraph format you defined first, N1. The system then automatically assigns outline level 2 to N2; N2 appears as a node directly beneath N1 in the style tree.

Now check the first outline paragraph again, N1. A reference to itself, N1, has automatically been entered for **Top Outline Paragraph**. Outline level 1 is also set.

Create another new paragraph format for another inferior level and assign the first paragraph format, N1, again for **Top Outline Paragraph**. The system now automatically assigns outline level 3 internally, and inserts the new paragraph format beneath N2 in the style tree.

Once you have completed this exercise, you have created all the necessary paragraph formats for outputting outline texts (see Figure 3.9). You now need only the additional formatting information that was indicated in Figure 3.8. You will now deal with these settings in detail.

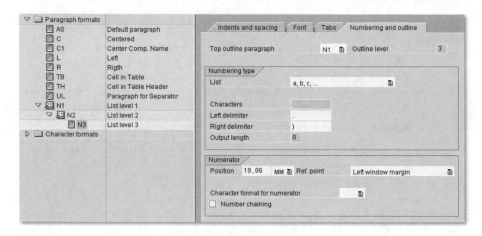

Figure 3.9 Attributes for numbering and outline

Special characters for the outline

Normally, each new paragraph within an outline starts with a special character. You choose the type of indicator with the **List** attribute. The following options are available:

▶ In a *List*, the special character is the same in each paragraph. You can use any character from the keyboard.

▶ In a *Numbering*, the special character is increased automatically for each new paragraph during output. The paragraph format determines only the type of the counter (for example, *Numeric* 1,2,3 or *Alphabetical* a,b,c). In a numbering, the system can also insert left and right delimiters such as parentheses for each level.

▶ You can also choose to not use any special outline character; in this case, the outline ensures only the proper formatting (through indents, for example).

To output the counter, choose from the following options in the **Numbering and Outline** tab page:

▶ You can define the horizontal output position of the counter relatively or as a distance from the page margin. The indent of the subsequent text is calculated from the general settings under tab page **Indents and Spacing**.

▶ You can specify a different formatting (such as *Bold*) for the counter. Please note, however, that the selected character format must already be defined in the style.

▶ An option for all list types is for the counter to include the counter from the superior paragraph in addition to the current level (**Number Concatenation** attribute).

Compare the attributes with the information in the example in Figure 3.8.

Testing the outline functions

First check the various output options for the outline levels with different lines in a text node. These will be your outline texts. To do so, create a new window with this text node somewhere in your sample form and assign your paragraph formats (N1, N2, …) to the individual text lines. Activate the form and test the output.

If you want to change an option in the outline paragraphs and then check it directly, a change in the style will suffice. The next output of the form will contain your changes automatically.

3.2.7 Character Formats

You use character formats to assign special output attributes to sections of texts within a paragraph. A paragraph format overrides the corresponding definitions in the paragraph format (see Figure 3.10).

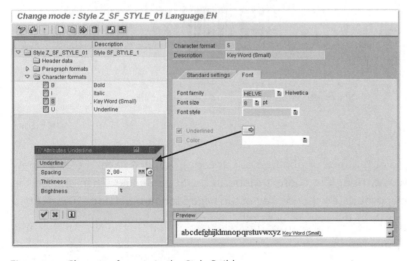

Figure 3.10 Character formats in the Style Builder

The information in the **Character Format** involves primarily the selection of a font, its size (font size), and other attributes such as *Bold* and *Italic*. The available selection options are partially dependent on the installed font families and ultimately dependent on the output devices used (also see Section 13.6.6). In particular, Smart Forms supports colored fonts on color printers.

The **Underscore** function has a special feature: you can use the multiple selection to define the height, width, and shade of the underscore. You can also choose *Strikethrough*. Make sure your printer supports the defined formatting, however.

You do not have to set all the attributes of the character format; the settings are taken from the valid paragraph format or from the header data of the style, if necessary.

Bar Code

A *bar code* consists of a series of horizontal bars that can be read reliably with a bar code reader (see Figure 3.11).

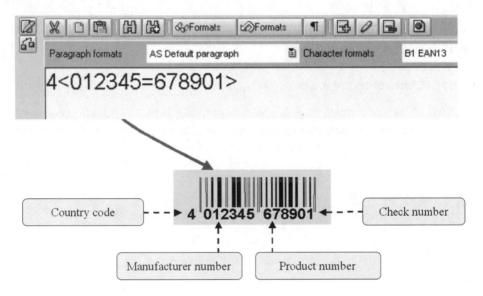

Figure 3.11 Bar code output

If you want to output text or numbers as bar codes, you first have to create a new character format, using the context menu in the Style Builder. Then choose the name of the appropriate bar code key in tab page **Standard Settings**. The defined height and width of the key are entered automatically.

A bar code is simply a special character format for text in Smart Forms, which means you assign the format like any other. Please note, however, that the space required to output the bar code cannot always be determined correctly, which may result in miscalculation (in the page breaks, for example). In the print preview, a bar code appears as merely an outlined graphic, although the size of the graphic is approximately the size of the selected bar code.

Usually, bar codes can be output only on specially equipped printers; you also have to adjust several settings in transaction SE73 (also see Section 13.6.6).

3.2.8 Sample Exercises: Style Content

Some of the exercises that involve your flight invoice form will require enhancements in the style, which you can define here.

Paragraph Formats (for the Form Header)

Three new paragraph formats are needed to output the header information for the flight invoice. Define these paragraph formats using the context menu, either from scratch or as a copy of an existing paragraph format, such as C (centered).

Name of paragraph	Change compared to paragraph format "C"
L (left-aligned)	Alignment *Left*, left margin 3 mm
R (right-aligned)	Alignment *Right*, right margin 3 mm
C1 (centered company name)	Space before 5 mm, font *Times* with size 36 points and *Italic*

Table 3.1 New paragraph formats

Name the new paragraph formats as listed in Table 3.1 and maintain the attributes in the **Indents and Spacing** and **Font** tab pages as described above.

You have to assign the font family only for paragraph format C1. You also have to specify a Space before, to ensure sufficient distance from the top margin for the given font size.

Character Format

Create a new character format U (Underscore) to underscore texts in the later exercises without requiring any other information, such as font family. When you are finished, don't forget to activate the changed style.

3.3   Form Builder

3.3.1   Editing Functions

The *Form Builder* provides a full graphical user interface for editing a form layout and the corresponding form logic. Only rudimentary ABAP skills are required, and only in special cases.

To call the Form Builder, choose SAP menu path **Tools · Forms · Smart Forms** and then select the required form.

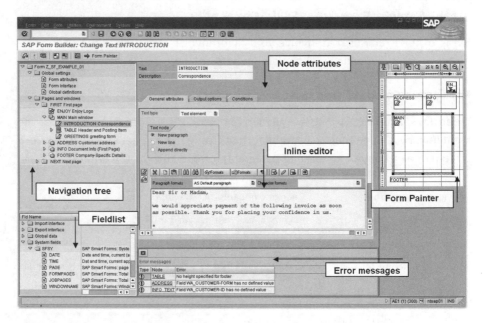

Figure 3.12 Form Builder editing screen

You can see the following tools of the Form Builder in Figure 3.12:

▶ The *navigation tree* in the upper left displays the form as a hierarchy in which each form element is represented by a node. The navigation tree gives you direct access to these elements (double-click the mouse) and their position in the form logic.

▶ The *field list* in the lower left shows all the data that is currently defined in the form. It is described in detail in Section 6.2.1.

▶ The middle screen area serves to maintain the attributes of the currently selected node in the navigation tree.

▶ A separate screen window, *Error messages*, appears below the node attributes if error or warning messages occur during a form check.

▶ The *Form Painter* on the right is a graphical tool for designing the layout using output areas (window sizes and locations).

The *Table Painter*, which you use to create templates and output tables, is not shown in the figure. It can be called only for specific node types (see Section 4.5).

Use the *inline editor* to enter texts and fields in a text node.

> **Note:** The inline editor is used in almost all SAP system modules in which users can enter texts. Therefore, with the exception of a few special functions, this is a standard application component that you should be familiar with already. If you would like to learn more about the inline editor and managing texts in the SAP system, refer to Section 13.3 for the relevant information.

Appearance of the Form in the Navigation Tree

The form is described in the Form Builder as branches in the navigation tree. The top hierarchy level contains the following nodes:

▶ Global settings
- ▶ Form attributes (see Section 4.2)
- ▶ Form interface (see Section 6.4.1)
- ▶ Global definitions (see Section 6.4.2)
▶ Pages and windows
- ▶ %PAGE1 New Page (with a main window, MAIN)

The additional subnodes are created automatically when you create a form. As a result, the structure of the navigation tree is already given:

▶ You cannot add any subnodes to the **Global Settings** branch. The attributes of the existing nodes are described in detail further below.

▶ You create the actual form by creating nodes under **Pages and Windows**. When you navigate through the structure of the hierarchy tree, you should bear in mind that subnodes assume some of their attributes (such as output areas) from their respective superior node.

Nodes in a level are also referred to as *superior nodes* and *inferior nodes*. As these designations indicate, the sequence plays a role during form output (processing). In general, the nodes in the navigation tree are processed sequentially from top to bottom as if all the nodes in the tree were expanded. The exact rules for processing and functions for affecting the flow are described in detail in Chapter 7.

Therefore, designing a form is the same as creating and maintaining the individual branches within the navigation tree. To create specific functions in the form, create one or more nodes whose node type corresponds to the required functionality (text or graphics node, for example).

Each node in the navigation tree has a graphical symbol (icon) in the Form Builder that indicates the defined node type. Figure 3.13 shows a list of the icons used.

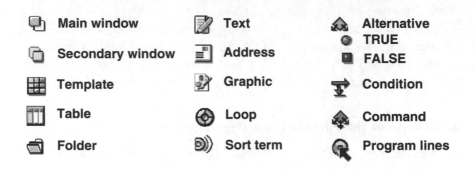

🗐	Main window	📝	Text	🔺	Alternative
				●	TRUE
🗐	Secondary window	📑	Address	■	FALSE
▦	Template	📝	Graphic	⤓	Condition
▥	Table	◉	Loop	🔺	Command
🗀	Folder	⫩))	Sort term	🔍	Program lines

Figure 3.13 Icons in the Form Builder navigation tree

In a few special cases, the Form Builder creates new subnodes in the navigation tree automatically. These nodes are called *event nodes* and can be created only by the system. They are executed whenever specific events occur during form output—for example, to output footer lines when a certain output area is exited. Event nodes are available only as a supplement for certain node types (such as **Loops** or **Folders**).

Editing Functions in the Navigation Tree

When you double-click to select a node in the navigation tree, the system automatically updates the display of the corresponding node attributes. You can also select a window in the Form Painter; the system then highlights the corresponding node in the navigation tree.

The operations that are possible for a specific node are shown in the corresponding context menu (right mouse button). In particular, the types of nodes you can insert at a certain point are highly dependent on the current cursor location in the navigation tree. For example, you can display a text node within a window or template, but not directly on a page. The items in the context menu vary accordingly (see Figure 3.14). The defined functions are self-explanatory.

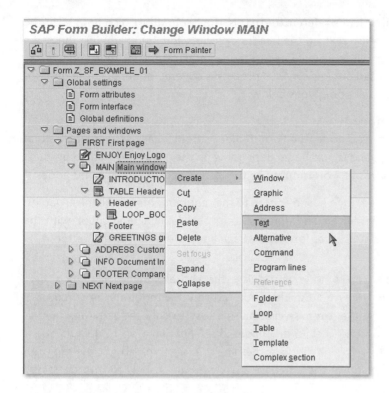

Figure 3.14 Editing functions in the navigation tree

The context menu also displays a list of all node types that can normally be inserted. This list is described in detail below, in the sections on form content.

Copying and moving nodes

Typical activities in form design involve copying and moving entire nodes, including the corresponding subnodes. The familiar functions to cut, copy and paste—via the clipboard—are available in the context menu. It is even easier to drag-and-drop with the mouse: hold the left mouse button to move a node; press the **Ctrl** key to create a copy of the node in the new location. The cursor may change appearance, depending on whether insertion at the selected target is allowed or not.

Unfortunately, the clipboard can be used only within the same form. It is not possible to copy parts of a different form (for example, through a second display window).

Copying nodes over multiple pages

You can create copies from one page to another, however. The system response in this case depends on the type of node involved. For windows, for example, the full contents are treated like a reference—that is, the contents are also output on the new page (for identical texts in the header or footer line, for example). The name and content of the window are copied to the target page; the location and size can be changed in the target window. This process is covered in detail in the descriptions of the individual node types below.

Name for a new node

When you insert a new node, the Form Builder automatically assigns a name that starts with a % sign and is numbered depending on the respective node type (such as %PAGE1). As a result, you cannot use the % sign at the start of other nodes.

Generally, the ID of a node has to adhere to the requirements for technical names: it can consist only of letters and numbers (no special characters), along with the underscore (_) as a substitute for blanks. Each code must start with a letter.

> **Tip:** When you delete a node, you delete the entire branch, including all its inferior nodes. In Release 4.6C, the node is deleted without a prior confirmation prompt. Therefore, exercise caution: it's easy to choose the wrong menu item with the mouse. The Form Builder does not have an undo function. Therefore, iIf you accidentally do something wrong, think about reverting to the last saved version in the database; (if necessary, cancel form processing and start over).

Node Attributes

Each node has several tab pages to display the corresponding attributes. The Form Builder determines the exact divisions depending on the current node type. The individual node attributes are grouped by subject in the various tab pages. Please note that changing a certain attribute can change the structure of a whole tab page, such as when you change the text type in a text node.

Event node

The Form Builder also generates subnodes directly in the navigation tree for some automatic processes, depending on the attributes. These *event nodes* represent a special node type. They have fixed definitions, and you can set only a few attributes for them.

> **Example:** In the case of folder and table nodes, you can call a function for header and footer lines in the **Events** tab page. When you activate the functions, the Form Builder automatically generates two inferior nodes, **Header** and **Footer**, where you can insert additional subnodes with the actual content.

Designing the input fields

In most cases, an input field in the node attributes can be filled in two ways:

▶ *Statically*, by specifying a fixed value

▶ *Dynamically*, by specifying a variable field

You may have to change the type of input field accordingly. Figure 3.15 shows an example of an include text node.

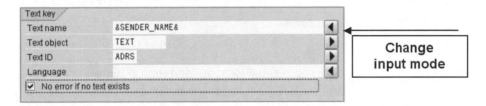

Figure 3.15 Functions in the input field

The attributes **Text Object** and **Text ID** are set to fixed values by default. If the arrow points to the right, the input field is set to a short version. If the arrow points to the left, the input field can be extended. The value help, **F4**, for selecting possible fixed values, is available only in the short version.

The attributes **Text Name** and **Language** are set to the long version. This means you can use field names. In our example, the text name is determined dynamically through a field. An additional ampersand (&) is included, which is usually the case only when you output a text in the field. Unfortunately, the output procedure here is not quite uniform. In most cases, the ampersand is not required to input node attributes (also see Section 6.2).

> **Tip:** In general, the extended SAP clipboard (**Ctrl + Y,** and so on) is also available for all node attribute entries. In practice, it makes sense to use them for table input (*table controls*)—, under the **Conditions** tab page, for example.

Basic Settings for the Form Builder

You can define a number of basic settings for the Form Builder, in addition to its tools, and adapt the Form Builder to the way you work. Use menu path **Utilities • Settings** to change the settings for all the tools at once (see Figure 3.16). The setting for the page format is automatically copied to each new form, where you can change it as necessary.

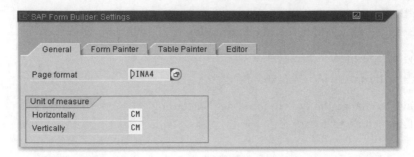

Figure 3.16 Settings for the Form Builder

Units of measure

The full layout of the form comprises the locations and sizes of the pages and windows, along with their subnodes. When you define the unit of measure here, you define which unit you generally want to use in forms. Of course, you can choose a different unit of measure for each input field.

The following units of measure are generally available in the Form Builder:

CH	Characters, see form attributes
LN	Lines, see form attributes
CM	Centimeters
MM	Millimeters
IN	Inches
PT	Points (1/72 inch, usual for font sizes)
TW	Twip (1/20 point, usual for bar code widths)

The values CH and LN are calculated values based on inches, and can be determined individually for each form (see Section 4.2).

> **Tip:** If possible, you should use the same measurements throughout the form. Otherwise conversions will have to be performed throughout. This Using the same measurements throughout not only makes things easier, but also helps you avoid potential errors, (especially when the references between the nodes are complex).

Other Settings

The configuration options in the **Form Painter**, **Table Painter**, and **Editor** tab pages are covered in the descriptions of the individual tools.

3.3.2 Form Painter

You can use the *Form Painter* to change the layout of a form—or simply check it—in a graphical view. You may have to call the Form Painter automatically when you start the Form Builder, depending on your last setting. To do this, choose menu path **Utilities · Form Painter On/Off** or press the corresponding pushbutton in the toolbar.

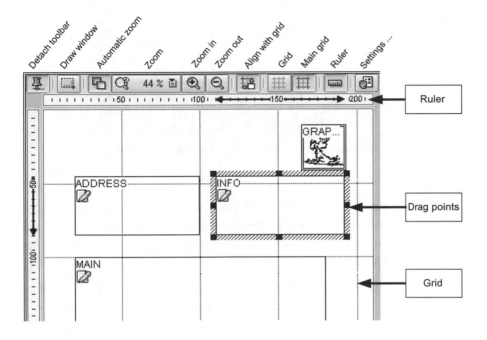

Figure 3.17 Window in the Form Painter

The Form Painter (Figure 3.17) displays the selected draft page in the navigation tree, with page dimensions, windows, and any defined background graphic. Simply click the mouse to choose a different window. Your selection is immediately highlighted in the navigation tree.

The Form Painter displays windows in symbolic frames that reflect the current size of each respective window. Therefore, the windows will not necessarily have borders in the output; to create borders, you have to configure the corresponding settings in the node attributes. Graphics are also displayed directly. If not, this function may be deactivated in your installation for performance reasons. In this case, deactivate the **Placeholders for Graphics** attribute under the settings for the **Form Builder** in the **Form Painter** tab page (not in the settings for the Form Painter).

Settings

The Form Painter has its own toolbar that contains the most commonly used functions. You can use the **Settings** icon to adapt many aspects of the Form Painter to your individual needs.

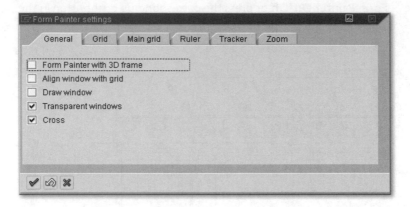

Figure 3.18 Settings for the Form Painter

As you can see in Figure 3.18, most of the settings apply to the appearance of the graphical user interface. Their respective meanings are usually obvious from the context; simply try out a function if its meaning is not obvious. The following options are especially useful:

▶ You can overlay a two-level grid for orientation in the Form Painter (as gray dotted lines or crosses; can be activated in the toolbar). You can adjust the grid spacing in the settings of the **Grid** tab page.

▶ As in most graphic editing programs, you can change the position and size of a window by dragging their handles (click and hold the left mouse button). In the process, the Form Painter can optionally align the new coordinates of a changed window to the grid automatically (see the **Align with Grid** attribute in the last diagram).

▶ Set the **Cross** attribute if you want to change your form graphically. You can check the coordinates of a point directly in the rulers at the top and left of the screen. This makes it easier to align a new window based on existing windows.

▶ Set the **Transparent Window** attribute if you want to have overlapping windows in your form. This makes it easier to spot the positions of the individual windows. Otherwise, if a large window completely covers a small window, the small window will no longer be visible.

Note: This setting only affects the display in the Form Painter. During output, all windows are always printed transparently on top of one another. Therefore, you can generally overlap any content by distributing it among several windows.

You have to set the display as a transparent window when you want to draw windows or templates based on a background graphic. In this context, an additional function also appears in the context menu of the Form Painter (right mouse button). If you choose **Send to Back**, a window is arranged such that you can modify other (smaller) windows with the mouse again.

Otherwise, the items in the context menu of the Form Painter correspond to the options for page and window nodes that you are already familiar with from the navigation tree.

3.3.3 Table Painter

The Table Painter enables the display and maintenance of template layouts and output tables. Both node types support the formatted output of texts and data that resembles the use of tabs. The attributes of the node types are described in detail in Section 4.5. The only important thing here is that you define output by line types, which in turn are divided into columns. This results in the individual cells in which the actual information is output. You use the table painter to design these line types at the graphical level.

You call it from the first tab page of a template or table node. Press the **Table Painter** button. The contents of the tab page change when you press the button. The table input form of the line types displays the graphical representation shown in Figure 3.19.

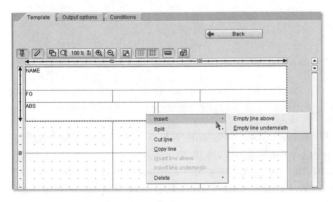

Figure 3.19 Table Painter

The design area is as wide as the corresponding template/table; existing line types are displayed directly. If no line types have been defined yet, the Table Painter automatically creates the first line—whose height corresponds to the total output area—during the initial call.

Mouse Functions

You can change the dimensions of existing rows and columns with the mouse. For example, position the mouse on one of the horizontal lines that separates two cells in a line. Hold down the left mouse button and move the line.

You can also create new rows and columns directly with the mouse. To do so, simply drag the cursor (as a pencil) horizontally or vertically to an existing line. Hold down the left mouse button while doing so. Once again, all the other editing functions are available in the context menu.

> **Tip:** You can only split only one existing line type into additional rows or columns with the mouse. Accordingly, no input is possible in the screen area below the last line type. Unfortunately, this external area in the Form Painter is not indicated, which you may find frustrating the first few times you use the tool.

Using the Grid

Like the Form Painter, the Table Painter offers a displayable grid with which you can automatically align the line and column spacing. To configure this, click the corresponding icon in the toolbar. You will probably find it easiest to use the Table Painter with the following options active:

▶ Transparent tables

▶ Cross

▶ Align with grid

Form and Background Graphic

It may make sense to insert a sample form as a background graphic and then trace a suitable template from it, especially when you create complex templates.

To display a background graphic in the Table Painter, you have to set the **Display Background Graphic** option (the first attribute in the Table Painter input screen). In this case, an excerpt from the background graphic appears in the Table Painter, which you can use to trace rows and columns. The excerpt is determined through the position and size of the superior window that contains the template. Please make sure that the **Vertical Alignment** attribute for positioning the template within the window is set to **Absolute**.

Exiting the Table Painter

When you exit the Table Painter with the **Back** button, your changes are immediately updated in the list display of line types. The Table Painter always aligns the last column such that the last line is exactly as wide as the corresponding template/ table. This prerequisite must be met for both node types, and is also verified in the check routine for the node.

3.4 Checking, Testing, and Activating Forms

Smart Forms differentiates between saved forms (via **Form · Save**) and forms that have also been activated (via **Form · Activate**). Any form that you plan to output through a main program must have status **Active**. The same applies to styles. You can see the status of the form in the Form Builder, after the form name, for example.

When you make changes to an active form and then save, the status is reset to **Inactive**. The last active version is retained in the system, along with the function module that was generated for it. Therefore, if you start output via the main program in this situation, the system uses the last active version. This also applies to the function for testing the form.

If you choose menu path **Utilities · Back to Active Version**, the Form Builder rejects any changes made so far and restores the last active version.

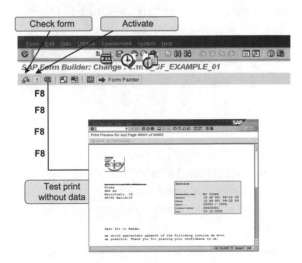

Figure 3.20 Checking, activating, and testing the form

3.4.1 Activating the Form

When you activate a form, the following functions are executed:

▶ Overall check of the form
▶ If no errors are found
  ▸ Generation of the function module
  ▸ Deletion of the previous active form
  ▸ **Active** status set for the current version of the form

The overall check for the form involves the consecutive individual checks of all its contained nodes; the Form Builder also checks the interaction among the nodes. This is described in detail further below.

If the form check does not find any errors, a suitable function module is generated and the form is set to **Active** status. Warning messages do not block the activation. You can then run an additional test of the form.

Error List

If the Form Builder reports errors or warnings during the check of a form or an individual node, an additional display area appears below the node attributes. All the messages appear in a list here. The list also contains the name(s) of the node(s) in which the error(s) occurred. Simply select a node with the mouse (second column). The system then goes to the corresponding position in the navigation tree and you can correct the error.

> **Tip:** In some cases, the Form Builder may not detect that the cause of an error has already been corrected. The corresponding message is obviously still present in the internal program buffer, and is displayed again during the next check. If you suspect that this may be the case, save the form, exit processing, and then start the Form Builder again. The check should no longer find any errors.

Individual Node Checks

An individual check exists for each node, and can be called using the *Check* icon in the respective node attribute. We recommend checking a node whenever you have made major changes to it. The main advantage of the individual check is that it is much faster than the overall check.

The components of the checks depend on the node type involved. In templates, for example, the system checks whether the dimensions of the individual rows correspond to those of the superior window. In a program node, in contrast, an ABAP syntax check is performed. The components of the respective checks are covered in detail under the descriptions of the individual node types.

Overall Check

Choose menu path **Form · Check** to subject the form to an overall check. This check is performed automatically when you activate the form. The overall check comprises:

▶ The individual checks of all nodes

▶ Additional checks that make sense only in the overall context of the form

If an error occurs in the form interface or the global data during the overall check, only the first error is reported; all further checks are cancelled. Follow-on errors are a given in this case, which makes it senseless to perform any additional individual checks.

Data flow analysis

The overall check also contains a data flow analysis. During the data flow analysis, the Form Builder checks whether a specific field that is used in a text has a defined value when the output takes place. Because there is no direct connection to the corresponding main program, however, the Form Builder can only perform this check based on assumptions. Please note that 100% certainty is not possible in this case; the Form Builder displays warning messages if a problem is supposed.

Assumptions of the data flow analysis:

▶ The system generally assumes that appropriate data is available for all the parameters that are defined in the form interface.

▶ If a variable has been defined in the **Global Definitions** (e.g., not in the form interface), it must be supplied with data in the form itself. As a result, the following conditions are also checked:

  ▶ Was a default value assigned during the definition? Of course, this check is performed only when a field, not a structured data type, is involved.

  ▶ Is the variable entered as an output parameter in a program node that has already been processed? If so, the system assumes that it has also been supplied with data there; the actual program code is not checked.

  ▶ Is a header of an internal table involved and is this internal table processed as a loop in a node?

The check ends without warnings when one of the above conditions is met. Because the processing sequence is also relevant for the data flow analysis, it is performed individually for each node.

In the case of globally defined data, the check also considers cases in which data assignment is dependent on the runtime conditions (if a prior data statement is subject to a condition, for example). In such cases, a warning message appears with the proviso that a field may not be filled.

> **Tip:** An independent table area is usually provided with the current data record of an internal table in loop nodes. This type of data assignment is not taken into account during the check. Therefore, the overall check may issue unjustified warning messages due to missing data in a work area, as (like you saw with the flight invoice in the Getting Started chapter). To avoid such warning messages, you should specify the work area as the output parameter of a program node beforehand (or under tab page **Initialization** in the global definitions).

3.4.2 Testing the Form

When you test a form, you are really testing the generated function module. This Smart Forms function is borrowed from the *Function Builder*, a tool in the ABAP development environment.

Choose menu path **Form · Test F8** for the activated form. The initial screen of the Function Builder appears (transaction SE37; see Section 13.7.3 for more details on this tool). From there, choose **Single Test F8** to enter the test mode for the generated function module.

A fast way of calling the test function is pressing the **F8** function key four times in a row (also see Figure 3.20). The main program for data collection is not called during this process; accordingly, the function module does not contain any data. Therefore, this test function is especially useful for checking the layout.

For more complex forms with data inclusion, you should use the test via the main program. When you open the main program in a second session, the call will be even faster than the internal test function for the form, provided the main program already exists.

3.4.3 Generating the Form

Generation means creating the appropriate function module for the form. This function is performed automatically when you activate the form; you cannot test the form via the function module until you have activated it.

When you transport a new form into another SAP system (via transport request, for example), no function module is available in the new system yet. However, it is generated automatically the first time you call the form via the corresponding main program. You can also trigger generation manually through menu path **Smart Forms · Generate** in the Smart Forms initial screen (you cannot call the test functions for the form or the function module until you have done so).

In contrast to activation, you do not have to call the form in change mode here, which means that no additional authorization is required. You can repeat the manual generation at any time; any existing function module is overwritten.

3.5 Form Documentation

Smart Forms itself does not contain any tools for documenting form contents. You can insert comment lines only in program and text nodes.

Smart Forms does not contain a specific function for change management, either. The system merely saves when the last change was made and who made it (see the **General Attributes** tab page in the form attributes). Because documenting the form contents is important, however, a practical solution is described below.

> **Tip:** When you design a form yourself, you should at least write brief documentation with a reference to the corresponding main program. Notes are available in SAPNet for the forms designed by SAP, which describe the combinations and installation (see the Appendix).

You have probably already discovered that documents that are saved independently of the actual object, the form in this case, are not read very often. Therefore, it makes sense to use a standard function within the form to document it: the text node (see Section 13.3.2 on instructions for use). This node type has useful functions for this application:

▶ The inline editor is ideal for short comments.

▶ Switch to the SAPscript editor for longer texts (optionally in graphical form or as a line editor).

▶ Use the SAPscript editor to print the text.

Because the text is intended only for documentation purposes in this case, it has to be suppressed during form output. You could achieve this by flagging all the documentation lines with the special character format /*. No other text formatting options are available in this case, however, it is better to flag the entire text node as a comment section by defining a suitable condition.

Suggestions for simple, straightforward form documentation:

1. Create a separate window for the documentation—for example, at the top of the first form page.

2. Position the window in a remote location on the page, such as in the upper right (not in the upper left, where all new windows are automatically placed).

3. Link the window node with an output condition that is never met (such as 'A' = 'B' or 'Text' = 'Docu'). Alternatively, you can also create a complete draft page exclusively for the documentation, but it must not refer to any other page in this case.

4. Create one or more text nodes below this window. Multiple nodes are recommended—if you want to list the basic documentation separately from changes, for example.

5. Create a separate style for the documentation that contains the necessary paragraph and character format. This makes the formatting for documentation independent of the respective form involved. Then assign this style to each individual text node. Please note, however, that a corresponding style also has to be defined for SAPscript if you want to print the text.

In some cases, it may make sense to enter comments directly for a form component. In this case, simply use additional text nodes directly in the respective positions—for example, at the start of each window (but don't forget to define the never-fulfilled output condition).

4 Form Layout

4.1 Overview

In the *Getting Started* chapter, you learned about the basic elements of the layout: *pages* and *output areas*. The latter are also referred to as *windows* in Smart Forms. To refresh your memory, Figure 4.1 shows the layout of your flight invoice again, as it looks when displayed in the Form Painter:

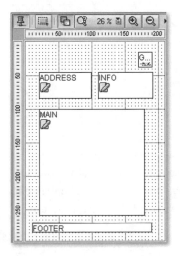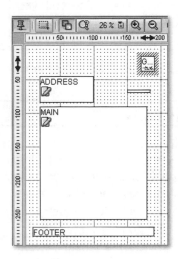

Figure 4.1 Layout of the sample form

The form layout in the sample form contains two draft pages. The division of the two pages into windows differs only slightly in the example, however: the second page does not contain an INFO window, and a page number appears in its place.

The invoice form is supposed to output all of a customer's flight bookings, with their prices, in a window in table form. The flight postings are output consecutively in the MAIN window. There are additional windows (as secondary windows) with information on the company logo, sender, customer address, and other properties (such as processing clerk, customer number, reference, and date; see also the sample printout in the Appendix).

The page division in the flight invoice corresponds to the most frequent application case: after the first page is output, the next page is repeated until all the data (the flight bookings, in this case) has been output.

Please note, however, that the Form Painter only shows the defined windows as output areas in the layout overview. You can use templates and output tables to divide these windows into smaller output areas, which give you additional design options. Accordingly, the output areas have a hierarchy with a maximum of three levels (see Figure 4.2).

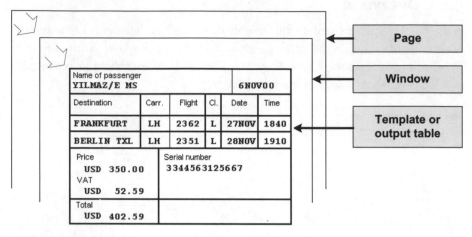

Figure 4.2 Definition of output areas

Each layout level (page, window, template, and so on) has its own individual attributes, which are described in the sections below. First, however, you will read about general layout definitions—such as units of measure or boxes and shading—which you can apply to nearly any node.

4.2   General Layout Definitions

You can define general layout information in various places in the form. This information is summarized here. In particular, you can define:

▶ General form attributes in the global settings

▶ Boxes and shading in the output options of the different node types

4.2.1   Global Settings

The node **Global Settings** and its three inferior nodes **Form Attributes**, **Form Interface**, and **Global Definitions** always exist for any newly created forms. You can configure several basic parameters here that apply to the entire form.

However, only the information for the form attributes is relevant to the layout design. Choose the **Output Options** tab page as shown in Figure 4.3.

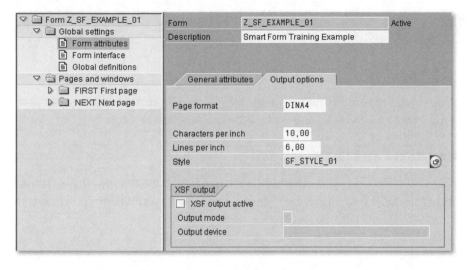

Figure 4.3 General form attribute

The individual form attributes are:

▶ **Page format**

The page format is taken from the basic settings of the Form Builder whenever you create a new form (see Figure 3.18). You can change this setting here. The value help, **F4**, displays all the page formats that have been configured in the spool administration transaction. You can also define for each page whether you want to output that page in portrait or landscape format.

▶ **Characters per inch**

This setting (*characters per inch, cpi*) does not have any direct effect. You define the unit CH (characters) only where it is available in fields with horizontal units of measure. If, for example, you define a window width of "1 CH", Smart Forms converts this entry to a tenth of an inch (approx. 2.54 mm).

▶ **Lines per inch**

You can configure the same definition as above in **lines per inch** (*lpi*) for the vertical unit of measure LN (lines).

Tip: The system defaults are 10 cpi and 6 lpi. You should not change these values unless you really have to, since they are supported by every printer.

▶ **Style**

The style you define here is the foundation for all output nodes (texts, addresses, and so on), unless you define a different style for individual subnodes (in a template, for example, or directly at the text node level).

▶ **XSF output**

This special type of output is mentioned here only to round things out. The options for XSF output are described in detail in Section 10.3.

4.2.2 Boxes and Shading

All selectable node types—with the exception of the program node—have **Output Options** tab page in their node attributes with a **Boxes and Shading** section (see Figure 4.4).

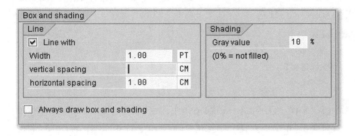

Figure 4.4 Boxes and shading

Shading

You can specify a gray tone to define a shading for an output area that is surrounded by a node element. However, in this case the system response also depends on the settings in the superior node. For example, shading in the window will override shading in the inferior text node.

Box

By specifying the settings for the line, you can draw a box around the entire node element (such as window, text). The offset values refer to the outer border of the superior output area, which means they are dependent on the node type used there.

Tip: Smart Forms offers direct support only for simple lines. If you require special boxes, such as with double lines, you should create separate windows specifically to display the box. You can also use such windows to create extremely wide boxes by configuring the gray scale value. The individual entries then overlap during output. Refer to the sample printout of the freight order in the Appendix to see an example of such formatting.

A box always surrounds a rectangular output area; Smart Forms does not have a simple option for outputting only horizontal or vertical lines. You can, however, define the box with a very narrow window node. It is even easier to use templates with an appropriate pattern.

Because a node is printed only when content is present, under the default settings a defined box is not output when a window is blank. To negate this, set attribute **Always Draw Box and Shading**.

Note: Window nodes are always displayed with boxes in the graphical Form Painter. These only serve to improve the display, however, and do not affect the boxes during output.

4.3 Page Node

To emphasize the importance of the draft page for the layout of the form, review the process for outputting the flight invoice:

▶ The customer's address is usually output in the FIRST draft page. This is followed in the MAIN window, after an introductory text, by an output table containing all flight bookings, in which the output length is dependent on the number of flight postings (*dynamic table*).

▶ If the first page does not have enough space for all the items, the table is continued on the next page and the column headers are printed again at the top.

The following information about the flight invoice is applicable to the layout of nearly every other form:

▶ The output consists of one or more pages. The start page is the first page; form processing always begins with this page.

▶ If the data for output in the MAIN window does not fit on the first page, the system automatically creates another page. Which page this is depends on the **Next Page** parameter of the respective page.

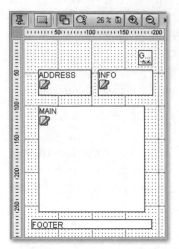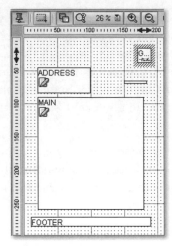

Figure 4.5 Page layout of the sample form

The usual names of the draft pages are:

▶ **FIRST**
First page (with NEXT as next page)

▶ **NEXT**
From print page 2 (with NEXT as next page)

Page breaks are triggered automatically when the space for the item list in the main window is not sufficient. Alternatively, you can force a manual page break. This is necessary, however, if you want to output a page with your business conditions after the last page of data output. These cases are covered in detail in the descriptions of the form logic in Section 7.4.

4.3.1 Creating a New Draft Page

You can create any number of draft pages for a form. If you create more than two pages, however, you also have to define a custom flow logic for the dynamic page break.

To create a new page, choose **Create · Page** in the context menu of an existing page. The new page immediately appears as the selected page in the navigation tree and in the Form Painter. Each new page has itself as the next page by default.

When you create a page as a copy of an existing page, the entire page contents are also copied. The windows that already existed on the first page appear with the same names in the copied page. The Form Builder assigns the same contents to the identically named windows (like a reference). This response is described in detail in Section 4.4.

Attributes for the Page Node

The most important item on the **General Attributes** tab page is the specification of the next page. When a form has two draft pages, this is always the draft page that will be output from page 2 onward. You can also specify parameters for page numbering in the **General Attributes**. This option is described in detail in Section 7.4.

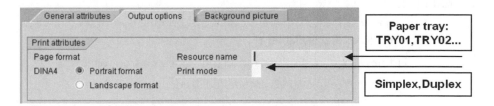

Figure 4.6 Page setup: Output options

The **Output Options** tab page (see Figure 4.6) contains basic print attributes for configuring the output of a page:

▶ **Page format**
You can choose here between portrait and landscape format. You can change only the print orientation for each draft page, not the actual paper format. This latter value is defined uniformly for the entire form under the form attributes; in our example, all pages are output with paper size ///DINA4.

▶ **Resource name**
This item enables you to enter a custom paper source for the printer—for example, to access a specific paper tray when using preprinted forms. The following values are available:

  ▶ TRY01 (first paper tray)

  ▶ TRY02 (second paper tray)

  ▶ TRY03 (third paper tray)

  ▶ TRYEN (envelope tray)

  ▶ TRYMN (manual paper feed)

  ▶ TRYME (manual paper feed for envelopes)

These entries are called the *print controls* and are defined in printer management (transaction SPAD). Make sure that the print controls for your destination printer are maintained to ensure that the correct tray is selected.

Note: You will see later that these print controls can also be entered through a command node anywhere in the form. This node type is defined in detail in Section 7.5.2. The paper tray must be selected at the start of the page, and therefore appears in the page node.

▶ **Print mode**
This attribute affects printers that are capable of printing both sides of a page. The following values are available:

- ▶ S: Start new page in SIMPLEX mode (one-sided on front page)
- ▶ D: Start new page in DUPLEX mode (dual-sided)
- ▶ T: Start new page in TUMBLE DUPLEX mode (dual-sided, but "upside-down" on the reverse side)

If you do not specify a **resource name** or **print mode**, Smart Forms uses the default values for the output device. Of course, these attributes are correct only when the printer meets the necessary prerequisites and the appropriate settings have been defined in transaction SPAD. Refer to Section 13.6 for more information.

You can use the **Background Graphic** tab page to assign a graphic to an entire page; the procedure is equivalent to creating a graphics node. This process is described in detail in Section 5.3.

4.4   Window Nodes

Window nodes divide each draft page of a form into output areas (see Figure 4.5). The direct assignment of elementary node types, such as text nodes, to a page is not possible. The only exceptions are graphic and address nodes; they can also be assigned the attributes of a window.

You can freely define the position and size of a window on a page. You enter the margins, height, and width in the **Output Options** tab page. You can also manipulate the windows with the mouse in the Form Painter. In this case, the alphanumeric node attributes are adjusted automatically.

Different windows can also overlap or even completely cover each other. This enables you to deliberately overlay the contents of specific windows (text over a graphic, for example). There are no dependencies between the windows themselves. Accordingly, all the windows appear at the same level under a page node in the navigation tree. This exact level is also displayed for processing in the graphical Form Painter.

The draft page can have two different types of windows: main and secondary . Each form can have only one main window. A window becomes the main window when you set the corresponding attribute in the **General Attributes** tab page.

The most important attributes are summarized below:

▶ **Secondary window**
In a secondary window, you output text and data in an output area with a strict definition. Text and data that do not fit in a secondary window are cut off, since a page break is not supported here. You can create any number of secondary windows within a given page.
If a secondary window with the same code appears on several pages, it is output with the same contents on each page, starting from the first line each time. However, the direct node attributes of the window, such as different position and size, may vary.

▶ **Main window**
In a main window you display texts and data, which can cover several pages (continuous text). As soon as the main window is completely filled, the remaining content is output in the main window of the next page. Page breaks are inserted automatically. Other special features:

  ▶ You can flag only one window in the form as the main window, using the corresponding attribute in the **General Attributes** tab page.

  ▶ When you create a new form, a main window already exists on the first page.

  ▶ You have to create a main window on the first two pages when the form has the usual page sequence. If necessary, configure the window on the first page and then use the copy function to copy it to the second page; see the next section for more details. The main window must have the same width on each page to ensure that the output by line is uniform throughout the form. In contrast, you can define any length.

  ▶ A page without a main window must not call itself as next page, as this would create an endless loop. Please note, however, that Smart Forms automatically cancels output after three pages to prevent this very situation.

4.4.1 Creating a New Window

To create a new window, choose **Create · Window** in the context menu of a page node or in the Form Painter. In the latter case, you can also directly configure the window position and size.

Either you enter the position and size of the window in the **Output Options** tab page, or this information is recorded automatically by the Form Painter.

If you draw the form in the Form Painter, we recommend using utilities such as the grid and crosshair to ensure a uniform design throughout the form (see Section 3.3.2).

You can also create a new window as a copy of an existing window (with the mouse while holding down the **Ctrl** key, for example). If you make a copy within a page, the Form Builder assigns a new, random name to the copied window, as for any other new window. The contents of the window are copied as subnodes, in addition to the node attributes (such as **position**). These subnodes are also created as copies under new names, which you can change as necessary.

Windows Across Several Pages

A different system response results when you copy a window from one page to another. You can use the copy function (**Ctrl** and mouse, for example) to create a window in several pages at the same time. In this case, it will have the same code in all the pages. When you copy a complete page, this effect copies all the windows at the same time. The result is:

▶ In this case, Smart Forms assumes that you want to output the same window contents. If a window contains subnodes, these also appear in all pages in the navigation tree. The content is identical in all pages (like a reference). If you make changes to a subnode in the FIRST page, for example, these changes are automatically duplicated in the corresponding subnode in the NEXT page.

▶ In contrast, the direct node attributes of the windows—such as position, size, box and conditions—can vary between the pages. Therefore, a window in the NEXT page can have a different position and/or size—or even be output under different conditions—than in the FIRST page. Please also note the following:

  ▶ Because both windows have identical contents, the output of these contents will be cut off if a window is too small in a given page. This applies only to secondary windows.

  ▶ The width of the main window must be identical on all pages, since the output of tables would not otherwise be possible.

You can create this type of node (with reference in subnodes) only with the copy function. If you try to create a new window, not a copy, with the same name as an existing window, the Form Painter will report an error.

Checking the Window Definition

Checking a window will result in error messages in the following situations:

▶ The window does not fit in the assigned page.

▶ The width of the main window is not identical in all pages.

4.4.2 Sample Exercise: Creating Windows

A picture (graphic) of a dog is defined as the logo of the issuing travel agency in your flight invoice. You will now add an appropriate text to the invoice for the sender.

Create a new window, SENDER, at the top margin. You can enter the text later. Enter the name and position data as shown in Figure 4.7. When you enter the coordinates as shown in the diagram, the margin of the window will be identical to the size of the graphic.

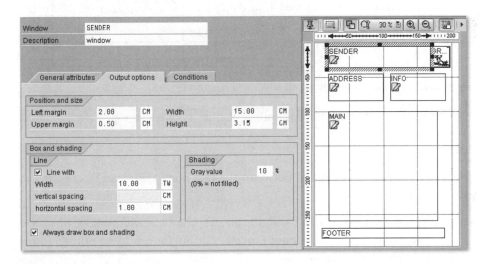

Figure 4.7 Creating a window

Experiment a bit with the box and shading functions. Please note, however, that the results will not appear directly in the Form Painter. You will see them only during actual output (the print preview will suffice) or during the form test. Make sure to erase any defined shading when you are finished, however, because you will use this window to create a template whose pattern function is incompatible with shading.

4.5   Templates and Output Tables

4.5.1   Overview

You can use the layout of templates and output tables in table nodes to break down a window further and create a table display. Although tabs are also frequently used to create table output, a fixed definition in a layout makes it much easier to design the form—and to maintain it later.

Table

Template

Your bookings					
Flight	Date			Price	
AA017	16.12.2000		1.200,00	USD	
AA017	31.12.2000		1.200,00	USD	
Sum for AA			2.400,00	USD	
LH400	17.11.2000		581,00	DEM	
LH402	17.11.2000		669,00	DEM	
LH403	12.12.2000		610,00	DEM	
Sum for LH			1.860,00	DEM	
Total sum			2.400,00	USD	
			1.860,00	DEM	

Name of passenger YILMAZ/E MS				6NOV00	
Destination	Carr.	Flight	Cl.	Date	Time
FRANKFURT	LH	2362	L	27NOV	1840
BERLIN TXL	LH	2351	L	28NOV	1910
Price USD 350.00 VAT USD 52.59		Serial number 3344563125667			
Total USD 402.59					

Figure 4.8 Differences between output tables and templates

Let's first examine the differences and similarities between the two design types.

Differences

The most important differences between the two node types can be seen in the examples in Figure 4.8:

▶ *Templates* have a fixed layout and a fixed size; the type and number of cells is not changed at runtime. They are especially useful for modeling printed forms (flight tickets, tax forms, and so on).

▶ *Output tables* are output using table nodes and have dynamic specifications for all height information. When you design the form, you do not know how many data records will be output later. Therefore, the length of the output table is calculated at runtime and results from the quantity and type of the data. This data is usually output through loop nodes (like the items in the flight invoice, for example).

Templates are used primarily in secondary windows. In contrast, table nodes are normally used in the main window, which is dynamic and which provides the necessary page breaks automatically.

Note: The term *Table* has several different meanings in Smart Forms. To avoid confusion, here is a brief overview:

▶ When the result of outputting a form—that is, what appears on paper or on screen—is involved, we refer to an *output table*. However, the node that provides this type of output is not called an output table, just a *table*.

▶ You will read a great deal about tables later on, but these involve the storage of data in the SAP system. In this case, we speak of *internal tables* or *database tables*, depending on where the data is located. The table node can use the built-in loop function to directly access data in the internal table. Therefore, data from *internal tables* is printed via *output tables* in this case.

▶ The information that a template describes in a layout is also frequently referred to as a *table*.

Similarities

Despite the differences described above, these two node types also have many similarities, especially regarding their maintenance in the form. The most important similarity is the line-based structure of the templates or output tables defined as *line types*:

▶ Each line type can be divided into any number of cells by defining columns. These cells are used later as output areas for the actual information, like a group of small windows, one next to the other.

▶ By arranging several line types, you create the entire template or output table. The sequence definition is fixed in a template, while it depends on the structure and number of output data records in an output table.

▶ This approach with line types enables you to use the Table Painter (which you learned about in Section 3.3.3) here as well.

Application Area of the Output Table

You will usually use output tables when you do not know how many rows a table will have when you design the form. Accordingly, output tables and the corresponding table node are described in detail in the context of loops in the main window (see Section 7.2).

However, it is easy to forget that table nodes are also useful for strict layout tasks that do not involve dynamic data access. We will come back to that aspect at the end of this chapter. But first you will use a template node to illustrate how to use these node types to your advantage in the flight invoice.

Creating Templates

You can create a template node only as the subnode of a window. You define the layout of the template using any number of line types in the node attributes. You can use the graphical Table Painter or directly enter the dimensions for the column widths and line heights.

The node type itself does not output any content; you have to define additional subnodes for the template to do so. In this case, each individual template cell assumes the function of an output area. You can output the same contents (texts, fields, graphics) as in a window.

You describe the following information in the template layout (Figure 4.9):

▶ The number of lines and columns (cells)

▶ The height of each line

▶ The width of each cell

▶ The alignment of the table in the window

▶ Whether and where to display separator lines or boxes

The defined layout of the template makes it easier for you to position the content to be output. You can also output the layout itself using separator lines and boxes. To do so, use the pattern function, which you will also learn about in the next exercise.

4.5.2 Sample Exercise: Configuring Template Nodes

You previously created a SENDER window for the flight invoice in order to output information for the sender there (also see the sample printout in the Appendix). You will now use a template to structure this window. Therefore, create a new template node below SENDER, with menu path **Create · Template** in the corresponding context menu.

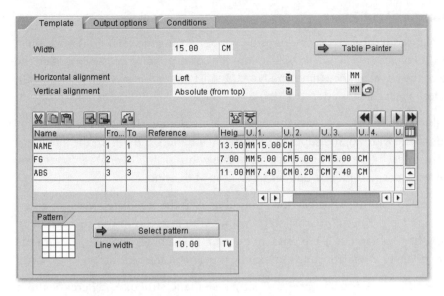

Figure 4.9 Template for sender information

The information required for the layout in the example is shown in Figure 4.9. The first attributes involve the positioning of the template and are largely self-explanatory. The reference point is always the upper left corner of the superior window. The template must always fit completely in the superior window. Therefore, pay attention to the following thresholds when you design the template:

▶ The template width, combined with the left margin, may not exceed the total width of the window.

▶ The sum of all defined rows equals the template height; this figure plus the defined vertical spacing must not exceed the height of the window.

▶ The check function of the node ensures that you stay within the threshold, with one restriction: you can also enter **Current** as the vertical alignment. In this case, the starting point of the template depends on the previous output in the same window. This setting is important when you previously output a text whose length is not limited, for example. If the entire template no longer fits in the corresponding window, form output is terminated with a runtime error. In this case, the resulting message does not name the node that causes the error in the form, which can make troubleshooting an arduous task indeed.

▶ Therefore, set the Vertical Alignment to **Absolute (from top)** whenever possible. In this case, the template will at least not be shifted due to other nodes in the same window, aside from the fact that the specified position is usually fixed for secondary windows anyway. Absolute positioning also enables you to define multiple templates in a window. This special case is discussed later in this chapter.

Configuring Line Types

A template with three rows is responsible for outputting the sender information in the flight invoice (see Figure 4.9). Later on, the corresponding cells will contain the name of the travel agency (line type NAME), a list of the represented airlines (FG), and the travel agency's address (ABS).

Each line type is defined with the appropriate columns. The total width corresponds to the width of the superior window; in addition, the sum of the individual columns in each line must correspond to the width of the overall template. The height you specify for a line applies to all cells of this line.

The **From/To** columns specify which output lines in the template are set to a particular line type. The numbering starts with 1. The intervals in the line definition may neither overlap nor leave gaps. In our simple example, however, each of the specified line types corresponds to exactly one line in the output.

Because templates usually have a strictly systematic structure, different output lines can have a similar line type in complex templates. If these lines are output consecutively, you can use the suitable line type as multiple lines. If you enter **From 2/To 4**, for example, a total of three lines are output.

> **Tip:** When you create a new template, neither the width nor a line type are initially defined. If you need only a single template in the corresponding window, you can use the useful initialization function in the Table Painter. Click the *Initialization* button and then return to the previous screen. The Table Painter has set the width of the template to the value of the superior window and—at the same time—created a single line type with one cell, whose dimensions also correspond to those of the window. You can then divide this first line further in the Table Painter and adjust the layout to your requirements.

If the similar rows are not consecutive in the layout you need, you have to define a new line type. In this case, you can enter the original line type as a reference. The system then automatically copies the values you specified for the line height and the individual cell widths from the referenced line type.

Maintenance in the Table Painter

You can enter the template data by line in the table editing screen, as shown in Figure 4.9. Alternatively, you can use the Table Painter, which you access through the corresponding button in the **Template** tab page. This changes the display form in the tab page. Figure 4.10 illustrates the sample template.

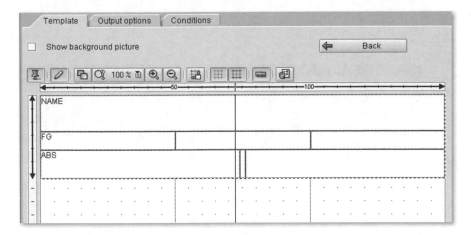

Figure 4.10 Template in the Table Painter

In the Table Painter, you can alter the design of the template graphically with the mouse in order to make changes like changing measurements or inserting new lines and columns. Please see Section 3.3.3 for general instructions for using this tool.

Unfortunately, in Release 4.6C the Table Painter cannot edit line types that are defined to display several lines (with from/to definitions) or which have a reference. You cannot call the Table Painter in these cases; a system message indicates this fact.

> **Tip:** When you define templates, it is critical that all the columns of a line together add up to the exact width that is defined as the template width. If a large number of columns are involved, this can involve time-consuming calculations. The Table Painter relieves you of this task. Just call one function, and the last column in all rows is automatically aligned to the template width.

Boxes and Patterns

Frequently, you want the cells (output areas) that you define in the template to be recognizable as such. To achieve this, you can draw boxes around cells in the template, similar to the box function for windows. To simplify this process, you use *patterns* to assign such boxes.

To access the selection of defined patterns, choose the **Template** tab page for the template node. An area with patterns appears below the list of table types. Click the **Select Pattern** button. A dialog box with a list of defined patterns appears (see Figure 4.11).

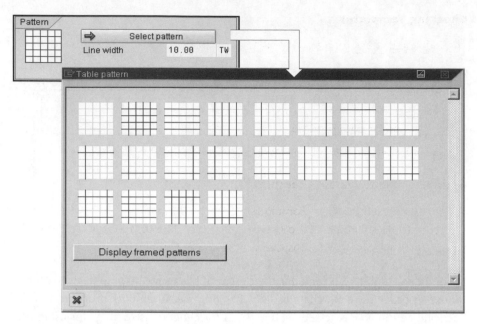

Figure 4.11 Selecting patterns for the template

You can choose between patterns with or without a full box. The structure of the patterns is self—explanatory.

In your example, you want each cell to have a box.

1. To accomplish this, choose the second pattern in the first row; you can choose the version either with or without an overall box. You already defined the box in the superior window, which means it will be output in any case.

2. When you select a pattern with the mouse, the dialog box closes automatically.

3. You are now back in the superior level for editing the node attributes. Now define a line width, such as "10 TW".

You cannot define any other boxes or shading in either the **Output Options** tab page for the template or its subordinate nodes. In particular, this means you cannot define a gray background, whether for the entire template or for individual cells.

> **Tip:** Smart Forms does not have a simple option for outputting horizontal or vertical lines, either. However, you can use a blank template with a corresponding pattern, as no contents are required to output the pattern. If complex patterns are involved, use multiple, overlapping templates (also see Section 4.5.3).

Checking Templates

The individual check for a node reports errors in the following situations:

▶ A template is larger than its superior window.

▶ The template exceeds the limits of a window due to incorrect offsets. This check is possible only for *absolute* positioning; otherwise, the error message will not appear until runtime.

▶ The sum of all columns does not agree with the width of the template.

Assigning Subnodes to a Template

The template itself does not contain any output information. You have to define subnodes to do so. You can also use the same template to output different node types, which enables you to position text next to a graphic, for example.

You have to specify the destination cell for each subnode in order to indicate where its contents should be output. You address it by specifying the line and column numbers as coordinates, where the line is derived from the **From/To** information. Each of these subnodes has two additional input fields, **Line** and **Column**, in the **Output Options** tab page to define the coordinates.

> **Tip:** The node check cannot monitor whether cells actually exist for the specified coordinates. Therefore, make sure you enter the values correctly; otherwise form output will terminate with a runtime error. This can happen often when you make subsequent changes to the template layout.
>
> A simple trick can help you keep track of the cell addresses in complex templates: print out the blank template with all its boxes and write down the coordinates in each individual cell to refresh your memory.

You can also output several subnodes in the same cell—for example, a sequence of different texts. The output sequence within the cell is determined by the sequence of the nodes in the navigation tree. In general, if there is not enough space in a template cell, the remainder of the content is simply cut off, as in secondary windows. Using an additional folder node for each line can help you to avoid this in many cases.

Tip: You can also use folder nodes to output several subnodes in a shared template cell. Folder nodes have additional output options for the template cell; however, you may not assign any output option for the individual subnodes. This joint assignment to a cell also applies to all node types with folder properties—that is, for loop and table nodes as well. This makes it simple for you to generate a list within a cell, for example (see the example for calculating the grand total in the flight invoice in Section 8.6).

You can define a separate style for the template in the **Output Options** tab page. This style then applies automatically to all the subnodes unless you define something else there.

4.5.3 Combining Several Templates

You can define an absolute position in the window to set several templates, adjacent or even overlapping (controlled through the offsets). This can make sense in the following cases:

▶ You want to achieve a special graphic design by overlaying templates with a defined pattern. In some cases, it may make sense to insert additional graphical elements, such as dashes, that do not directly involve the template contents. You can achieve this by overlaying a suitable blank template.

▶ You can position several templates next to one another. In particular, this is necessary when uniform line types are not available for the planned output format—that is, at least one line does not have a uniform height.

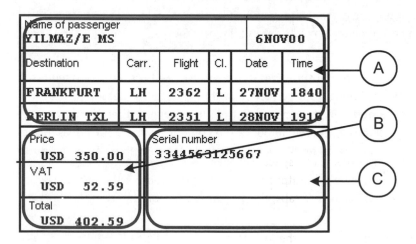

Figure 4.12 Combining several templates

Figure 4.12 shows an example of the second case: the lines with flight price and tax do not have a uniform line height. As a result, at least three templates (called A, B, and C) are required to model the form. Alternatively, you can create three different windows, each with a template as necessary.

4.5.4 Output Table Without Direct Data Access

A special feature of a template is that it defines a fixed output layout for both lines and columns.

In contrast, a table node only fixes the design of the columns. The number of lines that are generated—and their heights—depend on which of the subordinate nodes generate output, how much output the subordinate nodes generate, and which formats apply. Accordingly, table nodes are normally used to output lists whose length is not known beforehand, as is in the case with the flight invoice and its flight bookings as invoice items. For this reason, this table node is described in detail in the context of loops in the main window (see Section 7.2.6).

Still, we would like to point out here that you can use a table node without a loop altogether—that is, without direct access to data. In this case, only the layout functions are available. Once again, you can address cells within the output table of subordinate text nodes.

Example

In your flight invoice, the INFO window is intended to output general invoice information. At the present time, however, the single text node INFO_TEXT is responsible for output. INFO_TEXT achieves table output through the use of tabs.

Instead of using a single text node, you can output the text by assigning a separate text node to each text element. You can then position the texts through a superior table node without table access. To do so, you merely have to define a suitable line layout, consisting of a line type with two columns in this case. This gives you the following benefits:

▶ The height of a row is based on the contents, and changes in text formatting are taken into account.

▶ If the text length exceeds the space provided, a new line is automatically added to the involved cell in the output table, without disrupting the overall layout. In the current solution with tabs, the text would be continued at the start of a new line.

▶ In each line of our example, the information is output together with a preceding label (for example, "Phone 12344"). The output in the new variant uses two text nodes, with the actual information provided through data fields in the normal case. If the information to be output is missing (the phone number "12344" here), the corresponding data field in the second text node is also blank. If you now define a suitable condition for querying the data field in each text node, the entire line may be suppressed; the remaining elements are shifted upward in this case.

In the example described above, the table node is used within a secondary window. Please note that the entire output also has to fit inside the window here. If the output table becomes so long that it exceeds the height of the window, this will cause error messages at runtime and terminate the form output.

5 Elementary Node Types

This chapter introduces the elementary node types, such as text and graphic nodes, that are contained in nearly every form. It concentrates mainly on the modules that require little experience with database queries—or at least no ABAP skills—since both this book and Smart Forms are aimed at users with a corresponding skill level.

5.1 Text Nodes

5.1.1 General Attributes

You display all texts in the form using text nodes. The only exception to this are addresses, which are represented by a separate node type. You can enter custom texts for a form or read them from text modules in the database, which provides for centralized text maintenance.

You can include fields in the text that are then replaced by the appropriate data during form output. This feature is described in detail in Chapter 6.

Formatting

To format texts and fields (data), you use *paragraph* and *character formats*. As the names imply, the respective formatting information applies to either an entire paragraph or a sequence of individual strings (words, for example) that you want to define as a special format in the form design. A format contains the following attributes:

▶ **Paragraph formats**
Font family, color, and size; indents and spacing; text alignment in the paragraph; outline options, such as numbering; keep lines together on the same page

▶ **Character formats**
Font family, color, or size differing from the paragraph format; underscore; format as bar code

All the required paragraph and character formats must already be defined in a style. You can assign the style to a node at different levels in the navigation tree—for example, under the form attributes, in a template node, or directly in a text node. The definition at the lowest hierarchy level is always used.

You create styles using the Style Builder tool, separate from the form editing functions (see Section 3.2). This central definition lets you use the same styles for different forms, which enables you to define a uniform design for your forms and preserve your corporate identity.

Output Area

A text node is always the subnode of another node with layout attributes, such as a **window** or **template**. Text nodes cannot themselves have further subnodes. The superior node is responsible primarily for determining the output position of a text:

▶ If a subnode is in a window, the window position is used.

▶ If output involves a template or an output table, you also have to enter the cell (in the **Output Options** tab page) in which you want to output the respective text.

If you output a text through an output area that has fixed borders (secondary window, template), output control will cut off all text that does not fit within the defined space. A text also disappears completely when the selected font family is too large for the output area. The output area is then empty when you output or test the form.

If a text is located in an output area without a height limit (main window, output table), that text is not cut off. Instead, output control generates as many lines as are needed. Accordingly, you can set the **Page Protection** attribute for a text node in the main window to ensure that the respective text appears as a whole within the print page, and is not split by a page break.

Continuous Text Across Multiple Text Nodes

You can define any number of consecutive text nodes within a given output area—if you want to use different *text types*, for example. You can still output a single, continuous text despite the separation into individual text nodes. In this case, the nodes are combined in accordance with predefined rules. These rules enable you to create uniform formatting across multiple nodes, for example. The superior continuous text overrides the formatting of the individual text nodes if necessary.

You define the necessary settings in the **General Attributes** tab page of the **Text Nodes** input area.

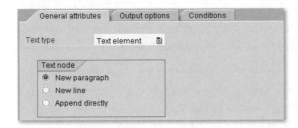

Figure 5.1 Text flow across multiple nodes

▶ **New Paragraph**
This option creates a new line at the start of the current node. All text formatting is defined as assigned in the text of the current node. A new paragraph corresponds to a "hard" line break within an individual text node (created with **Return**).

▶ **New Line**
This option creates a new line, but the paragraph format from the previous text node is copied and applied to the current text node. Therefore, the node's own formatting information is overridden. This entry corresponds to a "soft" line break within an individual text node (created with **Shift + Return**).

▶ **Append Directly**
In this case, the first character of the current text is appended directly to the last character of the previous text node; the formatting from that node is also used. If a blank character is required between the two text elements, you should enter it at the start of the second text, since the system trims trailing blanks in texts automatically.

There is an exception to these rules: if a box or shading is defined for the first text node, the second text node is always inserted as a **new paragraph**, regardless of what is defined.

Text Types

You can choose one of the following three text types in the **General Attributes** tab page:

▶ **Text element**
Supports direct entry of texts and fields, using the inline editor.

▶ **Include text**
Links the form with SAPscript texts, which are defined for a variety of objects in the SAP system. Among other things, this type enables you to reuse standard texts that were used as text modules in previous SAPscript forms. This is helpful for tasks such as migrating SAPscript forms to Smart Forms.

▶ **Text module**
Defined as a standardized text in the system, which means you can use it in several different forms (as a generally valid header or footer text, for example) at the same time.

In addition, you can consider the output of formatted address data to be a special text type, which is modeled in Smart Forms as the address node, a fully independent node type. This node type is described in detail later in this book.

Box and Shading

Before we discuss the above text types in detail, we would first like to point out several rules that apply to boxes and shading in text nodes. Like the other text nodes, the corresponding items are located in the **Output Options** tab page.

▶ Boxes and shading always refer to a rectangular area whose height is defined by the number of output lines. Even if the last line of a text is blank, the entire line is included in the box/shading.

▶ Under the default settings, a space of some 25% of the font height appears between the top line and the start of the text; the bottom line appears immediately below the end of the text.

▶ The left and right margins are also equal to the margins of the text. You can define additional spacing through the paragraph format.

If a text node has a box or shading, it cannot be continued with additional text nodes. If the first text node has a box or shading, the contents of the second text node are output with a new paragraph format (that is, in a new line, and so on), even if you choose **Append Directly** as an attribute for the second node. Box/shading information applies only to the first text.

5.1.2 Text Element

To create a new text, node, choose **Create · Text in the context menu**. A node with text type **Text element** is created by default. You can then change it to a different text type if necessary.

In the flight invoice in the example, choose page FIRST, window MAIN and node INTRODUCTION.

You edit the output text in an editor that appears directly in the **General Attributes** tab page, hence the name *inline editor*. It provides simple word processing functions that you will be familiar with from most WYSIWYG editors.

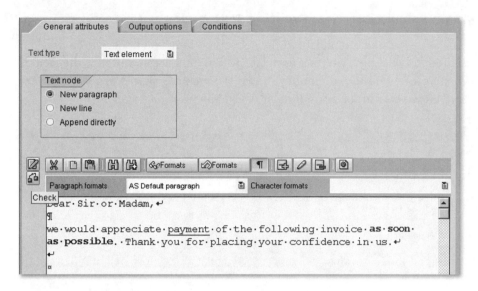

Figure 5.2 Text in text node

The inline editor is also used for similar purposes elsewhere in the SAP system. As a result, you are probably already familiar with it. If not, you will find a detailed description in Section 13.3.

In the inline editor, the display in the input area (with character formats such as *Bold* and *Italic* or with different font families; see Figure 5.2) largely corresponds to what the later output will look like.

Text nodes also frequently contain placeholders for fields, which are not filled with the corresponding data until the form is output. These placeholders not only determine the position of the output characters, but also their formatting (see Chapter 6 for more information).

> **Note:** When you input new texts in the form, the current language setting is also saved. All texts in a form can then be translated into other languages in with the SAP translation tool (see Section 13.2).

To familiarize yourself with text nodes, you will enter several sample texts in the form header of your flight invoice. To do so, use the template that you created as an output area in Section 4.5. Sample printout 2 in the Appendix shows how the text and formatting you enter look in the printout.

5.1.3 Sample Exercise: Creating Text Nodes

You already created a template in the section on template nodes in the previous chapter. You will now use this template to output suitable texts for the sender. When you are finished, the nodes shown in Figure 5.3 should appear under the SENDER window in the Form Builder navigation tree.

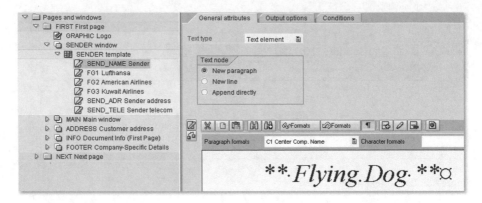

Figure 5.3 Texts for form header

To create the new text nodes, first click on template node SENDER to select it. Then choose **Create · Text** in the context menu to create a separate text node for each cell in the template. Please note that you also have to assign each template cell, with line and column, in the **Output Options** tab page.

Please refer to the sample printout in the Appendix to see which texts you should enter. To format the texts, use the three new paragraph formats C1, L, and R. If you have not created these paragraph formats yet, instructions for defining them are contained in the sample exercise in Section 3.2.7.

5.1.4 Include Text (SAPscript Texts)

You use text type **Include text** to include existing texts that have been defined in the system with the SAPscript text editor. This text type corresponds to the SAPscript statement INCLUDE. You already created a standard text in the *Getting Started* chapter, because the SAPscript text that is used in your sample form did not exist yet (see Section 2.2.2).

Creating a New Text Node

When you create a new text node, a node with text type **Text element** is created by default. To access a SAPscript text, you have to change the text type to **Include text**. A confirmation prompt appears when you change the text type. Answer it with *Yes*. The confirmation prompt appears because any text that you have already entered is lost when you change the text type.

Changing the text type also changes the structure of the **General Attributes** tab page. The inline editor disappears and you can now specify the attributes of a SAPscript text (text name, text object, text ID and language). Figure 5.4 shows an example.

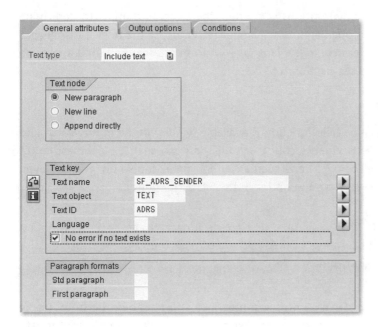

Figure 5.4 Text node with include text

Text Attributes (Text Key)

SAPscript texts are saved in the system under a name and various classification attributes. You have to specify all the relevant key attributes to uniquely describe a text and locate it in the system.

▶ Text object TEXT represents a SAPscript standard text in the example.

▶ The entry ADRS for the text ID stands for a subgroup of standard texts that are defined specifically for printing address information (see Section 13.3 for the definitions of these attributes). The standard indicator for a general SAPscript standard text is ST as the text ID.

The actual text module is found through the text name within this classification.

There are three ways to define the output language of the include text:

▶ You can specify a fixed language in the corresponding field (if you always want to output the text in the same language, for example).

▶ The entry for the language can be defined dynamically through a field. Usually, this field is then determined through a parameter in the form interface—that is, specified by the main program.

▶ If neither of the above options is defined, the system attempts to determine the include text through an internal language vector. All the relevant languages from the form interface, logon language, or form are scanned until a suitable text is found (also see Section 5.5).

Assigning Texts

A comprehensive value help function is available (via **F4**) in the input line to find individual text objects when creating a node. You can search by the attributes listed above, as well as by criteria such as author, date, and so on. You can even display individual texts from the hit list in the SAPscript editor.

> **Tip:** The contents of the included text are no longer visible in the text node itself. To check the contents of the text, you can call the value help again with the corresponding attributes.

In the standard case, Smart Forms assumes that a form should be output only when the required include texts in the text nodes are available in the appropriate language. If not, the entire output process is terminated with a runtime error, as described in the *Getting Started* chapter. If you want the form to be output anyway in this case, set the attribute **No error if no text exists**.

Formats for an Include Text

Just as you can only access formats in the corresponding style in Smart Forms, each existing SAPscript text also has its own defined style. By default, this is the SYSTEM style, which allows only basic formatting. You already saw an example of it in the *Getting Started* chapter (see Section 2.2.2).

Therefore, each include text can already contain several different formats, based on this defined style. The format ID is retained when the texts are output in Smart Forms, but the contents are read from the style of the include text node.

Tip: During form output, the system attempts to read the formats of an include text from the style that is active in the respective text node of the form. Therefore, make sure that all the formats you use are available in this style under Smart Forms. It is entirely possible that the contents of these formats differ from the contents defined in the previous style in the SAPscript text. As a result, the formatting of the included texts can be dependent on the form.

Here is an example: The address window of the flight invoice contains a standard text, SF_ADRS_SENDER, for the sender line. When you edit and print this text in the SAPscript editor, you will see that the text is defined in a small font without underscores. It is output with underscores in Smart Forms, however. The reason for this is paragraph format SD, which is defined in style SAPADRS. This style is also assigned in the text node under Smart Forms, and the characters are also defined as underscored there. You can check the paragraph format yourself by calling up style SAPADRS in the Style Builder.

You also have the option of replacing individual paragraph formats in the include text with paragraph formats from the form. Two options are available:

▶ If you specify a value for attribute **Standard Paragraph**, this overrides all the paragraphs that are formatted as a standard paragraph in the include text.

▶ You can use the **First Paragraph** attribute to configure a paragraph format for the first paragraph of an include text. If the **Standard paragraph** field is empty, all standard paragraphs in the include text are also formatted with this paragraph format.

Dynamic Text Names

It is also possible to define a text node as an include text, but to not know the actual text name until the form is output. This is the case, for example, whenever the text name depends on the respective document that is output—for example, texts that are entered as supplementary information for a sales documents or material texts that are dependent on the item. In this case, the text name must be defined dynamically through a variable field (see Section 6.2.3 for information on the general use of fields).

To illustrate this process, consider a delivery document. A text will be output for each item in this document. Suitable node attributes for calling the include text are shown in Figure 5.5.

Figure 5.5 Include text with dynamic name assignment

The code *VBBP* in this case indicates the general object type **Delivery**. The entry for the text ID refers to text type **0001**, which you also have to define in the respective item. If no entry is made, however, no error message is output in your case (see the corresponding attribute at the bottom of the screen). The text language is determined by the calling main program. This parameter is described in detail later in this book, along with the interface parameters.

In this case, the special entry for the text name is important. Because it is enclosed in ampersands (&), you can see that TEXT_NAME is not the name of the required text, but instead is a placeholder that is filled with the correct name when the form is output.

The text for a delivery item is always saved in the SAP database in such a way that the exact code of the item is contained. Therefore, the name of the text contains the delivery number (ten digits) and the item number (six digits).

This individual text name must be known in order to read the text from the database during form output. There are two possible ways of accomplishing this:

▶ The text name is provided by the form interface. This method is described in Chapter 9.

▶ The value is assigned within a program node by combining the document and item numbers (before the include text is called, of course). The contents of a program node of this type are discussed in detail in Section 13.3.4.

5.1.5   Including Text Modules

A text node with type **text module** refers to an existing text module in the system. This allows you to use such text modules easily in multiple forms. You maintain the text modules independently of form editing. Changes to text modules are reflected automatically during form printout. This means you do not have to activate the form again, as is the case when texts are entered individually for a specific form.

Therefore, text modules are similar to standard texts that you maintain in the SAP-script editor. Smart Forms text modules have two major advantages, however:

▶ They can be used across clients.
▶ They can be transported and translated.

Therefore, standard texts are the preferable application within Smart Forms. This does not mean that include text nodes are superfluous, however; they still have to be used to access object-specific texts for a material, vendor, or sales document, for example.

You can use text modules in a form only when those modules are defined in the same language as the form itself.

> **Note:** If a text module is not found during form output, the system responds with a runtime error and terminates the entire spool request. Therefore, make sure that the addressed text modules have been maintained in the target language.

You manage text modules through the initial screen for Smart Forms. You enter the actual text just like a text node in the form. If you want to create text modules in the system first, skip to Section 5.1.7 to read up on the procedure.

There are two options for including text modules in a form:

▶ **Address the text module as a reference.**
In this case, the text module appears write-protected in the inline editor, and is retrieved anew each time the form is output.

▶ **Copy the text module completely.**
In this case, the contents are copied and the inline editor treats the text as if you entered it directly in the form (changes are possible). Therefore, the text module acts as a template here. Later changes to the text module do not affect the form.

5.1.6   Sample Exercise: Including Text Modules

In this example, you will replace the introductory text of the flight invoice with a flight invoice, to illustrate the editing functions.

Open the MAIN node in the FIRST page of the flight invoice form. Then create another text node *above* INTRODUCTION with context menu **Create · Text**. Because INTRODUCTION is the first node under MAIN, you should position the cursor on MAIN; the new node is then inserted in the top position.

The node is created as a standard text element by default. Change the text type to **Text module**. The system prompts you to confirm that you want to change the text type. Answer **Yes**. Figure 5.6 shows the corresponding section of the navigation tree.

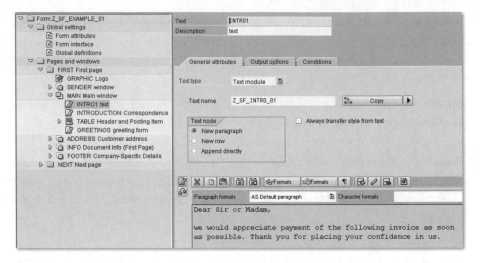

Figure 5.6 Inserting a text module

Enter the name Z_SF_INTRO_01 as the text module for the new node in the **General Attributes** tab page. If this text does not exist in your system yet, read Section 5.1.7 to find out how to create it.

Dynamic Text Name

In some cases, it may make sense to define the name of the text module dynamically. The addressed text module can then vary from case to case—for example, a dunning text that is dependent on the dunning level. In this case, instead of a text name, you enter a field whose contents are defined with the name of the respective dunning text (see Chapter 6).

Style Information

You can define paragraph and character formats for the included text by referring to either the style in the text module or the style in the form:

▶ When you add a new text module, the name of the style is automatically copied to the text node (as the entry in the **Output Options** tab page). If the paragraph formats you use are also contained in the superior style in the form, you can delete the entry for the style in the text node, which may change the formatting.

▶ The **Always Copy Style from Text** attribute has been defined especially for dynamic assignment of the text module name. After all, different styles may be needed for different text modules. If you set this attribute, you cannot enter a style in the **Output Options** tab page. Instead, the system automatically uses the entry for the text module.

Copying Texts

If you want to change the contents of a text module for your current form, click the **Transfer** button. The Form Builder automatically changes the text type back to **Text element** and copies the contents of the text module.

You can now edit the contents in the inline editor as usual. The original text module remains, of course, but any subsequent changes to it will not be reflected in the form.

5.1.7　Creating and Maintaining Text Modules

You just learned how to include existing Smart Forms text modules in a form. You will now find out how to create and maintain these text modules in Smart Forms.

One of the primary attributes of text modules is that they are managed independently of the forms. Accordingly, Smart Forms provides a transaction for maintaining these text modules that is completely separate from, yet almost identical to the editing options of the inline editor in the text node of a form.

The most important attributes of text modules include:

▶ They are valid in all clients, in contrast to include texts, which you create in the SAPscript editor.

▶ They have a link to the transport system, which is why you have to assign them to a development class.

▶ They have a link to the translation tools in the system; the current logon language when you create a text module is defined as its original language.

Your starting point for maintaining text modules is the usual initial screen for Smart Forms, as shown in Figure 5.7. Any customer-defined text modules must lie in the customer namespace, which starts with Y or Z.

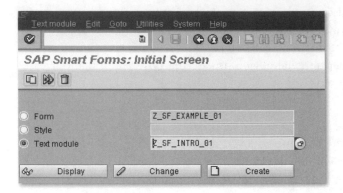

Figure 5.7 Maintaining text modules

> **Background:** Text modules are saved as reduced forms and therefore use the same database tables. To differentiate between text modules and forms, text modules have the flag T (= text module) in the database field for the form type. When searching for text modules with the **F4** value help, you will occasionally see all the (regular) forms in the hit list as well. You can then limit these results to the required type in the corresponding selection screen.

Because text modules, like forms, can be transported to other SAP systems, they are integrated in the SAP development environment. Therefore, the first time you save a new text module, the system prompts you to select a development class (see Figure 2.12 for comparison). During the exercise, use $TMP or **Local Object**.

The processing screen for text modules has two tab pages:

▶ **Text**
The options that are available for entering a text are also available as in the individual text nodes of a form. You can also enter fields for outputting data. Please note, however, that the system does not check at this point whether a field entry actually exists in the destination form. If you call up a module of this type in several forms, you have to define the same field name in all the forms.

▶ **Administration**
You have to assign a style to each text module. This style is assigned automatically whenever you include the respective text node in the form. This ensures that the formats you use are also available in the form. Whether or not they are actually used depends on your definitions. You can also define the languages (if any) into which you want a given text module to be translated. You specify this information in the form attributes.

Text modules do not have to be activated separately. When you create or change a text module, it is immediately available for use in a form.

5.1.8 Sample Exercise: Creating a Text Module

Create a new text module that will replace the previous, custom introductory text in your invoice form (suggested name: Z_SF_INTRO_01, as shown in Figure 5.7). Write a text of your choice.

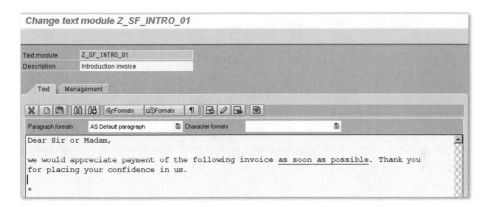

Figure 5.8 Text module for the flight invoice

Assign style Z_SF_STYLE_01 to the text module in tab page **Administration**. This makes the same formats available as in the form (see Figure 5.8). The introductory text in the form was previously set to paragraph format TB.

5.2 Address Node

Forms that you create in Smart Forms often contain a recipient, for delivery notes or invoices, or other references to an address (in posting documents, for example).

This recipient address has to be formatted correctly, especially if you intend to mail a form. Smart Forms features the **Address** node type for this application. It guarantees that the address is formatted according to the postal regulations of the sender country (ISO 11180 or Universal Postal Union guidelines). This default system formatting defines, for example, the number of lines used to output the address.

The functions of the address node are based on *CAM* (= *central address management*) in the SAP system, which is described in detail further below. This function is referred to as *BAS* (= *Business Address Services*) in Basis Release 6.1 and later.

An address in CAM is accessed through its unique address number, which has to be known when the node is processed. You do not need to have any technical knowledge to configure an address node.

> **Tip:** Most of the modules that utilize the CAM (such as the customer master) provide an icon directly in the input screen that lets you display which address format is used.

5.2.1 Creating Address Nodes

You can create an address node directly for a page node or within a window. The advantage of the first option is that the address node appears as a window in the Form Painter, and you can adjust its position and dimensions there.

In many cases, however, you will define a separate window—whose position and dimensions are designed for a window envelope (which has its own standards)—to display the address. In addition to the recipient's address, this window usually contains a text node with the sender's address in fine print as the first line in the address window.

Choose **Create · Address** in the context menu for a node of a page or window to insert the address node.

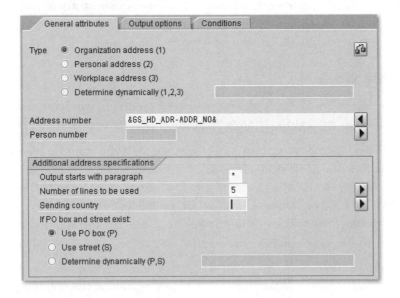

Figure 5.9 Address node (General attributes)

The options in the **Output Options** and **Conditions** tab pages are the same as in other node types. The additional entries for window position and size are available in the **Output Options** tab page only when you create the address node directly in a page.

Address Type

The first option in the **General Attributes** tab page is the address type:

▶ **Organization addresses**
These addresses are the conventional business addresses; they are assigned to customers, vendors, or a company code. Such addresses are uniquely identified through a single (ten-digit) *address number*.

▶ **Private addresses**
These addresses are assigned to a specific person. Private addresses contain additional attributes, such as title and additional name components. A person can have several addresses; therefore, both a *person number* and an *address number* are required to identify an address.

▶ **Workplace addresses**
These addresses involve people at companies (defined as *contact persons* in the SAP system). They contain person-specific attributes such as department, phone number and extension, room number, and so on. Once again, both an address number and a person number are required to identify an address.

You can also specify the address type dynamically. To do so, you use a field as a placeholder, which is filled with a suitable value at runtime. The application could be a newsletter that you send to both companies and individuals, for example. In this case, the address type also has to be determined from the available data and defined as a field.

Address Number and Person Number

The next attribute is the actual address number. This specification is almost always defined as a field, because you want to be able to send a form to more than one address. You enter the corresponding field name enclosed in ampersands (&).

> **Tip:** The field for the address number must have a valid value during output. Otherwise, the system terminates the output process with an runtime error that you may not be able to interpret correctly. Therefore, you may find it useful to define a condition for the address node that checks whether the required address number possesses a value at all (see Section 7.3.1).

You also have to specify a person number for private and workplace addresses. Once again, it only makes sense to determine the value dynamically through a field.

> **Tip:** When you create a new address node, the input field for the person number is set to the mode for entering the number directly (see Figure 5.9). You can even use the **F4** value help function for this field. To enter the (longer) field names, however, you have to switch the input field to the extended display (by clicking the arrow to the right of the input field).

Structuring the Address

The other attributes in the **Additional Address Specifications** box involve the structure of the address during later output:

▶ **Output starts with paragraph**
This value determines the paragraph format. No value help is available for this field. The code for the paragraph format must exist in the configured style, but this is not verified during the form check. The default paragraph format of the style is used when you enter "*".

▶ **Number of lines to be used**
If space is limited, it may make sense to limit the address output to a certain number of lines. In this case, the formatting routine in CAM suppresses the appropriate number of lines in the address. The maximum value of this field is "10". The system proposes a default value ("5" in the example).

▶ **Sender country**
Generally, the address format is dependent on the recipient country (including language-specific components such as "P.O. Box"). The specification for the sender country at this point enables the CAM address formatting to determine whether the recipient's address differs from the sender's country. In this case, the international address version (with the additional specification of the recipient's country, for example) is defined automatically.

If you leave the field blank, the system formats the address in accordance with the Customizing settings in Central Address Management. The default sender country here is the value specified when the address was entered.

▶ **If both PO box and street address are defined**
When an address has either a street address or a PO box, the system always selects the proper entry. If both entries are defined for an address, however, you can use this option to define which entry you want Smart Forms to use.

You can also define this value dynamically with a field entry (which must contain either "P" or "S" in this case).

If you insert the address as directly inferior node of a page (in the Form Painter, for example), the system displays a separate output area for the address in the Form Painter.

Address Format (Customizing)

The address is converted to postal format in the address node based on an ABAP function module, ADDRESS_INTO_PRINTFORM. The procedure used for formatting is described in detail in both the documentation for this function module and the chapter on CAM in the SAP Library.

You can adjust the type of address formatting individually in Customizing (using address versions, for example). To do so, choose the IMG menu path **Basis · Services · Address management** or **General Settings · Configure Countries · Define Countries** (Address Formatting Routines).

If you have special requirements, user exits are also available that enable you write ABAP programs for your own customer-specific address formats. These changes are passed through to the address nodes in Smart Forms.

Function module ADDRESS_INFO_PRINTFORM can also be addressed directly through a program node in Smart Forms, which activates additional formatting options in some cases. This procedure is described in Section 8.5 as an example of using a program node, but you should rarely need it for standard applications.

5.3 Graphics and Background Graphics

Smart Forms features several options for outputting graphics in the form (as a company logo, for example, optionally in color or in black and white). The only prerequisite is that the graphics must be imported into the SAP system first, through the graphics management transaction (SE78). See Section 13.4 for a detailed description of this process. You've already had some practice in working with graphics in the *Getting Started* chapter (Section 2.2.5).

5.3.1 Integration in the Form

The following options are available for integrating graphics in a draft form:

▶ **As a background graphic for a page**
You assign the graphic directly in the corresponding tab page of the page node. You can also use a background graphic to trace a scanned sample form in the Form Painter and Table Painter, for example.

► **As a graphic node directly within a page**

In this case, the node also contains the attributes of a window and is displayed directly in the Form Painter, like the logo for the flight invoice. The position of this graphics window is determined as an offset from the upper left margin. Please note, however, that the size of the graphic—with height and width—is calculated directly by the system, based on the selected resolution, and cannot be changed by the user.

► **As a graphic node within a window**

In this case, the position of the graphic can depend on other nodes, such as texts. If the text length changes, the graphic node is moved, and may disappear completely from a secondary window if not enough space is available.

► **As a graphic node below a template/output table**

In this case, you also have to specify the coordinates of the cell, as for text nodes. Only left-aligned format is possible in this case.

The flight invoice contains a logo graphic, which you configured in the *Getting Started* chapter. You define the required graphic, similar to include texts, in the **General Attributes** tab page (see Figure 5.10).

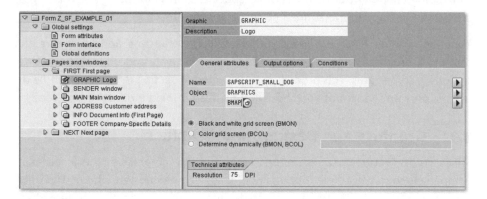

Figure 5.10 Graphic node

Graphics are saved similarly to include texts in the SAP system, with a name and additional classification attributes. The *Getting Started* chapter described in detail how to locate a graphic in the system. The corresponding selection parameters for the value help are shown in Figure 2.14.

> **Tip:** The value help returns a list of all the graphics that meet the specified criteria. If a large number of graphics are defined in your system, you may find it helpful to use the **restriction** function in the hit list, which enables you to select by author, for example.

In contrast to include texts, a standard SAP installation has only one attribute for both the graphics object and the graphics ID: GRAPHICS and BMAP. The latter value indicates that only pixel-based bitmap/raster graphics can be processed.

In addition to entering a fixed name for a graphic, you can define the selection dynamically. In this case, you use data fields that include different graphics depending on the situation—for example, to make a logo dependent on the sales organization or output pictures of materials (see also the notes for include texts).

> **Tip:** You can also overlay graphics and texts for output. To do so, create two different windows: one for the graphic and one for the text. To output graphics and texts adjacently, you can also use two window nodes or—even better—a superior template.

5.3.2 Graphics in a Window, Template, or Output Table

When graphic nodes are output in a window or in a cell of a template, the vertical output positioning always depends on the previous output in the respective output area. Accordingly, you can only specify the **Horizontal Position** of a graphic node in the **Output Options** tab page, as shown in Figure 5.11.

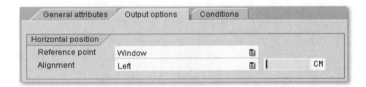

Figure 5.11 Horizontal position of a graphic

The reference point for the horizontal position can be either the border of the output area (with the typical alignments *Left*, *Centered*, or *Right*) or the end of the previous paragraph. If necessary, enter the distance to the left or right border (input field after the alignment specification).

The same select options apply to outputting the graphic in a template or an output table. In this case, reference point **Window** refers to the cell as the output area. The options for choosing an alignment are limited in this case, since only *Left* will produce sensible results. Of course, the **Output Options** tab page contains information on the coordinates of the corresponding cell, like the text node previously.

Tip: The vertical output position of the graphic is always determined by the previous output in the window. If there is no previous node, the graphic is output at the upper window/cell border. To move the graphic down, insert other nodes that generate blank output (such as a text node with blank lines) above the graphic node. Of course, if you use a template for the output, you can also include a blank template line.

5.3.3 Background Graphic for Page

You can also define a single graphic as the background graphic for an entire page, instead of a graphics node. You define this entry in the **Background Graphic** tab page of the respective page node (see Figure 5.12).

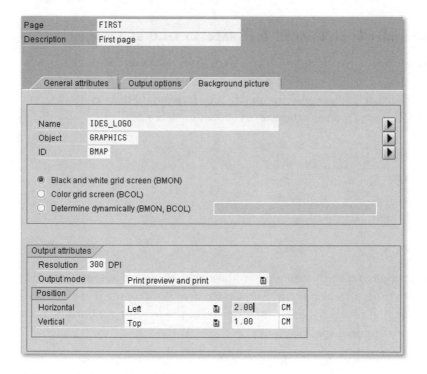

Figure 5.12 Background graphic for a page

You define the position of the background graphic with a direct reference to the page format. You define the other attributes the same way as in a graphic node.

The background graphic was implemented in Smart Forms primarily to enable you to display and trace a scanned, preprinted form. This can greatly simplify the positioning of windows and other output elements such as templates and output tables. Therefore, you can also display a background graphic in the Form Painter and the Table Painter. To ensure that other windows do not cover the image in the Form Painter, you should set the **Transparent Window** option in the corresponding settings.

The **Output Mode** attribute is also provided for preprinted forms. The options are:

▶ Blank (= no output)

▶ Print preview (for verification purposes only, no printout)

▶ Print preview and print

This attribute is blank by default, which means nothing is output. This corresponds to an application case in which you use the background graphic only to trace it. If you want to print the graphic, you have to select the latter option.

> **Tip:** You can overlay windows with any contents over the position of the background image. You can use the option, for example, of inserting additional text in a background image, for example.

5.3.4 Optimizing Print Output

If you repeatedly output forms that contain the same graphics, such as a logo, you can achieve much better performance by using the printer memory. In this procedure, the graphics are sent to the printer only once at the start of the spool request and remain there until the entire request is processed.

To use this option in Smart Forms, you have to set the appropriate attribute for the graphic in graphics management (transaction SE78, see Section 13.4).

5.4 Folder Node

As the number of nodes in a form increases, so does the risk that you will lose track of what is going on in the navigation tree. To mitigate this effect, you should decide on a uniform system for naming the nodes. This will make it easier for you to recognize the nodes in the navigation tree. Please note that Smart Forms does not have a search function for locating a specific node.

Another way to keep the display tidy is to use folder nodes. You can assign nodes whose contents or form are related to this node type as a shared subnode. They are then grouped together in this node in the navigation tree. For example, you can group the subnodes of a template or an output table together in the navigation tree by lines, columns, or even cells.

The folder also features additional functions, such as header and footer lines and the shared definition of a style.

Example: You want an invoice to contain additional texts, dependent on the payment conditions. In this case, you will create several text nodes, and assign conditions to each of them. To improve clarity, you can group the text nodes together in a folder called "Texts for payment conditions", for example. In other cases, it can make sense to define a condition for a folder node itself, which then applies to all the subordinate nodes in that folder.

Events Tab Page

In this tab page, you can configure the header and footer areas for the folder node. This information is output at the beginning/end of the area described by the contents of all the corresponding subnodes. You also have to specify a height for the footer area, which output control needs in order to calculate the page length.

If the header and footer areas are active, additional event nodes named **Header Area** and **Footer Area** appear automatically beneath the folder node in the navigation tree. You can then create additional nodes under each event node in order to output headers or calculate sums, for example.

Please note that these event nodes may not be stacked. Once you have activated a header or footer area, you cannot define these areas in any other node. Moreover, if you want to use both header and footer areas, both must always be defined in the same node. The Form Builder checks these conditions.

Note: The functions for the header and footer areas are also available with extended features in loop and table nodes. These are described in detail in Section 7.2.

Output Options Tab Page

The box and shading are equivalent to the corresponding options in other nodes. The folder node features the following additional options:

▶ You can assign an individual style that applies to all the corresponding subnodes.

▶ If you output through a template or output table, additional output options appear to define the attributes for assigning a cell. An entry in the order node ensures that all the corresponding subnodes are output in this cell, as long as no other cells are addressed in this node.

5.4.1 Sample Exercise: Creating a Folder

In the previous exercises, you created the SENDER window in the flight invoice, which contains information on the travel agency. You output three airlines in one template line within the assigned template. You could logically group these nodes together within a folder. The structure in the form should then look like Figure 5.13.

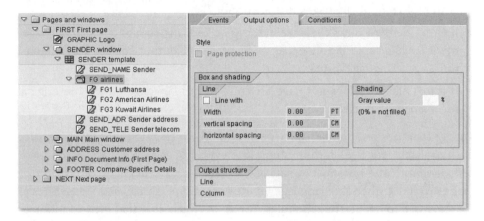

Figure 5.13 Attributes of the folder node

Choose menu path **Create · Folder** in the context menu of the navigation tree. Then move the existing texts FG1 through FG3 to the area below the new folder (simply drag and drop with the mouse). Make sure that the existing sequence of the texts is retained.

5.5 Language in a Form

When you create a new form, the Form Builder automatically enters the user's current logon language as the original language in the form attributes. As a result, all the long texts used in the form are saved with this language setting. These include:

▶ Node names

▶ Contents of text nodes (continuous text)

You can use the main SAP translation tool later to translate these texts into other languages. Please note, however, that even after translation, you can edit the form only in its original language in the Form Builder. The only exception to this rule is a subsequent change of the original language (see Section 13.2). You can use the form attributes to define whether or not you want a given form to be translated and, if so, into which language.

5.5.1 Language for Form Output

When you output a form, the node names are no longer pertinent; only the contents of the text nodes and their language-specific information are relevant. The language for this output can come from different sources:

▶ In many cases, the main program defines the output language. A corresponding parameter is available for this purpose in the form interface (possibly even with replacement languages; see Section 9.7).

▶ If a text element is not available in the specified language or one of its replacement languages, or if no language was specified, output control uses the current logon language instead.

▶ If a text element does not have an entry in this language either, the original form language is used.

The system uses an internal language vector, in which priorities are assigned to each available language in the system. If a text is not available in the highest-priority language, the system automatically searches for the language with the next-highest priority. The same language vendor procedure is also used for text nodes that are used to include text modules. Therefore, make sure that the text modules you use are also available in the required language(s).

You can only assign the output language as a custom node attribute for include texts. If no language is specified, the language vector is processed as usual, which means the specification from the interface has the highest priority. You already saw in Figure 5.5 how an include text can be defined for the language requirements of the form interface.

Date Output

A special case of "language dependence" is the country-specific format for outputting dates. This is especially true of the current date, which is available in a system parameter. The system uses the defaults recorded for the current user unless a different country was configured in an ABAP statement (see Section 6.4.3).

6 Form Data

6.1 Overview

Almost all forms are used to output variable data that is known only when you output a form (that is, at runtime), but not when you design it. The main program normally passes this data on to the form. In turn, the main program retrieves the data from the database and/or prompts the current user to enter it.

> **Example:** A delivery node always contains the ship-to party's address, the delivered materials as items, and various assorted background information such as the delivery date, delivery note number, and so on. This information is not known until the actual form is output.

To integrate this variable data in the form, you use placeholders in text nodes as substitutes for the data. You can also use placeholders in text modules, which makes them extremely flexible. A further use for placeholders is as an attribute of a given node (as a condition to be queried, for example).

These placeholders are called *fields* in Smart Forms. When you output a form, the system replaces all fields in the text with their currently valid values.

Data Sources

Of course, the system has to know how to retrieve the contents in order to fill the fields correctly during form output. The following options are available:

▶ The main program selects the data from database tables and then passes it on to the form through a defined form interface.

▶ The data is provided by the SAP system (the current date, for example, or the current page number in the printout).

▶ The data is determined in the form itself during output (for example, outputting sums in a list or making calculations within ABAP program coding).

The common factor in all three cases is that the fields that provide the required information at runtime are included with their names as placeholders in the text node. You can treat these placeholders like normal text (and define a suitable format, for example).

Data Definition

Before you can use a field as a placeholder in a text, however, that field must be known in the system. You do this in the data *definition* (or *declaration*). Analogous to the above three cases, Smart Forms provides the following three options for defining data in a form:

▶ Parameters in the form interface describe data that can be substituted by the main program.

▶ System fields have defined meanings, such as *date* and *page number*.

▶ *Global data*, whose contents are derived from the form itself (by calculating internal totals, for example), is defined within the form. These fields are often also required to output parameters with a desired format of the form interface.

Data Structure

The data used in the form can differ in other ways than its possible origins. It can also have very different contents. For example, a date value is saved differently than a complete address, which is different from a list of items in an invoice.

Accordingly, different *types* of data are involved. These different data types affect how you design the form, which is why you have to understand the basic differences in order to use data (and the corresponding fields) sensibly in the form.

Structure of This Chapter

The subject of *form data* is covered in three sections in this chapter:

▶ You will first see how data is integrated in the form (Section 6.2), which means starting with the result. This approach will help to familiarize you with the general subject.

▶ You will then learn in detail how data is defined under Smart Forms (Section 6.3). You will also learn several basic concepts.

▶ Smart Forms can retrieve data from different sources. The most important of these is the form interface, which the last section of this chapter introduces (Section 6.4), along with the form interface's most important attributes.

6.2   Fields as Placeholders

6.2.1   Field List

To use data in a form, you first have to define how this data will be addressed. Smart Forms uses *fields* for this purpose.

The *Field List* in the Form Builder contains an overview of which fields exist in any given form under. You can display or hide this additional display window through menu path **Utilities · Field List On/Off,** or through the corresponding icon. Figure 6.1 shows an example.

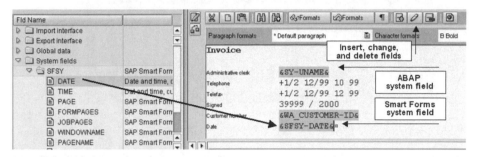

Figure 6.1 Text node with fields for variable data

The field list is displayed in the lower left screen area. It lists all the available fields, sorted by umbrella term. The information is displayed as a navigation tree.

You will read more about the umbrella terms later. First, you will see how easy it is to integrate fields in a text node.

6.2.2 Fields in a Text Node

You can move individual fields directly from the field list to a text by dragging and dropping with the mouse. To do so, you first have to select the appropriate text node and its **General Attributes** tab page. Figure 6.1 shows text node INFO_TEXT from the flight invoice as an example.

Dragging fields with the mouse is both the easiest and the safest way to insert fields, as it ensures that all the field names are spelled correctly. You can even choose the exact position in the text.

After you copy the fields to a node text, they are highlighted in gray there and enclosed in ampersands (&) to help you distinguish them from the normal text. You can format the fields with paragraph and character formats, just like regular text. You cannot change a field name directly, however; you have to use a special function in the inline editor to do so.

Editing Fields in a Text

The Smart Forms version of the inline editor provides three special icons for editing fields (illustrated in the upper right corner of Figure 6.1). You can use these icons to insert, change, and delete fields. You will probably use the change function most often: position the cursor on a field in the text and click the center icon for **Change Field**. A dialog box appears in which you can edit the field name freely, as shown in Figure 6.2.

Figure 6.2 Text node: Changing a field in the text

You can change the field name directly or add formatting options, which are described further below. Of course, you can also use this method to create new fields. However, this is recommended only if the field name is short or if you can insert it easily—from the clipboard, for example. You can also use this method to insert ABAP system fields (such as SY-UNAME)

Field Output with Text

The first ampersand does not have to appear directly before the field name. You can also enter any other characters that would normally be output as text. Figure 6.3 shows an example of this.

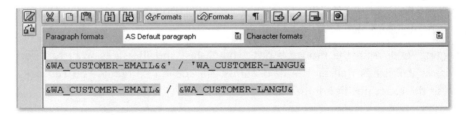

Figure 6.3 Additional text characters in a field name

As a result of the included fields, both lines generate the same output of the customer's e-mail and language for the flight invoice. A slash and blank are used as the separator between the two values. In the first line of the example, the string is included in the field with the language value. Please note that you have to enclose these additional characters in single quotes when you enter them between the ampersands, in order to enable Smart Forms to distinguish them from the field name.

Including such strings within the ampersandsfor field names makes sense when you want to output blank characters along with the values, for example. Another benefit: if the data part of the field name is blank, the corresponding blank character is not output either. Use the field functions in the toolbar as described above to enter these strings.

Fields in Text Modules

If a text node is defined as a text module or include text, all the fields from the *referenced* text are also copied and filled with the appropriate contents during form output.

Please note, however, that when you maintain such texts outside of the form, the system cannot verify whether all the fields that are recorded there are actually defined in the forms where the texts will be output. If you specify an incorrect field name, this will result in a runtime error and termination during form output.

6.2.3 Fields as Node Attributes

You can also use fields directly as entries for a node attribute, in addition to text nodes. Because in this case the contents of the corresponding attribute are not assigned until the form is output at runtime, this approach is also called *dynamic assignment*. The easy-to-use drag-and-drop mouse functions are not available for this application, however.

When you use fields as node attributes, you have to distinguish between two cases, each of which is characterized by different field display and input methods:

▶ If node attributes are represented in *list form*, such as in conditions or loops, the field names are entered without the surrounding ampersands. The header for such input fields is then usually the **field name**. If you want to enter a character string instead, you have to enclose it in single quotes. This notation corresponds to ABAP programming standards (see Figure 6.4).

▶ In contrast, *individual* node attributes must be entered as in the text of a text node. In this case, enclose the fields in ampersands (to assign a variable address number to an address node, for example). You can then enter values directly, as a string, without single quotes.

Figure 6.4 illustrates an example of the former case. Because a condition is used, the node is executed only when print page 3 is processed.

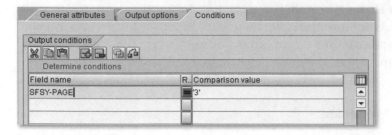

Figure 6.4 Fields as node attributes

Field SFSY-PAGE (= page number) is not enclosed in ampersands; instead, the comparison value is enclosed in single quotes. You can omit the single quotes for numeric values.

6.2.4 Fields with Formatting Options

In the example in Figure 6.1, field &SFSY-DATE& is contained in the text as the current date. When the form is output, the field contents are inserted as is appropriate for the current country. The formatting of the field does not contain any information for the number of places for the year, for example.

In many cases, however, it makes sense to modify the field contents again for output. The system features *formatting options* for this purpose. You append them directly to a field name. The formatting objects are controlled by codes, which you always enter in uppercase. Some of these codes can be combined. In this case, the system interprets the individual options in the defined sequence.

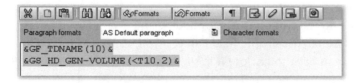

Figure 6.5 Fields with formatting options in a text node

Figure 6.5 shows two examples of fields with formatting options:

▶ The field in the first line was defined alphanumerically. Therefore, it can contain any number of characters. In this example, output is limited to 10 characters.

▶ The field in the second line was defined numerically. Therefore, it contains digits—weight information in this case. The output has a maximum of 10 places, of which two come after the decimal point, without a thousands separator (option T) and with a +/- sign in front of the number (option <).

As you can see in the examples, the output options are simply appended to the field names in parentheses. You can combine the individual options. The following output options are available:

▶ **&field+ <offset>&**
When the field contents are output, the number of places specified in <offset> is skipped. (This is sensible only for character fields.) If the offset is greater than the length of the value, nothing is displayed. Example: &GF_TNAME+5& outputs the full contents of the text variable, starting with the sixth character.

▶ **&field(<nNumber>)&**
Sets the output length to <nNumber> as a natural number. Example: &AMOUNT(8)& returns an output with eight places, without any rounding information for numeric field contents. You can also specify the length with an offset: &TYPE(1)+2& will only return the third character of field TYPE.

▶ **&field(.<nNumber>)&**
Limits the number of decimal places to <nNumber> as a natural number. Example: &AMOUNT(8.2)& returns an output with eight places, including two decimal places.

▶ **&field(*)&**
If the field is defined through a type in the ABAP Dictionary, the output length is taken from there.

▶ **&field(S)&**
Output without +/– sign—that is, as a strict value.

▶ **&field(<)&**
Output +/– sign to the left of a number; the default setting in SAP outputs the +/– sign to the right, after a number.

▶ **&field(E <nNumber>)&**
Displays the field value with the fixed exponent <nNumber>. The mantissa is adapted to this exponent by shifting the decimal character and inserting zeros.

▶ **&field(T)&**
Suppresses the thousands separator; makes sense only for fields with type DEC, CURR, INT, and QUAN, which are output with thousands separators by default.

▶ **&field(Z)&**
Suppresses leading zeros of numbers.

▶ **&field(I)&**
Suppresses the output of initial values; only fields with actual contents are output. Under the default settings, an initial numeric field is treated like the num-

ber zero during output. You can achieve the same effect as this formatting for an entire node by defining condition **field <> initial**.

▶ **&field(R)&**
Right-justified display. Use this option only if you also specify an output length. *Right-justified* only refers to the display within this output length. The corresponding specification in the text format (left/right-justified, for example) determines how the generated field contents are integrated into the surrounding output area.

▶ **&field(F<X>)&**
Replaces leading (left-justified) blanks in the value with the defined fill character. Example: &AMOUNT(F-)& generates leading hyphens.

▶ **&field(L)&**
Converts the date to the local Japanese date format (makes sense only in Japanese SAP systems).

▶ **&field(C)&**
The system takes the field value as a sequence of words separated by blanks. These words are merged to the left and then separated by one blank character each. Leading blanks are omitted completely, as with ABAP statement CONDENSE. This formatting option can also be used for numbers. For example, the formatting &NUMBER(C.2)& enables you to output numbers with two decimal places that are suitable for inclusion in continuous text—that is, which have no blanks at the start.

▶ **&field(K)&**
All previously defined formats are ignored when a fixed conversion routine is defined for a data type in the ABAP dictionary. You can use the (K) option to deactivate this fixed routine and make the other formatting apply instead.

Interpreting the Formatting Options

As you can tell from the above descriptions, not all the formatting options are appropriate for all field types. For example, the display with exponent is logical only for numbers, not for character fields. Accordingly, the system differentiates between *numeric* fields (numbers) and *character fields* (text contents) when interpreting the formatting options.

▶ **Application to numeric fields**
At first, the <length> specification—if any—is evaluated. If no length is specified, the field contents are output in the full length defined in the field declaration. The trailing blank indicates a positive sign. You can use formatting option C to suppress it. The <offset> makes sense only for character fields, and is ignored if specified here.

The following evaluation sequence applies to the formatting options:

<length>	Specification of output length in number of characters
<	+/– sign to the left
L	Japanese date format
C	Suppress blanks
R	Right-justified
F	Insert fill characters

▶ **Application to character fields**

Under the default setting, field contents are output in their full length; only trailing blanks at the end of the string are trimmed. The following evaluation sequence applies to the formatting options:

C	Suppress blanks <length> and <offset>
R	Right-justified
F	Insert fill characters

6.3 Data Structures and Data Definitions

6.3.1 Procedure

In the previous section, you learned how to use fields in text nodes or as attributes in any other nodes. Before you can use a field as a placeholder for data, however, it has to be known to the form. This process is referred to as the *definition* or *declaration* of the data. In accordance with the applications described above, Smart Forms provides the following three options for declaring data and inserting it in the form:

▶ Information in the form interface defines the data that can be substituted by the main program.

▶ System fields, such as the date or page number, are always available and have fixed meanings. You do not have to define these fields in the form yourself.

▶ The specifications in the global definitions define data whose contents can be assigned to the form, such as the result of calculations.

You can also define local data within a program node, but such data is available only in the respective node in this case (to save subtotals, for example). You use the appropriate ABAP statements to declare this data (see Chapter 8). In the following section, you will learn the skills you need to work with data and their definitions in Smart Forms.

6.3.2 Overview of Data Structures

All data in the SAP system is stored in the database system in the main server. To output this data in Smart Forms, you first have to load it into the working memory in the system.

The data in the database system is stored in *transparent tables*. This data is normally transferred to the working memory in the data collection section of the main program that calls the form. This data is then passed on via the form interface to the form, where it can be inserted through its field names.

Of course, a form developer has to know which data the main program makes available via the form interface. To do so, the names of the *interface parameters* have to be known. A form developer also has to know that the data can exist as different *types*. This requires basic understanding of the data types that are used in the SAP system. Such knowledge is a basic prerequisite for using data in forms.

> **Note:** Users who have experience with Customizing or ABAP programs should already be acquainted with the different data types. Therefore, you may already be familiar with much of the information in this section.

At this point, you have to consider only the data located in the working memory of a program. Figure 6.6 shows three main cases that are based on general customer data.

The differences between the three data storage variants are obvious; therefore, consider the consequences of outputting the information they contain.

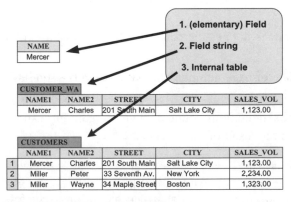

Figure 6.6 Basic types of variables

(1) (Elementary) field

A simple field consists of only one piece of information, and is indicated by its name format NAME. The variable has content "Mercer" for the selected customer. If a corresponding field is defined in the form, the output can take place directly in a text node in the example with &NAME&. Because the field can contain only one piece of information, it is also called an *elementary* data object.

(2) Field string

The field string contains several pieces of information for the selected customer at the same time. It therefore consists of several fields in sequence (hence the term *field string*). Such fields are also frequently referred to as *data components*.

The above example contains five specifications. Each data component has a label (NAME1, STREET, and so on), and the field string itself also has a name (CUSTOMER_WA in this case).

The names of the data components are unique only within a single field string. Therefore, another field string with the same structure called VENDOR_WA could exist for managing vendors' addresses. Accordingly, the system can locate the specific information for a customer only when the name of the involved field string is known.

This affects the display in the form under Smart Forms: to read and output a piece of information, you have to concatenate the specifications in the field (for example, &CUSTOMER_WA-STREET&). You always use a hyphen to define the link between the two levels. These conventions apply generally under ABAP.

Take another look at Figure 6.6—specifically, at the information regarding the data contained in the field string. You see character strings with information on the address (NAME, CITY) on one hand, and a numeric field with a sales value on the other hand. The differences between these data types also have to be known in the system.

> **Note:** The term *field string* is somewhat outdated; more modern terms are *structured data object* or simply *structure* (although the latter term is also used to describe other objects).

(3) Internal table

An internal table enables you to save information on several customers at the same time. The individual data records are numbered in a line index, comparable to a worksheet in a spreadsheet program. The line number has to be specified in order to uniquely identify a data record. The name of a piece of information is derived from the name of the *data component*, which corresponds to a column.

The combination of line and column information describes a unique cell. It contains the actual information. Instead of using the term "cell", however, the place where the actual information is stored is once again referred to as a *field*.

To address the contents of a field in an internal table, you have to name the required data record in addition to the data component. Therefore, the fields in an internal table cannot be addressed directly in a form (in a text node, for example). Instead, the practical procedure involves two steps:

▶ Before the actual output, the required data record is initially copied into an additional field string (as a line) with the same structure.

▶ In the second step, the required information is output as described in the previous section, using the corresponding field in the field string.

Field strings and internal tables are also referred to as *non-elementary data objects*.

> **Note:** Although the term *field* is also assigned other definitions in other contexts, this book concentrates on the conventional meaning defined above.

Summary

You have now learned about the basic variants for saving data in the program memory. Of course, the corresponding program (or form under Smart Forms) also has to know how to retrieve the respective data—as a simple field, for example, or an internal table. For this reason, you always have to define the required data in the first step.

The result of a definition is the specific *data objects*, which can then be addressed in the form or via ABAP. A further criterion is whether the data should be modifiable or not. The data is referred to as *variables* or *constants*, accordingly.

> **Note:** Even though forms are used primarily to output data that does not change, you will define the form as though the corresponding data were modifiable. As a result, the descriptions below speak of *variables* instead of data objects (which is closer to the modern terminology in any case). Therefore, *variable* is the umbrella term for all the types of data described above. In many cases, as well, *data* is simply used to describe the contents of the variables.

Defining the data always involves a *typing*, in addition to assigning a name. This method gives the system information about the structure of the variable created under the new name.

You now have enough basic information to continue with the definition of data in the next step (see Section 6.3.3). In some cases, however, you will come across variables during form development that are much complex than anything you have seen so far. Therefore, you may find it helpful to read about complex structures in the next section.

Variables with Complex Structures

The previous descriptions were based intentionally on a simple example, in order to make the differences between the different types of variables obvious. In practice, however, you will occasionally come across data structures that are quite a bit more complicated. The information in the following steps will help you to master this challenge as well.

As you already learned, a special property of a *field* is that it contains a single piece of information that cannot be broken down further. Because of this characteristic, fields are sometimes described as *elementary*. Previously you assumed that the information in the field string was stored equivalently in the corresponding fields (data components). This includes the name components "Charles" and "Mercer", for example, which are also elementary fields.

However, this restriction no longer applies to modern IT systems. Instead, each field in a structured variable can itself be an independent data component, like a reference.

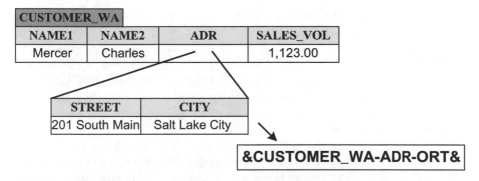

Figure 6.7 Extension 1 for the field string

You will now study two examples that illustrate how useful this technique can be. A data component (piece of information) in the field string can be defined like a reference to another field string (see Figure 6.7).

You can then define a new component ADR in field string CUSTOMER_WA that is defined as a structure that groups together all the information for the customer's address (STREET and CITY in this case). To retrieve a new piece of information from there, the field name also has to contain a new intermediate level in Smart Forms: &CUSTOMER_WA-ADR-STREET&. The previous components STREET and CITY can be deleted from CUSTOMER_WA.

The advantage of this solution is that you can achieve more clarity in field strings that consist of a large number of individual data components. If you include several inferior structures, they can even contain components with the same names, if necessary.

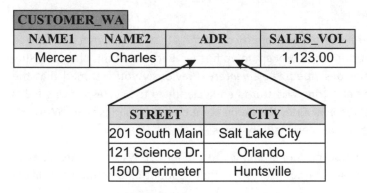

Figure 6.8 Extension 2 for the field string

Alternatively, you can also define a data component in the field string like a reference to an internal table (Figure 6.8).

In this example, you assume that a customer can have several residences, and therefore several addresses as well. The superior field string, CUSTOMER_WA, still contains only a single data record with a single customer's data. The additional component, however, can contain any number of addresses because it is an internal table.

Because the customer's name is not dependent on the address, the name is still listed in CUSTOMER_WA. It can therefore be addressed as before using the concatenated field name under Smart Forms. In contrast, in order to output the address (or possibly several addresses), you have to define individual logic for retrieving each data record individually as described above.

This procedure can also be applied to components within internal tables; references to other data structures can also be defined there. You can even nest internal tables if necessary.

Although this logic can result in an infinite number of combinations, all of them have a similar structure. As a result, the process remains clear.

> **Note:** The description of the form interface also contains individual parameters that involve data with complex structures as described here.

6.3.3   Data Definition

As you saw in the examples in the last section, data can have a wide range of attributes in the system. To use data, you have to define variables that reserve space for it in the program memory, which can then be filled with data. When you define a variable, you also define a *data type* (*typing*). The typing defines the attributes of the variable, which enables the system to reserve the appropriate memory.

Variable name	Type assig...	Reference type	Default value	Constant
NUMBER	TYPE	I		☐
NAME	TYPE	CHAR20		☐
WA_CUSTOMER	TYPE	ADDR		☐
CUSTOMERS	TYPE	TABLE OF ADDR		☐

Figure 6.9 Definition of global data

Some individual data definitions are listed in Figure 6.9. The individual lines are described in detail in the sections below. The entries themselves have no direct reference to the flight invoice from the sample form. However, you also enter the type definitions there to experiment.

Each data definition must contain at least three specifications:

▶ **Variable name**
You must observe certain restrictions that apply to naming:
the first character must always be a letter, and you may not use any special characters except the underscore "_". These rules are checked during the overall check for the form.

► **Typing**

Defines how the following reference type will be interpreted. The following values are available:

LIKE   For reference to existing variables in the form

TYPE   For reference to data types that are defined in the system (ABAP types or entries in the ABAP Dictionary)

TYPE REF   For reference to reference data types (used particularly for developing object-oriented programs)

Only the first two type definitions are described below.

► **Reference type**

These specifications involve new variables. Depending on which value you define in the **Typing** column, they may be data types defined in the system or other data already defined in the form.

When fields (elementary variables) are involved, you can enter a value in the **Default Value** column. If you enter a value as text, you have to enclose it in single quotes; you can omit the single quotes for numeric values.

If you set the **Constant** attribute, the data element cannot be set to a new value in the form. You set a constant when you want a field to always contain a defined default value in order to address it more easily in the text through its name, for example.

The following sections describe several options that are available for typing through TYPE and the corresponding data types. This information is by no means complete, however. For comprehensive information, refer to the documentation in the SAP Library or the corresponding printed documentation.

6.3.4 Using ABAP Data Types

The first line in the last example (see Figure 6.9) types variable NUMBER as I (= integer), which means it can only take the values of whole numbers at runtime. This basic type is supplied by the ABAP development system. The most important ABAP types are:

C	Character string
I	Integer (whole number)
D	Date
T	Time
F	Float (floating-point number)
STRING	Character string of any length

The definitions within the form are automatically translated into appropriate DATA statements in the ABAP programming language when you generate the corresponding function module. Therefore, you can also read about the exact application of type definitions through ABAP types in the SAP Library (term TYPE or DATA).

During the translation into ABAP statements, the standard length defined in the system is used for all the ABAP types (for example, one character for type "C"). You cannot define any other length information, such as NAME(29) under ABAP, in the form. Any such specifications are rejected during the form check. Of course, this also limits your options for using the ABAP types directly.

On the other hand, you really don't have to define the typing through the built-in ABAP types at all, since you can almost always define a typing through a reference to other components that already exist in the SAP system, through the central ABAP Dictionary, or through variables in the form itself.

6.3.5   Reference to the ABAP Dictionary

The *ABAP Dictionary* in the SAP system describes, among other things, the properties of all the database tables used in the system. It is frequently called the *Data Dictionary* or simply the *Dictionary*.

In addition to descriptions of true (*transparent*) database tables, the ABAP Dictionary contains entries that can be used only to define variables (*data types*). You should consider these data types to be like patterns or samples that enable you to define variables with uniform characteristics. One example of this is the uniform length of a name field in all programs, which allows you to use a name field without having to know how many characters the name in the database actually has.

The reference to the ABAP Dictionary is established with the addition TYPE, as with ABAP data types. If no suitable ABAP data type is found, the system automatically searches in the ABAP Dictionary. Figure 6.10 illustrates several examples of this.

In the second line of the example, variable NAME is defined as a text field. Reference type CHAR20 is used for this typing, as defined in the ABAP Dictionary. This entry tells the system that a text field with 20 characters will be defined.

> **Tip:** When the reference type comes from the ABAP Dictionary, you can display the respective entry in the ABAP Dictionary directly by double-clicking in the cell for the reference type (see example in Figure 6.11).

Variable name	Type assig...	Reference type	Default value	Constant
NUMBER	TYPE	I		☐
NAME	TYPE	CHAR20		☐
WA_CUSTOMER	TYPE	ADDR		☐
CUSTOMERS	TYPE	TABLE OF ADDR		☐
VENDOR	TYPE	ADDR		☐
WA_MATERIAL	TYPE	MARA		☐
MATERIAL	TYPE	TABLE OF MARA		☐
WEIGHT	TYPE	MARA-BRGEW		☐

Figure 6.10 Typing via the ABAP Dictionary

Unfortunately, no value help is available to search for suitable entries for the data type. If necessary, switch to the direct display of the ABAP Dictionary in transaction SE11. In many cases, the data type is derived from other information, as you will see below.

A data type in the ABAP Dictionary can also describe several fields simultaneously, or can even include other data types. You can define complete field strings or internal tables with a type assignment based on these central definitions. We will not consider the more complex nesting options yet.

The definition of WA_CUSTOMER in the example illustrates this case: the field string is defined through a data type, ADDR. Although the field labels are slightly different than in the first example address, the system should be clear. Double-click on data type ADDR to display the corresponding entry in the ABAP Dictionary, as shown in Figure 6.11. The involved fields are listed as components with their individual type definitions.

The label **Structure** appears in front of ADDR, the name of the data type. This is a reference to the classification as variable, field string, and internal table described at the beginning of this chapter. This division of data types is also reflected in the ABAP Dictionary; the corresponding terms are *data element*, *structure*, and *table type*.

This approach, using the ABAP Dictionary, is a valuable aid for typing in the form. Complex variables, such as field strings or internal tables, frequently have to be defined with a similar structure. You can define this structure as a data type completely in the ABAP Dictionary. When a typing refers to this data type entry, the complete field string or internal table is defined in the internal table.

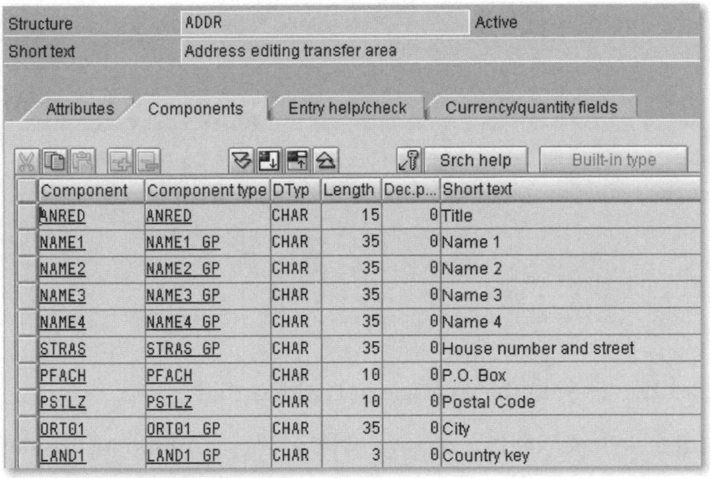

Structure: ADDR — Active

Short text: Address editing transfer area

Attributes | Components | Entry help/check | Currency/quantity fields

Srch help | Built-in type

Component	Component type	DTyp	Length	Dec.p...	Short text
ANRED	ANRED	CHAR	15	0	Title
NAME1	NAME1_GP	CHAR	35	0	Name 1
NAME2	NAME2_GP	CHAR	35	0	Name 2
NAME3	NAME3_GP	CHAR	35	0	Name 3
NAME4	NAME4_GP	CHAR	35	0	Name 4
STRAS	STRAS_GP	CHAR	35	0	House number and street
PFACH	PFACH	CHAR	10	0	P.O. Box
PSTLZ	PSTLZ	CHAR	10	0	Postal Code
ORT01	ORT01_GP	CHAR	35	0	City
LAND1	LAND1_GP	CHAR	3	0	Country key

Figure 6.11 Data type in the ABAP Dictionary

Examine the fourth line in the example in Figure 6.10. An extension for TYPE there creates an internal table, CUSTOMERS, whose line structure, in turn, is defined through data type ADDR and is therefore the same as in WA_CUSTOMER. The addition TABLE OF generates this internal table automatically.

Note: The type definition with TABLE OF did not work properly in the first versions of Release 4.6C; therefore, make sure you have installed the appropriate service packs.

Alternatively, you can create a data type in the ABAP Dictionary for the last definition line, which is intended specifically for this application. Please note that you have to define the data type as a table type in this case. You can then define the typing normally, using TYPE and a reference to that data type.

Database Tables

So far, you have assumed that special data types are defined in the system—that is, in the ABAP programming language or the ABAP Dictionary.

In many cases, however, field strings or internal tables are filled with data that is read directly from existing database tables. In this case, the source and destination have to have the same field structure.

Therefore, it makes sense to define a variable with reference to such a database table and then import the required data into this table. The ABAP Dictionary is also useful for this application, as it also stores all the database tables (as *transparent tables*) with its attributes. Once again, you define the reference with TYPE, even though types are not involved, strictly speaking.

> **Note:** You should always use TYPE for references to the ABAP Dictionary (that is, not only for data types). You will only be able to navigate to the Dictionary only by double-clicking the mouse in this case. To maintain compatibility to with previous versions, you can also generally use LIKE. Please note, however, that this key is only intended only for references to internal variables, as you will see below.

Take a look at the last two lines in the example in Figure 6.10:

▶ The structure of the defined field string, WA_MATERIAL, corresponds to that of database table MARA for material data. Accordingly, you can transfer only one material record there.

▶ You can also use the addition TABLE OF to generate an internal table. In this case, the internal MATERIAL table can take on more data records for the material master.

▶ Typing with TYPE can also be applied to individual fields. A variable, WEIGHT, is defined in the last line, and has the exact same definition as the database field for the net weight in the material master record. The individual field is located through its multilevel field name, just like when you output fields in the form.

Result

After all this work, you will be happy to see the result of the definitions in the field list of the Form Builder. The entries are located under the **Global Data** group, as shown in Figure 6.12.

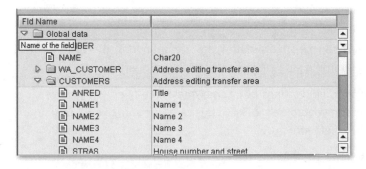

Figure 6.12 Field list in the screen display

You can enter the variable NAME directly as a field in the text, as indicated by the text symbol in front of the entry. The system has created a folder for WA_CUSTOMER and CUSTOMERS. The individual fields are listed underneath. When you add a field of this type in the text, the complete field name is combined automatically—for example, &WA_CUSTOMER-NAME1.

Note: At this point, you might be tempted to copy a field from table CUSTOMERS directly to the text, as the display in the field list does not indicate whether a field string or an internal table is involved. Give it a try and start the check of the text node.: the error message "CUSTOMERS is a table without header line and..." will appears.

Because the internal table consists of several lines, a unique assignment is not possible. Readers with ABAP experience will know that internal tables also have header lines, which enable direct assignment with some preparation. Accordingly, an error message like the one described above is displayed.

Suggested approach: assign clear names to all the tables (starting with the letter "T", for example). Also use field strings as work areas for these internal tables, and fill them with the corresponding data first with a loop or program node. This should prevent confusion (see Section 7.2 for more information).

6.3.6 Reference to Internal Data

When you design forms, you frequently have to copy the contents of one variable into other variables. To do so, you need variables with an identical field structure:

▶ You could use the procedure described above and use TYPE to create a reference to the original entry in the ABAP Dictionary, which was used to create the original variable as well.

▶ Alternatively, you can use the LIKE addition to refer directly to the existing variable of the source.

Note: You should only use type definition with LIKE and reference to existing data under 4.6C only if you have installed the appropriate service packs. Otherwise, the defined variables will not be displayed correctly in the field list.

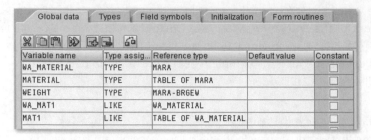

Global data	Types	Field symbols	Initialization	Form routines		

Variable name	Type assig...	Reference type	Default value	Constant
WA_MATERIAL	TYPE	MARA		☐
MATERIAL	TYPE	TABLE OF MARA		☐
WEIGHT	TYPE	MARA-BRGEW		☐
WA_MAT1	LIKE	WA_MATERIAL		☐
MAT1	LIKE	TABLE OF WA_MATERIAL		☐

Figure 6.13 Defining data with LIKE

To complete the descriptions of the options available here, the last procedure is outlined below. You already know the first three entries for the material master record in Figure 6.13 from the previous examples.

▶ You also see a new field string, WA_MAT1, with reference to WA_MATERIAL (which you previously defined via the ABAP Dictionary). Therefore, both field strings have an identical structure.

▶ MAT1 is declared as an internal table with the TABLE addition; it therefore has an structure identical to that of the previous entry, MATERIAL.

Note: You normally cannot use LIKE to define individual variables such as WEIGHT in Smart Forms. The node check requires an internal table with header as the reference type, while these tables are usually defined without headers in Smart Forms.

6.3.7 Individual Data Types in the Form

In most cases, the data definitions from the ABAP Dictionary or the built-in ABAP data types will suffice for form development. In some cases, however, it can make sense to create separate data types. In this case, you assign it to variables through the typing, TYPE, as described above.

You define internal data types for forms in the **Types** tab page of the *Global Definitions*. Figure 6.14 shows several examples.

Even though ABAP coding is involved, the definition of a data type is relatively clear-cut: it is introduced with the TYPES statement. This is followed by the name of the data type and then the addition TYPE to define the structure.

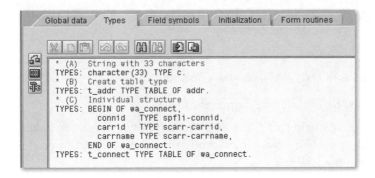

Figure 6.14 Global definitions: Types

Notes on the contents in the examples:

(A) In this case, a data type CHARACTER is defined, which can take a string of 33 alphanumeric characters. A variety of such data types is already defined in the ABAP Dictionary; you used CHAR20 in the example above. The entry CHAR33 does not exist yet in the Dictionary, however; you could therefore use CHAR-ACTER as the reference type here in the form (see Figure 6.10).

(B) This entry generates a table type based on the structure of ADDR. In the example above, you could then create the internal table CUSTOMERS with reference to T_ADDR. You can then omit the addition TABLE OF in the data definition.

(C) This example initially generates an individual structure with three fields. This makes it possible to save the code and name of the airline for a flight connection at the same time. You use a second TYPES statement to create a suitable table type for saving several data records, if necessary. In both cases, you only need to use TYPE, without any additions, to define the suitable variables.

Of course, the definition of individual data types through ABAP coding offers additional, flexible configuration options, which are described in detail in the ABAP keyword documentation (call with F1 on TYPES in the ABAP editor).

6.3.8 Field Syntax

Taken together, the descriptions and other system information described above constitute the rules that you have to follow when entering field names. In summary, the following rules apply:

▶ The name must not contain any blanks. The characters ' + ( ) may not be used in the name, as they are reserved for specifying input options.

▶ The name can be up to 130 characters long. However, the system uses only the first 32 characters to distinguish between existing fields.

▶ The field names are not case sensitive—that is, the names &myfield&, &MYfield&, and &MYFIELD& are identical.

▶ You cannot use the names of existing system fields to define your own fields.

When you output fields in text, also note the following:

▶ The field name must be enclosed by ampersands (&).

▶ To output a column in a field string, the involved components must be linked in two stages with a hyphen (minus sign). You can use this format to model structures with multiple layers.

6.4   Data Sources

Remember that there are several ways that data can reach a form:

▶ Information in the form interface defines the data that can be substituted by the main program.

▶ System fields provide data with predefined contents, such as the current date or page number.

▶ The entries in the global definitions creates the variables that you use within the form for calculations and so on, including, for example, the work areas for reading internal tables from the form interface.

The specifications in the global definitions were discussed in the previous chapter to describe how data is handled. The individual properties of the described cases are now described in detail below.

6.4.1   Form Interface

When you activate a form, Smart Forms interprets the definitions of the individual nodes to generate an ABAP function module. This function module contains the full form description and can be called for output directly by a suitable main program.

Function modules of this type always have a defined interface, which describes how data reaches the function module or returns it to the calling program—as a reaction to error messages, for example.

The logic of this defined interface is reflected directly in the form interface. The node is created automatically, under the global settings, whenever you create a new form. Figure 6.15 shows the form interface of the flight invoice as an example.

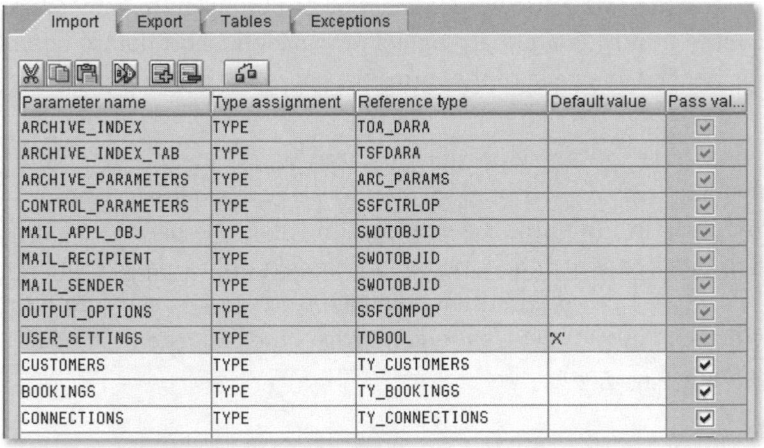

Parameter name	Type assignment	Reference type	Default value	Pass val...
ARCHIVE_INDEX	TYPE	TOA_DARA		☑
ARCHIVE_INDEX_TAB	TYPE	TSFDARA		☑
ARCHIVE_PARAMETERS	TYPE	ARC_PARAMS		☑
CONTROL_PARAMETERS	TYPE	SSFCTRLOP		☑
MAIL_APPL_OBJ	TYPE	SWOTOBJID		☑
MAIL_RECIPIENT	TYPE	SWOTOBJID		☑
MAIL_SENDER	TYPE	SWOTOBJID		☑
OUTPUT_OPTIONS	TYPE	SSFCOMPOP		☑
USER_SETTINGS	TYPE	TDBOOL	'X'	☑
CUSTOMERS	TYPE	TY_CUSTOMERS		☑
BOOKINGS	TYPE	TY_BOOKINGS		☑
CONNECTIONS	TYPE	TY_CONNECTIONS		☑

Figure 6.15 Form interface in the sample form

Four different tab pages are available for defining the parameters that will be reflected in the definition of the ABAP function module. You define the settings as described in the previous chapter. Because all the parameters can be addressed through the field names as soon as they are defined in the form, you can also consider them to be global data.

Furthermore, all the parameters defined here must also be defined in the call through the main program, otherwise the system will respond with a short dump when you attempt to output the form. The activation of the interface through the main program is described in detail in Section 9.4.

Tab Page for Import Parameters

The **Import** tab page contains the typing of all interface parameters that the main program passes on to the form. The data listed here can only be read in the form; no modifications are possible.

The parameters highlighted in gray are entered automatically when you create a new form, and cannot be removed. These parameters control the general functions for form output. See Section 9.7.2 for a comprehensive description. Although the parameters are defined in every form interface, they do not necessarily have to be supplied with data by the main program. If necessary, the function module utilizes the corresponding default values during output. Accordingly, these values are often called *optional interface parameters*.

The highlighted lines are filled during the form design. These parameters contain the application data that will be processed in the form. The main program always has to provide these application parameters (*required interface parameters*). However, because you can create a form independently of the main program, Smart Forms cannot verify this. Ultimately, a program termination (short dump) occurs if a parameter is defined in a page of the form, but not in the main program.

> **Tip:** The opposite case is entirely possible: you can supply parameters in the main program that are not (yet) used in the form. These parameters do not even have to appear in the form. The sequence in which the parameters are named can also differ between the form and the coding of the main program. This feature is useful when you use the same main program for several forms; it means you do not have to revise every form each time you extend the data supplied by the main program.

Import Parameters with Centralized Data Transfer Structure

Figure 6.15 shows the import parameters in the flight invoice. In comparison, take a look at the form interface for the delivery note to see what the data transfer looks like in an extremely complex form. The form for the delivery note is called LE_SHP_DELNOTE. Figure 6.16 shows the import parameters of the form interface.

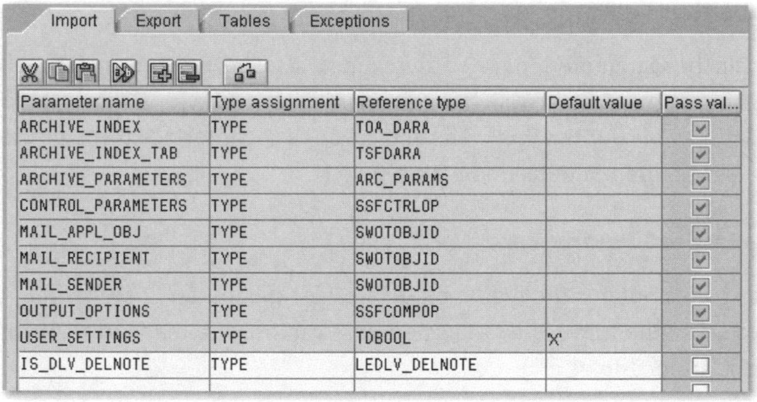

Parameter name	Type assignment	Reference type	Default value	Pass val...
ARCHIVE_INDEX	TYPE	TOA_DARA		✓
ARCHIVE_INDEX_TAB	TYPE	TSFDARA		✓
ARCHIVE_PARAMETERS	TYPE	ARC_PARAMS		✓
CONTROL_PARAMETERS	TYPE	SSFCTRLOP		✓
MAIL_APPL_OBJ	TYPE	SWOTOBJID		✓
MAIL_RECIPIENT	TYPE	SWOTOBJID		✓
MAIL_SENDER	TYPE	SWOTOBJID		✓
OUTPUT_OPTIONS	TYPE	SSFCOMPOP		✓
USER_SETTINGS	TYPE	TDBOOL	'X'	✓
IS_DLV_DELNOTE	TYPE	LEDLV_DELNOTE		☐

Import   Export   Tables   Exceptions

Figure 6.16 Form interface for the delivery note

The optional standard parameters, which are repeated in every form interface, once again appear highlighted in gray. Despite the complexity mentioned above, only one definition line for data transfer exists (with parameter IS_DLV_DEL-NOTE). You define the typing by assigning the appropriate data type in the ABAP Dictionary—LEDLV_DELNOTE in this case. The structure of this data type contains definitions for all the necessary components. Instead of listing the individual variables, field strings, and internal tables that are needed, the structure groups them all together in one shared variable for transfer. You can double-click on the reference type to display the structure of the data type.

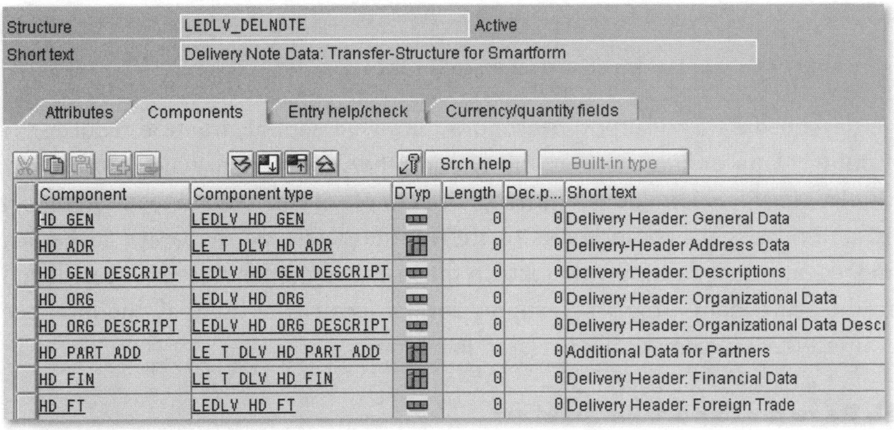

| Structure | LEDLV_DELNOTE | Active |
| Short text | Delivery Note Data: Transfer-Structure for Smartform | |

| Attributes | Components | Entry help/check | Currency/quantity fields |

Srch help   Built-in type

Component	Component type	DTyp	Length	Dec.p...	Short text
HD_GEN	LEDLV_HD_GEN		0	0	Delivery Header: General Data
HD_ADR	LE_T_DLV_HD_ADR		0	0	Delivery-Header Address Data
HD_GEN_DESCRIPT	LEDLV_HD_GEN_DESCRIPT		0	0	Delivery Header: Descriptions
HD_ORG	LEDLV_HD_ORG		0	0	Delivery Header: Organizational Data
HD_ORG_DESCRIPT	LEDLV_HD_ORG_DESCRIPT		0	0	Delivery Header: Organizational Data Descr
HD_PART_ADD	LE_T_DLV_HD_PART_ADD		0	0	Additional Data for Partners
HD_FIN	LE_T_DLV_HD_FIN		0	0	Delivery Header: Financial Data
HD_FT	LEDLV_HD_FT		0	0	Delivery Header: Foreign Trade

Figure 6.17 Transfer structure of delivery note in the form interface

As you can see from the entries in column **DType** in Figure 6.17, the superior structure contains both field strings and internal tables. The **Component** column shows the respective names as they will appear in the field list of the form.

Each component of the data type has its own definition in the ABAP Dictionary, which you see in the **Component Type** column. This information will be important later on when you attempt to pass on data from one component to other variables within the form, which occurs frequently during form processing. In this case, of course, the new variable has to be defined with the same typing in the form. As a result, you will not have to spend too much time searching for a suitable entry.

Tip: You can double-click on an entry in column **DType** in the window to display the exact structure of the respective component. This function is especially useful because the field labels do not always appear in the field list in Smart Forms, (and the field name does not always provide an indication of its contents).

In the above example, the central transfer structure illustrates the fact that data types can have any number of hierarchy levels in the Dictionary. Each new level also extends the field name that you have to use to output that field in the form. Figure 6.18 shows an example of this: the output of header information for the delivery (delivery number and creation date).

Figure 6.18 Data output with a central interface structure

The described data collection procedure through a central structure reduces the amount of type definitions that you would otherwise have to have in the form. This also simplifies form development. For example, if you need to, you can simply add additional data components to the central data type, and then make any changes necessary to supply the data in the main program in a second step. If you use the same main program to supply several forms with data, all the interface parameters are automatically declared in all forms.

Tab Page for Export Parameters

You can use the **Export** tab page to pass data back to the main program after the form has been output. This usually involves logs from the form output, including any errors that occurred during form processing. However, during pure electronic form processing (without printing or faxing the results), this can also be the entire form contents. In this case, the main program is also responsible for forwarding the contents of the output to the appropriate output unit (see Chapter 9).

However, in normal form development, the export parameters are much less relevant than the import parameters, for example. They are more important for changing or developing a main program. All the parameters are introduced in detail in this description (see Section 9.7.4).

Parameter name	Type assignment	Reference type	Pass val...
DOCUMENT_OUTPUT_INFO	TYPE	SSFCRESPD	✓
JOB_OUTPUT_INFO	TYPE	SSFCRESCL	✓
JOB_OUTPUT_OPTIONS	TYPE	SSFCRESOP	✓

Figure 6.19 Form interface, export parameters

When you create a form, three parameters are inserted automatically and cannot be deleted. These parameters are read and interpreted by the main program for specific applications (*optional parameters*):

- The first parameter always contains the number of pages that were output.

- JOB_OUTPUT_INFO contains log information on the form output—for example, flagging whether output took place, spool IDs, or even the entire form output in OTF or XML format.

- JOB_OUTPUT_OPTIONS contains the output options that were valid when the form was started. The system can compare these values with the second parameter to determine, for example, whether the user changed any print parameters.

The **Pass by Value** attribute is set in all cases. Therefore, the parameters are not passed on to the main program until form output is complete.

In some cases, it may make sense to define additional parameters and evaluate them in the main program. The parameters are required in this case, which means they also have to be listed in the main program when the function module for the form is called.

If you have defined your own export parameters, you may want to leave out the **value transfer**. In this case (*Pass by Reference*), the parameters are updated directly—which means that if an error occurs, the data collected up to the point of the error can still be evaluated.

> **Note:** When you pass by reference, the main program can also set values in the export parameters and pass them on to the form, (which means that data transfer is possible in both directions).

Tab Page for Tables

As the name implies, this tab page is used to pass on parameters that are saved in internal tables. However, as you saw above, you can also do this under the import parameters, for example. Therefore, a separate tab page for passing on tables is not really necessary, and is not actually used in most cases.

Nonetheless, it may make sense to use this tab page, because the transfer as *import parameters* involves only read access to the form. In some cases, however, you may have to return internal tables with changed values to the main program. You define these values in a similar way to the examples described above. Figure 6.20 shows an example from the flight invoice. Passing by reference is always involved, which means any changed values in the program are returned directly to the main program.

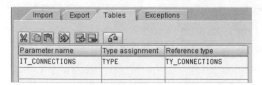

Figure 6.20 Form interface: Table definition

Tab Page for Exceptions

Errors can occur during form output and require an immediate response by the system. These errors are called *exceptions*. Four exception cases are already defined, and are entered as parameters automatically when you create a new form (see Figure 6.21).

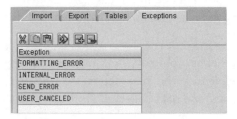

Figure 6.21 Form interface: Exceptions

In the function module for the form, each error is assigned to an *error class*, which in turn is assigned to an *exception*. When an error causes form processing to terminate, the precise exception is triggered. The main program can then query the exception number using system variable SY-SUBRC and can respond accordingly (with an appropriate message for the user, for example). See Section 9.8 for more information.

6.4.2 Global Definitions

This node groups together various definitions that are available in any form node as data or subroutines. Figure 6.22 shows all the tab pages of the **Global Definitions**.

Variable name	Type assig...	Reference type	Default value	Constant
GS_SERNR_PRT	LIKE	KOMSER		☐
GT_SERNR_PRT	TYPE	GT_TYPESERNR_PRT		☐
YES	TYPE	CHAR1	'Y'	☑
NO	TYPE	CHAR1	'N'	☑
				☐

Figure 6.22 Global data

The **Initialization** and **Form Routines** tab pages are described in detail in Chapter 8. An overview of the tab pages for the data definition appears below.

▶ **Global data**

In this tab page, you define the data that is needed in the form but is not provided by the form interface—totals values, for example. Because this data is normally blank after typing, the data also has to be retrieved within the form—through a loop or a program node, for example.

> **Note:** The parameters of the form interface (described above) are also addressed using fields that are available in the entire form, and which therefore can thus be used in any form node. Therefore, the parameters for the form interface are really **global data** as well.

▶ **Types**

You can define data types as user-defined ABAP coding here if no suitable type is available in the Data Dictionary.

▶ **Field symbols**

You can use field symbols as pointers for reading from internal tables. Please note, however, that this book does not discuss field symbols in any detail; instead, the method using field strings as work areas is recommended.

You learned about data structures as the foundation for outputting field contents in Section 6.3, which repeatedly refers to the definitions as *global data*. Therefore, only a few special features are listed here.

▶ When you type variables as (unstructured) fields, you can also assign a default value. You normally enclose the corresponding input value in single quotes. In the above example, the variables YES and NO are defined as default values to make the logical queries simpler. You can also enter a value directly for numeric variables.

▶ If a field is also flagged as a constant, it cannot be changed in the form. Of course, this makes sense only when you define a default value for the field as well.

▶ You can define default values for any variables in the **Initialization** tab page. The assignments are defined here using ABAP program coding, which enables you to define any calculations and default settings (also see Chapter 8).

▶ Global data can be read through fields in any form node, as well as changed. Accordingly, the sequence in which the nodes are processed can be relevant for the later contents of the variables. To ensure that a variable really contains the required data, the node that assigns the contents must be processed prior to output. This is determined primarily through the node's position in the Form Builder navigation tree. This is described in detail in Chapter 7.

Unfortunately, the Form Builder does not provide a direct option for checking the use of fields in a form, in contrast to the where-used list for ABAP programs. Therefore, make sure you document your form properly.

> **Tip:** A simple trick can help you create a type of where-used list. To do so, take advantage of the fact that fields that are addressed in the form are reported as errors during the overall check, if the definition does not exist. You can use the reverse case to display all the found locations: simply make a minor change to the name in the *data definition* (add an additional letter, for example). The previous name now no longer exists, and the overall check lists all the nodes in which the variable is addressed.

6.4.3 System Fields

Each form contains a list of system fields that Smart Forms replaces with specific values when the form is processed. The field values either come from the SAP System or are the result of the form output. All these variables are grouped together in a shared field string, SFSY. The individual fields are:

▶ DATE (current date)
The display format is based on the country ID in the user master record. You can change the country ID with an ABAP statement (SET COUNTRY) in the main program or in a program node.

▶ TIME (current time)
Local time at output in format HH:MM:SS (HH: hours, MM: minutes, SS: seconds).

▶ PAGE (current page number)
The page counter is changed in each new print page in accordance with the defined attributes for the page node (*Increase*, *Hold*, *Reset*, and so on). You also define the display form for output here (*Arabic*, *numeric*, and so on). Also see Section 7.4.

▶ FORMPAGES (total number of pages in form)
Combined with the page number, this enables you to output information such as "Page 2 of 9".

▶ **JOBPAGES (total number of pages in print request)**
Total number of all pages in the forms from the current print request. Differs from FORMPAGES only when you group several forms together in one print request.

▶ **WINDOWNAME (name of the current window)**
Enables you to output the short name of the window (the name you entered in the **Window** field in the node attributes).

▶ **PAGENAME (name of the current page)**
Enables you to output the short name of the page (the name you entered in the **Page** field in the node attributes).

The following three system fields are intended for internal use only; therefore, you should not use them for your own applications:

▶ **PAGEBREAK (flag for page break)**
Automatically set to "X" when a page break occurs in the current print page.

▶ **MAINEND (last page)**
Set when the main window ends in the current page. The system queries this parameter when the condition **Only at/before End of Main Window** is set for a node.

▶ **EXCEPTION (number of the last exception)**
UIsed when individual error messages occur in the form and cause output to terminate (see Section 9.8).

When you use fields SFSY-FORMPAGES or SFSY-JOBPAGES, the SAP system has to keep all the output pages in main memory until the end of the form or the print job in order to allow these fields to be replaced with their respective values. Accordingly, large-volume output will require a large amount of main memory on the SAP application server.

You can also access these system fields in any program node—without having to name them explicitly as input/output parameters, as is the case for other variables. Moreover, all the ABAP system variables in system table SYST are also available in the program node. These variables are normally addressed in the program coding starting with "SY-"—for example, SY-SUBRC for the error status.

7   Form Flow Logic

7.1   Overview

So far, you have learned how to design the layout of a page and to integrate texts, graphics, and even data by using the corresponding nodes.

Thus far, however, you have not thought much about the *processing* sequence of the nodes during output, how outputs of several pages take place, or how you can control these processes. These functions are located in the flow logic of the form, which is often simply referred to as the *form logic*.

Before you examine in detail the various options available in designing the form logic, we first want to give you a brief summary of the basic functions involved in the form logic.

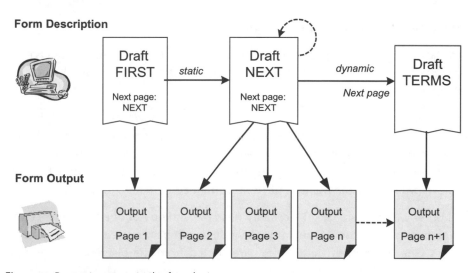

Figure 7.1 Processing pages in the form logic

Each form consists of one or more draft pages (see Figure 7.1). The first page in the navigation tree is the start page. This page is usually called FIRST, and is sometimes referred to as such in this book. The processing of the form starts with this page. Within the page, processing takes place in the sequence in which the assigned nodes are defined in the navigation tree of the Form Builder.

When a print page is full, output control has to determine whether additional pages are required. This determination depends on whether all the texts and/or data have already been output or not. The specification for the next page—in the attributes of the previous draft page—determines which page layout is used for the new print page. The usual code for the next page is NEXT. Because the next page has a fixed definition, this approach is sometimes called *static* processing.

Alternatively, a next page can be generated *dynamically* through a manual page break—that is, as the result of defined conditions at runtime. This is the case in Figure 7.1, for example, when outputting a concluding page that lists your company's conditions for doing business, TERMS. The dynamic page break occurs as soon as all the data records are processed.

> **Note:** When we talk about outputting the form, we mean generating an intermediate document that contains all the statements necessary to enable further processing in the SAP spool system. The program section in the Smart Forms runtime environment that converts the form elements into this intermediate document is also called the *form processor* or *composer*.

Main Window and Secondary Windows

The layout of each draft page contains one or more windows. These windows contain the texts and data, while all formatting information is taken from the defined style.

Only one window in the form can be flagged as the *main window*. Only in this window can the system monitor the contents of the output and determine whether it fits in the current print page or whether a new page has to be created. If a different layout is used for the next page, the main window must also exist in that layout, in order to enable the output to be continued in that window.

All other windows are called *secondary windows* and do not directly influence the page breaks. Nonetheless, secondary windows can be repeated in different draft pages. The contents of the window are started from the beginning (instead of being continued from the previous page) on each new print page.

Therefore, the contents of the main window can be distributed across multiple pages (continuous text and data with automatic page breaks), while the contents of secondary windows are repeated on each respective page.

Processing a Draft Page

A page (and the nodes it contains) is processed in the sequence in which the nodes are defined in the navigation tree. If you want to determine this sequence, you will find it useful to completely expand the navigation tree for a page. The individual nodes then appear in the order in which they are used (Figure 7.2 shows an excerpt).

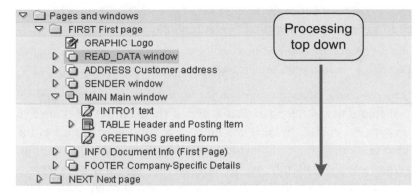

Figure 7.2 Form processing during output

The processing sequence is not dependent on the position of the nodes in the page during output. The only exception is the relative positioning of text or graphic nodes. In this case, the relative position depends on the previous output.

You have to pay special attention to the processing sequence when you use fields. You have to make sure that the required data is assigned to a node that is located above the node where that data is output in the navigation tree.

You can move individual nodes (or even entire branches) in the navigation tree to change their sequence; we recommend using the mouse functions in the Form Builder (context menu, drag-and-drop). With a little practice, you will develop a feel for choosing the destination. In some cases, the system prompts you to choose whether you want to insert a node as the next node or an inferior node in a location.

Custom Form Logic

Various options are available for influencing the processing of the form. Use the general node attributes or the special node types, which are described in more detail below:

▶ Use loop nodes to repeat an output as often as necessary. This is an easy way to output data from internal tables, for example. The table node is available for formatting the output in table form. Data output using a loop in a main window is the most common way of generating output with automatic page breaks.

▶ You can define conditions for each form node. If a condition is not met during form output, the respective node, including all inferior nodes, is not processed in the current print page.

- ▶ Use alternative nodes if you want to choose between different branches (and their inferior nodes) in the navigation tree at runtime.
- ▶ You can use a command node and its conditions to configure when a dynamic page break with a custom next page is triggered.

The sections below cover this and other options for influencing the form logic in detail. The first step starts with loop and table nodes. These output types are also referred to as *dynamic* output, because the number of data records (such as the number of invoice items in the flight invoice), and thus the length of the output, is unknown when you design the form. The fact that the number of data records is unknown represents its main difference from a template. During dynamic output, the page breaks have to be generated automatically by output control at runtime.

7.2   Dynamic Data Output

7.2.1   Overview

When a form is output, the data retrieval part of the main program usually reads the required data from database tables, transfers it to internal tables, and then passes it on to the form via the form interface. In special cases, the data retrieval can also take place in a custom program node in the form. You will read about this in more detail later in this chapter.

These internal tables consist of information regarding the columns, which contain the actual field names, and any number of lines (similar to a worksheet in a spreadsheet program). In contrast to the contents of variables or field strings, these internal tables **cannot** be placed directly in a text node. Instead, output must take place by line and must use work areas.

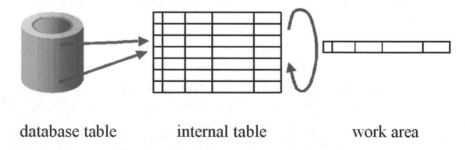

database table   internal table   work area

Figure 7.3 Loop for an internal table

Internal tables are processed in the following steps:

▶ Each line of the internal table is read once and, in the process, copied to a field string with the same column structure. This field string is called the *work area* or the *output area*.

▶ After each read operation, the required fields in the work area can be output in the form.

▶ When all the output is processed, the system automatically continues to the next line in the internal table.

This pass of all entries in an internal table is called a *loop*. Smart Forms uses a loop node (or, alternatively, a table node) for this function, as you will see below. Two important options are available for the loop pass:

▶ If not all of the data records in the internal table are relevant for output, you can define selection conditions. Only those lines that satisfy the conditions are read and copied. These are called WHERE conditions in the node attributes. In special cases, you can also define conditions to read only a single data record.

▶ You can define sort criteria for an internal table to determine a specific output sequence. When you sort the output, you also have the option of inserting intermediate variables for each sort level.

When you use a loop to output an internal table, you usually do not know how many data records it contains. Therefore, you will generally output internal tables in the main window, to ensure that the output control can insert the required page breaks.

In most forms, the data records will be output in table format—that is, the format of the first output line is simply repeated (like the items in the flight invoice, for example). Consequently, it makes sense to describe individual lines in order to describe this tabular output format in the form. In the simplest case, you can do so using a text node with tabs or with a sequence of several text nodes. A table node is even better, however. In this case, you can define the output lines as line types, much like a template.

7.2.2 Node Types for Outputting Internal Tables

The following node types are available for outputting the data in internal tables:

▶ Loop
Accesses data in an internal table. The internal table is processed in a loop, which enables you to output each individual data record through a work area. The type of output is not defined here; you have to create the appropriate inferior nodes. The node attributes contain selection conditions and sort information. Because the loop groups together all the inferior nodes, it can also exe-

cute the functions of a folder node—for the automatic generation of headers and footers, for example.

▶ **Table**
The table node controls the structured output of data within output tables. For this purpose, the node attributes contain a tab page with information on the table layout (in the form of line types). The entry method is similar to that of a template. You have to define references to the defined cells in the layout of the output table for all corresponding inferior nodes that are relevant for output.

If necessary, the table node can also control access to data in an internal table. As a result, it also possesses all the functions of a loop. In fact, the combination of these two functions is the most frequent method for using this node type.

▶ **Complex Section**
This node type simulates the attributes of node types **folder**, **loop**, **table**, or **template**. Which of these alternatives is activated depends on the entry in the first tab page. This node type stems from the early days of Smart Forms development and should no longer be used. Therefore, it is not described in any detail here.

> **Note:** The original flight invoice uses several nodes with type **Complex Section** to output the items. In one of the exercises below, you will replace these nodes with loop and table nodes, and smooth out the structure in the main window at the same time.

Complex forms frequently include combinations of different node types:

▶ You can assign several table nodes as inferior nodes of a loop node, in order to design the output format.

▶ Alternatively, you can create one or more loop nodes within a table node, which then all use the shared attributes for the output table.

Which structure you choose depends on the specific application at hand. The table node itself cannot be nested; you cannot define a table node as an inferior node of another table node.

This Chapter

In the sections below, you will learn about the options for outputting internal tables in detail, once again based on your sample flight invoice form. The following subjects are covered:

▶ The loop is introduced as the main element of all described nodes; this also involves the equivalent functions in node types **table** and **complex section**.

▶ You can use the functions of the output table in node types **table** and **complex section** to design the output format of all involved texts, data, or even graphics.

▶ In all three node types, you can use event nodes to execute specific inferior nodes in a header or footer. You activate event nodes by defining the corresponding events for which they are executed.

▶ Finally, you modify the your flight invoice to see how you can completely change the output of the items (flight bookings). This will make your form much easier to understand.

7.2.3 Loop

Each of the above three node types (**loop**, **table**, and **complex section**) can perform loop functions. Use the **Data** tab page to describe the pass of an internal table and its attributes. Because the attributes for the loop function are identical for all three node types, you only have to describe them once.

In the flight invoice, flight bookings are output as invoice items (see the sample printout in the Appendix). Figure 7.4 shows node LOOP_BOOK in the MAIN window (somewhat hidden, under the TABLE node), which describes the attributes of the corresponding loop.

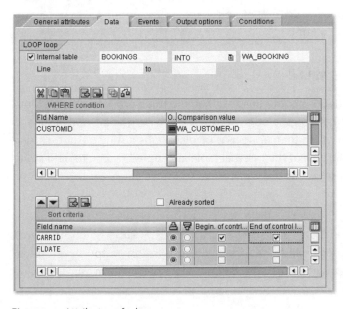

Figure 7.4 Attributes of a loop

Node LOOP_BOOK is a **complex section**: As a result of the definitions in the **General Attributes** tab page (**Simple** output type and **repeated processing**), it functions like a loop node.

Data for Loop

The **Data** tab page contains all the attributes required to access the data within the loop. The first and most important specifications involve the internal table that will be read. The most obvious of these is the flag in front of the **Internal Table** attribute:

▶ It is set by default and ensures that the specific internal table is actually processed.

▶ If you deactivate loop execution in the attribute, the loop is not run. In this case, only the other functions in the node are active, which means that it probably works like a folder. If a table node is involved, the output layout will also be retained. This means you can continue to use the line types to output inferior nodes (as a replacement for a template, for example; also see the notes in Section 4.5). If a **complex section** node is involved, as in this example, the entire **Data** tab page is removed from the display if you deactivate the flag. You can reactivate it afterward in the **General Attributes** tab page.

> **Tip:** If the flag in front of the **Internal Table** attribute is deactivated, the previous contents still remain in the background in all node types. This can be useful during the text phase of your form if you want to temporarily disconnect a loop from its data, for example.

Defining the Internal Table

In the example, BOOKINGS is configured as the table to be processed in the loop. It contains all the flight bookings, along with their characteristic attributes such as airline, date, and price, which then appear as invoice items during output. During loop processing, the contents of the internal table are copied by line to field string WA_BOOKING, which serves as the work area.

> **Tip:** In your example, the name of the field string that serves as the work area consists of the abbreviation "WA" (*work area*) and the name of the internal table for which it is used. You should use such conventions when developing your forms, as it will provide for clarity even in highly complex forms.

Once the loop has been processed completely, the last data record is present in the assigned work area. You can also access these contents outside of the loop.

The internal table, BOOKINGS, is supplied in the flight invoice via the form interface; the field string is defined under the global data in the form. The reference to a uniform data type in the ABAP Dictionary ensures that the field structure of both components is identical. You can check the names of the fields at any time in the field list in the Form Builder.

Special Case 1: Internal Table with Header Line

You can define a special typing to define an internal table such that it has its own work area. This work area has the same name as the internal table. This case is also called an **internal table with header line**. When you enter an internal table of this type in the **Data** tab page, the Form Builder identifies it and automatically copies the header line into the specification of the work area.

Even if the internal table has a header line, however, you can still enter a different, independent field string as the work area. This will improve the clarity in your form. After all, according to SAP's recommendation, you should not use internal tables with header lines anyway.

Special Case 2: Using Field Symbols

You use assignment type INTO to transfer the data into the work area. The alternative, with ASSIGNING, is provided in case you want to model the work area with a *field symbol*. In this approach, the system uses pointers, which means that the individual lines do not have to be copied to a separate field string. This can speed up the program runtime, especially when large internal tables are involved.

If you want to use a field symbol, you first have to enter it in the appropriate tab page under the global definitions. This approach is not described in any detail below, however.

Limiting Data Selection

As shown in Figure 7.4, two options are available for limiting the number of address data records during the loop of the internal table: by line number or with WHERE conditions.

Restriction by line number
Because each data record in an internal table has a unique number, you can specify the line numbers in **From/To** to limit the number of data record. This option is only rarely useful, however. You can leave these input fields blank to include all the data records in the loop.

Tip: If you specify a loop **From line 1 to line 1**, only the first line of the internal table is read. This can make sense, for example, if you want to access a single field that has the same contents in all table lines. When you output the field, you want to output its contents like superior header data (that is, outside of the actual loop over all the data records). In this case, you can use a additional loop node to read only the first table line, in order to output the required field.

Restriction using WHERE conditions

A much more frequent application is to limit selection of the data records using a WHERE condition. In this case, only those data records that correspond to the defined conditions are copied to the work area and output. You input the conditions just like the logical expressions in the **Conditions** tab page (this is described in detail in Section 7.3.1). The only difference is that a logical expression here in the loop may query only components of the internal table.

Note: As you can see in Figure 7.4, the field name for the component of the internal table always appears in the left-hand column. Enter the field name in its short form—that is, without the name of the internal table in front of it. Users often forget this rule in their first experiments with Smart Forms. The node check returns an error message in this case.

Because internal table BOOKINGS can also contain other customers' data in the example, a WHERE condition has been defined for the loop (see Figure 7.4). Field CUSTOMID contains the customer number for each flight booking; its contents are compared with the intended customer number for the invoice. This customer number is located in the *ID* field of work area WA_CUSTOMER, which also takes care of outputting the address.

Sorting and Grouping

You often have to output the data records in a specific sequence. However, the data records in the internal table do not necessarily have the required sort sequence. You can define your sorting requirements as attributes for the loop. You enter this information in the bottom section of the **Data** tab page (see Figure 7.4).

Example

You have defined a sort sequence in the example that is not present in the original flight invoice.

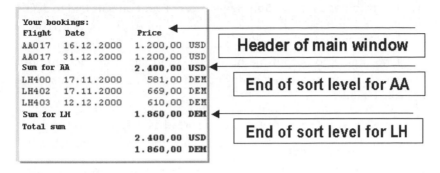

Figure 7.5 Sorting and grouping

When you output the items, the node attributes in the example have the following effects:

▶ The first sort level with the CARRID sorts the flight bookings by airline (code).

▶ The second level with FLDATE then sorts the bookings by flight date (for each respective airline).

In the sample printout, the code of each airline appears in the **Flight** column, followed by the flight date. The items are sorted *in ascending order* in both cases (see the corresponding definitions in the node attributes). Please note, however, that the output is not a continuous list:

▶ A new header appears before each airline with the long name of that airline.

▶ At the end of each airline's section, its part of the invoice amount is displayed as a subtotal.

This is controlled using *event nodes*, which the Form Builder inserts automatically whenever the attributes **Start Sort** or **End Sort** are set (for sort level CARRID in this case).

General Information

Because the sort sequence is always based on the active internal table in the loop, the fields that you want to sort by must exist in this internal table. Once again, you have to enter the field names in their short form—that is, without the name of the internal table in front of it.

If you enter several fields, the sequence of field names determines their sort priority. You can change the sort priority later using the black arrows/icons (upper left). Each entry in the list represents one sort level.

You can use the attributes **Event on Sort Begin** and/or **Event on Sort End** to define a *control level* for each sort level. In this case, one event node appears for each level in the navigation tree in the Form Builder, as in the example. You can then create additional inferior nodes to output the headers or subtotals in the desired positions. The event nodes are addressed during output whenever the contents of the addressed field change.

If you do not specify a sort sequence, the data is read as it appears in the active internal table, which means the sorting performed by the main program is used.

> **Note:** It is entirely possible that the main program has already supplied the necessary sorting in the internal table. If you want to generate a control level with event nodes, for example, you have to enter the sort fields in the loop node anyway. In this case, however, output control in Smart Forms cannot detect that the internal table has already been already sorted and sorts it again, resulting in unnecessary runtime. Set the **Already Sorted** checkbox to avoid this.

Output in a Loop

Now take a look at how the contents of work area WA_BOOKING, with the individual flight bookings, are output in the inferior nodes in the flight invoice. To do so, open inferior node LOOP_CONNECT. You see five text nodes for the individual columns of the output table, starting with BODY_COL1. Open the last text node. You see the field specifications for price and currency. Both are contained in WA_BOOKING.

If you look at the *Output Options*, you see the information that is needed to assign the individual text nodes to the cells of the output table. This is discussed in detail in Section 7.2.6, when the handling of output tables is described.

7.2.4 Reading a Single Data Record in a Loop

As mentioned in the previous section, you can use a loop to read an individual table item by specifying a line number. However, more often, the specific data record will be determined using a WHERE condition. In this case, as well, the contents of the queried fields are not known until runtime. Therefore, in contrast to the first case, this situation involves dynamic access to a data record in the internal table. Return to your sample invoice form to illustrate this case.

Open node BODY_COL4 in the flight invoice. Obviously, the departure time is not read from the work area, WA_BOOKING, but instead from WA_CONNECTION.

The reason for this is simple: when regularly scheduled flights are involved, the departure time is always the same. Accordingly, it is not saved in the flight information, but instead in the superior flight connection (also see the notes for the flight data model in the Appendix).

To ensure that the correct time can be output for each flight connection, WA_CONNECTION must contain a link to the current flight booking. Node LOOP_CONNECT, which also has type **Complex Section**, takes care of this. The text nodes mentioned above are defined here. Choose the **Data** tab page under the node attributes, as shown in Figure 7.6.

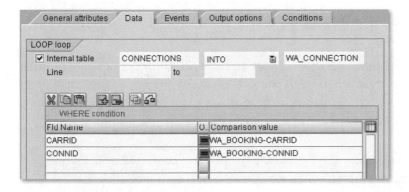

Figure 7.6 Loop for reading a data record

Once again, the settings in the **General Attributes** define this node as a loop. Due to the defined WHERE conditions, however, only a single data record is read from the internal flight connections table and copied to the corresponding work area. Two properties for the current flight booking restrict the selection:

▶ Field CARRID with the current airline
▶ Field CONNID with the current connection number

Because a flight booking can be assigned to only one connection, only a single data record is read. As a result, the departure time for the connection, which is defined in field DEPTIME, can be output in text node BODY_COL4.

Loop in Program Coding
In this example, the loop node is "misused" in order to read a specific data record from an internal table. Otherwise, a function of this type is possible only in a program node, which requires some basic ABAP skills.

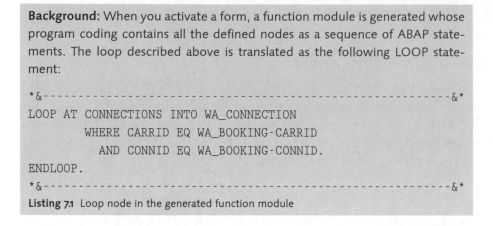

Background: When you activate a form, a function module is generated whose program coding contains all the defined nodes as a sequence of ABAP statements. The loop described above is translated as the following LOOP statement:

```
* &-----------------------------------------------------------&*
LOOP AT CONNECTIONS INTO WA_CONNECTION
        WHERE CARRID EQ WA_BOOKING-CARRID
          AND CONNID EQ WA_BOOKING-CONNID.
ENDLOOP.
* &-----------------------------------------------------------&*
```

Listing 7.1 Loop node in the generated function module

The result of the read operation in work area WA_BOOKING is not only available within the loop; it remains until its contents are overwritten by a subsequent operation. Therefore, the information in the loop work area can be output in any node, not only in the inferior nodes of the loop.

Note: When a work area is read in a loop node and addressed by fields that are not defined within that node, the overall form check may trigger a warning message. In this case, the Form Builder assumes that the involved work area does not contain a valid value. You should specify the work area as an output parameter elsewhere in the form—for example, in the **Initialization** tab page under the global definitions (also see the notes in Section 3.4). This case also occurs in the sample exercise below.

7.2.5 Sample Exercise: Loop

As you have seen in the information above, the LOOP_CONNECT node does not represent a true loop, but instead merely serves to retrieve the data for the variable that contains the flight date.

The actual output of the items is controlled in node LOOP_BOOK, which runs through each flight booking consecutively. Accordingly, all the inferior nodes that involve output should be assigned to this node; they currently appear in LOOP_CONNECT.

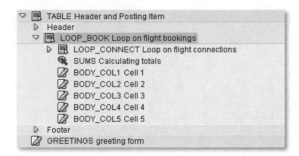

Figure 7.7 Position output after LOOP_CONNECT

Using the mouse, move the nodes from LOOP_CONNECT to LOOP_BOOK (see Figure 7.7). Make sure that the existing node sequence is retained. Output the form with program Z_SF_EXAMPLE_01 (don't forget to activate it first) and check whether the departure time now appears.

> **Note:** Unfortunately, the overall form check now displays a warning message: "Field WA_CONNECTION-DEPTIME does not have a defined value". This phenomenon—and the appropriate solution—was mentioned above: enter WA_CONNECTION as an output parameter in tab page **Initialization** under the global definitions. This will eliminate the error message in the overall check.

In the exercise at the end of this chapter, you will make major changes to the structure of the branch that outputs the invoice item (see Figure 7.8). In the process, you can create new nodes with type **Loop** to replace the existing **Complex Section** loops.

7.2.6 Output Table

In the previous section, you learned how the items of the flight invoice are read in a loop and output using text nodes. You have not learned, however, how to output this information as a table. To do so, you use the layout of an output table, which you learned about in Section 4.5.

Accordingly, first check the **Table** tab page in the TABLE node, as shown in Figure 7.8.

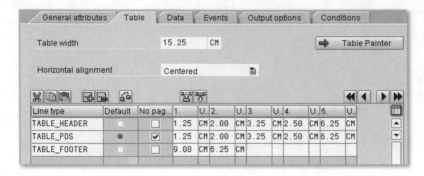

Figure 7.8 Output table

This is another case of a node with type **Complex Section**. In this case, it is configured as a table node with **repeated processing** in the **General Attributes** tab page. As a result of this definition, the entries in the **Data** tab page are used to read an internal table. You will deal with the contents later. Ultimately, you will reconfigure this node as well.

Each table node has a special tab page, **Table**. It defines the layout of the output table that can be addressed by the corresponding inferior nodes. You define it using line types, similar to a template. You will immediately be able to recognize the three line types defined in the example in a sample printout of the form. One special feature is that row types TABLE_HEADER (for the header information) and TABLE_POS (for the individual items) have the same column definitions in this case, which means you could theoretically get by with just one line type.

Once again, the individual columns are specified with their widths. In contrast to a template, the line height is not specified. It is determined dynamically, and thus depends on the contents and defined style of the cell. The cell with the greatest height determines the height of the entire line. Therefore, the individual cells can have different heights after output, depending on their respective contents.

You have to specify the required line type for each output-relevant inferior node of an output table. You can set the **Default** attribute in the table layout to define which line type you want to use if no line type is specified for the output of an inferior node.

You can set the **No Break** attribute to define whether you want to protect the respective line type from page breaks. In this case, the full contents of a line are always output in a single page.

Before you enter the row types, you have to define the total table width and the positioning within the superior window, just like in a template. Once again, the output table may not be wider than the window. The total width of all the cells together must agree with the column width. The graphical Table Painter is again available for designing the row types; it ensures that the line types agree with the overall width.

Assigning the Cells in Inferior Nodes

You've already learned how to define the layout of the output table. You will now find out how to assign the output-relevant inferior nodes of the cells within the output table. To do so, open text node BODY_COL1, which outputs the airline, and select the **Output Options** tab page. You now see an additional section for assigning the text within the output table (see Figure 7.9).

Figure 7.9 Output options for a table

When you read about templates in Section 4.5, you already learned that text and graphic nodes are assigned to the template lines through fixed line and column specifications. This is due to the fixed structure of a template. In contrast, output tables do not have line specifications, since the number of lines varies according to the data quantity. Accordingly, the text nodes must be assigned dynamically:

▶ Because the node in Figure 7.9 outputs the code of the airline, which is the first column in the output table, the attribute for **New Line** must be set.

▶ The lower attribute **New Cell** triggers the creation of a new cell (the first cell in this case, since no cells are skipped).

Now check the next nodes, BODY_COL2 and so on: The **New Cell** attribute is set in each.

If neither a **new line** nor a **new cell** is set for an output-relevant node, its contents are appended to the previous node. If a text node is involved in this case, you have to watch out for the **New Paragraph** and other settings in the first tab page of the node. In contrast, when a new cell starts, the formatting always starts with a new paragraph (like the settings in the current text).

7.2.7 Events (Event Nodes)

Because each node type that supports dynamic data output also groups together inferior nodes, it is also equipped with the functions of a folder node. This enables the automatic generation of event nodes for headers and footers, to output headings or final totals, for example.

You define the corresponding settings in the **Events** tab page under the respective node attributes. Open the TABLE node in the flight invoice (as shown in Figure 7.10), in which the existing header and footer are defined.

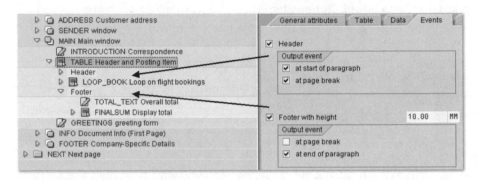

Figure 7.10 Event nodes in dynamic data output

You can output event nodes for the following events:

▶ At the start and end of a section (the section is defined as the sequence of all inferior nodes)

▶ For a page break (at the beginning or end of a page)

You have to specify a height for the footer in the form, to ensure that sufficient space is left for the footer when calculating the page breaks.

When you activate a header and/or footer, the Form Builder automatically generates the suitable event nodes (named **HEADER** or **FOOTER**) in the navigation tree. You can then insert additional inferior nodes as necessary. The texts for the table headers and the invoice totals are already defined in the currencies of the individual flight bookings in the example.

> **Note:** Footers are normally used to output subtotals. To do so, you have to make sure that the corresponding sums have been fully calculated beforehand. The calculation of grand totals is described in detail in the next chapter (see Section 8.6).

You cannot nest event nodes. Therefore, when you have defined a header or footer for a section, you cannot define any inferior sections with separate headers or footers. Moreover, if you define both a header and a footer, you must define both in the same node.

> **Tip:** If you combine table and loop nodes in a form design, please note that the event nodes are not available at every level; they can be used only in the superior node.

7.2.8 Sample Exercise: Revising the Flight Invoice

In the previous section, you only checked the design of the output table in the TABLE node. Now open the node again and select the **Data** tab page. In this node, the information for the current customer is copied from an internal table to the corresponding work area, WA_CUSTOMER.

Because a given form is intended for only a single customer, however, this node does not involve true loop processing either. This special case for the loop was mentioned previously in Section 7.2.3.

Moreover, the filled work area is not actually needed for the item data; instead, it serves primarily to print the customer's address in the ADDRESS window.

> **Note:** Until now, you have been able to output the address properly only because the corresponding address node, ADDRESS, appears after MAIN—and thus after TABLE—in the navigation tree. Try moving the entire address window above MAIN in the navigation tree and output the form again with the main program. The address no longer appears.

The function for retrieving the recipient address in the TABLE node is one that you wouldn't necessarily expect in the MAIN window. As a result, the branch that outputs the invoice items has a structure that could be improved in several aspects. All you really need is:

▶ A single table node that conducts the entire loop processing for the flight bookings and outputs the items.

▶ A node for retrieving the time of a flight connection. You can use a loop to read a single data record, as before.

▶ A node outside of MAIN to retrieve the address; the node that outputs the address must appear **below** the retrieval node. You can use a loop to read a single data record, as before.

Overview of the Structural Changes

In the next exercise, you will define a new, more apparent node structure to output the item table. Here are the basic requirements:

▶ You want to use a single new, main table node to control the output, as described above.

▶ The inferior nodes that are output will be moved to the new structure, which means you can reuse them in their present form.

▶ You will create true table and loop nodes to replace the nodes with type **Complex Section**.

Figure 7.11 illustrates the result of these changes. In particular, the structure of the MAIN window has become much more complex, as it now has fewer nodes. The address data is now retrieved where it should be: in the same window where it is output.

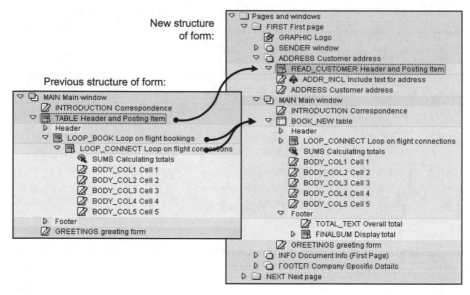

Figure 7.11 Form optimization

Now proceed step by step. Because most of the required nodes are already available, you should have no difficulties in following the example. You will make more changes in later chapters based on the new structure.

Step 1: Create a Table Node

Upon closer examination of the TABLE node, you can see that you do not need it in order to output the flight bookings in the main window. You will want to keep it there, though, because it contains the recipient address. To output the actual invoice items, however, you will now create a new table node that contains both the formatting for the output table and the loop over the flight bookings.

Create a new table node in the MAIN window above GREETINGS, using **Create · Table** in the context menu. Enter BOOK_NEW as the name, along with a suitable description. The table width is 15.25 cm. The **Data** tab page is active by default in the table node. Fill in the following tab pages, one after another:

▶ Table

Copy the design of the output table (width, line types, line pattern) from the previous TABLE node. You can also use the fast SAP copy function with the extended clipboard (**Ctrl + Y** and so on). If you want your items to appear with visible frames, as before, you should also select the appropriate pattern.

▶ Data

The loop should process the internal table with the flight bookings as in the previous LOOP_BOOK node. Copy the settings.

▶ Events

Copy the settings for the header and footer from the TABLE node.

Check the individual nodes. The overall check should not report any errors either.

Step 2: Move the Existing Inferior Nodes

Now move the inferior nodes into the new branch in the navigation tree (drag and drop with the mouse):

▶ Start with the inferior nodes in the header and footer, which were previously located under the TABLE node. Make sure that the sequence of the inferior nodes under BOOK_NEW is the same as it was before.

▶ Now move the nodes that are responsible for outputting the positions directly into the new BOOK_NEW node. You will find them under LOOP_BOOK. You already moved the nodes for outputting the nodes into this node (from the level below LOOP_CONNECT) in the exercise in Section 7.2.4.

The new branch in the navigation tree should now look approximately like the one in Figure 7.12.

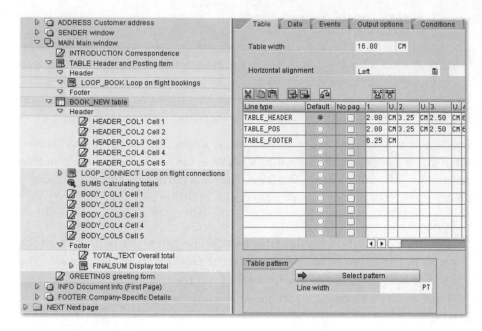

Figure 7.12 Changed item output

All the relevant contents of the previous TABLE node have been copied to BOOK_ NEW. Because the previous loop processing of TABLE no longer has any contents, you will remove it in the next step.

Run the overall form check. No new errors should occur. Test the output with main program Z_SF_EXAMPLE_01. The result should be identical to the previous outputs.

Step 3: Remove the Old Nodes and Settings

To complete the exercise, you will clean up the form a bit:

▶ The previous LOOP_BOOK node has been transferred completely to the new node; you can delete it.

▶ Also remove the header and footer below TABLE; they will now only generate blank lines during output (in the **Events** tab page), at most.

▶ Because the previous TABLE node now serves only to retrieve the customer data, change its name to READ_CUSTOMER.

▶ It makes more sense to retrieve the address where it is needed. Therefore, move the READ_CUSTOMER node to the ADDRESS window. Make sure it is the first item there, to ensure that the subsequent text nodes are assigned contents.

Because the design of the output table is no longer relevant for this node, you should change the output type to **Simple** in the **General Attributes** tab page; otherwise, the overall check will report that the table won't fit in the window. When you set this option, the node with type **Complex Section** now acts like a loop node.

▶ Finally, move the entire ADDRESS procedure above MAIN.

There are two reasons for doing this:

   ▷ It is easier to navigate in the navigation tree when the windows that appear at the top of the page are also listed first in the navigation tree.

   ▷ The customer number must be known before the MAIN window is executed, because you use the customer number in WA_CUSTOMER-ID to find the flight bookings in table node BOOK_NEW.

The new structure in the navigation tree should now look like the structure illustrated in Figure 7.11 at the beginning of this section.

Optional Changes

Both the READ_CUSTOMER and the LOOP_CONNECT nodes below BOOK_NEW are still implemented as node type **Complex Section**. Yet each of them now serves only to read a single data record and copy it to a field string. They do not have any inferior nodes. Replace the nodes with true loop nodes. To do so, proceed as follows:

▶ Create a new loop node after each of the existing nodes. As a result, the new node is executed after the old one. Therefore, the data record that is read always comes from the new node.

▶ Assign the attributes as you did in the previous nodes (**internal table**, **work area**, **conditions**).

▶ Check the form and test the output.

▶ Delete the previous nodes with type **Complex Section** and give each new node the names of the node it replaced.

7.3 Logical Queries

The most common way to influence the flow logic in the form is to define logical queries. Two options are available:

▶ You can define *conditions* for any node in the form below the page node. This enables you to release or block the execution of the respective nodes, along with any inferior nodes.

▶ An *alternative* node is basically an extension of the conditions, and defines the node to be executed if the defined condition is false. This node type provides for a more concise representation and reduces your input efforts.

7.3.1 Conditions

All manual node types below a page, with the exception of the program node, have a **Conditions** tab page to adapt the node execution to the respective form logic.

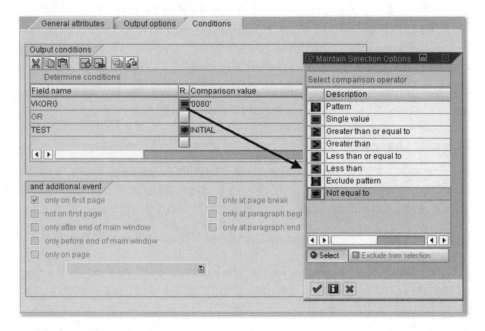

Figure 7.13 Conditions for a node

When you create a condition, the corresponding node immediately appears in the navigation tree. Smart Forms distinguishes between two types of conditions:

▶ Logical expressions

▶ Output events

The properties of each type are described below.

Monitoring Logical Expressions

You can enter a logical expression with two operands in each line of the conditions. Each of these operands can be either a field or a value, as both columns are equivalent despite their labels **Field Name** and **Comparison Value**. Do not enclose the field names in ampersands, but enclose the values in single quotes. You can omit the single quotes for numerical values.

The comparison operator, which you select from the defined list (as shown in Figure 7.13), appears between the two operands. If you do not specify an operator, the equality check is selected by default.

You can enter multiple conditions to configure complex logical queries. The individual queries in the lines are linked with a logical AND. To configure an OR link between two lines, choose the corresponding button in the toolbar or enter OR in the first column. Once you confirm your entry, the line is automatically displayed in gray in both cases, to prevent further additions.

> **Tip:** In addition to the comparison operators for logical queries, ABAP also supports a query for the condition **is initial**. In this case, the system checks whether the defined field has been assigned a valid value after its declaration. You can also define this check as a condition in Smart Forms by entering INITIAL in the second operand (see example in Figure 7.13).

Monitoring Events

You can use the **Additional Event** box to link the execution of the node with special events in form processing. Because these conditions are largely self-explanatory, they are described only briefly below:

▶ The attributes **Only/Not on First Page** always refers to the individual print pages, not the draft pages.

▶ The conditions **Only at/before End of Main Window** make sense only for nodes in secondary windows that appear after the main window in the navigation tree. The defined condition is based on a query of system variable SFSY-PAGEBREAK. This variable is set when the main window has been completely processed. Sample application: Outputting subtotals within a secondary window that will appear on all pages except the last page.

▶ If you activate **Only on Page**, you have to specify a draft page. In many cases, you can delete the corresponding node in the draft page instead. You can only do so, however, if the corresponding window exists only on that page. Otherwise, if it exists as a copy on several pages (as is usually the case with MAIN, for example), the node would be deleted on all pages.

The settings to the right for **page breaks** and the **start/end of sections** can be selected only for nodes that are defined below event nodes. In turn, event nodes exist under node types Folder and Loop, and enable the automatic creation of headers and footers (see Section 5.4 for an example).

Linking the Monitoring Operations

The results of the individual monitoring of the logical expressions and the output events are linked internally with a logical AND. Therefore, a given node is processed only when the overall conditions are met. If not, this node and all its inferior nodes are ignored.

In general, all the inferior nodes are also linked with their respective superior nodes with a logical AND when the conditions are evaluated. You can use this fact to define query logic of nearly infinite complexity in the form.

> **Tip:** The use of conditions is also recommended for the development phase of a form—to find the cause of runtime errors, for example. You can use conditions to selectively deactivate entire branches, in order to localize the error.

7.3.2 Branching with Alternative Nodes

The alternative node is a handy solution for situations in which two nodes are to be performed under opposing conditions.

When you create this type of node, the Form Builder automatically generates two additional event nodes, TRUE and FALSE, as direct inferior nodes in the navigation tree. You then add the actual inferior nodes, which will be executed depending on the result of the logical query. You can define further alternative nodes here as necessary.

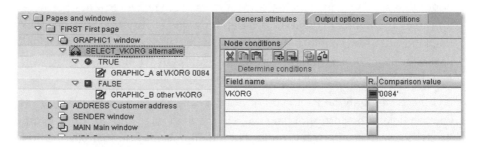

Figure 7.14 Branching with alternative nodes

In the simple example in Figure 7.14, one of two alternative graphics (defined in the TRUE and FALSE branches) is selected, depending on the query of the sales organization.

> **Important:** You determine the contents of the query in the **General Attributes** tab page of the alternative node. The possible values here are identical to those in the **Conditions** tab page, which may confuse you at first. You can also use the **Conditions** tab page to define a condition for processing the entire alternative node.

You could achieve the same result as in the example in Figure 7.14 by defining two graphic nodes. In this case, you merely have to define opposing conditions for the query of the sales organization, setting one to *Equality* and the other to *Inequality*.

> **Note:** The alternative node is translated as the ABAP statement IF ... THEN ... ELSE ... ENDIF in the source text of the generated function module.

7.4   Page Sequence and Numbering

You can use system field SFSY-PAGE to output the current page number in the text node of a form, as well as to query it in other node attributes (such as the conditions; also see Section 6.4.3). The contents of the page counter depend on the sequence of pages in the form. This sequence, in turn, is dependent on the following factors:

▶ The number of data records to be output and the amount of space available In the main window

▶ The configured node attributes of the respective draft page

▶ The use of dynamic page breaks through a command node

Page Sequence

Normally, a page break occurs whenever the main window in a page is full. The system then processes the page that is defined as the next page in the current page node (in the **General Attributes** tab page). In the example of the flight invoice, the FIRST and NEXT draft pages follow this static logic. This form of processing was also discussed at the beginning of this chapter.

Alternatively, you may want to output an additional page—with your general terms and conditions for doing business, for example—at the end of regular form output. In this case, output control must be able to calculate dynamically which page should be accessed and when. You can define this information in a command node in the form.

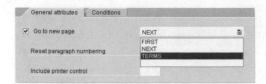

Figure 7.15 Dynamic page break in a command node

Activate the option **Go to New Page** and enter the code for the required page (see Figure 7.15). You use the **Conditions** tab page as usual to define when the command node will be executed.

Generally, you can insert a command node at any point within the navigation tree (see Section 7.4). Please note, however, that two additional prerequisites must be met for you to use the **Go to New Page** option:

▶ The command node must be defined in the main window. Otherwise, a runtime error will occur during form output.

▶ The dynamic page break must not be located within a loop. As a result, it is not possible, for example, to interrupt the output of items for a flight invoice under a certain condition and continue on the next page.

All the nodes that follow a command with a manual page break within the main window are no longer processed in the current page. Therefore, a command node with dynamic page break is usually the last node in the main window. The defined secondary windows are still output in the same page, however.

Page Counter

You can use the following system fields to query the current status of the page numbering in the form:

SFSY-PAGE   For the current page number

SFSY FORMPAGES   For the total number of pages in the form

SFSY-JOBPAGE   For the total number of pages in all forms in the print job

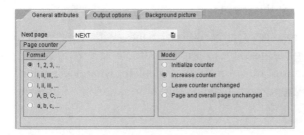

Figure 7.16 Attributes of the page counter

You can use these system fields to query the internal page counters from output control. You can define several attributes for these internal page counters in the **General Attributes** tab page in the attributes for the page node (see Figure 7.16):

▶ Define the format for the page numbers (Arabic digits, Roman numerals, or letters) in the **Format** box.

▶ Define how the values of the various page counters can be modified in the **Mode** box.

  ▶ The options **Initialize**, **Increase**, and **Hold** change the current page number only in SFSY-PAGE. The totals figures in SFSY-FORMPAGES and SFSY-JOBPAGES are always increased by one, regardless of this setting.

  ▶ If you set **Page and Overall Page Unchanged**, both &SFSY-PAGE& and &SFSY-FORMPAGES& will remain unchanged.

7.5   Command Node

7.5.1   Overview

A command node is a collection of different functions, some of which have already been described.

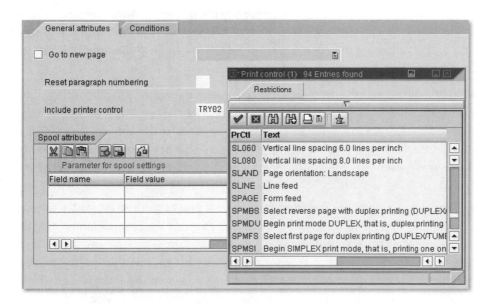

Figure 7.17 Command node with list of print controls

Overview of the individual functions:

▶ **Go to New Page**
You can use this function only within the main window, and only outside a loop there. This was discussed previously in Section 7.4.

▶ **Reset Paragraph Numbering**
If a paragraph format contains outline functions, numbering is reset to the initial value. The outline functions were explained in detail in Chapter 3, *Style Builder*.

▶ **Insert Printer Control**
You use this function to insert a print control to use specific functions of the output device.

▶ **Assign Spool Attributes**
You can assign spool attributes for the generated output request; these are used to evaluate the requests in the spool.

Because the first two options have already been dealt with in detail, only the latter two are described below.

Overview of Output Control

The previous chapters of this book frequently discuss "**outputting** the form," usually ignoring the fact that output consists of two separate steps. A critical way station in this process is the spool program, which manages all the print requests in the SAP system:

▶ In the first step, the output is passed on to the spool program as a spool request. Although the contents of the request are the result of form processing, it does not yet have formatting that the destination device (printer, fax machine, and so on) can interpret directly. At this point, the generated document is present in a device-independent interim format, the *Output Text Format*, or OTF for short.

▶ The spool requests are collected in the spool program. Their attributes can be changed there if necessary; for example, you can assign a different output device. After final confirmation by the user, the spool program generates the actual output request and sends it to the output device. To do so, the *printer driver* is normally used to convert the existing document from the intermediate OTF format to a custom format for the specific destination device.

Step 2 is where *print controls* are used. They translate the general format instructions of the OTF format into specific control sequences for the output device. Therefore, the print controls describe the actual functions of the output device.

This automated procedure does not consider all the possible functions of the output device; otherwise, almost every device type would require its own, extremely specific printer driver. Moreover, the Form Builder would have to support each of these custom functions, which would increase its complexity exponentially. Nevertheless, to enable the use of individual features of an output device, Smart Forms supports the call of print controls through the command node.

7.5.2 Print Controls

Print controls in the command node give a form direct access to individual functions of the output device. However, their use involves dependencies and even hazards, such as:

▶ They make a form dependent on a specific output device. Therefore, different devices may produce different results.

▶ The check routine in the form cannot determine which function is invoked by a given print control. Moreover, it cannot check whether a given print control is even supported by a specific output device.

▶ The printer commands contained in the print control must not affect the current printer settings, because the printer driver does not have any information about which changes a given print control will trigger. The printer driver assumes that the print control will not have any effect on the texts and graphics that are output afterward. You may need to define another print control to reset the change.

▶ If the defined print controls use the line feed, the automatic calculation of the page break will no longer work.

Despite these risks, print controls can help you find solutions for even the trickiest problems. Therefore, their technical background is described in detail below.

> **Note:** All the print controls that you can integrate in a form with a command node are managed centrally in the spool administration transaction. To start this transaction, choose SAP menu path **Tools · CCMS · Spool · Spool Administration SPAD**. Choose the **Print Control** button in the **Device Types** tab page. This button is available only in extended administration mode.

Print controls consist of a five-character code and a description. The first letters of a code indicate the grouping of the print control for the respective application case. Examples include:

BAR..	Bar code functions
CI...	Settings for the character spacing
COL..	Settings for the print color
LI...	Settings for the line spacing (lines per inch)
S....	Print controls for SAPscript (used in the printer driver)
TRY..	Selection of the paper tray

Specific print controls are defined in each of these groups. Examples include:

CI010	Set character spacing 10 characters per inch
COL2V	Inverse type
TRY02	Use printer paper tray 2 for the printout

Normally, the appropriate print controls are used automatically when converting form output into the command set of the output device. The *SAPscript printer driver* is responsible for converting output from Smart Forms. It uses primarily print controls that start with the letters "S" and "T". These include the following print controls for controlling fonts and bar codes:

SBPxx	Activate bar code with number "xx"
SBSxx	Deactivate bar code with number "xx"
SFxxx	Choose printer font number "xxx"
SLxxx	Configure line spacing "xxx"

You maintain the specific printer fonts and bar codes in SAP font management (see Section 13.6.6).

When the spool request is converted to an output request for the specific output device, each print control is converted to the appropriate command (escape sequence) for the respective device type (also see Section 13.6).

Note: Only one print control can be output for each command node. To display a list of all the print controls that have been defined in spool administration, use the value help in the input field. This is a complete list; you will have to make sure that the selected print control is also defined (with the required control function) for the active output devices.

7.5.3 Attributes for the Spool Request

As mentioned above, whenever a form is output, a spool request is initially generated and saved in the spool program. Spool requests may contain a variety of administration information. This information is discussed in detail in Section 13.6.

You can also specify freely definable attributes for each spool request as additional administration information, such as supplying custom attributes for analysis. To display these attributes in spool administration (SP01), choose menu path **Goto • Request Information** and then the **Free Attributes** tab page, which exists only if attributes have been defined. You can also use a command node to generate these spool attributes directly within the form.

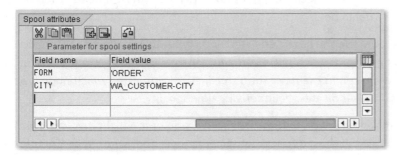

Figure 7.18 Command node with spool attributes

The individual spool attributes consist of a freely definable name for the corresponding field as well as its contents (field value). Two attributes are defined in the example:

▶ FORM reflects the contents of the form, with field value ORDER (AUFTRAG) as an indication of the order confirmation.

▶ Parameter CITY contains the sold-to party's city; it is defined dynamically through a field here, as this specification is dependent on the current sold-to party.

A subsequent evaluation of the spool file could contain the following query: List all order confirmations (that is, field name FORM = "AUFTRAG") that were sent to a specific city—such as NEW YORK (that is, additional field name CITY = "NEW YORK").

Note: If you dynamically assign field contents in Release 4.6C, you have to surround the field name in ampersands (&); this condition is considered to be a program error (see the SAP Notes in the Appendix).

One possible use of the spool attributes is for postage optimizing: in this case, you can specify an (abbreviated) ZIP code as an attribute. See report RSPOPRNT, for example; the spool attributes are saved in database table TSP02A.

7.6 Complex Section

A **complex section** unifies the attributes of node types **Folder**, **Template**, **Table**, and **Loop** in a single node type. You configure the options in the **General Attributes** tab page to determine which node type you want to simulate. Therefore, you cannot combine attributes of different node types.

Node type **Complex Section** stems from the early versions of Smart Forms and should no longer be used. Because it does not provide any new functions, it is not described in any detail here.

Instead, you should use the new, dedicated node types to implement the function you need. Using this approach gives you another small advantage in the display: the corresponding icon in the navigation tree instantly indicates which node type is involved, and thus indicates its underlying functionality.

You will remember, however, that the original version of the flight invoice, which you have been using in the exercises, contained several nodes with type **Complex Section**. You replaced these nodes with their dedicated counterparts in the exercise in Section 7.2.8.

7.7 Postprocessing

A regular requirement in form development is the need to output data on the first page of a form that isn't known until form output is complete.

> **Examples:** Outputting sums that are calculated during form output, such as individual invoice totals or the total weight of a delivery note. Frequently, this information is also associated with special output formats, such as bar codes or information for enveloping machines. Another requirement may be a "Copy" notation, when several copies of a form are output.

As you read in the section on flow logic above, a field can be output correctly only if its contents are already known at the time of output. This is not the case in the above examples. To enable this type of output, at least two passes are required to process the form:

▶ All the required values are calculated in the first pass.

▶ These values are then available from the start of the second pass, and can be output accordingly.

> **Note:** Earlier in this chapter, you learned about system fields SFSY-FORM-PAGES and SFSY-JOBPAGES (total number of print pages in a form or spool request). Strictly speaking, these values are not known until form processing is complete. However, the form processor generally treats these fields as special cases, and does not insert them in the print pages until a second processing pass.

In Basis Release 6.1, it will be possible to output any variable in a second pass. The control takes place in a special window node, which must be defined as a secondary window for this purpose. You can then set the **Postprocessing** node attribute, which triggers processing in the second pass, for this window. This enables you to implement the examples mentioned above (also see Chapter 12).

This special node attribute is not available in Release 4.6C. The postprocessing logic is already implemented, however, and is already used to output the total number of pages. Support Packages 12 and later for Release 4.6C provide a workaround that enables you to implement the required postprocessing for an entire window.

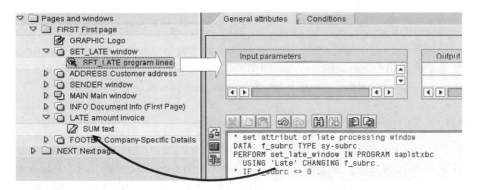

Figure 7.19 Postprocessing

If you have installed the support package, you can also set the attribute for post-processing of a window in an additional program node, instead of using the node attributes, as in Release 6.1 and later. Here is a brief explanation of the procedure:

1. Define all the windows in the node, including the secondary windows that will not be processed until the second pass (for example, with names LATE1, LATE2). You can use all of the form fields in the inferior nodes of these post-processing windows. The contents present at the end of the first pass (with calculated grand totals, for example) are output.

2. Always create another secondary window at the top of the navigation tree on the first page, such as SET_LATE in the above diagram. This window will not generate any output itself.

3. Instead, create a program node underneath this window node. In this program node, you have to call a FORM routine that sets the additional attribute for each defined postprocessing window. The sample coding below involves two windows (LATE1 and LATE2) that should not be processed until the second pass:

```
*&-------------------------------------------------------------&*
* Set attribute for postprocessing window
DATA: f_subrc TYPE sy-subrc.
PERFORM set_late_window IN PROGRAM saplstxbc
  USING 'Late1' CHANGING f_subrc.
* IF f_subrc <> 0 .
PERFORM set_late_window IN PROGRAM saplstxbc
  USING 'Late2' CHANGING f_subrc.
*&-------------------------------------------------------------&*
```

Listing 7.2 Postprocessing

Please read the corresponding notes in SAPNet (see Appendix) for more details. In Basis Release 6.10 and later, you should use the provided item in the node attributes of the respective window instead. Therefore, you will need to delete any additional program nodes you have defined when you upgrade your release.

7.8   Summary of Form Processing

In this chapter, you learned about all the node types and attributes that can influence form processing. In closing, we would like to summarize all these processes from the perspective of the flow control for form output. Please note, however, that this information is not directly relevant for form design.

We differentiate between two processing levels:

▶ Control of output by page
▶ Processing of the individual nodes within a page

Take another look at the branches of the navigation tree in the Form Builder:

▶ Output starts with the first page—that is, the first page in the navigation tree—unless a different first page is explicitly specified in the form interface parameters.

▶ The windows in each draft page are processed in the sequence defined in the navigation tree. In turn, each individual window is processed in the sequence of the assigned inferior nodes.

Information is output in a secondary window until one of these two situations occurs:

▶ All the nodes in the window have been processed.

▶ The window in the print page is full.

Page Output Control

If the current draft page contains a main window, its response determines whether output control creates a new print page or whether the current page is the last page. The flow control for page output is activated when one of the following conditions is met:

▶ All the nodes in the main window have been processed.

▶ All the nodes in the main window have *not* been processed yet, but there is no more room in the print page.

▶ A manual page break is triggered in a command node.

In all cases, output of the current page is completed. Any remaining secondary windows are output, since they follow the main window in the navigation tree. In the two latter cases, a new print page is created automatically:

▶ If there is no more room in the print page, the statically defined next page is created.

▶ If a manual page break is triggered in a command node, the dynamic next page defined in the triggering command node is created.

Because no further print page is needed when all the nodes contained in the main window have been processed, overall processing of the form is also complete at this point.

If a draft page does not have a main window, the next page is always read from the static specification of the next page. A manual page break with dynamic next page is not possible here because the corresponding command node cannot be executed here; this feature is supported only in the main window. If no next page has been specified, the current print page is the last page.

Processing Individual Nodes

The nodes in the navigation tree have different types and, accordingly, different characteristics (type of processing, number of inferior nodes, and so on). Output options and conditions can be defined for all nodes. The processing of an individual node involves the following steps:

▶ If a condition is defined for a node, that node and all its inferior nodes are processed only when this condition is met.

▶ If the condition is met or no condition is defined, the action assigned to the respective node, such as outputting a text or processing program coding, is performed. All the configured output options are also taken into account. These include:

  ▶ Output of boxes and shading

  ▶ Assigning cells of a template or output table

  ▶ Specifying a style for custom paragraph and character formats

  ▶ If page protection is set, all the contents of a node and its inferior nodes are output in the same page

▶ If a node has its own inferior nodes, these inferior nodes are processed first. The processing sequence is dependent on the node type; the following sequences are possible:

  ▶ Sequential from top to bottom

  ▶ Only upon certain events

  ▶ As an alternative, based on logical queries

  ▶ Repeated when controlled by a loop

8 ABAP Programs in Forms

8.1 Why Use Program Coding in a Form?

A special feature of Smart Forms is that it contains a defined form interface to transfer data between the main program and the form. The advantage of this approach is that a single main program can be used to retrieve data for several different forms. Consequently, the main program should be as independent from the individual form as possible.

> **Note:** When the functions of the main program are described (see Section 9.6), you will also read learn how you can customize the data retrieval in the main program for an individual form.

But what happens when you have to output data in a form, but the main program cannot supply this data as required through the form interface? This is possible in the following cases, for example:

▶ The data is available in tables in the SAP database. These tables were not intended for use in the current application, however, and thus were not read by the main program or provided for use in the form.

▶ You want to output data in the form that is calculated from other existing data, such as subtotals and grand totals.

▶ The data has to be output in a specific format—only certain characters of a text variable, for example, or the contents of a field in all caps.

The first case is the most frequent, and also the most challenging. There are two possible ways to retrieve the data under Smart Forms in this case:

▶ The determination of the data is added to the main program; the contents are passed on to the form interface as usual.

▶ The data is determined through ABAP program coding in the form.

Factors for Choosing the Data Retrieval Method

Therefore, you first have to decide which method you want to use. You should consider the following factors:

▶ Does any additional data have to be retrieved from database tables? If so, are the involved database tables already read in the main program? In this case, you should add the extra fields there.

▶ Is the data also required in other forms?

▶ Will the ABAP coding involved require relatively little effort? If so, you should always implement it in the form. This will save you from having to modify the form interface.

▶ Is the main program a standard program from SAP? If so, avoid making changes to it whenever possible, because it would be necessary to copy the program. And in this case you can loose the advantage of maintenance by SAP for the main program.

In light of these factors, the form is the preferred choice for the development in many cases. Accordingly, you will need to implement program coding in the form.

> **Note:** You may have heard that subsequent reading of data in the form results in worse performance than data retrieval in the main program (for database queries, for example). This statement is only true, however, when the data is read from the same sources that were already queried in the main program (but due to different contents). In this specific case, you have duplicate functionality that can slow down program execution. Otherwise, a database query in the form has the same execution time as a query in the main program.

Entering Program Coding in the Form

You enter program coding in different places in the form, depending on the task at hand. The supported ABAP statements are the same everywhere. The following options are available:

▶ **Program node**
You can use this node type to place program coding anywhere in the form (below any window).

▶ **Global definitions, Initialization tab page**
The program coding at this point is executed before any other node. The statements are particularly suited for basic data assignments, such as:

  ▶ Initializing variables or conversions

  ▶ Reorganizing internal tables that are supplied through the form interface

  ▶ Retrieving additional data from database tables

▶ **Global definitions, Form Routines tab page**
In this case, subroutines are managed as FORM routines, which you can call from any other program node using the PERFORM statement. In turn, FORM routines can execute other subroutines, or even complete function modules, in the system with infinite nesting.

► **Global definitions, Types tab page**
  Individual data types are required in the form when equivalent entries are not available in the ABAP Dictionary in the system. You can use these data types for data declaration anywhere in the form, except in the form interface—in the **global definitions**, for example, or in a program node.

You have already considered several factors to clarify whether data retrieval should take place in the main program or in the form. If you choose in favor of the form, you now have to decide whether to create the corresponding programs centrally during form initialization or in individual nodes. Factors that you should consider for this decision include:

► Central data retrieval, such as reading from the database, should always take place during form initialization.

► It may seem advantageous to write as much coding as possible in the initialization and then merely use the results as variables in the form. While this approach gives you a main overview of all ABAP programs, it also has some key disadvantages:

  ► Some calculations are performed in direct interaction with nodes in the form—for example, calculating totals for an item within a loop). Therefore, you will have to define these calculations in the individual node anyway.

  ► If a large number of routines is involved, you will want to document where each respective routine is used in the form. In this case, you might as well insert the program directly for the individual node.

You will generally make use of all the above options.

Further Steps

You use the same input function to maintain program coding in all the locations described above. Therefore, this chapter starts with information on how to use the ABAP editor and on the special features associated with its use under Smart Forms. You will then learn about the individual ABAP statements that are most frequently required in form development. Please note, however, that this chapter is not a beginner's guide to ABAP programming, as that would go far beyond the scope of this book.

> **Note:** If you need more information on ABAP programming, refer to the information in the SAP library and the specialized books on this subject (such as *ABAP Objects—The Official Reference* by Horst Keller and Joachim Jacobitz (1st Edition, SAP PRESS 2003, ISBN 1–59229–011–6) and *ABAP Objects* by Horst Keller and Sascha Krüger (2nd Edition, SAP PRESS 2001, ISBN 3–89842–147–3)).

The last two sections of this chapter introduce two examples of applications for program nodes:

▶ Including an address using the function module that controls the functions of the address node

▶ Calculating a grand total for the flight invoice in a program node

8.2   Editing Functions in the Program Node

You generally use the *ABAP editor* to maintain programs in the SAP system. You already used it in the *Getting Started* chapter, for example, to change the main program (transaction SE38).

In contrast to this full-page version, the program node in Smart Forms provides a version with a reduced input area. The individual functions have also been reduced to the specific demands of Smart Forms. No matter where you enter program coding within the form, the input area always looks the same (see Figure 8.1).

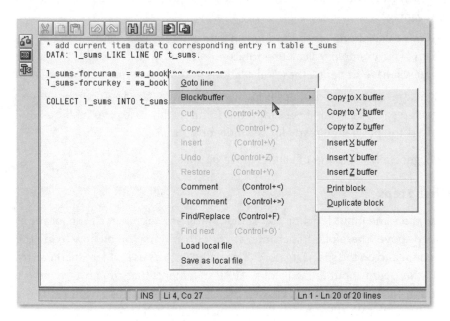

Figure 8.1 Entering program coding

The editor has an input area with a fixed size, in which mouse functions are also supported. For example, select a block of several lines of source code. You now have the following options:

▶ You can press the tab key to shift the lines two characters to the right, or press **Shift + Tab** to move them to the left.

▶ You can move the selection with the mouse by dragging and dropping, that is, while holding down the left mouse button.

These and other functions are also available through menu items, which are discussed further below.

The editor has a status bar at the bottom of the input area. The current position of the cursor (line/column information) is displayed here. This is particularly useful for processing with error messages.

The toolbar above the input area features standard editor functions, such as **cut**, **copy**, **paste**, **undo** and **restore**, **search and replace**, and **load/save as** local file.

The toolbar to the left of the input area features special functions that can be very useful when entering source text:

Check

The node check utilizes the syntax check from the ABAP development environment to locate formal errors in the specified source text. The syntax check reports any errors found, along with the corresponding line numbers. This enables you to find the source of the error quickly in most cases. If necessary, choose **Goto Line** in the context menu. The line specification may be incorrect in some situations; therefore, ABAP beginners may have to exercise patience to track down the actual cause.

> **Tip:** When you create a new program node, its contents initially consist of around 25 unnecessary blank lines, which are not immediately visible. Select several lines with the mouse; they appear as an inverted column. Delete these lines before you start entering any source text. Several programmers have reported that this trick eliminates several inexplicable error messages that previously appeared during the syntax check!

Statement Pattern

This button inserts patterns for complete ABAP statements, as well as function module calls. The statement pattern function automatically inserts the appropriate program coding in the source text at the current cursor position. This configures a function module call with (for example) a number of interface parameters, which you can then modify to suit your needs (see Section 8.5).

▓ Pretty Printer

This function formats the source text to make it easier to read. For example, it automatically indents subordinate lines and converts statements and other objects to all caps. You can specify the desired formatting in the settings for the full ABAP editor (transaction SE38). The basic functions in the upper toolbar are also available in the context menu (right mouse button) during text input. The context menu also contains other useful functions:

▶ **Goto Line**

This function is especially useful in case of syntax errors, since the syntax check lists any errors it finds in the source text together with the respective line numbers.

▶ **Block/Buffer**

The most important function here is probably **Print Block**, which you can use to print a selected text block directly. The **Copy/Paste X/Y/Z** buffer functions give you access to the extended clipboard in the SAP system in order to copy several text blocks at the same time, for example.

▶ **Comment/Uncomment**

In ABAP source text, single lines are treated as comment lines whenever an asterisk (*) appears in the first column. The editor displays the corresponding lines in a different color, to better distinguish them from active coding. You can use the **Comment** function to insert asterisks for each row of the selected block, and **Uncomment** to remove them. This function is especially useful during the test phase, to temporarily deactivate specific program functions.

Help Functions

When you enter the source text, you can press **F1** to retrieve the ABAP keyword documentation for an ABAP statement. For example, position the cursor on the COLLECT statement in Figure 8.1 and press **F1**. A new window appears with the documentation of the keyword and all its options.

If you press **F1** for a blank line, an additional selection screen appears as your gateway to the extended documentation, as shown in Figure 8.2.

You can specify any object in the upper screen area, which enables you to display ABAP keyword documentation for keywords that do not appear in the source text, as well as the ABAP overview and new features.

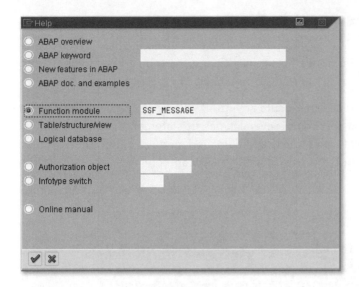

Figure 8.2 Help in a program node

The selection of function modules, tables, and so on is based on the items in the Repository or ABAP Dictionary. These options take you directly to the display mode of the corresponding maintenance tools, such as the Function Builder. From there, choose menu path **Goto · Documentation** to display the information for the respective object.

ABAP Line Editor

The ABAP editor described above features basic functions, such asgraphical support and mouse functions, that are standard in most modern word processors. A line-based version of the editor is also available. To toggle between the editors, choose menu path **Utilities · Settings** in the Form Builder and then select the **Editor** tab page. The terms used are somewhat cryptic; here is a translation:

▶ The option **Text Edit Control** corresponds to the graphical editor (default setting).

▶ The option **Table Control Editor** corresponds to the alternative line-based display.

The line editor has several additional functions in the toolbar that stem from the line-based display; the line number also appears to the left of each line. Please note, however, that the context menu is not available in this version of the editor.

8.3 Special Features in the Program Node

You will now learn about several special features involved in entering ABAP program coding in program nodes. To simplify things, the term "program node" also refers to the contents of the **Initialization** tab page in the global definitions.

In theory, a program node can execute any ABAP statements. Nonetheless, due to the architecture of Smart Forms, several types of statements are not possible, especially the ones that cannot be used in function modules either. These include direct error output and the use of interactive components such as selection screens.

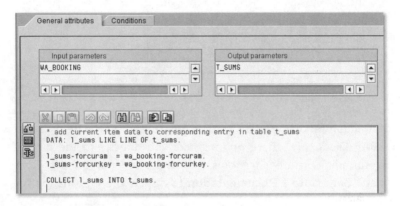

Figure 8.3 Program node

Input/Output Parameters

A special feature of program nodes in Smart Forms is that all global data that is addressed in the program coding must be declared as input or output parameters. This specification is not required for execution, nor is it included in the generated function module. The assignment of input/output parameters simplifies subsequent troubleshooting, however, as they are taken into account in the following situations:

▶ You can use only global fields that have been declared as parameters in the coding. Otherwise, an error message appears during the local check of the program node.

▶ Before a given field is output the first time — in a text node, for example — the system checks whether it has been assigned a value. This check also covers the program node. Please note that the source text is not checked specifically; the field merely has to be specified as a parameter.

▶ The superior main program can also access the input/output parameters, to determine which fields are really needed in the form.

The input/output parameters do not have to agree with the details in the program coding. If you output a specific field in a field string, for example, you can specify either the complete field name or merely the name of the field string as the parameter. You can also enter more parameters than are really needed in the source text.

The division into input and output parameters only serves to improve clarity. Therefore, you can also make changes to input parameters in the program coding.

Translation in the Function Module

When you generate a function module for a form, each program node is created as a subroutine and encapsulated with FORM and ENDFORM statements. Because the function module itself is made up exclusively of ABAP coding, you can also see the translation of the program node there.

> **Tip:** If you want to check where and how your program node appears in the form, open the generated function module in display mode in the Function Builder. Now call the extended search and enter the search term as the ID of the node, or another unique term such as the name of a local variable or a reference in a comment line (also see Section 13.7.3).

8.4 ABAP Basics

8.4.1 Overview

A comprehensive description of all the options available in ABAP programming is not currently possible. Plenty of specific literature is available on this subject, however, as well as the documentation in the SAP Library (BC-ABAP). Still, this section contains a brief overview that Smart Forms novices without ABAP experience should find especially useful.

First, there are several basic rules that you need to observe when writing program coding:

▶ Every ABAP program consists of *comments* and *statements*. A comment line starts with an asterisk, while a statement ends with a period.

▶ The ABAP editor automatically displays *comment lines* in a different color. Alternatively, you can also enter a short comment at the end of any *statement line*, which you have to start with a double quote. This variant is not displayed in a different color, however.

▶ Every ABAP statement is concluded with a period, although statements can also run over several lines, which means that the period will appear at the end of the last line. Conversely, several statements—each of which is concluded with a period—can also appear in a single program line.

> **Note:** Many ABAP beginners forget the period. But however, the syntax check often has trouble diagnosing this simple case. Therefore, so a given error message will not necessarily point out the cause immediately.

▶ Every ABAP statement starts with an ABAP keyword that describes which operation will be performed. This keyword is followed by operands, operators, and additions. Blank characters appear between each element of the statement.

▶ The operands of an ABAP statement normally involve variables such as **fields**, **field strings**, and **internal tables**. These are the same elements that were described in detail in Chapter 6, so you should already be familiar with them.

A program node in Smart Forms can address all the global data that is defined in the form. One special feature applies, however: the data must be defined as input or output parameters. Only the system variables from SFSY and SY are available directly as "true" global data. You can then define additional, local data within a program node—to save interim values, for example—which is then only known within that node.

Conventions for ABAP Statements

This section describes several key ABAP statements that you will probably use frequently in Smart Forms, and which are especially well-suited to explaining the conventions for their use.

Let's start with a brief overview of the conventions for the following statements:

Statement element	Code	Meaning
Keyword	ABC	Indicates the keyword in the ABAP statement or addition (in all caps)
Variable	fld	Indicates an elementary field
	str	Field string (derived from a structure here)
	itab	Internal table
	var	General variable (independent of type)
Data type	tyfeld	Elementary data type (Dictionary or ABAP data type)
	tystr	Structure (in the Dictionary or user-defined)
	tytab	Table type (in the Dictionary or user-defined)
Database	dbtab	Transparent database table

Table 8.1 Conventions for ABAP statements

8.4.2 Data Definition

From the previous information in this book, you know that two steps are required to use variable data:

▶ You first have to define (and type) the required data. If internal form variables are involved, you do this in the global definitions. The DATA statement is always used to define data in ABAP. In addition to assigning a name, it is used to type the data, with the additions mentioned in the previous chapters.

> **Note:** When you generate the function module for a form, the globally defined variables of the form are also translated into equivalent DATA statements.

▶ The actual processing of the data takes place in the functions that are defined in the other nodes of the form. In program nodes, these are the recorded ABAP statements.

This two-step process also applies in an ABAP program:

You define the data with ABAP keyword DATA and the additions TYPE or LIKE. You already learned about these additions when you defined the data in the form. As a result, the syntax of the examples in Table 8.2 should be familiar.

Syntax of data definition	Remarks
* Create field	
DATA fld1 TYPE tystr.	Reference to a data type
DATA fld2 TYPE tystr-fld.	Reference to a field in a structured data type
DATA fld3 TYPE dbtab-fld.	Reference to a field in a database table
DATA fld4 LIKE fld.	Reference to an existing variable
* Create field string	
DATA str1 TYPE tystr.	Reference to a structure in the Dictionary; this structure can consist of any other data types
DATA str2 TYPE dbtab.	Reference to a database table, although only one field string is created
DATA str3 LIKE LINE OF itab.	Reference to an internal table; enables "str3" to be used as a work area for this table
* Create internal table	
DATA itab1 TYPE tytab.	Reference to a table type in the Dictionary or created with TYPES

Table 8.2 Syntax for data definition

Syntax of data definition	Remarks
`DATA itab1` `    TYPE TABLE OF tystr.`	Reference to a structure in the Dictionary; also equivalent to the following statement
`DATA itab2 TYPE tystr` `    OCCURS 10.`	Reference to a structure; the addition OCCURS ensures that an internal table is created
* Statement chain	

`DATA: fld1 TYPE tystr1,`
`      fld2 TYPE tystr2,`
`      fld3 TYPE tystr-fld.`
	A statement chain links statements that have an identical beginning. The keyword is listed only once, followed by a colon; the remainder of each single statement is concluded by a comma. The last statement ends with a period.

Table 8.2 Syntax for data definition (continued)

You can use a *statement chain* to combine multiple statements that have an identical beginning. This can save time and improve clarity. Because this type of input is especially common in data definitions, a corresponding example is shown in Table 8.2.

8.4.3 Value Assignments

When a variable is defined, it is blank—or, more precisely, *initial*, unless default values are included in the definition. Consequently, one of the main tasks involved in writing programs is assigning values to the defined data. You will now learn about the syntax of basic value assignments:

Syntax of assignment	Remarks
* Delete contents	

`CLEAR fld .`
`CLEAR str .`
`CLEAR itab .`
	Reset to initial values—that is, the default values immediately after definition. If structured variables are involved, each component is deleted individually.

* Assign field contents	
`MOVE fld1 TO fld2 .`	Copy the contents of fld1 to fld2; a direct assignment using the equals sign is preferred to this outdated ABAP statement (see next statement).
`fld2 = fld1 .`	Copy contents, possibly with format adjustment.
`fld3(2) = 'xy' .`	Set the first two letters of a text variable.
`fld4 = LEFT(fld3) .`	Determine the contents using a character operation.

Table 8.3 Data assignment

`fld5 = 11 .`	Directly set the contents of numeric field fld5, with or without single quotes.
`fld6 = fld5 + 1.`	Calculate contents with an arithmetic operation.
* Fill field string	
`str2 = str1 .`	Copy a complete field string; the strings must have an identical field structure.
`MOVE-CORRESPONDING` `   str1 TO str2 .`	Copy only identically-named fields.
`str-fld = var .`	Copy a single field in the field string (data component) from another variable, possibly with format adjustment.

`READ TABLE itab`
`   WITH KEY fld1 = 'xyz'`
`            fld2 = var`
`   INTO str .`
	Read a row of an internal table, with field specifications as selection criteria.

`LOOP AT itab INTO str.`
`   WHERE fld1 = 'xyz'`
`   AND    fld2 = var .`
`      "Statement block`
`ENDLOOP .`
	Loop of an internal table, itab: each line is copied to a work area (identical field structure). A loop always ends with ENDLOOP; any other ABAP statements can be used within the loop.

* Fill internal tables	
`itab1[] = itab2[] .`	Copy the contents of tables with identical field structure; the square brackets are required as special indicators.
`APPEND str TO itab .`	Append a line to an internal table (identical field structure required).

Table 8.3 Data assignment (continued)

8.4.4 Querying Database Tables

The data assignments above assume that the required contents either have fixed definitions or can be derived from other data. This is often not the case, however. Instead, the data has to be read from the database tables of the SAP database system. These database table queries are usually implemented as SQL queries.

> **Background:** To use database content in a form, it first has to be read from the database tables and stored in the working memory. This interim storage involves the variables used in the form, for example, which can then be addressed through their field names in a text node or as an attribute of other nodes.

An autonomous database server is responsible for managing the database tables in the SAP system. This server must support the database language *SQL* (*Standard Query Language*), the current standard for high-performance databases. These language elements inform the database server when contents of database tables have to be read, changed, or created. For this reason, many SQL statements have been integrated in the ABAP programming language; SAP has even adapted several aspects of the SQL conventions to meet the specific system requirements (*Open SQL*).

Because forms will generally output data, but not actively change contents of database tables, the information below is also limited to reading database tables. In the SQL database language, the SELECT statement is used to implement such read operations. This statement also requires three basic specifications, in addition to the keyword itself:

▶ The source—the database table from which you want to read the data (FROM)

▶ The destination—variables that have been defined locally in a program node or in the global definitions (INTO)

▶ The conditions under which the data records will be read (WHERE)

Common examples:

Syntax	Remarks

SELECT *
  FROM dbtab
  INTO TABLE itab
  WHERE fld1 = 'xyz'
  AND   fld2 = var .
	Copy multiple records simultaneously from a database table to an internal table; the source and destination must have an identical line structure.
	
	The fields in the WHERE condition must already exist in the database table.
	
	You can also add WHERE conditions to any other database query below.

SELECT SINGLE *
  FROM dbtab
  INTO str
  WHERE ... .
	Copy a single data record from a database table to a field string (identical field structure required); used primarily with a unique key in the WHERE condition.

SELECT SINGLE fld
  FROM dbtab
  INTO var
  WHERE ... .
	Read a single field from the database and copy it to an existing variable.

Table 8.4 Querying database tables

Syntax	Remarks

`SELECT SINGLE fld1`
`fld2`
`  FROM dbtab`
`  INTO (fld1, fld2)`
`  WHERE ...   .`
	Read several fields simultaneously and copy into existing internal fields.

`SELECT SINGLE *`
`  FROM dbtab`
`  INTO CORRESPONDING`
`      FIELDS OF str`
`  WHERE ...   .`
	Read the contents of a database record and copy them to the identically-named fields of a field string.

`SELECT *`
`  FROM dbtab`
`  INTO str`
`  WHERE ...   .`
`  "Statement block`
`ENDSELECT .`
	Read database tables by line and copy contents to a field string as work area (identical field structure required). This SELECT variant works like a loop, which is why you always have to end it with an ENDSELECT statement. You can use any other ABAP statements between SELECT and ENDSELECT—to process contents from the work area, for example.

Table 8.4 Querying database tables (continued)

8.4.5 Loops

Loops enable the repeated processing of statements. They consist of at least two individual ABAP statements: one each at the beginning (LOOP) and end (END-LOOP) of the program block to be repeated.

You already learned about one variant of loops in the section on loop nodes. This node type is translated into a LOOP/ENDLOOP statement block in the generated function module of the form (also see Listing 7.1).

Syntax	Remarks

`LOOP AT itab INTO wa.`
`  "Statement block`
`ENDLOOP .`
	The LOOP statement passes over an internal table and copies the current data record to a work area each time. Any other ABAP coding can appear within the loop. A loop node in Smart Forms is translated into a LOOP statement.

`WHILE log_expression`
`  "Statement block`
`ENDWHILE`
	Conditional loop: The statement block is processed as long as the queried logical expression is fulfilled.

Table 8.5 Control structures

Syntax	Remarks

`DO [n TIMES] .`
    `"Statement block 1`
    `EXIT.`
    `"Statement block 2`
`ENDDO .`
	Unconditional loop: In this case, the statement block is processed until the loop is exited with an EXIT statement. You can use the addition with TIMES to restrict the number of passes in advance.

Table 8.5 Control structures (continued)

As you already read above, a LOOP statement in the program node implements the same functionality as a loop node in the form. There is an important difference, however: in the former case, additional ABAP statements appear between LOOP and ENDLOOP; in the latter case, these are the inferior nodes of the loop node.

8.4.6 Control Structures (Using Conditions)

You already learned in Section 7.3 about alternative nodes and the attributes in the **Conditions** tab page as important form logic functions in Smart Forms.

These functions are also available in ABAP program development; after all, a program flow has to be able to follow the conditions that apply at runtime.

Syntax	Remarks

`IF var = 'xyz' .`
    `"Statement block`
`ENDIF .`
	This statement block is executed only if the condition in the first line is fulfilled. You can define a condition for each node in a form design, which represents the equivalent of this statement.

`IF    fld1 = 'X'`
    `AND fld2 = 'xyz' .`
    `"Statement block`
`ENDIF .`
	As in a node, an IF query can contain several conditions, even additional arithmetic operations, in Smart Forms.

`IF var = 'xyz' .`
    `"Statement block 1`
`ELSEIF.`
    `"Statement block 2`
`ELSE .`
    `"Statement block 3`
`ENDIF .`
	If the query is true, the first statement block is executed; if not, the second block is executed. This query corresponds exactly to alternative nodes in Smart Forms. You can optionally use ELSEIF to query further alternatives.

Table 8.6 Control structures (Querying conditions)

Syntax	Remarks
| ```
CASE var1.
  WHEN var2.
    "Statement block 1
  WHEN 'xyz'.
    "Statement block 2
  WHEN OTHERS.
    "Statement block 3
ENDCASE
``` | Variable var1 is compared to other variables. The statement block is executed when the compared contents agree.<br><br>If the compared statements do not agree, the statement block under OTHERS is executed. |

Table 8.6 Control structures (Querying conditions) (continued)

Logical queries form the foundation of the control structures. They are frequently based on fields whose contents can represent only two states, *true* and *false*. In ABAP, these fields are typed as text with a length of one character; the content is typically "X" (true) or blank (" ", false). Several standard data types, such as BOOLKZ, have been defined for this in the ABAP Dictionary.

8.4.7 Subroutines

You can use subroutines (FORM routines) to modularize the source text of a program. This both improves clarity and enables you to reuse statement blocks in different places. You can call subroutines from within any program node in Smart Forms.

> **Note:** Function modules offer even greater encapsulation of program coding, (such as the generated function module for the form). Please note, however, that function modules are not defined within an ABAP program, nor within a form. You use the Function Builder to develop them. However, you can also call the function modules that are available in the system. Use the **pattern function** in the program node to ensure that the syntax is correct.

Every call of a FORM routine is normally associated with the transfer of parameters that are defined in the subroutine. This definition also includes the type. In contrast to function modules, the name of the parameter is not relevant here. As a result, the calling program must pass on the required parameters in the exact sequence and with the identical type defined in the subroutine.

You can use the **Form Routines** tab page in the global definitions to define the valid subroutines for a form. In addition, a program node can call subroutines that are contained in other programs in the SAP system, such as standardized data retrieval routines.
```

Syntax	Remarks
* Set up subroutine	
```FORM data_check USING var1 TYPE ty_fld var2 TYPE ty_tab CHANGING ret_code TYPE I. "Statement block * ret_code = 1. ENDFORM .```	In this case, two internal tables are passed on to the subroutine as parameters. The calling program must supply these tables in the same sequence and with the same type. The only return parameter from the subroutine is the error code, ret_code.
* Call subroutine	
```Data ret_code TYPE i. PERFORM data_check USING var1 var2 CHANGING ret_code. IF ret_code <> 0. * Error handling ENDIF .```	Calls the subroutine mentioned above, provided it has been defined as a form routine in the form. Includes definition of the return parameter as a local variable and a check of the return value after execution of the subroutine.
```Data ret_code TYPE i. PERFORM data_check IN PROGRAM zwhtest USING var1 var2 CHANGING ret_code. IF ret_code <> 0.```	The same call as above, with the exception that the subroutine exists in a program/report outside of the form ("zwhtest" in this case).

Table 8.7 Logical queries

8.4.8 Test Function

You use the *debugger* in the ABAP development environment to execute a program in individual steps. You can also set a breakpoint to call the debugger in a program node; in this case, however, you always have to create an additional statement in the source text to set the breakpoint, which means you have to have change authorization for the form. An alternative method, using jump points in the Function Builder, is described in Section 13.7.4, along with instructions for using the debugger.

Syntax	Remarks
`BREAK-POINT.`	Sets a breakpoint in the current line.

Table 8.8 Test function for setting a breakpoint

8.5 Example: Including an Address with a Function Module

8.5.1 Overview

Using an address node to include an address in the form (see Section 5.2.1) will meet your requirements in most cases. In rare cases—if you want to use special options, for example—it may make sense to access the underlying function module, ADDRESS_INTO_PRINTFORM, directly. Like the address node in Smart Forms, the most important input parameter for the module is the specification of the address to be used. Two different procedures are available:

► In most cases, you will specify an address number to include the address. In this approach, the module reads the corresponding address information from CAM, generates a correctly formatted postal address, and returns it as the result.

► Alternatively, you can pass on all the components of an address to the function module individually. The function module reads this information and generates and returns the correct postal formatting.

You will have to use the latter procedure, for example, when the address data for the corresponding object is not available in CAM yet. In this case, the address components have to be read from an individual database table and passed on to the function module through a standard field string, in order to format it there. Once again, this is illustrated with the sample flight invoice. Both procedures are described below.

Return Parameters

In both methods, the values are returned as a field string with ten fields, each of which contains one line of the formatted address. You only have to output the corresponding field names in a text node.

The function module also provides one-line and two-line fields for brief descriptions of the address components, which you can include as alternative or additional information in a field. Therefore, the following steps are involved in outputting an address:

► Definition of variables to store the address number or individual address data

► Definition of a field string with line information of a formatted address (as return parameters)

► Determination of the address number or the individual information for the address

▶ Call of ABAP function module ADDRESS_INFO_PRINTFORM to convert the address information into the correct postal output format (with the address number or the information for the address as input parameters)

▶ Output of the formatted address fields in a text node

Form Modifications

Figure 8.4 shows the type definitions that you need for the following example. They will be described in more detail further below.

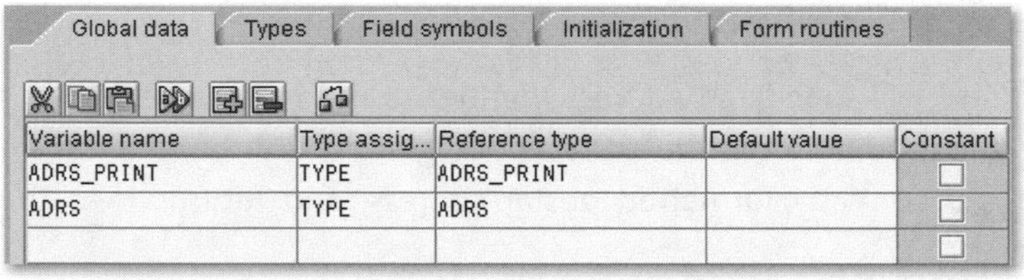

Global data	Types	Field symbols	Initialization	Form routines		

Variable name	Type assig...	Reference type	Default value	Constant
ADRS_PRINT	TYPE	ADRS_PRINT		☐
ADRS	TYPE	ADRS		☐
				☐

Figure 8.4 Data for the example address (Global definitions)

The function module is called in a program node. The easiest way to do this is to use the **statement pattern** function, which you can call from the toolbar in the program node. The **Function Module** option is already selected in the subsequent selection screen. You only have to enter the name, ADDRESS_INFO_PRINTFORM. The call of the function module is then automatically included in the source text, along with all the relevant transfer parameters.

8.5.2 Using an Address Number from CAM

Listing 8.1 shows the call of a function module when the address is passed on as an address number. Most of the transfer parameters are not required in this case, and have been deleted from the source text as a result.

```
*&---------------------------------------------------------------&*
* Address number exists
* all variables declared in main definitions
CALL FUNCTION 'ADDRESS_INTO_PRINTFORM'
  EXPORTING ADDRESS_TYPE        = '1'
            ADDRESS_NUMBER      = GS_HD_ADR-ADDR_NO
            NUMBER_OF_LINES     = 5
  IMPORTING ADDRESS_PRINTFORM   = ADRS_PRINT
*           ADDRESS_SHORT_FORM =
*           ADDRESS_DATA_CARRIER =
```

```
*              ADDRESS_DATA_CARRIER_0 =
*              NUMBER_OF_USED_LINES =
*&--------------------------------------------------------------&*
```
Listing 8.1 Including address formatting from CAM

This call corresponds to the specifications that you selected for the address node in Section 5.2.1 (see Figure 5.9). The following input parameters are set:

▶ ADDRESS_TYPE is set to 1 (= organization address).

▶ The address number in ADDRESS_NUMBER is derived from the same variable you used in the example for the address node.

▶ The NUMBER_OF_LINES parameter restricts the maximum number of lines in the formatted address to 5.

Return Parameters

The field string, ADRS_PRINT, receives the formatted postal address as ten fields (field names LINE0 to LINE9) for the return parameters. This field string was typed in the global definitions with reference to the identically named table in the Dictionary (see Figure 8.4). Remember, you can double-click on a data type in the global data to display the contained fields.

In the above example, three additional return values are included as comment lines for your information:

▶ If necessary, ADDRESS_SHORT_FORM contains the address summarized in a single line, consisting of name and city.

▶ The two variables for "…CARRIER" return a two-line entry for the address that is generally used in bank transfer forms (for DME—data medium exchange— for example).

▶ The last parameter returns the number of lines that were actually required to format the full address. You can use this value to trigger or prevent the output of additional blank lines after the address as necessary, for example.

Thus far, you have determined the address and formatted it properly. All that is missing now is the last step, the output. To output the address, the fields of the return parameters are inserted successively into a text node, as shown in Figure 8.5. The sender information is output in the first line, in small type, followed by the lines with the recipient address. Because the maximum number of lines is set to five in the above example, only five lines are output.

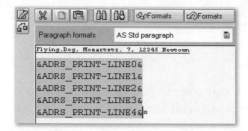

Figure 8.5 Outputting an address in a text node

8.5.3 Integration with Direct Transfer of Address Information

In this case, the contents of the address (name, city, and so on) are known, but not the address number in CAM. Listing 8.2 shows the corresponding function module call.

This is the case in the flight data model, for example: the customer addresses are saved in database table SCUSTOM here. In this case, the calling main program supplies the current address, with all the fields, in a field string (WA_CUSTOMERS), in order to print the invoice. (You already learned how data is read from the database in Section 9.3.1.)

The relevant fields from WA_CUSTOMERS can be passed on to the function module, which provides for the correct postal formatting. To keep things simple, only the most important interface parameters are shown below:

```
*&--------------------------------------------------------------&*
* Address without existing number
ADRS-ANRED = WA_CUSTOMERS-FORM.
ADRS-NAME2 = WA_CUSTOMERS-NAME.
ADRS-STRAS = WA_CUSTOMERS-STREET.
ADRS-PSTLZ = WA_CUSTOMERS-POSTCODE.
ADRS ORT01 = WA_CUSTOMERS-CITY.
ADRS-ILAND = WA_CUSTOMERS-COUNTRY.
CALL FUNCTION 'ADDRESS_INTO_PRINTFORM'
  EXPORTING ADRSWA_IN          = ADRS
*              ADDRESS_1         =
*              ADDRESS_2         =
*              ADDRESS_3         =
*              ADDRESS_TYPE      = ' '
*              NUMBER_OF_LINES   = 5
  IMPORTING ADRSWA_OUT         = ADRS
```

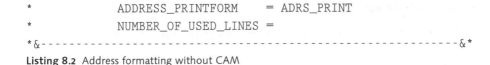

```
*                    ADDRESS_PRINTFORM     = ADRS_PRINT
*                    NUMBER_OF_USED_LINES =
* &- - - - - - - - - - - - - - - - - - - - - - - - - - - - - - - - - - - - - - - - - - - - - - - - - - - - - - - -& *
```

Listing 8.2 Address formatting without CAM

To prepare, you create a field string, ADRS, in the global definitions and type it with reference to the identically named structure in the Dictionary (Figure 8.4). This field string contains all the common fields of an address, which the function module uses to format the address.

The program node then fills the fields of ADRS with the appropriate contents of the work area from the flight data model, WA_CUSTOMERS. The result is passed on as input parameters for the function module; the parameter name is ADRSWA_IN.

Return Parameters

Field string ADRS has another special feature: it contains ten additional fields (LINE0 through LINE9), which the function module can use to return the formatted address directly. Accordingly, you can also use ADRS as return parameters. Alternatively, you can use ADRS_PRINT, as in the first example. Because a field string like ADRS requires only a single definition operation, however, this is the faster method.

Individual parameters of the function module are included above as comment lines for your information:

▶ The field strings with the internal identifiers ADDRESS_1 through ...3 reflect the case in which the specified address exists in a record structure that corresponds exactly to the individual address types (1 through 3). You can then use one of these field strings as the input parameters. Please note, however, that you also have to set the appropriate address type in ADDRESS_TYPE in this case.

▶ Once again, you can use NUMBER_OF_LINES to restrict the formatting to a certain number of lines (such as 5).

The address is outputted just like in the previous example, with the exception that you now have to enter ADRS in the text node, instead of ADRS_PRINT and its field names.

8.5.4 Sample Exercise

You can apply the case described above directly to the flight invoice. To do so, use the following procedure:

▶ First define the required variables in the global data (see Figure 8.4).

▶ Create a program node in the ADDRESS window that calls the function module for address formatting, using the assignments shown in Listing 8.2.

Then replace the existing fields for WA_CUSTOMERS with the entries in ADRS for the output in text node ADDRESS.

8.6 Example: Calculating Totals in the Flight Invoice

You will now learn how to use a program node to calculate the total price of all the items in the flight invoice. This involves the following steps:

▶ Define the global data required for the calculation.

▶ Create the program node to add the prices in all the bookings.

▶ Create the event nodes to output the totals.

> **Note:** The totals calculation involves a special case that you have not dealt with yet: the flight data module supports the entry of flight bookings in different currencies. Strictly speaking, the invoice total therefore involves a list of several total values with one entry for each currency, which calculates the totals calculation and output.

Defining the Data

First open the **Global Data** tab page of the flight invoice in the global definitions, as shown in Figure 8.6.

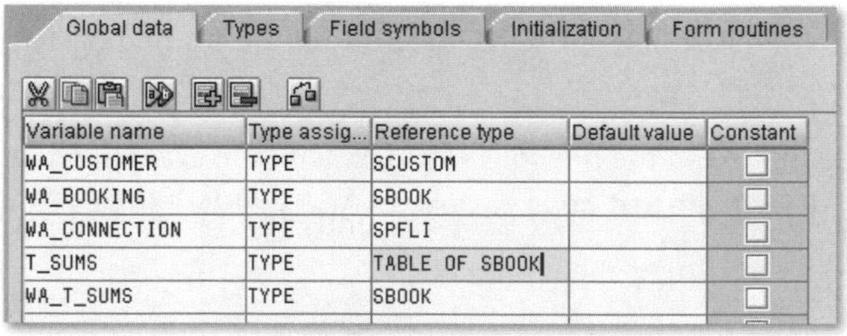

Variable name	Type assig...	Reference type	Default value	Constant
WA_CUSTOMER	TYPE	SCUSTOM		☐
WA_BOOKING	TYPE	SBOOK		☐
WA_CONNECTION	TYPE	SPFLI		☐
T_SUMS	TYPE	TABLE OF SBOOK		☐
WA_T_SUMS	TYPE	SBOOK		☐

Global data Types Field symbols Initialization Form routines

Figure 8.6 Global data in the flight invoice

You will want to store the list of totals values for each currency in internal table T_SUMS. As a result, it has been typed based on database table SBOOK, which is usually used for the single bookings. Only the fields for currency and currency amount are used to calculate the totals. The work area used to output the totals values is WA_T_SUMS.

Calculating Totals

Each new item in the flight invoice will change the corresponding total for the flight prices. Therefore, the calculation in the main window has to take place in the same loop that is used to output the items. Choose program node SUMS in the navigation tree; its contents are similar to the illustration in Figure 8.7.

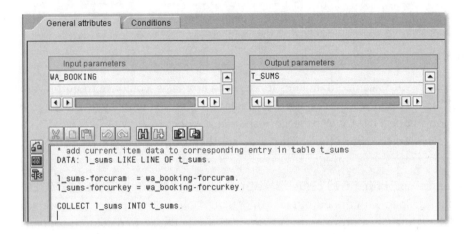

Figure 8.7 Calculating totals in a program node

A local field string, L_SUMS, is first defined to calculate the totals. The currency and currency amount from the current flight booking are saved here. This entry must then be added to the totals value in T_SUMS that has the same currency as L_SUMS. Therefore, programming the single steps means:

▶ Checking whether the current currency is already listed in T_SUMS

  ▶ If the currency is already listed, increase the total value by the current flight price.

  ▶ If the currency is not already listed, create a new entry for this currency and copy the price from the current flight booking.

The COLLECT statement performs this function (press **F1** to display detailed documentation for the syntax). Once all the items are passed, internal table T_SUMS contains one totals line for each different currency in the flight invoice.

Configuring the Output

Now you only need to output the results. To do so, open the footer for the main loop in the MAIN window.

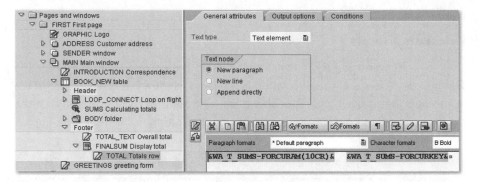

Figure 8.8 Outputting totals

Because T_SUMS can contain lines for several currencies, you have to output the results in a loop in which each individual line is copied sequentially to a work area (see loop node FINALSUM; the corresponding work area is WA_T_SUMS). The two relevant fields from the output area are then output in a conventional text node, TOTAL.

The entire output has two columns, with reference to line type TABLE_FOOTER, which is defined with the output length of BOOK_NEW. The first column receives the label "Total Sum" from node TOTAL_TEXT, while the second column contains the individual total amounts and the corresponding currencies.

> **Tip:** Pay special attention to how this two-column output is executed. It is an excellent example of how to combine the results of a loop in a single cell.
>
> The specific problem here is that the label "Total Sum" is only supposed to be output only once in the first column, whereas the second column can contain multiple entries. This constellation does not really correspond to the line-based structure of the output table.
>
> To enable this output format anyway, the full contents of loop node FINAL-SUM are transferred to the second column of the output table as a superior value (see the assignment in the *Output Options* tab page of the loop node). The actual text line, TOTAL, does not have a separate assignment to the output table, and only writes only to the second column. Because each new data record starts a new paragraph, each currency line is separated by a line break, but they are all contained in the same cell.

8.6.1 Sample Exercise: Output in the Local Currency

Now that you have learned the basics of calculating totals, you can improve your form by adding additional information in the local currency. Calculating the total for the local currency is easier than solving for multiple currencies, and is also more like typical business requirements.

Please note that this change is only a suggestion. To implement it, you can use several of the functions that have already been introduced in the previous chapters. Two alternative implementations are possible:

▶ In the first approach, you add an additional column to the existing item overview, and output each price twice—once in the original currency and once in the local currency.

▶ In the second approach, you can optionally replace the existing currency information with the local currency. In this case, the currency you want to display must be known as an additional criterion in the form, and the parameter with this value must be supplied logically by the form interface.

Approach 1

The first approach involves the following steps:

▶ Make minor changes to the column definitions of the existing items, in order to provide sufficient space for an additional column with the local currency. Add the additional column to the output table for all line types.

▶ You can output the local currency through a new text node and field &WA_ BOOKING-LOCCURAM&. Because the currency is the same for every item, you can omit its output.

▶ Define another global variable to calculate the total. Because the total has a value for only a single currency, you do not need an internal table to store the totals values. Defining a field string (typed with SBOOK, for example) is enough in this case.

▶ Calculate the total in the local currency for all items. Use the existing program node, SUMS, to do so. Because this calculation is much simpler, calculating the total now involves only adding the individual prices, which no longer requires the COLLECT statement.

▶ Create a new text node in the footer of the loop to output the calculated total in the local currency. Make sure the cell in the output table is assigned properly.

- Insert a reference to the local currency in an appropriate position.

  - If you add the reference to the INFO window, for example, you can read the currency code directly from work area WA_BOOKING. In this case, however, you have to output the INFO window immediately after MAIN, as was the case in the original form.

  - If you want to output the currency in the column header for the output table, you have to determine the currency code first. For example, you can read the contents of field LOCCURRKEY for the first data record in BOOK-INGS in an additional loop node. Yyou learned about this procedure in Section 7.2.4.

The sample printout of the flight invoice in the Appendix also contains an extra column to display the local currency.

Approach 2

The second approach involves the following steps:

- In the main program, extend the call of the function module for the form with a parameter that specifies the category of the currency. For example, set to "X" if the local currency is to be used. This step enables you to continue using the existing form.

- Add a suitable query for the currency category in the selection screen of the main program, and pass its contents on in the form interface parameters.

- Define the new parameter in the form interface (in the form page).

- Create a second text node for the "Price" column in the form, in order to output the item prices in the local currency. After this node (or in the existing node), define a condition that queries the parameter you defined above. You can also use an alternative node here.

- Implement the totals calculation in the local currency as described in the first solution approach.

Output the total dependent on the interface parameters as well. In this case, you can completely replace the previous output, which used the loop in node FINAL-SUM, since you now have only one value.

9 Main Program

9.1 Overview

To output the form, you need an application program (*main program*) that primarily performs two tasks (see Figure 9.1):

▶ Retrieve the data for the form

▶ Trigger and control output through function module for the form

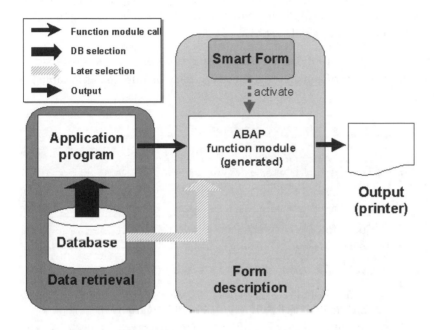

Figure 9.1 Main program and form

The main program can be a conventional ABAP report, but it can also be a function module, depending on the specific case involved. All the general rules for program development apply. Accordingly, this chapter deals only with the specific aspects of form processing. This involves three components:

▶ Reading the required data (from the database, for example) and supplying it in the same structures that are defined in the form

▶ Determining the name assigned to the generated function module for the form

▶ Calling this function module as the trigger for form output

Of course, the main program also has to know the attributes for which the form will be output, such as the number of an invoice or other document. The main program also has to be told which form to use for output.

The main program normally starts with the setting of these parameters. Two basic procedures are available for determining them:

▶ The user is prompted to enter the attributes of the data to be output in a dialog (the *selection screen*).

▶ An upstream application program supplies the main program with this data—during output through message control, for example.

Before thedata is actually retrieved from the database, the main program can check, if necessary, which data is required in the form. This function is used to output the delivery note, for example. In some situations, this check can significantly improve performance during data retrieval.

Function modules or subroutines are usually called to perform the single steps. Therefore, the structure of a main program can roughly be outlined as in Table 9.1 below:

Step	Meaning
A	* Question: Which form will be used and which * parameters for data selection will apply there? * Read from output control or individual selection screen.
B	* Optional: Which data does the form need? CALL FUNCTION 'SSF_FIELD_LIST'
C	* Read database tables to retrieve the data, * grouped together here in one subroutine. PERFORM GET_DATA
D	* Determine name of the function module for the form. CALL FUNCTION 'SSF_FUNCTION_MODULE_NAME'
E	* Execute function module for the form (output). CALL FUNCTION func_mod_name

Table 9.1 Components of a main program

In the sections below, you will read more about these individual components, using individual elements from the main program for the flight invoice as examples. A complete printout of the program coding is available in the Appendix. In some cases, you will also examine the main program for the delivery note because the flight invoice is not complex enough to describe all the relevant aspects.

9.2 Defining the Properties for Data Retrieval

As mentioned above, the main program first has to determine which data will be output (number of an invoice or delivery note, for example). Generally, two different procedures are available to set these parameters:

▶ The user is prompted to enter them in a selection screen.

▶ The information is passed on by an upstream application program.

This chapter will teach you the basic skills for both methods. Once again, the corresponding ABAP statements can be encapsulated in subroutines.

9.2.1 Flight Invoice: Selection Screen for Data Entry

When you output the flight invoice with program Z_SF_EXAMPLE_01, a selection screen like the one in Figure 9.2 always appears in the first step.

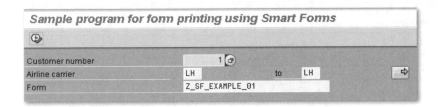

Figure 9.2 Main program with parameter prompt

This example program contains queries for:

▶ Customer number

▶ Airline (possibly a multiple selection)

▶ Form name

The selection screen has been kept simple, yet still provides several useful features. For example, a value help function has been defined for the customer selection, while multiple selection is possible for the airlines. The corresponding source text has been implemented with just a few ABAP statements.

```
*&- - - - - - - - - - - - - - - - - - - - - - - - - - - - - - - - - - - - - - - - - - - - - - - - - - - - -&*
DATA: carr_id TYPE sbook-carrid,
      fm_name TYPE rs38l_fnam.
* Start selection-screen
PARAMETER:      p_custid TYPE scustom-id DEFAULT 1.
SELECT-OPTIONS: s_carrid FOR carr_id    DEFAULT 'LH' TO 'LH'.
```

```
PARAMETER:        p_form    TYPE tdsfname DEFAULT 'Z_SF_EXAMPLE_01'.
* End selection screen
*&-------------------------------------------------------------&*
```
Listing 9.1 Selection screen for the flight invoice

You can use three basic ABAP settings for a selection screen:

▶ **SELECTION-SCREEN**
Enables the entry of general formatting information—for example, to display headings in a selection screen or separate with blank lines. It is not used in the above example, however.

▶ **PARAMETER**
Enables you to query parameters that can take only a single value.

▶ **SELECTION-OPTION**
Enables you to query parameters that can be restricted through "From/To" values or other user input, and can therefore accept multiple values for each parameter.

> **Note:** When the main program is initiated, the system searches the source text for all three of the above statements, which can appear anywhere in the program coding. For clarity's sake, however, we recommend grouping these statements together in a single block, enclosing them in comment lines (as in the above example) and placing the statements for the selection screen at the start of the program.

All these statements are grouped together for the selection screen in the order in which they appear and are automatically displayed on the screen when the report is called.

If you are an experienced ABAP user, the program coding will be self-explanatory. Novices can refer to the summary information for interpreting the individual statements below:

▶ The first PARAMETER statement queries the customer for whom the flight invoice will be generated. After the return from the selection screen, the user's entry appears in variable P_CUSTID. The field was initially set to the default value 1. Variable P_CUSTID is defined directly in the statement with the TYPE addition, which means it does not have to appear in any additional DATA statement.

▶ The second statement with SELECT-OPTIONS goes even further: it is used to select the airlines, and enables the user to perform tasks like specifying a range of values with *From/To* specifications. After the return from the selection screen, the user's entries appear in internal table S_CARRID.

One property of the SELECT-OPTIONS statement is that naming its assigned parameter simultaneously declares that parameter as an internal table. The statement always contains four fields, including LOW and HIGH fields for saving a single "From/To" combination. Because an airline code will appear in both fields, they have to be set to an appropriate data type. You achieve this using the addition FOR, which copies the required data type from variable CARR_ID (which generally corresponds to typing with LIKE in a DATA statement). CARR_ID, in turn, was previously defined in a DATA statement, in accordance with the ID field of the database table.

If the user enters only one *From* and one *To* value, the corresponding internal table has only one data line. Multiple lines are created only when the user has activated the optional multiple selection with the corresponding pushbutton on the screen. In this case, each value specified by the user is saved in a separate data line. The differentiation of the user entries by single values and intervals, as well as inclusion and exclusion, is determined for each data line through additional control parameters in the OPTION and SIGN fields of the internal table. The user's entries in this selection screen become the input parameters for selection from the corresponding database tables later on.

Because the form will be selectable in this case, the name of the form is queried in the last PARAMETER statement. Variable P_FORM is set to a default value with the DEFAULT addition, but can be changed by the user. The type of the variable is determined based on the fact that names of forms can be up to 30 characters long in Smart Forms. Data type TSDFNAME has been defined for this in the Dictionary.

9.2.2 Processing with Output Control

During processing with output control in the SAP system, a user dialog like the one described above cannot take place, due to automatic processes during output. Instead, the required information is always taken from the corresponding management tables for output control.

Brief Overview

The functions of output control are described here only to the extent that they are relevant for creating the main program. Refer to Section 13.5 for detailed information.

All the outputs defined for a document are saved in a centralized database table in the SAP system, NAST:

▶ Every output is identified through client number, application code, and document number in table NAST.

▶ Table NAST contains all the information required for a single output, including language, output object with document number, partner information (addressee), output device, and so on.

Each time you assign a new output to a document, a new entry is created in table NAST. This can happen in several different ways, depending on which application is involved. For example, most logistics applications use the condition technique for output control, which is described in detail further below (output determination).

Most of the information in table NAST has its origin in the respective document or in the condition records of output determination. When an NAST entry is generated, the responsible output type is also saved in table NAST. This value is then used to determine the assigned main program in Customizing, as well as the form, which is saved in database table TNAPR.

> **Note:** The delivery note is used below to illustrate the process flows in output control, since integrating the flight invoice would require an unreasonably large effort.

Process Flow in the Main Program

In the output control framework, the main program is not called directly by the user, but instead by a higher-level application program.

The main program is responsible for the following:

▶ **Start of processing:** Accept all the relevant processing information from output control; determine the form name from the output type.

▶ **End of processing:** Return status information to the calling application program; supplement the error-handling program if necessary.

A static interface to the higher-level application program is normally used to resolve these activities. It contains both global data definitions and transfer parameters for a subroutine call. The most important components are:

NAST	The work area for this database table is set to the contents of the current output by default.
TNAPR	Database table TNAPR contains all the information that is defined as the processing routines for the output type (such as the form name) in Customizing. The current output type is the default setting for the work area.
US_SCREEN	Transfer variable as logical value; if it is set ("X"), output the form in the print preview.
RETURN_CODE	Return value that documents the result of the output (numeric like SY-SUBRC; the initial value is "999"). The calling application program records the success of the output in NAST based on this value. Any return value other than "0" indicates an error during output.

The last two variables are passed on as parameters through a defined program interface. To do so, the higher-level application program calls a FORM routine directly in the main program of the form, which is given the two variables as parameters. The name of this FORM routine, usually ENTRY, must be defined in output determination, together with the name of the main program (in table TNAPR).

Call by the Application Program

The call by the higher-level application program then has syntax like that of the following example:

```
*&-------------------------------------------------------------&*
* Call main program in higher-level application program
Form_name = TNAPR-RONAM.    "FORM subroutine is usually 'ENTRY'
Prog_name = TNAPR-PGNAM.
PERFORM Form_name IN PROGRAM Prog_name
        USING RETURN_CODE
        US_SCREEN.
*&-------------------------------------------------------------&*
```
Listing 9.2 Call of form routine through output control

The name of the main program is read, together with initiating FORM routine, from Customizing table TNAPR.

Structure of the FORM Routine

Because the corresponding FORM routine is usually called ENTRY, the main program itself has the following structure at the top level:

```
*&--------------------------------------------------------------&*
REPORT RLE_DELNOTE.
* declaration of data
INCLUDE RLE_DELNOTE_DATA_DECLARE.
FORM ENTRY
     USING RETURN_CODE US_SCREEN.
     DATA:   LF_RETCODE TYPE SY-SUBRC.
     PERFORM PROCESSING USING US_SCREEN CHANGING LF_RETCODE.
     IF LF_RETCODE NE 0.
        RETURN_CODE = 1.
     ELSE.
        RETURN_CODE = 0.
     ENDIF.
ENDFORM.
*&--------------------------------------------------------------&*
```

Listing 9.3 Form routine called during output control

The actual top-level program coding consists only of the basic data definitions here, defined in an appropriate include. The FORM routine was created with the same parameters as those above. In the above example, however, further processing takes place in the PROCESSING subroutine, which is not listed above. The specification for the print preview is also passed on to the PROCESSING subroutine. Any confirmations from the PROCESSING subroutine are only differentiated between "1" and "0" (that is, error *Yes/No*) and passed on to the higher-level application program in RETURN_CODE.

Utilized Data Definitions

The current table entries (work areas) in NAST and TNAPR are provided by the higher-level application program; therefore, you only have to declare them as global data in the main program. A TABLES statement takes care of this. Because such declarations are needed in many programs, they have already been defined in a centralized location in the system: they are integrated in the main program as include RVADTABL (see the last program excerpt). Here is an excerpt from the include program:

```
*&-----------------------------------------------------------------&*
* Declaration of global data in include RVADTABL
TABLES:
  NAST,            "Message status
  *NAST,           "Message status (temporary table entry)
  TNAPR,           "Processing routine for output type
                   "with parameters like control prog., form
  ITCPO,           "Used as data type for the spool interface
  ARC_PARAMS,      "Transfer parameter for optical archiving
  TOA_DARA,        "Transfer parameter for optical archiving
  ADDR_
KEY.       "Address structure with address type, address no.
                   "i.e. for recipient information (no default)
TYPE-POOLS SZADR."Data types for central address management
*&-----------------------------------------------------------------&*
```

Listing 9.4 Data definition to output a delivery

The sample program also defines several parameters, such as the ones required to control form output through the spool.

> **Background:** When automatic output control is used, you may want to output the form without requiring user intervention (spool dialog). The corresponding parameters then have to be specified by the main program. These involve, for example, fields in the transfer parameters, OUTPUT_OPTIONS, and the CONTROL_PARAMETERS in the form interface, in addition to the parameters for controlling archiving. The corresponding single parameters can once again be taken from NAST.

The transfer of these parameters is described in more detail in Section 9.7, which also introduces the standard parameters for the form interface.

Form Name

The current work area for database table TNAPR supplies all the information that is listed for the output type under *Processing Routines*. Therefore, you can use statement LF_FORMNAME = TNAPR-SFORM to copy the name of the form to be executed into an internal variable. This internal variable is later used to determine the name of the function module to be called.

9.3 Data Retrieval

9.3.1 Flight Invoice: Reading the Database Tables

The flight invoice is an example of extremely simple data retrieval. Three database tables in internal tables are read in accordance with the user's entries and then passed on to the form interface. The internal tables are defined equivalent to the form. Excerpt:

```
*&-------------------------------------------------------------&*
DATA: customers   TYPE ty_customers,
      bookings    TYPE ty_bookings,
      connections TYPE ty_connections.
* Get Data
SELECT * FROM scustom INTO TABLE customers
        WHERE id = p_custid
        ORDER BY PRIMARY KEY.
SELECT * FROM sbook INTO TABLE bookings
        WHERE customid = p_custid
        AND    carrid   IN s_carrid
        ORDER BY PRIMARY KEY.
SELECT * FROM spfli INTO TABLE connections
        FOR ALL ENTRIES IN bookings
        WHERE carrid = bookings-carrid
        AND    connid = bookings-connid
        ORDER BY PRIMARY KEY.
*&-------------------------------------------------------------&*
```

Listing 9.5 Data retrieval for the flight invoice

The first SELECT statement copies the master record from the customer selected by the user to internal table CUSTOMERS.

> **Note:** A special feature of the sample form is that CUSTOMERS is defined as an internal table, even though it contains only a single data record. If you want, you can alter the main program in a later example to enable the selection of an invoice for several customers at the same time. The user query at the start of the program must then take place equivalent to the airline.

The second SELECT statement copies all the flight bookings for this customer to an internal table, BOOKINGS, but only the airlines that the user already selected are considered. The addition "AND carrid IN s_carrid" is designed specifically for the use of such internal tables, which can be filled with data by a multiple selection in a selection screen. The structure that you read about in Section 9.2.1, in the description of the selection screen, is required.

The third SELECT statement now fills internal table CONNECTIONS with a list of all the connections found for the bookings selected in the second SELECT statement. In this case, the addition "FOR ALL ENTRIES IN bookings" enables you to read all the data in one pass, since the invoice may be generated only for one connection. You can use the table to output attributes of the flight connections that are not saved in the individual bookings, such as the departure time, in the form.

These compact SELECT queries provide all the data that you need for the flight invoice. Of course, data retrieval is much more complex in most cases. For this reason, you will now read about the process flows involved in the delivery form.

9.3.2 Delivery Combining Data

Subroutine GET_DATA, which retrieves delivery data, is programmed to provide all the data that could possibly be needed for form output. The fact that data that is not actually needed in the form may be retrieved was already mentioned above. Excerpt from the data retrieval call:

```
*&      - - - - - - - - - - - - - - - - - - - - - - - - - - - - - - - - - - - - - - - - - - - - - - - - - - - - - - - -&*
* definition of data
DATA: LS_ADDR_KEY     LIKE ADDR_KEY.
DATA: LS_DLV_DELNOTE TYPE LEDLV_DELNOTE.
* select print data
PERFORM GET_DATA
        USING     LS_PRINT_DATA_TO_READ "list of required data
        CHANGING LS_ADDR_KEY            "address from NAST
                 LS_DLV_DELNOTE         "data for delivery note
                 CF_RETCODE.            "error messages
*&- - - - - - - - - - - - - - - - - - - - - - - - - - - - - - - - - - - - - - - - - - - - - - - - - - - - - - -&*
```

Listing 9.6 Data retrieval for delivery

Subroutine GET_DATA provides all this data in a single structured variable, LS_DLV_DELNOTE. It has a comprehensive collection of field strings and internal tables as its components. The structure of the component was already mentioned as an example in Section 6.4.1. Where the individual data is read is a complex issue that you will not consider at this point.

Subroutine GET_DATA also has an input parameter, field string LS_PRINT_DATA_TO_READ. It contains a list of all the components that are used in the current form (its creation will be described in more detail in Section 9.6). The corresponding contents are read from the database within GET_DATA only when a data component is flagged as required here. In the simplest case, an IF query is defined for every field in LS_PRINT_DATA_TO_READ. If the condition is not met, the corresponding database tables are not read, and the corresponding data component in LS_DLV_DELNOTE remains empty.

> **Note:** LS_DLV_DELNOTE is typed as in a form, using a data type in the ABAP Dictionary. Therefore, if you make changes to this component, you do not have to revise the main program immediately; you can do so later instead. The interface remains functional in either case.

9.4 Calling the Function Module for the Form

The name of a function module for a form is unique only within a single SAP system. Normally, the function module is first generated in the system where the form was developed. When you transport the form to another SAP system, a new function module with a different name is generated the first time the form is called.

> **Note:** You can display the current name of the function module in the Form Builder with menu path **Environment · Name of Function Module** or by calling the test function with **F8**.

Despite this situation, you still have to be able to output the form, regardless of which SAP installation is involved. The solution is to call the form and its function module in two steps:

▶ The first step uses the form name to determine the exact name of the generated function module.

▶ That function module is executed in the second step.

9.4.1 Determining the Name of the Function Module

An addition function module is defined in the system to determine the name of the generated function module: SSF_FUNCTION_MODULE_NAME. Yet another example from the flight invoice:

```
*&--------------------------------------------------------------&*
DATA: fm_name   TYPE rs381_fnam.
CALL  FUNCTION   'SSF_FUNCTION_MODULE_NAME'
       EXPORTING  formname            = p_form
       IMPORTING  fm_name             = fm_name
       EXCEPTIONS no_form             = 1
                  no_function_module  = 2
                  others              = 3.
*&--------------------------------------------------------------&*
```

Listing 9.7 Determining the name of the function module

The name of the form must be declared as an input parameter. In this example, the corresponding variable, P_FORM, was queried from the user in the selection screen upon the program start.

9.4.2 Calling the Function Module for the Form

After this call, the required name of the function module for the form is set in variable FM_NAME. This field is a text field with 30 characters, as the result of its typing with RS38L_FNAM. It is now used to trigger the actual form output:

```
*&--------------------------------------------------------------&*
* now call the generated function module
CALL FUNCTION fm_name
       EXPORTING  archive_index        =
*                 archive_parameters   =
*                 control_parameters   =
*                 mail_appl_obj        =
*                 mail_recipient       =
*                 mail_sender          =
*                 output_options       =
*                 user_settings        = 'X'
                  customers            = customers
                  bookings             = bookings
                  connections          = connections
*      IMPORTING  document_output_info =
*                 job_output_info      =
*                 job_output_options   =
       EXCEPTIONS formatting_error     = 1
                  internal_error       = 2
                  send_error           = 3
```

```
         user_canceled          = 4
         OTHERS                  = 5.
*&- - - - - - - - - - - - - - - - - - - - - - - - - - - - - - - - - - - - - - - - - - - - - - - - - - - -&*
```

Listing 9.8 Calling the function module for the form

You should immediately recognize all the parameters, which you already saw in the form interface of the Form Builder. Because the standard parameters that are generated automatically when you create a new form are optional, you can also flag them as comment lines. In this case, these output parameters are not controlled by the main program. The internal default values of the function module are used instead.

In this example, the decisive parameters for passing the data on to the form are internal tables CUSTOMERS, BOOKINGS, and CONNECTIONS. The same names are used in both the form and the main program for the flight invoice.

When you call the function module, you can also supply parameters that are not defined in the form itself, which means the list in the form does not have to be complete. This feature is especially useful when a main program uses different several forms, but the forms do not all need the same data.

Calling the Function Module with the Pattern Function

Of course, entering the call of the function module by hand is somewhat labor-intensive, especially when many parameters have been defined. The ABAP editor offers a helpful tool here, which you already know from the program node. Press the **Pattern** button in the toolbar to insert the pattern of a function call automatically. You only have to know the name of the function module. But there's the hitch: in this case, the name not only depends on the form, but has also been assigned completely randomly.

But there is an elegant solution to the problem, because you can determine the name required for the function module directly and manually in form processing. This involves the following steps:

▶ Call the Form Builder for the involved form.
▶ Press **F8** to call the test function; the name of the function module appears.
▶ Copy the name to the clipboard (**Ctrl + C**).
▶ Call the program editor (SE38) with the main program.
▶ Use the **Pattern** function to insert the pattern.
▶ Choose option CALL FUNCTION with the existing clipboard contents as the function name.

The appropriate function call, with all interface parameters, is automatically added to the source text. All the names used in the form appear to the left of equals signs; therefore, you now only have to add the corresponding parameters that are valid in the main program on the right-hand side.

The standard interface parameters in the system (see Section 9.7) are always optional, and are therefore initially flagged as comment lines. Individual parameters in the form are always required; the main program has to supply the corresponding data.

Assigning the Correct Name of the Function Module

With the approach you have used so far, you are still dependent on the specific SAP system. Due to the name assignment, the main program will work only in this system. Because you want to avoid this situation, you now have to replace the name of the function module in the source text with the corresponding variable (FM_NAME in this case) in the last step.

9.5 Sample Exercise: Flight Invoices for Multiple Customers

In the previous sections, you learned about several basic elements that are used in almost every main program that outputs forms.

To round out this subject, you will now make several enhancements to the existing main program for the flight invoice. These enhancements also create the foundation for testing several of the form interface parameters in the next chapter.

Thus far, the main program can output only a single flight invoice. You will change that now by implementing the customer query as a multiple selection in the selection screen, as is already the case with the airlines.

Conversion

Thus far, the individual customer has been passed on to the function module of the form in interface parameter CUSTOMERS. Because this parameter is an internal table, you can also use it to pass on several addresses.

A major disadvantage here is that you cannot create a loop in the form that processes all the customers in sequence and starts a new first page for each customer.

To output individual invoices for several customers in sequence, the required loop has to be performed in the main program itself. In the process, the function module for the form is called individually for each customer. You will now enhance the form interface such that each individual customer is now passed on directly in an appropriate work area, WA_CUSTOMER, which has thus far only been assigned in the form . To work with several customers, however, you first have to extend the existing selection screen.

Step 1: Enhanced Customer Query

The selection screen in the main program should now enable the entry of several customers. Therefore, you will replace the existing PARAMETER statement with SELECT-OPTIONS:

```
*&---------------------------------------------------------------&*
DATA: cust_id TYPE scustom-id.
*  PARAMETER:      p_custid TYPE scustom-id default 1.
SELECT-OPTIONS: s_custid FOR cust_id  DEFAULT 1 TO 1.
*&---------------------------------------------------------------&*
```
Listing 9.9 Enhanced selection screen

The previous PARAMETER statement is already flagged as a comment line in the source text shown above. In the future, the user's specification of the customer selection will be contained in parameter S_CUSTID. You are already familiar with the syntax of the SELECT-OPTIONS statement from the query of the airlines. Because the FOR addition always has to refer to internal variables, you inserted a suitable DATA statement first. As a result, the From/To fields in S_CUSTID are defined with the type of the customer number in SCUSTOM_ID.

Step 2: Enhanced Data Retrieval

Because users can now enter several customers, and the corresponding selection options now appear in an internal table, S_CUSTID, the SELECT statement used for data retrieval, has to change as well. The old and new versions appear below:

```
*&--------------------------------------------------------------&*
* get data
*  SELECT * FROM scustom INTO TABLE customers
*            WHERE id = p_custid
*            ORDER BY PRIMARY KEY.
*  SELECT * FROM sbook INTO TABLE bookings
*            WHERE customid = p_custid
*            AND   carrid   IN s_carrid
*            ORDER BY PRIMARY KEY.
* now with more than one customer
SELECT * FROM scustom INTO TABLE customers          " (1)
         WHERE id IN s_custid
         ORDER BY PRIMARY KEY.
SELECT * FROM sbook INTO TABLE bookings             " (2)
         WHERE customid IN s_custid
         AND   carrid   IN s_carrid
         ORDER BY PRIMARY KEY.
SELECT * FROM spfli INTO TABLE connections          " (3)
         FOR ALL ENTRIES IN bookings
         WHERE carrid = bookings-carrid
         AND   connid = bookings-connid
         ORDER BY PRIMARY KEY.
*&--------------------------------------------------------------&*
```

Listing 9.10 Retrieving data for multiple customers

The addition IN for the first SELECT statement now copies the data of all involved customers to internal table CUSTOMERS, as is the case with the airline. The Internal table CUSTOMERS was previously only a single entry.

The same change is made in the second statement for the structure of the booking table, BOOKINGS, which now also has to take multiple customers into account.

The change does not have any effect on the internal table of flight connections in the last statement. It is included above only to give you the full picture.

Step 3: Create the Loop

Each customer will now be passed on to the form interface individually. As a result, the main program has to loop over the corresponding internal table, CUSTOMERS, once for each selected customer. You implement this with an ABAP LOOP statement, which generally functions like a loop node in Smart Forms. Accordingly, you will also need a suitable work area here.

Every LOOP statement is concluded with an `ENDLOOP`; in between are the actual statements to be processed within the loop. The following listing shows how to implement a multiple call of the function module:

```
*&-----------------------------------------------------------------&*
* several customers
DATA wa_customer  TYPE scustom.
LOOP AT customers INTO wa_customer.
* now call the generated function module
  CALL FUNCTION fm_name
      EXPORTING  customers              = customers
                 bookings               = bookings
                 connections            = connections
                 wa_customer            = wa_customer
      EXCEPTIONS formatting_error       = 1
                 internal_error         = 2
                 send_error             = 3
                 user_canceled          = 4
                 OTHERS                 = 5.
* Error handling
ENDLOOP .
*&-----------------------------------------------------------------&*
```

Listing 9.11 Function call within a loop

You first defined the work area, WA_CUSTOMER, then filled it in the LOOP statement and passed it on as an additional parameter in the form interface. Although this parameter is not currently queried in the form pages, the interface should still work, since the other transfer parameters are still there. If necessary, you can use the same functions as in the original program (which are indicated here as comment lines within the loop) for troubleshooting.

Test the main program with the changes you have made so far. The user dialog box should now look like this:

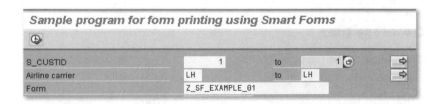

Figure 9.3 Enhanced selection screen

Choose only one customer at first. The output should then take place as before. Now try selecting several customers. In this case, the output is repeated, with a spool dialog box each time. As you can see, however, the flight invoice is created for the same customer each time. Try to figure out which logic in the form is responsible for this.

In the last step, you will now configure the form for the new, unique interface parameter WA_CUSTOMER.

Step 4: Modify the Form

Thus far, the form does not have any information about parameter WA_CUS-TOMER, which the main program specifies as the unique customer. Instead, with its present logic, the form attempts to determine the customer in internal table CUSTOMERS, which may now contain several customers. The form always reads the last table entry as the customer in the corresponding loop.

The form previously used a work area to actually output the address, since the contents of internal tables cannot be used directly as fields in text nodes. The name of this internal form work area is also WA_CUSTOMER, as in the main program/form interface. If you now also define the work area as an interface parameter in the pages of the form, the data specified by the main program will also be copied to this work area.

Therefore, this definition consists of two activities:

▶ First change the name of the existing variable to WA_CUSTOMER_O to remind you of its original definition. After all, you may need this entry again later.

▶ Then define WA_CUSTOMER as a parameter for the form interface with the same typing as before, with TYPE SCUSTOM.

After this change, WA_CUSTOMER must no longer be overwritten in the form. When you make the necessary changes, however, you will have to consider whether or not you performed the exercise in Section 7.2.8, which involved the assignment of the address data (among other things):

▶ **If you made the changes described in the exercise**
In this case, node READ_CUSTOMER in the ADDRESS window is responsible for assigning the address data. Depending on which modifications you have made so far, it is either a loop node or a complex section. Delete the node. If you prefer to deactivate it with a condition instead, you will also have to change the work area to WA_CUSTOMER_O in the **Data** tab page, since the check function of the node will display an error message otherwise.

▶ **If you have not performed the exercise**
In this case, the customer data is assigned in a **complex section** called TABLE in the MAIN window. This node also contains all the line definitions for the item output table. Therefore, you must not delete or deactivate it. Change the entry for the work area to WA_CUSTOMER_O in the **Data** tab page and then deactivate the entire loop. To do this, deactivate the flag next to **Internal Table** in the same tab page. Alternatively, you can deactivate the flag in front of **Repeat Processing** in the **General Attributes** tab page.

Note: You also changed the work area to WA_CUSTOMER_O, because the check function of the node would respond with an error message otherwise. This check only queries the field contents, and cannot determine if the loop—or even the entire node—was deactivated with a condition. The entry WA_CUSTOMER must not appear there any more; it is now write-protected because it is a parameter in the form interface.

Final Test

Now test the form output in the main program. When you select several customers, the corresponding number of flight invoices—with the correct addresses—should now be created.

9.6 Which Data Does the Form Use?

9.6.1 Overview

From the previous information on the form interface, you know that the generated function module is used to exchange the data between main program and form:

▶ When output starts, the main program supplies the data that is required by the form as import parameters.

▶ When the form is processed, the main program can verify its processing through the export parameter.

In both cases, standard parameters for general message control can also be used; these are described in detail in the next chapter.

At this point, we would like to point out a function that is not immediately obvious, but is often very useful. We have repeatedly mentioned that one main program can control different forms. The connection to the main program is made when output is started; it does not exist when you design the form.

In many applications, it can be beneficial for the main program to know which of the interface parameters are used in the function module for the form *before* the data transfer takes place. Because this information has to be known before the call of the generated function module, it cannot be defined as export parameters. Two examples:

▶ Because a main program can supply data for several forms, it often supplies interface parameters that an individual form does not need. If these parameters are known, the main program does not have to fill them with data. This can help you vastly improve performance during data retrieval.

▶ You often need to flag carbon copies during form output (*repeat print*). This function is available only in Smart Forms Release 6.10 and later (see Chapter 12). In earlier releases, you can use an interface parameter that flags the repeat page. If the parameter is not addressed in the form, you can use internal functions of the output device, such as the printer, instead.

An example of each application case appears below.

List of Output Parameters Used in the Form

An additional function module, SSF_FIELD_LIST, is available to determine which form interface parameters are used in the form. Here is an example of a call that you can use in the main program for the flight invoice:

```
*&-------------------------------------------------------------&*
* determine print data
DATA: fieldlist    type TSFFIELDS.
DATA: wa_fieldlist type TDLINE.
CALL FUNCTION    'SSF_FIELD_LIST'
     EXPORTING   formname             = p_form
     IMPORTING   fieldlist            = fieldlist
     EXCEPTIONS  no_form              = 1
                 no_function_module   = 2
                 others               = 3.
*&-------------------------------------------------------------&*
```

Listing 9.12 Checking data usage in the form

The input parameter of the function module is the name of the form, which you queried from the user in the flight invoice. The only output parameter of the function module is an internal table, FIELDLIST, which was declared in the first DATA statement. Each line of this internal table consists of a single text field. After the return from the function, FIELDLIST contains one entry for each interface parameter that is addressed in the form.

> **Background:** To prepare the list, the function module reads the entries in the text field for the import/export parameters of database table STXFCONTR.

Figure 9.4 shows FIELDLIST how it could be used in the flight invoice, as described in the last listing.

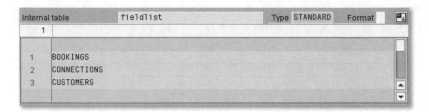

Internal table	fieldlist		Type STANDARD	Format	
1					
1	BOOKINGS				
2	CONNECTIONS				
3	CUSTOMERS				

Figure 9.4 List of interface parameters used

The displayed list was called through the debugger immediately after the execution of function module SSF_FIELD_LIST (information on this useful utility is available in Section 13.7.4). Obviously, all three internal tables that you pass on in the interfaces are also used in the form.

Criteria for Use in the Form

You still have to find out the criteria that function module SSF_FIELD_LIST uses to determine whether a data component is used actively in a form or not. To do so, at least one of the following conditions must be met:

▶ The parameter was inserted in the text node as a field.

▶ The parameter is defined as an attribute in any node.

▶ The parameter is listed as an input/output parameter in a program node.

Display in the Parameter List

If an interface parameter is involved in field output at several levels, both the single field and the superior level are included in FIELDLIST. In the flight invoice, the corresponding parameters are defined as an internal table. They are merely read using work areas in the form, and therefore do not appear as single fields for the output. As a result, Figure 9.4 shows only the superior level: the respective internal table.

9.6.2   Example: Transferring Connections on Demand

In the conclusion to this overview, you will see an example of how you can adapt data retrieval to the items in FIELDLIST. Your objective: the database query for the connections in the flight data model should take place only when this data is actually required in the form.

```
*&----------------------------------------------------------------&*
* Select data only if needed
READ TABLE fieldlist INTO wa_fieldlist
     WITH KEY table_line = 'CONNECTIONS'.
IF sy-subrc = 0.
   SELECT * FROM spfli INTO TABLE connections
            FOR ALL ENTRIES IN bookings
            WHERE carrid = bookings-carrid
            AND   connid = bookings-connid
            ORDER BY PRIMARY KEY.
ENDIF.
*&----------------------------------------------------------------&*
```
Listing 9.13 Retrieving only the required data (FIELDLIST)

If a "CONNECTIONS" entry exists in internal table FIELDLIST, the corresponding line is copied into a suitable work area, WA_FIELDLIST (see Listing 9.12 for its definition). In this case, the data component of the same name is also needed in the form. Note that the comparison value must be in uppercase in this statement. When the transfer is successful, system variable SY-SUBRC does not show any errors. Only in this case will the database be accessed in the SELECT statement as a result of the IF condition.

9.6.3 Reduced Data Retrieval for the Delivery Note

The strict separation between main program and form logic creates a decisive advantage for form output under Smart Forms: one main program can supply data for many different forms. Of course, all the forms have to belong to the same area—the same application, for example—to ensure that at least roughly equivalent data is required.

The data retrieval in the main program should be configured so that as little additional data as possible has to be added to the individual forms, to avoid the redundancy caused by duplicate functions.

> **Note:** You may have heard that subsequent reading of data in the form results in worse performance than data retrieval in the main program. This statement is true only when the data is read from the same sources that were already queried in the main program (but due to different contents). Only in this case do you have a duplicate function that slows down processing.

This universal requirement for the central data retrieval routine results in redundancies, however, because all the data is always provided, but is not always needed in the form. This has a negative effect on performance.

The solution to this problem is the subject-based grouping of the supplied data components at the higher level. You can then define whether or not to read the data by each subject. You should organize the subjects to directly correspond to one or more dependent read operations in the database. If the data for a subject is not needed, the corresponding read operations at the database level are omitted automatically.

You can use function module SSF_FIELD_LIST to determine which subjects/data components are required in a form. The process flow for outputting a delivery document illustrates this in the next example.

Querying the Interface Parameters Used

Data retrieval is controlled through a special field string, which reflects the subjects whose use you want to monitor in the form (see Figure 9.5).

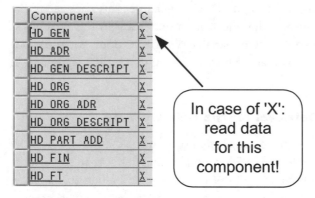

Figure 9.5 Controlling data retrieval in a delivery

The field string contains a field for each data component. Each of these fields represents a logical state that is set to "X" when data retrieval is required for the corresponding subject.

The structure of the field string is always dependent on the specific application. Accordingly, it has to be defined individually for each data retrieval routine, using the corresponding data type in the ABAP Dictionary.

> **Note:** The field string does not have to contain all the data components of the form interface, as long as data is generally supplied for the other components.

Call in the Main Program

Function module SSF_FIELD_LIST is executed again to set the logical states. To do so, you have to modify it slightly, to encapsulate the delivery as a subroutine in the main program:

```
*&------------------------------------------------------------&*
* name of Smart Forms form
DATA: LF_FORMNAME    TYPE TDSFNAME.
LF_FORMNAME = TNAPR-SFORM.
* list of all data-elements (read yes/no)
DATA:     LS_PRINT_DATA_TO_READ TYPE LEDLV_PRINT_DATA_TO_READ.
* determine print data with use of SSF_FIELD_LIST
PERFORM    SET_PRINT_DATA_TO_READ
   USING    LF_FORMNAME
   CHANGING LS_PRINT_DATA_TO_READ
            CF_RETCODE.
* example for reading data
IF LS_PRINT_DATA_TO_READ-CD_GEN = 'X'.
   SELECT ....
ENDIF.
*&------------------------------------------------------------&*
```

Listing 9.14 Logic for data retrieval in the delivery

The functions in Listing 9.14:

▶ The input parameter of subroutine SET_PRINT_DATA_TO_READ is the name of the form again, read from TNAPR in this case, which is usual when output control uses the condition technique. LS_PRINT_DATA_TO_READ is returned.

▶ You can use a simple IF query to link the retrieval of the individual data components with the result in LS_PRINT_DATA_TO_READ, the list of data components from Figure 9.5.

▶ Normally, the entire data retrieval process—reading the database tables—is also grouped together in a separate subroutine. The input parameter is field string LS_PRINT_DATA_TO_READ with the required data components, as you already saw in Section 9.3.2.

It can make perfect sense to always supply certain data components regardless of the results in SSF_FIELD_LIST. In this case, you have to set the corresponding field in LS_PRINT_DATA_TO_READ to "X" before the actual data retrieval.

9.6.4 Example: Flagging Carbon Copies

In the introductory section on carbon copies, you read about a second application case in which it is helpful for the main program to know which interface parameters are used in the form *before* data transfer takes place. Let's return to your familiar flight invoice to illustrate this case.

Obstacles

In order to use a corresponding function in Release 4.6, you have to overcome an obstacle:

▶ There is no parameter within the form that indicates which copy of the current form output is involved. The standard parameters of the form interface merely specify the number of identical copies (parameter OUTPUT_OPTIONS-TDCOPIES).

▶ However, the function module does not take advantage of this information directly; instead, it is passed on to spool control. As a result, the number of copies appears in the print parameters as **Number of Copies** (see spool dialog box in Figure 13.29). Therefore, the output device, such as the entered printer, is ultimately responsible for generating the copies.

But the output request itself contains only a single document that is the same for all copies. Under these circumstances, there is no parameter in the form that reflects which copy is currently being processed!

Controlling the Number of Copies Through the Main Program

To flag the copy anyway, you have to change an important aspect of the overall process flow. The main program must take over output control for multiple copies, and activate the function module for the form individually if necessary. This can take place in another LOOP statement, similar to the exercise in Section 9.5. In this approach, the main program can utilize an interface parameter to convey to the form which copy is currently being printed.

Under this changed process flow, the corresponding form is processed several times. This will reduce the output speed and increase the number of items in the spool. Therefore, it makes sense to monitor the form, to see whether the provided interface parameter for flagging the current copy in the form is queried at all; if not, the main program should use the control for multiple copies provided by the spool.

Here is the program flow, illustrated as an excerpt from the main program:

```
*&----------------------------------------------------------------&*
* ask user for copies
PARAMETER:   p_exemp   TYPE i DEFAULT 1.
DATA:        exemplar TYPE i.
DATA  output_options TYPE SSFCOMPOP.
* check whether parameter "exemplar" is used in form
  READ TABLE fieldlist INTO wa_fieldlist
       WITH KEY table_line = 'EXEMPLAR'.
* if not used, generate copies in the spool
  IF sy-subrc > 0.
    output_options-tdcopies = p_exemp.
    p_exemp = 1.
  ENDIF.
* start of loop in case of several customers
LOOP AT customers INTO wa_customer.
* start of loop in case of copies needed
  exemplar = 0.
  WHILE exemplar < p_exemp.
* now call the generated function module
    CALL FUNCTION fm_name
      EXPORTING
```

```
                output_options        = output_options
                user_settings         = ' '
                customers             = customers
                bookings              = bookings
                connections           = connections
                wa_customer           = wa_customer
                exemplar              = exemplar
*       IMPORTING document_output_info =
*                 job_output_info     =
*                 job_output_options  =
      EXCEPTIONS formatting_error      = 1
                 internal_error        = 2
                 send_error            = 3
                 user_canceled         = 4
                 OTHERS                = 5.
* next copy if more than one
    exemplar = exemplar + 1.
  ENDWHILE.
ENDLOOP.
*&----------------------------------------------------------------&*
```

Listing 9.15 Output of single form copies

In the flight invoice, the user is prompted to enter all the central control parameters in a selection screen. You used the PARAMETER statement to add an option for entering the number of copies; it is now saved in P_EXEMP. The additional variable EXEMPLAR will later indicate the sequence number of the copy currently being output. It has also been added as a parameter in the form interface.

Modified Loop Control

You should already be familiar with the LOOP for outputting several customers from a previous example (see Section 9.5).

You have now defined additional conditions within this loop for the function module call for the form. The process flow differs depending on whether or not the form uses parameter EXEMPLAR. The corresponding query for table FIELDLIST was explained in the overview in Section 9.6.1:

▶ If parameter EXEMPLAR is used in the form, the WHILE/ENDWHILE statement sets up an additional loop. In this loop, the function module for the form is called once for each loop pass, which is also the number of copies that the user specified. By including parameter EXEMPLAR in the form interface, you can define a condition to link any nodes in the form (windows, texts) with the current copy number, thus controlling their execution.

▶ If parameter EXEMPLAR is not used in the form, the regular interface parameter in OUTPUT_OPTIONS that is responsible for passing the number of copies on to the output device is set (see Section 9.7 for a detailed description of the standard parameters). At the same time, the WHILE/ENDWHILE loop is limited to a single pass. This is the same situation as before your changes.

Please note that the routine described above is not an example of highly optimized program coding. It would also be possible, for example, to pass on all the copies— after the original printout—in a shared spool request, assuming that each copy is to be flagged identically.

Functional Test for Form Output

As long as parameter EXEMPLAR is not used in the form, the total number of requested printouts is directly passed to spool control. To check this, enter 2 as number of printouts; this number appears under **Printouts** in the spool dialog box.

Single steps to trigger the single output mode:

▶ Include parameter EXEMPLAR in the interface, on the form pages.
▶ Enter the parameter as a field in any secondary window, such as the INFO window. The main program then registers this parameter as "in use" and you can monitor its contents in the print preview.
▶ Start the main program with several copies (carbon copies).

The spool dialog is now called several times and the number of printouts is 1 each time. In contrast, parameter EXEMPLAR is increased in increments of one until the requested total number is reached, which means you can use it to flag carbon copies in the individual forms.

9.7 Standard Parameters of the Form Interface

9.7.1 Overview

In the previous sections, you learned how the form and the corresponding function module interact with the main program, and how you can transfer data in the interface parameters. The interface was described from the perspective of the form in Section 6.4.1. You learned about the following parameters in the tab pages of the nodes:

► **Import**

For transferring data from the main program to the form

► **Export**

For reporting the output results to the main program

► **Tables**

For transferring internal tables that can be modified in the form

► **Exceptions**

For general error handling (described in Section 9.8)

Of these interface components, the import parameters are the most important for form development. All the data provided by the main program is transported to the form through these parameters:

► If a parameter has been defined specifically in a form, it must also be assigned in the main program (required).

► Additional standard parameters exist that are the same in every form interface. They are added to the interface automatically each time you create a new form. These parameters are used for general output control and are always optional; the main program can utilize these parameters, but does not have to.

> **Note:** Parameters of a function module are optional because the function module call also includes the names of the parameters that are valid within the function module. Because they are assigned specifically, the system always knows which parameters are involved. In FORM routines, in contrast, the sequence of the transferred parameters is the sole criterion and, as such, must always be followed.

Monitored Standard Parameters

Now consider the following two cases:

► Standard *import* parameters can contain information from the main program that involves output via printer, fax or e-mail, as well as storage in the archiving system. If no information is specified, the function module called for the form uses internal default values.

► Standard *export* parameters are returned by the function module following form output. They serve to check the output results, such as the number of printouts. You can use this method to return the generated intermediate document to the main program, just like it is given to the spool, in order to perform further steps such as download or conversion to PDF.

9.7.2 Standard Import Parameters

The main program passes the import parameters on to the form. This enables the main program to specify the default output destination through the corresponding options, as is necessary in automatic print processes or for fax dispatch, for example.

Several of the interface parameters contain structured, multilevel data. This section starts with a general overview of the parameters as they appear in the form interface and then continues with the more detailed levels. Some of the parameters are explained with the assistance of exercises below. Others are covered in the sections that deal with special output types, such as e-mail, fax, and XML (see Chapter 10).

The following import parameters are generated automatically when you create a new form. They are merely listed in a slightly different sequence there.

Parameter name	Meaning
CONTROL_PARAMETERS	The entries in this field string control several general specifications for form output, such as language, first page, selection of print preview instead of spool, and display/hide the print dialog box before each output.
OUTPUT_OPTIONS	You can use the fields in this field string to set defaults for many of the options that users normally see in the spool dialog box, such as the output device. If parameter USER_SETTINGS is active, however, the system takes this information from the user defaults instead.
USER_SETTINGS	Logical value that specifies the source of some spool control parameters: "X": User defaults (default setting) blank: Use OUTPUT_OPTIONS
MAIL_APPL_OBJ MAIL_RECIPIENT MAIL_SENDER	Parameters for sending the form by e-mail from the BCI (Business Communication Interface).
ARCHIVE_INDEX ARCHIVE_INDEX_TAB ARCHIVE_PARAMETERS	Parameters for archiving/document storage via ArchiveLink (see the manual entries for the storage mode in the spool dialog box). When output through output control, these fields are specified by the higher-level application program.

Table 9.2 Standard import parameters for the form interface

The requirements for output via e-mail and archiving are described in detail in Chapter 10.

Components of Standard Import Parameters

The CONTROL_PARAMETERS listed at the top of Table 9.2 are the most important parameters for controlling standard output via the spool or printer as output device. Table 9.3 lists its most important single components, with the corresponding field names and meanings.

CONTROL_PARAMETERS (data type SSFCTRLOP)	
General control parameters for form output	
NO_OPEN NO_CLOSE	Control fields that make it possible to group several forms together in one spool request (see explanation in text below).
DEVICE	Type of output device; possible values: PRINTER, TELEFAX, MAIL. If nothing is specified, the function module uses the default value, PRINTER.
NO_DIALOG	Logical value to deactivate the spool dialog box: blank: Display dialog box "X": No dialog box for user entry If the dialog box is not displayed, the output attributes specified in OUTPUT_OPTIONS or in the user defaults apply. Note that the output device is a required entry. If it does not contain a valid value, the spool dialog box is always displayed.
PREVIEW	"X": Print preview on the screen. If SY-BATCH indicates that background processing is involved, this value is ignored and the spool request is generated in any case.
GETOTF	Triggers output as OTF document: "X": Return as OTF document through the export parameter JOB_OUTPUT_INFO-OTFDATA; that is, no output on any other output devices. If XSF output is active (set with XSFCOMDE), this value is ignored. Also see the notes for the export parameters.
LANGU REPLANGU1 REPLANGU2 REPLANGU3	Language in which the form texts will be printed (and replacement languages if a text is not available in the previous language). The default value in the function module is SY-LANGU, the user's current logon language.
STARTPAGE	Code of the first page (the default value in the function module is the top page in the Form Builder navigation tree).

Table 9.3 Fields for the standard import parameters

OUTPUT_OPTIONS (data type SSFCOMPOP):

Information for controlling form output via the spool, similar to the way the user can configure these values in the spool dialog box. The list below contains only some of the available individual components:

Optical archiving (ArchiveLink)

TDARMOD	Defines whether or not to generate an object for archiving at the same time that the spool request is generated: 1 = Print only (default) 2 = Archive only 3 = Print and archive (see Chapter 10)
TDNOARCMCH	"X": User cannot change the archiving mode in the spool dialog box.

Print preview and dialog

TDTITLE	Title text displayed in the spool dialog box (default title is "Print").
TDNOPREV	"X": Generally block the print preview. The button does not appear in the dialog box.
TDNOPRINT	"X": Do not allow print output from the print preview; button is not active.
TDNOARCH	"X" (default): Archiving mode in the print preview cannot be changed (with the corresponding icon).
TDIEXIT	"X": Immediately return from print preview when output to printer or fax was triggered there.

Texts for output request

See the options in section "Spool request from the spool dialog box"

TDDATASET	Setting for part 1 of the name of the spool request (default is "SMART").
TDSUFFIX1	Part 2 of the name of the spool request (default is the name of the output device).
TDSUFFIX2	Part 3 of the name of the spool request (default is the user ID of the current user).
TDCOVTITLE	Setting for text on cover sheet.

Spool control

Some fields are ignored if USER_SETTINGS is also active; in this case, the information from the current user's master record are used instead (marked with "*" below).

TDDEST *	Output device (short form: printer); the default is the output device from the user master record, depending on the setting in USER_SETTINGS.

Table 9.3 Fields for the standard import parameters (continued)

TDPRINTER *	Type of output device: It makes sense to enter something here only if you want to restrict the printer selection to one device type in the spool dialog box (see list in spool administration).
TDNEWID	"X": Create a new spool request; otherwise search for a suitable spool request (see example below).
TDIMMED *	"X": Print immediately; otherwise, a subsequent user trigger is required (through entry in the spool).
TDDELETE *	"X": Delete spool request after output.
Cover sheet	
TDCOVER	Blank: No cover sheet. "X": Output cover sheet. "D": Use cover sheet defaults from output device.
TDRECEIVER	Output recipient on cover page. If blank, the current user name is used.
TDDIVISION	Indicate department on cover sheet.
Page selection and copies	
TDCOPIES	Identical number of copies to be output (default = "1"; "0" is also interpreted as 1). This entry is copied to the *No. of Copies* field in the spool dialog box (also see the example for flagging carbon copies in Section 9.6.4).
TDPAGESELECT	Blank: Print all pages; otherwise information for page selection (including combinations). Examples: 2: only Page 2 2–5: Pages 2 to 5 -5: All pages up to Page 5 2-: Page 2 to end 2,5,7–9: Print Pages 2, 5 and 7 to 9
XSF output	
XSFCMODE XSF XSFOUTMODE XSFFORMAT XSFOUTDEV	Controls for XML standard data exchange interface (see notes in Section 10.3).

Table 9.3 Fields for the standard import parameters (continued)

Comment: The fields marked with "*" above are used by the main program only when interface parameter USER_SETTINGS is blank. Otherwise, the function module for the form automatically uses the user defaults.

Output Options for Processing with Output Control

When output control is used, you may want to output the form without requiring user intervention (spool dialog). In this case, the main program must specify all the parameters for controlling the output. This is especially true of the fields in the standard transfer structures OUTPUT_OPTIONS and CONTROL_PARAMETERS in the form interface. Most of their contents are already available in table, NAST, and can be used there.

A suitable function module, WFMC_PREPARE_SMART_FORM, is already available in the system. It reads the relevant information from NAST and provides it in parameters that can easily be transferred to form interface parameters—for example, the printer, specifications in OUTPUT_OPTIONS, and even e-mail parameters. Here is a typical call:

```
*&---------------------------------------------------------------&*
SF_REPID = SY-REPID.                "Name of the current program
* Read parameters from NAST
CALL FUNCTION 'WFMC_PREPARE_SMART_FORM'
  EXPORTING
    PI_NAST        = NAST           "Message status and address
    PI_REPID       = SF_REPID
  IMPORTING
    PE_RETURNCODE = RETCODE         "Error code
    PE_ITCPO       = SF_
ITCPO      "Transfer structure (like SAPscript)
    PE_DEVICE      = SF_
DEVICE     "Communication type, output device type
    PE_RECIPIENT  = SF_RECIPIENT "e-mail recipient object
    PE_SENDER     = SF_SENDER.    "e-mail sender
* Set output options of form interface
IF RETCODE = 0.
  MOVE-CORRESPONDING SS_ITCPO TO OUTPUT_OPTIONS.
* Optional: Fill fields in CONTROL_PARAMETERS
  CONTROL_PARAMETERS-DEVICE    = SF_
DEVICE.    "Communication type
```

```
    CONTROL_PARAMETERS-NO_
DIALOG = 'X'.                "Printer dialog off
    CONTROL_PARAMETERS-PREVIEW   = US_SCREEN.     "Preview yes/no
    CONTROL_PARAMETERS-GETOTF    = SF_ITCPO-TDGETOTF. "OTF output
    CONTROL_PARAMETERS-LANGU     = NAST-
SPRAS.      "Language from NAST
ENDIF.
*&---------------------------------------------------------------&*
```

Listing 9.16 Copying form interface parameters from NAST

The most important input parameter for this function is the current entry in table NAST.

The appropriate fields of communication structure SF_ITCPO are filled depending on which communication type (printer, fax, e-mail) is involved. You can use them to directly derive the contents of OUTPUT_OPTIONS, the form interface parameter under Smart Forms. This is implemented with the MOVE-CORRESPOND-ING statement in the above example.

The main fields in CONTROL_PARAMETERS, such as the output device and the language, have been assigned default settings as examples in Listing 9.16. If necessary, you can also use the return parameters SF_RECIPIENT and SF_SENDER as parameters for e-mail dispatch in the Smart Forms form interface.

9.7.3 Sample Exercise: Standard Import Parameters

You will learn how to use interface parameters directly in the exercise below. You can consider the examples to be exercises and make the corresponding modifications to the flight invoice. Please note, however, that the main program should be able to handle several outputs in sequence in order to control the spool request. Accordingly, make sure you have implemented the last form enhancement from Section 9.5.

General Procedure for Spool Control via the Interface

When you output a form, the spool control information is read from the user master record by default. Alternatively, the main program can specify the values, using the various parameters in OUTPUT_OPTIONS. Interface parameter USER_SET-TINGS determines which source is used. This parameter itself is set to "X" by default, to use the user parameters.

To use the information from the interface, you have to perform the following steps in the main program:

► Define field strings in accordance with interface parameters CONTROL_
PARAMETERS and OUTPUT_OPTIONS and assign them in the function module
call.

► Set the required information in these parameters (for example, the printer in
TDDEST).

```
*&---------------------------------------------------------------&*
DATA  control_parameters TYPE SSFCTRLOP.
DATA  output_options     TYPE SSFCOMPOP.
output_options-tddest = 'LOCL'.
*&---------------------------------------------------------------&*
```

You also have to set USER_SETTINGS = SPACE in the interface call, to activate
interface control of the output.

Hiding the Spool Dialog Box

Under the default settings, the spool dialog box appears whenever you output a
form. This enables the user to individually change the current spool parameters.
You can suppress the call of the dialog box by specifying the corresponding settings in CONTROL_PARAMETERS:

```
*&---------------------------------------------------------------&*
CONTROL_PARAMETERS-NO_DIALOG   = 'X'.
CONTROL_PARAMETERS-PREVIEW     = 'X'.  "Preview anyway
*&---------------------------------------------------------------&*
```

Please note, however, that appropriate information also has to be defined for the
output device, for example:

```
*&---------------------------------------------------------------&*
OUTPUT_OPTIONS-TDDEST    = 'LOCL'.    "Local printer
OUTPUT_OPTIONS-TDCOPIES = 2.          "2 copies
*&---------------------------------------------------------------&*
```

If the entry is not a valid printer, however, the spool dialog box will appear regardless of the setting in NO_DIALOG.

Requirements for the Spool Request

When you output several forms in sequence, controlled by the loop in the main
program, a new, separate spool request is generated for each form by default. You
already saw this in the previous example from Section 9.5, when you output the
form several times in sequence for several customers; the spool dialog box was displayed separately for every single customer.

You can set the corresponding interface parameters to send all output to a single, shared spool request. In this case, the print preview also shows only a single, summary document, with the invoices of all the selected customers.

Two fields in CONTROL_PARAMETERS control this response, and have to be set according to the schema listed below:

	no_open	no_close
First form output	blank	"X"
Additional output	"X"	"X"
Last output	"X"	blank

Table 9.4 Controls for creating spool request

You have to configure these logical states within the loop processing. Suitable excerpts from the source text are:

```
*&---------------------------------------------------------------&*
DATA  control_parameters TYPE SSFCTRLOP.
LOOP AT customers INTO wa_customer.
* make sure spool is not closed
  control_parameters-no_open    = 'X'.
  control_parameters-no_close   = 'X'.
  AT FIRST.
    control_parameters-no_open  = ' '.
  ENDAT.
  AT LAST.
    control_parameters-no_close = ' '.
  ENDAT.
* output of form
  CALL FUNCTION fm_name
    EXPORTING
              control_parameters   = control_parameters
              customers            = customers
              bookings             = bookings
              connections          = connections
              wa_customer          = wa_customer
    EXCEPTIONS formatting_error     = 1
              internal_error       = 2
              send_error           = 3
              user_canceled        = 4
```

```
            OTHERS                      = 5.
ENDLOOP.
*&--------------------------------------------------------&*
```
Listing 9.17 Passing on the interface parameters

The fields for spool control in CONTROL_PARAMETERS are set within the output loop. The first two statements correspond to the case indicated as "Additional output" above. The AT FIRST and AT LAST statements serve to catch the first and last loop passes; the alternative settings are used only there.

> **Note:** A new spool request is appended to an existing spool request by default only in the following cases:
>
> ▶ The attributes such as name, output device, number of copies, and formatting type (paper format) agree.
>
> ▶ The existing spool request is not complete yet.
>
> ▶ Field TDNEWID in OUTPUT_PARAMETERS is not set to "X".
>
> If any one of these conditions is not met, spool control automatically generates a new spool request.

When you execute the main program now, a single spool request will be generated even if several customers are selected. You can see this in the print preview: all the output pages are grouped together in a single document and displayed in sequence. Previously, a new print preview was opened for each individual customer.

9.7.4 Standard Export Parameters

The main program can utilize export parameters to send information back to the function module of the form. Standard export parameters serve to check the output results, such as the number of printouts. You can also use this method to return the generated intermediate document to the main program, in the same way that it is passed on to the spool for additional steps, such as download or conversion to PDF file. All the standard export parameters are optional, which means that the main program can query them, but does not necessarily have to.

When you create a new form, the system always creates three standard export parameters (see Table 9.5).

Standard export parameters	
Parameter name	Meaning
DOCUMENT_OUTPUT_INFO	Number of form pages output
JOB_OUTPUT_INFO	Various information regarding the last output (actual information)
JOB_OUTPUT_OPTIONS	Structure similar to input parameter OUTPUT_OPTIONS. Enables the main program to determine, for example, whether the user made any changes in the spool dialog box.

Table 9.5 Standard export parameters

Structured parameter JOB_INFO_OUTPUT supplies the most important information regarding the output: it contains important information on the generated spool request, which the main program can optionally use to transfer the complete document. Table 9.6 shows the corresponding single components.

JOB_OUTPUT_INFO (data type SSFCRESCL)	
OUTPUTDONE	Flag for successful output; "X": Output was successful
ARCHDONE	Flag for successful archiving; "X": Archiving was successful
USEREXIT	Last user function before end of output: "C" = Cancel, "B" = Back, "E" = Exit blank = Other function
TDFORMS	Number of forms output in spool request; this value is greater than "1" only when several outputs were grouped together in one spool request (see notes for import parameters).
SPOOLIDS	Table with all IDs of the generated spool requests
FAXIDS	Table with all IDs for fax output
MAILIDS	Table with all IDs for e-mail output
OTFDATA	Table with all lines of the output document in OTF format (filled only when requested with GETOTF; see remarks below)
XSFDTA XSLDATA CSSDATA	Tables with all lines of an XML output if output mode "A" was selected (separated into sections for XML, XSL, CSS). Each table contains only one column with type *String*; each line entry is a line of the output document (is filled only when requested in the corresponding import parameter; see notes there). XSF output is described in detail in Section 10.3.

Table 9.6 Database components involved with export parameters

Each form output generates an intermediate document, which contains all the format information required for a correct print representation. This document is usually sent to the spool.

OTF Document as the Result of Form Output

This intermediate document exists in *Output Text Format* (*OTF*), unless XSF output was requested explicitly. OTF format consists completely of readable characters. It describes the formatted text in a uniform intermediate format. It is still independent of the control language used by the specified output device. The output/printer driver (PostScript, PCL, and so on) is responsible for converting from OTF format to the output device language.

The generated OTF document is saved together with the spool request. The print preview also uses the OTF document, which is why you can also call it within spool control.

A main program can request this OTF document from the function module, using import parameter GETOTF in CONTROL_PARAMETERS, and then copy it in the export parameters as entries in component OTFDATA, which itself is another internal table. In this case, the contents are not passed to the spool or the print preview. The main program is responsible for further processing—conversion to PDF or another format, for example, or download to the user's PC. The example below is also based on this case.

9.7.5 Sample Exercise: Standard Export Parameters

Only a few steps are necessary to return the intermediate document from form output in OTF format to the application program (instead of the spool; see Listing 9.18).

```
*-----------------------------------------------------------*
DATA control_parameters       TYPE SSFCTRLOP.
DATA job_output_info          TYPE SSFCRESCL.
control_parameters-getotf    = 'X'.    " Get OTF on
control_parameters-no_dialog = 'X'.    " Spool dialog off
* Additional statements
* i.e. determine name of function module
CALL FUNCTION    fm_name
     EXPORTING   control_parameters  = control_parameters
                 customers           = customers
                 bookings            = bookings
                 connections         = connections
```

```
            IMPORTING  job_output_info       = job_output_info
            EXCEPTIONS formatting_error       = 1
                       internal_error         = 2
                       send_error             = 3
                       user_canceled          = 4 .
WRITE 'Transfer in OTF format complete'.
* Further processing of OTF document in
* JOB_OUTPUT_INFO-OTFDATA i.e. with function module CONVERT_OTF.
*--------------------------------------------------------------*
```

Listing 9.18 Returning form output to the main program

Individual steps in the main program:

▶ Define the form parameters as specified above.

▶ To activate return of the output to the main program, you really only have to set GETOTF. We recommend deactivating the spool dialog with NO_DIALOG, however, because it is not needed here.

▶ Assign the parameters in the form interface.

▶ The query of errors has been omitted from the above listing; instead, a short text is output with the WRITE statement.

After execution of the function module, the main program can further process the output results (for conversion to ASCII or PDF with function module CONVERT_OTF, for example) using the line-based entries in component OTFDATA of JOB_OUTPUT_INFO.

9.8 Runtime Errors/Exceptions

9.8.1 Overview

Section 3.4 already described in detail how you can detect and correct errors in the form during the development process—using the built-in checks in the Form Builder, for example. The functions described in that section are usually entirely sufficient for form development. To complete your knowledge in this area, you will now deal with errors that occur only during form output, specifically during data retrieval. These errors are called *runtime errors*.

> **Note:** The functions described here are only rarely relevant for form development.

Interface Parameters

A standardized procedure for monitoring runtime errors has been defined in the function module for the form. The interface of the function module passes on the messages, which means the main program is ultimately responsible for dealing with them properly. The following options are available for the main program to monitor messages from the function module:

▶ Query SY-SUBRC to determine whether an error situation caused the function module to terminate.

The query of SY-SUBRC is a general procedure in the SAP system; any ABAP program can use it to monitor the correct execution of a subordinate function. If SY-SUBRC is not zero after the return from a function call, this means an error occurred during execution that caused that function to terminate. If a deviation from the regular program flow occurs within a function module, it is generally called an *exception*. The called program can respond to these exception situations by outputting appropriate messages, for example.

▶ Check other *system fields* (such as SY-MSG1), which may describe the contents of the last exception in more detail.

These system fields are also usually filled for the form function module. As a result, when you return from the function module in the previous examples of the flight invoice, you can start a query of SY-SUBRC <> 0 and then use the additional system fields to display an error message.

▶ Read a detailed *internal log*.

All the messages (errors, warnings) that occur during the execution of the function module are written to an internal log. The main program can use a defined function call to read and process this log.

Function modules do not normally generate any direct screen messages themselves. This is because they can be integrated in different types of programs and could, in the worst case, completely block a batch process. Instead, the module ends its own execution in case of error and sends a reference to the exception situation back to the calling program. The exception can also be passed across several levels depending on the specific situation, such as when one function module calls another function module.

Response in the Main Program

Therefore, the main program is ultimately responsible for determining how to proceed after an exception. Two types of response are typical for form output:

▶ **Output on screen**
If an error occurs, the main program displays an error message on the user's screen. It contains a brief reference to the cause of the error. You can frequently display the long text for an error message using the F1 help. This option also makes sense when testing forms.

▶ **Logging**
When you use message control for output, the entries from the internal error log are transferred to a central error log in case of error, and the current message is assigned. The user can evaluate the log using the individual menu paths in the respective application. At the same time, each message is assigned a new status, such as "Incorrect execution". This log contains all the error messages, including warnings, that occurred during form output. If you use this procedure, it may be possible to continue output with a different document.

The severity of the exception also plays a role in the handling of error situations—for example, distinguishing between actual error messages and mere warnings. For this reason, the errors are classified by category. Only actual errors cause the program to terminate; warnings are merely written to the internal execution log.

Standard Error Messages

A variety of error situations for Smart Forms form output are predefined and integrated in the function module for the form, including spool errors, user cancellation and text module not found, to name just a few.

Note: The design of the form can also affect how the system responds to specific events. For example, when you add an include text, you can set the option **No Error, If Text Does Not Exist**. If a corresponding text cannot be found in the current client, this fact is always recorded in the internal log. Depending on the settings in the node, an exception can also be triggered, which terminates execution of the function module.

The defined standard messages are generated by the output processor automatically when an error occurs. You can also generate individual messages as warnings or error messages—to prevent the form from being processed under certain conditions, for example. You can add the corresponding statements to the form in a program node. This approach is described in detail further below.

The handling of exceptions during the execution of an ABAP function module is also described in detail in the corresponding documentation in the SAP Library. Therfore, this section relates only the contents that are relevant for use in Smart Forms.

9.8.2 Error Handling in the Main Program

Every application area (work area) in the SAP system has its own (error) messages. To avoid overlaps, they are divided into message classes: a message number is unique only together with this class; an entry exists for each language. All the messages for Smart Forms are contained in class SSFCOMPOSER. You maintain the messages in transaction SE91. They are stored in database table T100.

Each message class is also assigned an exception in the function module of the form. If an error occurs, the defined exception is triggered. To trigger the exception, system variable SY-SUBRC is set to the exception number. The details (error number, work area, message text, and so on) are saved in other system parameters. Therefore, the query SY-SUBRC <> 0 in the calling program will always indicate immediately whether or not an exception has occurred. Reading the other system parameters may indicate the cause of the exception.

Exceptions are interface parameters in the function module and have to be defined accordingly in its call. Here is a sample call:

```
*&-------------------------------------------------------------&*
* calling Smart Forms function module
    CALL FUNCTION fm_name
        EXPORTING   customers           = customers
                    bookings            = bookings
                    connections         = connections
        EXCEPTIONS  formatting_error    = 1
                    internal_error      = 2
                    send_error          = 3
                    user_canceled       = 4
                    test                = 5
                    test1               = 6.
IF SY-SUBRC <> 0.
   MESSAGE ID sy-msgid TYPE sy-msgty NUMBER sy-msgno
       WITH sy-msgv1 sy-msgv2 sy-msgv3 sy-msgv4.
ENDIF.
*&-------------------------------------------------------------&*
```

Listing 9.19 Output of error message after form output

The exceptions that can be used are listed in the EXCEPTIONS block in the call of the function module. You will also find the same entries in form processing in the **Exceptions** tab page, under the attributes of the form interface.

Error Message Output in the Main Program

The listing above also illustrates a possible response by the main program when an exception occurs—that is, when SY-SUBRC <> 0: the MESSAGE statement outputs a message directly on the screen. The resulting display could look like this:

Figure 9.6 Error message with MESSAGE statement

The message parameters are the information returned by the function module:

SY-MSGID	Message class (always SSFCOMPOSER in Smart Forms)
SY-MSGTY	Message category with: A = Termination, E = Error, I = Info, S = Status message, W = Warning, X = Exit/short dump
SY-MSGNO	Current message number

The message number must be defined as an entry for class SSFCOMPOSER. The other fields indicate the component in the form to which the message refers. When an include text is missing, for example, the system responds with the following message number:

610 Include text &1 does not exist (object &2, ID &3)

The variables &1 to &3 in the message text are filled with the contents of the involved form component; these contents can also be read directly through the system variables. In the above example, they involve information on the include text node:

SY-MSGN1	Here: Name of the include text
SY-MSGN2	Here: Corresponding specification of text object
SY-MSGN3	Here: Corresponding specification of text ID

Outputting to an Internal Error Log

In the previous example, only a single error message from the function module is evaluated and output on the screen. This is not possible in many cases, however—during automatic printing, for example.

In this case, the logging approach is preferred. In this approach, the messages are collected in a central log table, to make them available to the user. This is the usual approach for execution using message control, for example. To ensure a complete log, the main program should also have access to the warning messages.

This requirement is met by an additional log function that collects all triggered messages in an internal table during execution of the function module. Various function modules support this internal processing:

▶ Function module SSFRT_WRITE_ERROR is used to save the messages; it is normally called only within the function module for the form. If necessary, a suitable exception is raised with the RAISE ERROR statement.

▶ Function module SSFRT_READ_ERROR lets the main program read the last entry in the internal error table. If an exception was triggered, the last entry is automatically the error message that belongs to the exception (equivalent to the entries in SY fields).

▶ Function module SSF_READ_ERRORS is available for reading all the runtime messages in the internal log. The only transfer parameter is an internal table that is based on data type SSFERRORS; it contains the exact fields that comprise the individual messages (with message class, message number, texts, and so on). The internal log from the last form output is read automatically.

The information in the internal log is transferred to application programs triggered via message control, for example. After a true output via the spool (not in the print preview), the corresponding status of message table NAST is updated. In addition, all the messages that occurred are copied to the message control log files, using a function such as NAST_PROTOKOLL_UPDATE; also see Section 13.6.

Example of the Internal Message Log

In the final example, you will see a short program routine that generates a simple list of all the messages that occurred, along with their parameters, on the screen (of course, a more elegant solution is also possible):

```
*&--------------------------------------------------------------&*
FORM print_ssfprot.
* Declaration
  DATA: errortab      TYPE tsferror.
```

```
      DATA: wa_errortab    TYPE LINE OF tsferror.
* get Smart Forms log
      CALL  FUNCTION  'SSF_READ_ERRORS'
            IMPORTING errortab = errortab.
* output log
      LOOP AT errortab into wa_errortab.
        WRITE: / wa_errortab-msgid,
                 wa_errortab-errnumber,
                 wa_errortab-msgty,
                 wa_errortab-msgv1,
                 wa_errortab-msgv2,
                 wa_errortab-msgv3,
                 wa_errortab-msgv4.
      ENDLOOP.
ENDFORM.
*&----------------------------------------------------------------&*
```

Listing 9.20 Reading and outputting the error log

A PERFORM for this subroutine, instead of the MESSAGE statement, could completely replace the error handling in the main program at the beginning of this section. The subroutine then displays a list of all the errors that occur, line by line, on the monitor. No other parameters are needed for the call itself.

9.8.3 Individual Error Handling in the Form

Previously, you learned about the typical information for a message that the user sees on the screen or in a log. In this section, you will learn how you can capture individual errors in the form and forward them to the main program as exceptions.

Internal Error Constants

To simplify processing in Smart Forms, all the messages used there are defined as constants in the source text. Excerpts from the corresponding include program, SSF_ERRORS (which is automatically included in the function module for the form) appear below:

```
*&----------------------------------------------------------------&*
*    INCLUDE SSF_ERRORS                                           *
*    errors numbers for SAP Smart Forms                           *
*----------------------------------------------------------------*
* error class 00: user canceled document processing
* exception    : user_canceled
constants:
```

```
  ssf_err_user_canceled            type tdsfnumber value '000001'.
* error class 01: send and convert output (spool, archive)
* exception      : send_error
constants:
  ssf_err_dest_no_authority        type tdsfnumber value '010001',
  ssf_err_spool_error              type tdsfnumber value '010002',
  ssf_err_unknown_device           type tdsfnumber value '010003',
*&--------------------------------------------------------------&*
```

Listing 9.21 Defined error messages during form output

Each constant contains a six-digit number. The first two digits represent the error class, while the last four digits represent a consecutive number within that error class. This number is then listed in the internal execution log, among other places.

The error class determines which exception is triggered and returned to the main program in SY-SUBRC. Five error classes are currently defined, and each has been assigned a different exception (see Table 9.7).

Class	Exception	Name	Application cases
00	4	user_canceled	User cancellation
01	3	send_errors	Output to printer, conversions in fax, e-mail, and so on
02	1	formatting_error	References to texts, graphics, fonts, and formats
03	2	internal_error	Composer and true runtime errors
99	Other	user_defined	Custom messages for the form

Table 9.7 Assignment of error classes to exceptions

Function module SSFRT_WRITE_ERROR provides a routine for saving a new message. If an error occurs, the RAISE ERROR statement also raises an exception within the function module for the form. The response from the main program is already described above.

Raising Exceptions in a Program Node

Normally, the form processor generates error messages automatically at runtime — if a text module does not exist, for example. In addition, it may make sense to generate individual messages in a program node in the form (to trap data-specific error situations, for example). Several possibilities of this are illustrated below.

Direct screen output is not possible within a function module. Because each form is translated as a function module, direct use of the MESSAGE statement is not an option. You can, however, write the required message to the internal log, as described above, as well as raising an exception if necessary. Listing 9.22 below illustrates three examples, one in each comment block.

```
*&---------------------------------------------------------------&*
*  (A): Use macro to raise exception
*     USER_EXCEPTION TEST.
*  (B): Output with internal error constant + message number
*     CALL FUNCTION 'SSFRT_WRITE_ERROR'
*       EXPORTING
**         I_ERRNUMBER        = ssf_err_unknown_device   "'010003'
*         I_msgid            = 'SSFCOMPOSER'
*         I_MSGTY            = 'E'
*         I_msgno            = '027'
*         I_MSGV1            = 'Test fax'
*         I_MSGV2            = ' '   .
*     USER_EXCEPTION TEST.
*  (C): Output with message number, etc.
*     CALL FUNCTION 'SSF_MESSAGE'
*       EXPORTING
*         I_MSGID         = 'SSFCOMPOSER'
*         I_MSGTY         = 'E'
*         I_MSGNO         = '027'
*         I_MSGV1         = 'Test fax'
*         I_MSGV2            = ' '   .
*     SFSY-EXCEPTION = 'TEST'.      " Also raise
*     RAISE TEST.                   " an exception
*&---------------------------------------------------------------&*
```

Listing 9.22 Error messages and exception in program node

These three examples are valid for use only within a program node.

The exceptions used must previously be defined in the global definitions, in tab page **Exceptions**. The exception is named TEST here. The program flow in the generated function module changes depending on whether or not an exception is defined there. Make sure you enter the correct spelling for each value precisely, since there is no check function in the form to monitor this. The names of the exceptions of the exceptions are available directly in a program node—that is, without requiring assignment as input parameters.

If course, the exceptions also have to be defined in the main program, under the same names, when the form is called. You also assign an internal number to the exception name here. If an error occurs, this number—which can be any integer— is available in SY-SUBRC following the return from the function module.

Raising an Exception with a Macro

Every form contains a defined macro called USER_EXCEPTION, which can raise an exception directly. The macro itself consists of ABAP program coding, much like a subroutine.

```
*&-------------------------------------------------------------&*
DEFINE USER_EXCEPTION.
  PERFORM RESET_ALL IN PROGRAM SAPLSTXBC.
  SFSY-EXCEPTION = '&1'.
  RAISE ERROR.
END-OF-DEFINITION.
*&-------------------------------------------------------------&*
```

Listing 9.23 Definition of macro USER_EXCEPTION

The parameters required to call the macro include the name of the exception you want to raise. This name is copied to system variable SFSY-EXCEPTION within the macro. The macro also deletes various status values from the Composer and then uses RAISE to raise the actual exception.

You can use this macro only in a program node, not during initialization.

Please note that this simple method for raising an exception does not provide any additional error information, either in the SY variables or in the internal log table, ERRORTAB. Therefore, a MESSAGE statement in the main program will likely trigger a random message that depends only on whether or not other messages, such as warnings, have been recorded in the internal log.

> **Background:** Before returning to the main program, the function module for the form always reads the last entry in the internal log and places it in the SY variables. It does this under the assumption that the last entry is responsible for raising the exception, but this results in a largely random message in the above case.

Therefore, the last saved warning can appear as the reference in some cases. If no warning message has occurred yet, message number "003" is assigned automatically. A message like "Non-classifiable error (unknown exception raised)" appears on the screen.

In light of this situation, it makes sense to pass on the reason for the exception situation as well. The two solutions introduced below show you how to do this.

Exception with Internal Error Constant + Message Number

Function module SSFRT_WRITE_ERROR is provided for outputting Smart Forms-compatible messages in the program node. It describes an internal log table for exchanging messages, ERRORTAB, and requires the usual information, such as message class, message category, message number, and so on as its input parameters.

You can optionally specify a six-place error constant for the function module in parameter I_ERRNUMBER. If this entry is not filled, the system automatically adds "990001" for form-specific error situations.

In the simplest case, you can use this module to write warning messages to the internal log.

If you also want to raise an exception, the USER_EXCEPTION macro has to follow this function call. SFSY-EXCEPTION is set to the name of the exception once again in the macro as the basis for forwarding the exception to the main program.

Exception with Message Number

As an alternative to the above solution, you can use module SSF_MESSAGE to write the error message to the internal log. The specification of the internal error numbers is not supported here. The function module itself calls SSFRT_WRITE_ERROR, which means that "990001" for form-specific errors is added automatically.

SSF_MESSAGE uses RESET_ALL to delete several status values from the composer for messages whose message category identifies them as errors; this method is also used in macro USER_EXCEPTION.

Therefore, if you then use USER_EXCEPTION to raise an exception, RESET_ALL may be executed twice. Alternatively, you can use the ABAP RAISE statement to raise the corresponding exception directly. Please note, however, that this exception will be forwarded correctly only if the name of the exception is also recorded in system variable SFSY-EXCEPTION (see last example in Listing 9.22), which is normally the case in the macro.

> **Background:** To ensure that an exception is passed from the program node to the main program, the generated function module has to call two additional function modules. The following program flow results:

- In the first step, the exception leads back to the call of function module SSFCOMP_TABLE_NEXT_ROW. This function module then raises an exception itself with RAISE ERROR. As a result, an OTHERS exception appears in the higher level function module, SSFCOMP_PROCESS_DOCUMENT.

- A %RAISE subroutine is then executed at this level, which uses function module SSFRT_READ_ERROR to read the last entry from the internal log and transfer its contents to the SY variables.

- %RAISE also checks whether individual exceptions have been defined in the global definitions of the form. If so, the contents of SFSY-EXCEPTION are evaluated.

- If a form-specific exception is defined there, that exception is raised again with its respective name (TEST in this example), and is thus passed to the main program of the form.

- If no form-specific exception is found, %RAISE derives the exception from the error number in the internal log (through an error constant, depending on the previous statement). This case corresponds to the regular handling of standard exceptions.

As you can see from this internal process flow, system variable SFSY-EXCEPTION always has to be set. If you use macro USER_EXCEPTION in the program node, this value is assigned automatically.

9.8.4 Monitoring Form Execution with TRACE

In some cases of advanced form development, it can make sense to use trace functions to monitor form output as an additional runtime analysis. In this case, each execution step is automatically logged in a text.

You can also configure the trace to record only certain events, such as error messages, in the log. The SMARTFORM_TRACE transaction provides suitable trace functions for use in Smart Forms. Because the functionality of these trace functions are similiar to those used elsewhere in the system, they are not described in any detail here.

10   Special Output Processes

In the previous chapters, you dealt primarily with examples in which forms are output to a printer or displayed on the screen as a print preview.

While printing a form on paper is certainly the most widespread output method, other output formats (output media) are also commonplace and increasingly important. These output methods include dispatching a form by fax or e-mail, as well as outputting in PDF format. The archiving of finished forms also involves a special output format. Moreover, with the growing number of Internet applications, XML and HTML output formats are increasing in importance.

Smart Forms supports all these different output formats. The most important of them are described in this chapter.

10.1   Sending Forms via E-Mail or Fax

10.1.1   Overview

To send forms by e-mail or fax, SAP Smart Forms uses the *BCI (Business Communication Interface)*, which has been renamed *BCS (Business Communication Service)* in Release 6.10. This interface sends documents autonomously to internal communication partners. To send documents to external partners, the BCI forwards the send objects to SAPconnect. This multilevel architecture ensures a uniform interface in Smart Forms as well.

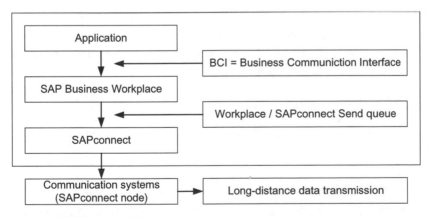

Figure 10.1 SAP communications system

Currently, the BCI is used primarily for e-mail communication. It can also use any other communication type supported by the SAP system, such as fax, Internet, X.400, remote mail, paging, and even printing. Please note, however, that these additional services usually require additional communication systems outside of the SAP system.

> **Note:** To simplify a complex subject, this chapter initially concentrates on communication using the internal SAP mail system. This approach enables you to check the results directly in the SAP Business Workplace.
>
> The other BCI services, (such as fax dispatch via the BCI, as an alternative to using the spool,) are covered at the end of this chapter.

From a technical standpoint, the BCI is implemented using *BOR* (*Business Object Repository*) *objects*. These objects also form the foundation for the SAP Business Workplace, as well as the SAP Business Workflow.

Basic Send Information

The following information is relevant for sending a document via the BCI:

▶ The BCI requires values for a *recipient* and a *sender*. Both values must exist as BOR objects. You will find out what these objects look like—and how to create new ones, if needed—based on practical examples further below.

▶ The BCI can also create automatic *links* between the send operation and the application object. This approach has two major advantages:

    ▶ You can use the application object to analyze all the send operations. Access is even possible directly during processing of the application object—for example, when maintaining a delivery document called from the system menu.

    ▶ Confirmation messages for the status are possible. This enables you to tell, for example, which format (such as PostScript or PDF) was used to send a document from the SAP system.

Parameters of the Form Interface

Therefore, the above parameters are the only ones needed in the form interface of Smart Forms to send forms by e-mail via the BCI.

Parameter name	Meaning
MAIL_RECIPIENT	Recipient of document
MAIL_SENDER	Sender of document
MAIL_APPL_OBJ	Links the application object with the send document

Table 10.1 E-mail parameters in the form interface

All three parameters are based on the same data type, SWOTOBJID. In the BCI terminology, these are BOR objects with object type **Recipient**. They are defined here as **flat** recipient objects. "Flat" indicates that each parameter can have only a single entry: only one recipient address, not a distribution list.

> **Background:** This object type represents a recipient to which a document—(that is, a MESSAGE object—) will be sent. This value can be an internal SAP user, an organizational unit, or a contact person at a company, (provided it has been assigned a standard communication type). The corresponding recipient object contains all the information needed to send the document, such as (the address, for example, as well as optional send attributes such as the send priority).

Examine the data components of a flat recipient object as it is used in Smart Forms.

MAIL_RECIPIENT (data type SWOTOBJID)	
LOGSYS	Logical system
OBJTYPE	Object type, such as: RECIPIENT for sender/recipient SOFMFOL for link
OBJKEY	Object key
DESCRIBE	Describe indicator

Table 10.2 Data components in the recipient object

You may be surprised by the simple structure of the parameters—just four fields—and be tempted to set their contents like you did the previous interface parameters. Unfortunately, it isn't quite that simple.

Take a look at the specific contents that are passed on to the generated function module in the case of output via e-mail for the recipient object in Figure 10.2. The entries in the objects are really only references to other objects in the BCI. The actual information is saved here. Therefore, if you do not know these objects and the corresponding object numbers, you cannot enter anything in the interface.

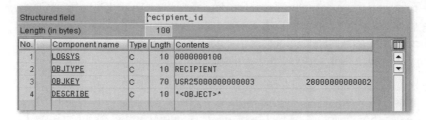

Structured field				recipient_id	
Length (in bytes)				100	
No.	Component name	Type	Lngth	Contents	
1	LOGSYS	C	10	0000000100	
2	OBJTYPE	C	10	RECIPIENT	
3	OBJKEY	C	70	USR25000000000003	28000000000002
4	DESCRIBE	C	10	*<OBJECT>*	

Figure 10.2 Contents of the e-mail recipient object

You could drop the subject at this point, as it is highly unlikely that you are familiar with the BCI. In turn, an introduction to the BCI would distract you from the main subject, Smart Forms. Moreover, the management of objects in the BCI is hardly relevant for conventional form development, because the contents are already provided by upstream systems (via table NAST, for example).

Despite these facts, if you wish to continue reading, you will learn below how to configure e-mail dispatch in Smart Forms, and become familiar with the parameters in the process.

10.1.2 Sample Exercise: E-mail Dispatch

It would be nice if you could show other employees at your company how successful you've been with the flight invoice so far. Via e-mail, of course. To make sure your co-workers remain friendly and undisturbed by your many e-mail attempts, however, you should mail your experiments to yourself first.

Therefore, the existing form will be output like before, with the exception that it is sent by e-mail this time. With this method, you can deactivate the additional function again at any time.

> **Tip:** Alternatively, you could also enhance the selection screen for the flight invoice with an additional parameter, "Also Send as Mail?" Although you've already covered the basics for doing so in the previous chapters, you will deal with this option in a second, later step.

You will find a printout of the corresponding program enhancement for the flight invoice in the Appendix. This program enhancement will be referred to frequently in this chapter.

First take a look at the program structure:

▶ The entire output as e-mail has been grouped together in one subroutine, MAIL_OUTPUT. It contains all the functions for supplying the BOR components of the BCI.

▶ The transfer parameters for the subroutine are the data required in the form interface, especially the name of the generated function module.

▶ Because the form is output in the subroutine, the generated function module is also included there. The corresponding parameters from the control structure inform the function module that the form will be sent as an e-mail. The specific e-mail objects are accepted only in this case.

> **Note:** You have already modified the form interface in many other examples in this book. The information in the listing here refers to the original form, which you can use for this exercise, as since it is not changed here.

Creating the E-mail Objects

Of course, the real question is how the e-mail objects in the form interface are generated:

▶ You will first see several data definitions in the MAIL_OUTPUT subroutine.

▶ These are followed by the blocks for sender, recipient, and application object. As mentioned above, you should be both the sender of the flight invoice and the recipient of the e-mail; accordingly, you assign the recipient through the user ID in SY-UNAME. Of course, you can also enter your user ID directly, enclosed in single quotes.

▶ In this special case, the sender and recipient are the same, which is why the entry for the user ID appears in both places.

Another note on the definitions in the recipient block: The recipient block contains, among other things, a line with information on the address type. Because value "B" is assigned to parameter "TypeID", the BCI knows that dispatch via e-mail is requested. The corresponding entry for fax dispatch, for example, is "F".

Once this program coding is processed, all the necessary objects for the BCI have been created. The remaining program coding serves, among other things, to modify the flat objects as required for Smart Forms.

Entering the Source Text

If you would prefer not to enter the entire example by hand, there is a much easier way. The program coding in the example is not completely new; it is based on report RSSOKIF2, which uses an example to illustrate e-mail output in SAPscript, and is also available in your system. You can use this example for your requirements here.

In the Appendix, the section following the listing contains exact instructions for moving the contents of RSSOKIF2 to the main program for the flight invoice. When you follow these instructions, you will receive an additional express document every time you output a form.

Figure 10.3 Express document received after sending from Smart Forms

The reference to the express document also contains the name of the function module for the form. Of course, you can also view the contents directly in the **inbox** of your Business Workplace in the SAP system.

Conclusion
Whether or not you optimize the program further is up to you. Here are a few helpful hints:

▶ You may be curious as to why the form is output within a LOOP. This is due to a function of the original program, which supports output for multiple recipients. In this case, however, only one recipient is filled.

▶ The source text in the Appendix largely corresponds to the template from program RSSOKIF1. Only the comment lines have been modified.

▶ The starting point for your activities involves the non-existent (or improperly filled) header data for the e-mail. The corresponding assignments for original fax dispatch are provided as an example. Now you only have to define appropriate default parameters for the form interface.

10.1.3 Additional Features with DEVICE='MAIL'

Even though the parameters MAIL_SENDER, MAIL_RECIPIENT, and MAIL_APPL_OBJ are designed primarily for sending e-mails, they also provide a general connection to the BCI. This means that you can use these parameters to address all of the types of communication that the BCI supports.

The communication type is configured through an attribute of the recipient object (as address type). It is specified in attribute **TypeID** when the RECIPIENT object is created. Fax output was already mentioned in the above example. The following address types are available:

B	SAP user ID
P	Personal distribution list
C	Group distribution list
F	Fax number
U	Internet address (URL)
R	Remote mail address (within an R/3-R/3 system group)
X	X.400 address
G	ID of an organizational unit
H	Name of an organizational unit

Note: Smart Forms primarily uses the OTF format to send forms. This setting is recommended for sending forms within the SAP system. Other formats are used to send external messages, (through forwarding to SAPconnect). Accordingly, you can specify a node for the supported address types in SAPconnect administration; this node converts forms, to formats like PDF for example, before they are sent (transaction SCOT).

10.1.4 Application Case: mySAP CRM

You can execute marketing campaigns in CRM that involve mass mailings. The messages can be dispatched through various communications channels, such as e-mail, printed letter, fax, and SMS. This mass processing is based on forms in Smart Forms.

Background: This situation involves a variant of Smart Forms that has been tailored specifically for use under mySAP CRM. The form output generates the content of the messages directly as *plain text* or in *HTML format*. To ensure that contents can be generated in HTML format at any time, some of the node types available in the standard version of Smart Forms are not available here.

Every marketing mail is created using a template that already contains the basic text blocks of the mail. The standard SAP template for this is CRM_MARKETING_MAIL_01. Different templates are available, depending on the destination and the communication method. Here are a just a few examples:

▶ E-mail as newsletter

▶ Fax for product information

▶ SMS for invitations to events

▶ Letters for product announcements

The addresses of the business partners are imported when the mails are sent to the defined target groups, using the contained fields as placeholders, which are called *attributes* in CRM.

Further personalization in the form is achieved by defining conditions for various text blocks. These conditions can come from the business partner's master data, from the current campaign, or from other system data.

When sent by e-mail, the forms can contain a hyperlink (a link to a Web page with the current campaign). An additional ID that is linked with this hyperlink enables you to track whether the business partner visited your page. More information on the use of these tracking IDs is available in the discussion of hyperlinks in Section 13.3.2.

10.2 Sending by Fax

The most current method of sending a form by fax utilizes the SAP spool, which is the same as print output.

> **Background:** The spool system has its own device types for fax dispatch. The send operation is processed in SAPconnect. Alternatively, you can also dispatch faxes using a fax machine connected to the local work center, a method which is (similar to output on the local printer).

To send a form as a fax in Smart Forms, you have to set the DEVICE parameter of control structure CONTROL_PARAMETERS to "TELEFAX" in the form interface. Smart Forms then starts a fax dialog under the default settings, instead of the usual spool dialog. The user can then enter the required fax number (see Figure 10.4).

As with the spool dialog (see Figure 13.29), you can preassign values for these fields using the output options, and skip the dialog by setting the NO_DIALOG field in the control structure.

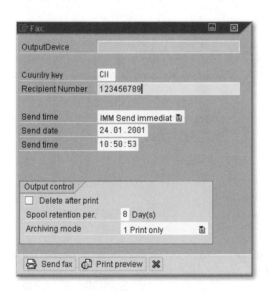

Figure 10.4 Fax dialog for spool processing

Table 10.3 shows the interface parameters for form control:

Fax parameters in OUTPUT_OPTIONS	
Parameter name	**Meaning**
TDTELELAND*	Country key, such as "US". Used for automatic determination of country code.
TDTELENUM*	Telecommunications partner; digits only, with /-.() and blanks as separators. If you set an ampersand (&) at the beginning, the internal number check is deactivated. Also see the documentation for data element SKTELNR.
TDTELENUME	Replacement telecommunications partner
TDFAXUSER	Name of SAP user
FAXFORMAT	Document format
TDSCHEDULE*	Requested send time: IMM: Immediate send (default) NIG: Send at night
TDSENDDATE*	Requested send date
TDSENDTIME*	Requested send time

Table 10.3 Interface parameters for fax control

You can use the components flagged with "*" to preassign the corresponding fields of the fax dialog. Use component TDARMOD to preassign the **Archiving Mode** field (see archiving in Section 10.4).

Information for the cover sheet design is especially helpful for fax dispatch. You can use the additional parameters in OUTPUT_OPTIONS to define this information.

10.3 XSF Output

10.3.1 Overview

The XML (eXtensible Markup Language) format is increasingly important for exchanging data over the Internet. This standardized format makes it possible to integrate different applications in a shared business process over the Internet. This makes XML a foundation for B2B (business to business) communication, for example.

XSF stands for *XML for Smart Forms*, and is an XML schema designed for the output of form contents. XSF output cannot contain any layout information, only the processed data and text from the form. Using XSF output, external applications outside the SAP System can access and process the contents of forms. This enables the integration of external form tools, as a replacement for the conventional RDI interface under SAPscript.

> **Note:** More information on the XSF interface is available in the Internet under *http://www.sap.com/spp* (search for "BC-XSF"). Software partners can receive a certificate from SAP for products that access the XSF interface.

In its simplest format, generated XML output can be displayed directly in a Web browser. The implementation in the output functions enables you to use the same forms for both print output and Web publishing.

> **Note:** If you want to output XSF using spool processing, you have to configure at least one printer with type "XSF" in the system.

You can activate XSF output both statically and dynamically under Smart Forms:

▶ Static output utilizes the form attributes.
▶ Dynamic output uses standard parameters in the form interface, overriding any static preassignments.

> **Note:** The generated function module additionally also returns a reference to an instance of type CLIXML_DOCUMENT. You can use the iXML Library with this instance to access the XML output.

10.3.2 Transfer Methods for the XSF Output

The XML data stream consists of pure text information that can be displayed as characters in any editor or browser. You will see an example of this at the end of this chapter (see Figure 10.5).

Smart Forms can also generate formatted XML output upon request, in which two additional components, CSS and XSL, are supplied as formatting information. The formatted output shows the complete form contents, with all contents and formatting, when displayed in a browser. In Basis Release 6.10 and later, you can also use XSF to output HTML directly (see Chapter 12).

You can output XSF format in two ways:

Return to the application program
The form interface passes XML output data passed back to the main program for further processing (see exercise further below). You can use export parameter

JOB_OUTPUT_INFO in the form interface for this purpose. It has three internal tables named XSFDATA, XSLDATA and CSSDATA as components. The table consists of a single data component: a field with type STRING (variable length), where the output data is written line by line. Data components XSLDATA and CSSDATA, with the same structure, are available for formatted XML output.

Spool request

Output takes place via the spool, like other print requests. A suitable output device (device type XSF) must be configured to output the contents.

You normally save the generated XML document for later exchange with an external system; this can also be a local file for test purposes. You can use the approach with the spool request in both cases.

> **Note:** When SAP Smart Forms sends XML documents to spool processing, it uses a binary format instead of OTF to ensure that no information is lost during conversion. When you save such a spool request as text using the export functions in spool output control (transaction SP01), the export function inserts line breaks. Due to these line breaks, the exported file frequently no longer conforms to the XML conventions and, consequently, cannot be displayed in the browser. Therefore, this spool output function is not suited for exporting binary data.

The following procedure is recommended for frontend printing:

▶ Use a device type with coupling type F. When you print with this device type, output is forwarded to a printer daemon. This may be another program, depending on the operating system.

▶ Configure a printer that diverts the output into a file as the frontend printer on your local PC. Under Windows NT, for example, you have to define a printer that uses the FILE: port.

This is only one possible procedure. There are other coupling types you can use to reroute output from the spool into a file. For more information, refer to the SAP Printing Guide.

10.3.3 Statically Activating XSF Output

If you want the output of a form to always be in XSF format, you can set this format statically in the Form Builder. You can override this setting in the main program if necessary.

You specify this information in the form attributes of the **Output Options** tab page (see Figure 10.5).

Figure 10.5 Form attributes: Control of XML output

When you configure these settings, Smart Forms outputs the form in XSF format:

▶ The **XSF Output Active** attribute sets the XSF output, deactivating the usual OTF output.

▶ The output mode indicates the output medium to output the XML information (see list above). The following values are available:

  ▶ S = Spool request

  ▶ A = Application

▶ If you set S (= spool request), you are prompted to enter a suitable device type (printer).

10.3.4 Specifying XSF Dynamically via the Form Interface

Another option is to control XSF output via the form interface. Once again, various fields in the OUTPUT_OPTIONS interface parameters are responsible (see Table 10.4).

Information for XSF output in OUTPUT_OPTIONS	
xsfcmode	XSF status set by calling program
	Controls which source (form or interface) provides the XSF settings. If it is set to "X", the later interface parameters override the settings in the form. In this case, the contents of component GETOTF in CONTROL_PARAMETERS are no longer relevant.
xsf	XSF output active
	If set to anything but "X", regular output continues in OTF format. Both settings at the same time are not possible.
xsfoutmode	XSF output mode
	S = Spool, A = Application. In the latter case, you should also deactivate the spool dialog in the control structure.

Table 10.4 Information for XSF output in OUTPUT_OPTIONS

Information for XSF output in OUTPUT_OPTIONS	
xsfoutdev	Output device
	Sensible only for output mode S = Spool. If component TDDEST is set to a value in OUTPUT_OPTIONS, the entry here is ignored.
xsfformat	Formatted XSF output
	If set to "X", formatted XSF output is active; otherwise, only a derived XML file is output, without any formatting information in CSS and XSL.

Table 10.4 Information for XSF output in OUTPUT_OPTIONS (continued)

The control parameters largely correspond to the three static entries that are possible in the form. You use XSFCMODE to determine which information should be used. Only XSFFORMAT enables you to request formatted XSF output under the control of the form interface. In this case, the output consists of two additional sections with formatting information for the form. You can also display the output in a Web browser, for example; see the example below.

10.3.5 Sample Exercise: Download XSF Output

You can use this exercise to start XSF output for the flight invoice form. The output is returned to the main program, where it is then downloaded to the local PC.

When output mode A = Application is set, the generated XML data stream is sent back to the main program. Export parameter JOB_OUTPUT_INFO is available in the form interface to forward this information. It has, among other things, three internal tables named XSFDATA, XSLDATA, and CSSDATA as components.

Each table consists of a single data component: a field with type STRING (variable length), where the output data is written line by line. Three individual tables are needed because the data stream can consist of three sections, XML, XSL, and CSS, when formatted output is involved.

To reuse the data within the main program—for a download, for example—you can process the tables in a loop.

Listing 10.1 below shows the necessary statements for:

▶ The data definitions
▶ The parameter settings to control XSF output via the form interface
▶ Returning the results to the main program
▶ Downloading the results to the local PC

```
*----------------------------------------------------------------*
* Additional definitions ---- -------*
DATA: output_options      TYPE SSFCOMPOP,
      control_parameters TYPE ssfctrlop,
      job_output_info     TYPE SSFCRESCL.
* Request XSF output -------------------------------------*
output_options-xsfcmode      = 'X'. " Get XSF params from prog.
output_options-xsf           = 'X'. " XSF output active
output_options-xsfoutmode    = 'A'. " Application
* output_options-xsfformat    = 'X'. " optional: Formatting ON
control_parameters-no_dialog = 'X'. " Spool dialog OFF
* Other assignments, data retrieval, etc.
* Form output ---------------------------------------------*
CALL FUNCTION    fm_name
    EXPORTING   control_parameters   = control_parameters
                output_options       = output_options
                user_settings        = ' '
                customers            = customers
                bookings             = bookings
                connections          = connections
    IMPORTING   job_output_info      = job_output_info
    EXCEPTION   formatting_error     = 1
                internal_error       = 2
                send_error           = 3
                user_canceled        = 4.
* download XML data -------------------------------------*
DATA: l_line(1024) TYPE c,
      l_table      LIKE TABLE OF l_line,
      xsf_line     LIKE LINE OF job_output_info-xsfdata.
LOOP AT job_output_info-xsfdata INTO xsf_line.
    l_line = xsf_line-xrdistr.
    APPEND l_line TO l_table.
ENDLOOP .
CALL FUNCTION 'DOWNLOAD'
    EXPORTING
        filename = 'C:\temp\test.xml'
    TABLES
        data_tab = l_table.


*----------------------------------------------------------------*
```

Listing 10.1 Downloading XML data

The steps in detail:

1. Define the usual structure to specify the output options (type: SSFCOMPOP), as well as a structure with type SSFCRESCL to retrieve the result.

2. Enter the following control parameters for the form interface:

   ▶ Set XSFCMODE to indicate that the XSF information in the form interface, not the information in the form, will be valid.

   ▶ Parameter XSF changes the format from OTF to XSF.

   ▶ Use XSFOUTMODE to indicate that the output results will be returned to the main program.

   ▶ You can optionally set XSFFORMAT to select formatted output. If you do this, however, you have to repeat the subsequent download separately for each section of the output. To compensate for your extra effort, you will also be able to display the results in the browser.

   ▶ To suppress the spool dialog, you should set NO_DIALOG in the control structure, as suggested above.

3. Call the generic function module and pass the structures OUTPUT_OPTIONS and JOB_OUTPUT_INFO to the identically named standard parameters in the form interface.

4. To download the returned output data, table L_TABLE is initially created with a single field, L_LINE, with 1024 characters in the example. In the subsequent loop, the lines with the XML data are all transferred to this table. The variable field lengths in the output table are automatically converted to the fixed field lengths of L_TABLE. You can then use this table as an input parameter for a standardized download function—in this case, to the TEMP directory on the local hard drive, C:.

When you execute the main program for the flight invoice with these changes, another prompt for the destination file appears prior to output (Figure 10.6).

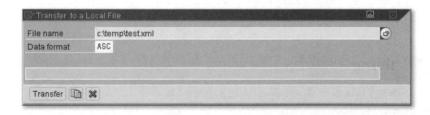

Figure 10.6 Prompt for destination file during download

Confirm the default value. Please note that the TEMP directory must exist on your hard drive. Now open the destination file in your Web browser to see the generated XML statements (Figure 10.7).

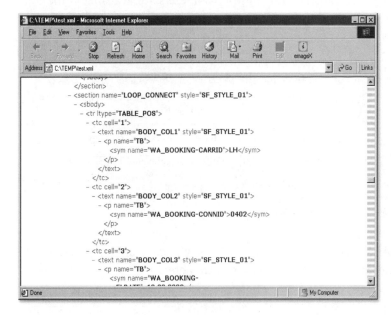

```
</section>
    - <section name="LOOP_CONNECT" style="SF_STYLE_01">
      - <sbody>
        - <tr ltype="TABLE_POS">
          - <tc cell="1">
            - <text name="BODY_COL1" style="SF_STYLE_01">
              - <p name="TB">
                  <sym name="WA_BOOKING-CARRID">LH</sym>
                </p>
              </text>
            </tc>
          - <tc cell="2">
            - <text name="BODY_COL2" style="SF_STYLE_01">
              - <p name="TB">
                  <sym name="WA_BOOKING-CONNID">0402</sym>
                </p>
              </text>
            </tc>
          - <tc cell="3">
            - <text name="BODY_COL3" style="SF_STYLE_01">
              - <p name="TB">
                  <sym name="WA_BOOKING-
```

Figure 10.7 XML output results in the browser

The browser automatically highlights keywords in the text, and generates additional indents to show the navigation tree for the text.

To see the output contents as the formatted invoice, activate parameter XSFFORMAT in the OUTPUT_OPTIONS. In this case, however, you have to repeat the download for all three components of the output. Create three individual files on your local PC with the extensions XML, XSL, and CSS, respectively.

> **Note:** The system already contains a model solution for the flight invoice for the latter case (main program: SF_XSF_DEMO).

10.4 Archiving

In many business processes, it is extremely important to archive the involved business documents, usually for legal reasons. This includes forms, which can be archived electronically. SAP ArchiveLink is the general interface for external archiving solutions. SAP does not have its own archiving solution, but a variety of certified partner products are available for this application. For more information, visit the *Partners* section at *www.sap.com*.

As far as Smart Forms is concerned, the external archiving system is treated like another logical printer. Accordingly, storage is triggered directly by the print operation. This means that the call also utilizes the generated function module for the form. Once again, several standard control parameters are available in the form interface (Table 10.6).

Parameter name	Meaning
ARCHIVE_INDEX	SAP ArchiveLink structure of a DARA line
	Index information for the print output to be archived. This information is saved in the archive along with the print output. As a result, you can access this print output in the archive directly through the index information.
ARCHIVE_INDEX_TAB	SAP Smart Forms: Table with archive indices
ARCHIVE_PARAMETERS	ImageLink structure

Table 10.5 Archiving parameters for the form interface

These parameters, as well as the document filled with data, are forwarded to SAP ArchiveLink. The contents of these interface parameters are not normally relevant for form development. Instead, these parameters are preassigned by the upstream application to form output. Therefore, you do not need to concern yourself with the details here.

Archiving information in OUTPUT_OPTIONS	
TDARMOD	This field entry determines whether to save an archive document when the spool request is output: 1 = Print only 2 = Archive only 3 = Print and archive
TDNOARCMCH	"X": User cannot change the archiving mode in the spool dialog box.

Table 10.6 Archiving information in OUTPUT_OPTIONS

There are two ways of configuring archiving for an output document:

▶ The user defines the storage mode in the spool dialog prior to output.

▶ If a form is output without the spool dialog, you have to preassign the setting in the form interface. It is controlled with component TDARMOD in the OUTPUT_OPTIONS (see Table 10.6).

The forms are linked with the application data entered in the SAP system. OTF is used as the archiving format.

11 Migrating SAPscript Forms

11.1 Overview

Up to and including Release 4.6B of the SAP system, SAPscript was the only available tool for developing forms. This tool continues to be supported, even though development has stopped, due to the large number of SAPscript forms that still exist. Smart Forms offers several decisive advantages over SAPscript:

▶ Form modification has been simplified, with both the graphical user interface and new function elements, such as templates.

▶ You do not have to learn a new scripting language just to perform certain commands. You can now use the Form Painter to draw a box around a text graphically, for example, whereas SAPscript requires a separate command to do so. Furthermore, while this box can be dynamically defined in Smart Forms, the SAPscript command can only render a static box.

▶ The interface to the main program has a clearer design, which makes it easier for you to use one main program with multiple forms.

▶ Completely new functions that SAPscript does not support, such as output via XSF, are available.

The Smart Forms installation includes basic forms for important business processes. However, if an appropriate standard form is not available, or if you have developed your own SAPscript forms, you need to know how to migrate these forms to Smart Forms.

Automatic Migration Functions

Smart Forms features an integrated migration function to help you with such situations. In order to properly appraise its potential, you have to have a basic understanding of form development under SAPscript. Therefore, if you have never had any experience working with SAPscript, a summary of the relevant features is listed for your information below.

Similarities between the systems

Despite all the differences between the two systems, there are also a variety of similarities that simplify the migration process. Here are just a few of the functions that are the same or similar:

▶ SAPscript uses the same *page* and *window* elements for the form layout, including separation into main and secondary windows. Because the attributes are identical, this information can be migrated directly to Smart Forms.

- ▶ Within the windows, SAPscript uses text elements for all output. During migration, each of these text elements is transformed into a text node under Smart Forms.

- ▶ SAPscript also uses paragraph and character formats to format texts. The contents of the formats are similar in both systems, and most of the information can be transported. Formats can also be grouped together to form styles in SAPscript forms. Unfortunately, this option was not used in many of the existing forms. However, automatic migration of the relevant formats is possible only if styles have been defined.

- ▶ A SAPscript application program provides a variety of control parameters that are equivalent or similar to the standard parameters of the form interface under Smart Forms.

As you can see, most of the similarities are concentrated in the page layout.

Differences between the systems

The primary differences involve the processing, or control, of form output. The two most important issues are:

- ▶ A text element in a SAPscript form can contain specific commands, which are interpreted when the text element is output. They affect the process flow of the output within the text element, such as logical queries and positioning and drawing boxes. A complete list of these commands appears further below. In Smart Forms, these commands are represented by node attributes or specific node types.

- ▶ The order in which the individual text elements are output is usually defined in the corresponding application program in SAPscript (this information is defined in the form in Smart Forms). To achieve this, a suitable function module—with the appropriate parameters—is called for each text element.

Overall, the interface between form and main program under SAPscript is very complex. One indication of this fact is the large number of function modules that are responsible for controlling output. As you have learned, a single, main function module performs this task under Smart Forms.

Recommended Procedure

As this brief comparison shows, the automatic conversion provided by the integrated migration function is suited primarily to copying the form layout. You will have to replicate the entire form logic, along with any necessary changes to the main program, manually. Therefore, in the present environment, migration is recommended only if you plan to implement major changes to existing SAPscript forms or want to replace them entirely with Smart Forms.

This chapter describes the ideal steps involved in a successful migration. In addition to general information, you will also work on a specific example of form migration: the QM complaint report, which consists of SAPscript form QM_COMPLAIN and main program RQQMRB01. See Section 13.5.4 for information on how to activate and output the report in QM Customizing.

> **Note:** Another important factor for the migration process is the question of how much your planned form under Smart Forms will differ from the SAPscript template. Logically, a 1:1 migration is assumed in the recommendations below.
>
> We also assume that the necessary information for the migration will largely be taken largely from the source form or main program. (The more additional documentation is involved, the easier the migration will be.)

11.2   Migrating Styles

You can define styles under SAPscript as well, to ensure uniform formatting of different texts. To this day, styles are used primarily to format texts. The SAPscript STYLE statement lets you use these styles in SAPscript forms as well. In addition, you can maintain style information individually in a SAPscript form. This represents the common practice today, and is most likely the result of legacy developments.

During automatic migration from SAPscript to Smart Forms, only the explicitly defined styles are transported, not the individual paragraph and character formats in a form. To start migration, choose menu path **Utilities · Migrate SAPscript Style in the initial screen for Smart Forms**. First enter the name that you want the style to have under Smart Forms. The usual prompt for development class and so forth appears. Don't forget to activate the new style before you use it in a form for the first time.

Because the migration function cannot help you with individual formats in a SAPscript form, you will often have to fall back on a strictly manual copy method: create a new style under Smart Forms and manually copy all the information from the existing SAPscript form in a second session. In most cases, you will start the overall migration process with this step.

The new style under Smart Forms should contain all the formatting information from the existing SAPscript form. Make sure you use the same identifiers in both source form and destination formats; after all, the text formats will be addressed directly through these identifiers when you migrate the form in the next step.

Although you have to copy the information by hand, this won't take too long, and will also give you a quick overview of the formats used in the form. In most cases, you don't have to worry about copying tab stops either. After all, this layout concept has been modeled as elements like the template node in Smart Forms, which renders most tab settings superfluous.

11.3 Migrating Forms

11.3.1 Automatic Migration Function

Two methods are available for migrating forms:

▶ Using SF_MIGRATE in reporting
You can use this program to migrate multiple SAPscript forms. The name of the original form is appended with "_SF" and proposed as the name of the new form. You can use this program only to migrate forms from the customer namespace.

▶ With menu path **Utilities · Migrate SAPscript Form** in the initial screen of Smart Forms

Because both methods use the same function module in the system, they both have the same result.

Steps Involved in Single Migration

Because we assume that single migration is the more common approach, the following information applies exclusively to this approach.

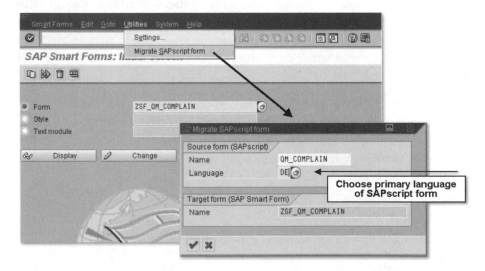

Figure 11.1 Migrating SAPscript forms

Perform the following individual steps:

▶ Enter the name of the destination form in the initial screen of Smart Forms, making sure it lies in the customer namespace.

▶ Choose menu path **Utilities · Migrate SAPscript Form**.

▶ Enter the name and language of the SAPscript source form in the dialog box (see Figure 11.1).

After the migration run, the new form is automatically displayed in change mode in the Form Builder.

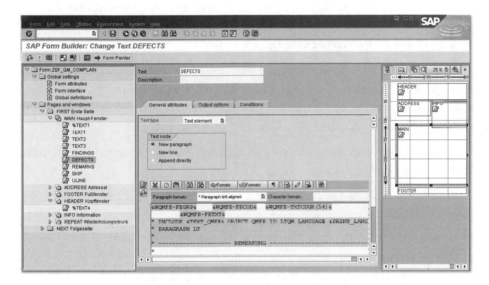

Figure 11.2 Form from SAPscript migration

When you see a screen like the one in Figure 11.2, all the automatic migration functions are already complete. The automatic migration functions include:

▶ All layout information for the draft pages and windows is copied, along with their attributes (position, and so on). The objects can be displayed in the Form Painter immediately. The main window always appears at the top of the navigation tree, followed by the secondary windows in alphabetical order.

▶ All text elements in the SAPscript form are migrated to text nodes. The contained texts have the same paragraph and character formats as in the source form. Please note that the assigned style of the form under Smart Forms must contain these formats. The text nodes appear in the corresponding window in the same order in which they were defined in the SAPscript form. This is often a long list in the main window.

► All fields (*symbols* in SAPscript notation) are output in the texts. At this point, none of the required declarations exist in the form interface or the global data. Therefore, running the form check now would result in a long list of errors.

► All SAPscript commands (such as IF...ENDIF, BOX, INCLUDE...) are formatted as comment lines in the text nodes and highlighted in gray accordingly.

The migration process creates a form without any flow logic in Smart Forms, since this logic is defined in the main program or in special SAPscript commands under SAPscript. You have to copy these contents manually. Consequently, migration with the system tool is only the first step in migrating forms from SAPscript to Smart Forms. All further steps are your responsibility as the form developer.

11.3.2 Manual Postprocessing

In most cases, you will need to open at least three SAP sessions in parallel for post-processing: one session each for the form and main program under Smart Forms, and one to display the original SAPscript form. You may also need another session with the transaction for executing the main program later on.

We recommend conducting the further activities for the automatically migrated form in the following steps:

1. Modify the form design to enable the tests in the form, i.e., define the necessary data and formats.
2. Implement the SAPscript commands in equivalent nodes under Smart Forms.
3. Modify the main program to enable output of the form.
4. Implement the form logic, especially the flows in the main window.

These steps are described in detail in the sections below.

11.3.3 Enabling the Form Tests

To enable an initial output test for the migrated form, you should first try to interpret the *fields* (*symbols* in SAPscript) contained in the form. You will find an overview table at the end of this section.

The individual steps involved are:

► Create a new style in the Style Builder in Smart Forms. This new style should contain all the formatting that was previously defined in the SAPscript form, assuming a comparable style is not available yet in Smart Forms. It is important to use the same IDs for paragraph and character formats as in the SAPscript form. Although IDs must be named identically, their contents can differ.

- Assign the new style in the form attributes of the migrated form. Under this condition, all the migrated texts immediately have the same formatting as in the original form. If you omit this step, the first check of the form will return a wide variety of error messages.

- Open a copy of the existing SAPscript main program in a separate session. This will serve as the basis for your future application in Smart Forms.

- Now define the variables used in the form. If no suitable documentation is available, you can also use the built-in checks in the Form Builder. Start an overall check in the Form Builder in Smart Forms. The system reports a series of fields that are not found. Please note that this list is not complete; more error messages will appear later on. Call up the individual nodes to determine which data structures are involved in the respective messages:

  - Replace the system fields, such as &Page& for the page number, with the equivalent fields in Smart Forms (&SFSY-PAGE& in this case).

  - In SAPscript forms, horizontal separators are usually output with the &ULINE& or &VLINE& symbol, a long character string consisting of individual underscores. This is described further below.

  - Check the other fields to see how they were declared in the SAPscript form. Declare the corresponding internal tables and field strings accordingly in the form interface in Smart Forms. You may be able to tell from the contents or the previous main program that some content is first assigned in the form. In this case, define the relevant objects in the global definitions instead of in the form interface.

  - If in doubt, simply deactivate a field (flag it as a comment line) until more information is available. To do this, use the full-page version of the line editor, which enables you to enter the special comment ID, "/*", directly as a paragraph format.

- If the overall check does not report any error messages, you can activate the form for the first time. First test only the generated function module (shortcut: press **F8** four times in sequence). This sometimes detects additional errors that would cause a termination at runtime, such as problems with field formatting options. Unfortunately, your search for the cause of the error is more difficult in this case.

- After a successful test of the function module, you will see the new form with its defined text elements for the first time in a print preview—without data, of course.

Your job from now on is **continuous optimization**: enhancing the modules in the form one step at a time.

Converting ULINE

As mentioned above, the &ULINE& symbol is used to output horizontal separator lines in SAPscript forms, which are generated with the special underscore character. Here are a few tips for dealing with this symbol:

▶ You will frequently use a different graphical function under Smart Forms. A template is one possible option: choose the same width as output by &ULINE&. The template should consist of only two lines, such as two lines with a height of "0.5 LN" each. Choose a single separator line between the lines as the pattern. You can use the line height to configure the space requirements as necessary. No additional text nodes for output are assigned to the template.

▶ If you want to continue using the same procedure for &ULINE&, define an appropriate variable in the global definitions (typed with CHAR80, for example). Assign an underscore as an appropriately long character string with ABAP in the **Initialization** tab page (for example, with ULINE = '_____'). This will even enable you to retain existing formatting options such as &ULINE(71)&. Make sure that the corresponding paragraph format, usually UL, is still configured to a fixed font; you may also have to modify the line spacing.

▶ As another alternative, you can use ABAP system field &SYST-ULINE&, which is also configured with the underscore as filler. Once again, make sure the font is fixed and the spacing is configured properly in the corresponding paragraph layout.

Converting Symbols

The correct interpretation of the symbols in the SAPscript form is crucial to the steps described above. The different symbol types are summarized in Table 11.1 below:

Symbols in SAPscript and their conversion	
General system symbols	Many system fields, such as &Page& for the page number, have equivalent fields in Smart Forms (&SFSY-PAGE& in this case). If a system symbol in SAPscript does not have a replacement in Smart Forms (&DAY&, for example), you should define a new field in Smart Forms and use ABAP in a program node to supply it with the appropriate contents. You may be able to use general system fields (see next line).
ABAP system symbols (SYST)	The system fields are also available under Smart Forms as node attributes, in program nodes, and as placeholders in text nodes. You can continue to use them as before. In this case, however, you cannot use the field list for new entries in a text node. Instead, use the field functions in the editor and enter the system fields directly, or simply copy the existing entry from SAPscript.

Table 11.1 Symbols in SAPscript and their conversions

Symbols in SAPscript and their conversion	
User address (USR03)	You may have to determine the data individually in a program node; the user name is available in SY-UNAME.
SAPscript system symbols	Some of the defined fields are available in the Smart Forms system fields, such as FORMPAGES, while others are taken from parameters in the form interface, such as the specifications for fax output.
Standard symbols	Smart Forms does not directly provide the entries in table TTDTG, but they can be read in a program node if needed.
Text symbols	Smart Forms does not use specific text symbols; instead, this function is covered completely by global variables, which you can configure with any texts.
Program symbols	These objects contain all the data that a SAPscript print program supplies to the individual form. Under Smart Forms, you should add this data as import parameters in the form interface.

Table 11.1 Symbols in SAPscript and their conversions (continued)

11.3.4 Converting SAPscript Commands

As you have seen, text elements in SAPscript can contain special commands that are modeled in node attributes or special node types in Smart Forms. You will continue the migration with this conversion. A table with a list of all SAPscript commands appears at the end of this section.

The automatic migration has created a text node in Smart Forms for every text element from SAPscript. The node contains all the information that was defined as commands or texts under SAPscript. Analyze each function unit in turn and copy the contents to the respective nodes and attributes in Smart Forms. For example, implement the INCLUDE command in a corresponding, individual text node.

> **Tip:** As you expand the form further, you may find it helpful to retain the existing text nodes—as they were originally migrated by the system—for documentation purposes. This will help you manage the transition. To accomplish this, you have to convert all the contents to new nodes in Smart Forms. Then completely deactivate the contents in the original node (with /* as paragraph format).

Based on practical experience, we recommend that you optimize the secondary windows of the form first, before you work on the actual form logic for outputting the data in the main window.

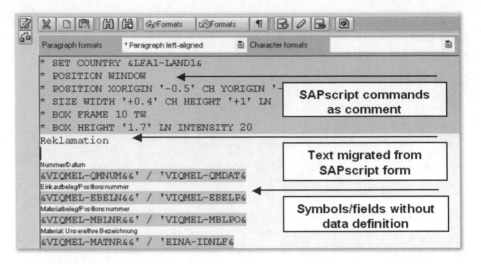

Figure 11.3 Text node after automatic migration

Figure 11.3 shows a typical text node after the automatic migration. Here are several examples of how to convert the SAPscript commands:

▶ SAPscript uses special commands to design an output area: BOX, FRAME, and so on. These lines are deactivated in the migrated text nodes, like all the other SAPscript commands. To activate these functions in Smart Forms, use the **Boxes** and **Shading** attributes, which appear in the **Output Options** tab page (including information for text spacing) of every node. The box can involve a whole window (BOX FRAME) or sections thereof. In the example in Figure 11.3, the "Complaint" heading is boxed and highlighted in gray by the second BOX command. To accomplish this in Smart Forms, you have to create a separate text node for the heading. You configure the suitable attributes for the box and shading there.

▶ Your migrated SAPscript form probably also used standard texts through INCLUDE commands. Decide whether you want to continue using these texts. If you do, you have to create a corresponding include text node for each call. You can copy the parameters directly from the deactivated INCLUDE command. Please note that the language of the text is usually defined by a variable that is passed on in the Smart Forms form interface. Of course, you can continue to use the existing variables, provided you define them in the global data. You can then pass the parameter on in the interface, if necessary.

Note: SAPscript commands and fields can also be components of a standard include text (such as &ULINE& for underscores). Some commands and fields can cause runtime errors under Smart Forms. In this case, changes to the standard text are unavoidable; simultaneous use in both systems is no longer possible.

▶ The standard texts that you specify in include text nodes are still client-specific and are not included in Smart Forms transport. You can create new Smart Forms text modules with identical contents as an alternative.

▶ If address data is output in the form (command ADRESS/ENDADRESS in SAPscript), check whether the addresses are managed in Central Address Management—that is, identified by an ID. If so, you can use the address node in Smart Forms. The address contents may also be passed on as individual fields; in this case, use an additional program node (as described in Section 8.5) to provide the correct formatting.

▶ When table information is involved, you may want to replace the previous tab-based formatting with template nodes, as in the attributes shown in Figure 11.3. In this case, you will have to divide the existing output text into individual text nodes and also assign them as inferior nodes for the individual cells in the template.

A list of all SAPscript commands and their equivalents under Smart Forms appears below:

SAPscript commands	Implementation in Smart Forms
NEW-PAGE	The manual page break is an attribute in the command node.
PROTECT	Sets page protection (*No Break*) in the attributes of a text node or in the paragraph layout.
NEW-WINDOW	Smart Forms supports only one main window. To implement functions like multiple columns, use output tables in the main window.
DEFINE	You now define variables under the global definitions.
SET DATE MASK SET TIME MASK	There is no separate date/time mask under Smart Forms; combine it individually with the surrounding text.
SET COUNTRY	You can specify the display of decimal places and date format in Smart Forms with the ABAP statement SET COUNTRY (optionally in the main program, during initialization or in a program node). If no value is specified, Smart Forms uses the country-specific formatting defined in the user master.

Table 11.2 Converting SAPscript commands

SAPscript commands	Implementation in Smart Forms
SET SIGN	Output +/– signs: Use the individual formatting options for fields with numeric information to define the position.
RESET	You use an option in the command node to reset an outline level.
INCLUDE	SAPscript texts can be integrated in a form in an include text node. This node offers the same options as the original command, which means you can transfer the parameters directly.
	In the Releases prior to 4.6C, graphics were converted to standard texts and could be integrated in a SAPscript form with an include command. These graphics cannot be used in Smart Forms. Instead, define the graphics again in the system and use the graphic node to output them.
STYLE	Changing a style is an attribute of the respective node, optionally possible through assignment to a superior node (folder, template).
ADRESS	Use the address node; in this case, only the address number is required (when managed in CAM).
TOP / ENDTOP	Header text in the main window; use the corresponding event nodes for folder, table or loop nodes.
BUTTON / ENDBUTTON	Footer texts (see above).
IF / ENDIF	Condition in node that triggers the output; alternative node optional.
CASE	Set conditions for differentiating between the nodes (possibly organized in folder nodes).
PERFORM	Execute ABAP coding in a program node; you can also define FORM routines in the global definitions that apply only to the respective form. Please note, however, that the method used to pass parameters in the SAPscript command differs from the standard procedure under ABAP.
PRINT-CONTROL	Specify as attributes of the command node.
BOX, POSITION; SIZE	Boxes and shading are available as attributes of various node types, including text nodes. Alternatively, you can use template nodes and their functions for creating patterns.
HEX / ENDHEX	You can no longer transfer hexadecimal codes directly to the printer; you must use print controls instead.
SUMMING	Use individual ABAP statements in program nodes to calculate totals.

Table 11.2 Converting SAPscript commands (continued)

11.3.5 Enabling Output with the Main Program

The most critical factor in the ongoing optimization of your migrated form is the structure of the flow logic in the main window. The text elements that were previously used in the SAPscript form were merely migrated as a succession of completely unrelated text nodes. Therefore, you will have to interpret the flow logic primarily from the SAPscript main program. To do this, however, you have to have an executable main program under Smart Forms.

Perform the following steps:

▶ In the above exercise, you created a copy of the existing SAPscript main program, which will become your future Smart Forms main program. Frequently, this program is not called on its own, but instead is called by another SAP application. First integrate your copy there. Check the output of your sample data again with the existing SAPscript form to make sure that the settings really work. Wait until then to change the entry for the form to the migrated version under Smart Forms.

▶ Search the new main program to determine which program blocks were formerly responsible for general data retrieval and which ones contained the output control routines. Even under SAPscript, most form developers observed strict separations of these areas in the source text.

▶ Deactivate the exiting program blocks for output control by setting them to comment lines. Instead, integrate the two function modules for calling the form for Smart Forms (as described in Section 9.4). This involves the following steps:

  ▶ Define all the required variables for the form name. A form name was required to output the SAPscript form as well, and is supplied by the data retrieval block. Copy the name to the new variable. When you have the form name, you can use it to derive the name of the function module for the form interface.

  ▶ Assign the parameters to the form interface that you have defined for the specific form (required parameters). In most cases, the data retrieval block fills these parameters with data. The names of the parameters are identical in the function module and program, provided you use the original data in the form as described above. These names must also be declared in the main program.

  ▶ Check the program for syntax errors and don't forget to activate it when you are done.

▶ Now output a form using the corresponding application (print preview). If you succeed, you've passed one of the most important milestones!

Even though you haven't implemented the flow logic in the main form window yet, you can now conduct tests within the application for all further modifications. This guarantees that the tests are realistic and avoids unpleasant surprises later.

11.3.6 Higher-Level Flow Logic

To implement the higher-level flow logic, you have to analyze the corresponding passages in the source text of the previous main program if no other documentation is available.

Once again, here are a few general notes for your information:

▶ The previous output block of the main program indicates the sequence in which the text elements were formerly output. You should configure the sequence of windows/nodes in the navigation tree in Smart Forms accordingly.

▶ Output in the main window normally involves a list of any number of items. Because they are kept in an internal table within the main program, a loop (with LOOP/ENDLOOP statement) has to appear in the source text there. You can also nest multiple loops, depending on the complexity of the form. Always start with the outermost loop.

▶ When you copy the flow control, you will have to add additional parameters, such as internal tables, to the form interface. Still, it makes sense to copy the complete function module into the main program (with the *Pattern* function) only if major changes are involved. Therefore, make sure you make all the changes in the form and the main program simultaneously; you will trigger runtime errors otherwise.

▶ In most cases, it makes sense to use a table node to start the main window of a form in Smart Forms. You specify the most important line layouts here, such as for item and header lines. Under SAPscript, column divisions were created with tabs; therefore, you will find the column widths in the corresponding paragraph layouts.

▶ Then start with the outermost loop of data output, which you can model in the existing table node or an inferior loop node, depending on your specific situation. Define the required work area in the global definitions. Define suitable text nodes (as inferior nodes) for the outputs you want to generate in this loop.

▶ Continue to refine the flow logic with other loop nodes, and so on.

▶ Determine the parameters that will be calculated in the form, such as grand totals and subtotals. Check whether a standard function of the loop node is available for this purpose. If not, create a suitable program node. In some cases, you can even copy the corresponding source text directly.

> **Tip:** Do not make too many changes at once during this phase. Instead, repeatedly test the output of the form through your main program. Otherwise, you may run into runtime errors that are difficult to interpret and will cost you a lot of troubleshooting time.

Example Migration

Figure 11.4 shows the migration from SAPscript to Smart Forms based on form QM_COMPLAIN from the Quality Management (QM) module. The form contents are a list of discovered material faults, which can be used to report to the vendor, for example.

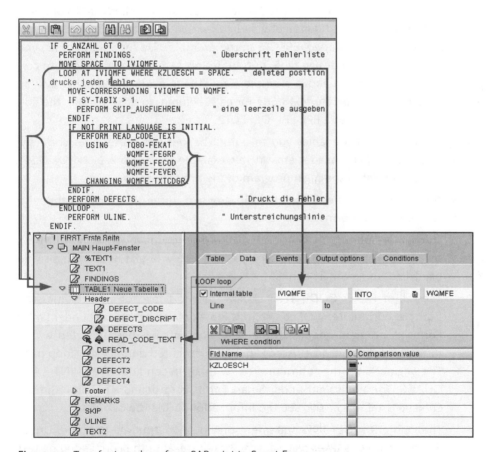

Figure 11.4 Transferring a loop from SAPscript to Smart Forms

Frequently, the contents of a LOOP statement in the main program can be copied directly into a loop node in Smart Forms, as in the above example. Additional information you can derive from the example is:

▶ Because the work area is always responsible for output, the internal table that is required in the loop was not mentioned in the form so far. Especially it is not defined in the form interface yet. Add this entry to the form and the main program. Consequently, work area WQMFE has functions only in the form. If you previously set the definition in the form interface, move the corresponding line to the global definitions (**Global Data** tab page) now.

▶ In the SAPscript main program from the above example, the work area is filled with statement MOVE-CORRESPONDING. It is equivalent to LOOP ... INTO ... and is used when the structures of the work area and internal table are not completely identical.

▶ To achieve table output of the items in the main window, tab stops were defined in the paragraph formats under SAPscript. The fields of a complete item line were defined consecutively in a text element and aligned with the tabs (shown as text node DEFECTS in the example). Under Smart Forms, you can use line types to design table output; in this case, use a table node to create the loop, as in the above example. To fill the individual cells correctly, you have to define a separate text node for each column. In the example, the columns were defined as DEFECT1, DEFECT2, ...

▶ The table node also enables you to output header and footer lines correctly. The contents of the header area in this example replace the PERFORM FINDINGS statement in the main program of the previous form.

▶ Within the loop in the SAPscript main program, three subfunctions that also exist under Smart Forms are executed:

▶ The call of subroutine SKIP_AUSFÜHREN generates a blank line from the second item onward; if necessary, you can output a text node with a single blank line under Smart Forms.

▶ The call of READ_CODE_TEXT checks the short text for an error message from the current item. Of course, this function also has to exist under Smart Forms. A program node with the same contents has been inserted within the loop for this purpose. Accordingly, it is executed during every loop pass. The original links the subroutine call with an IF condition for PRINT_LANGUAGE. The equivalent under Smart Forms is to define a condition in the *Conditions* tab page (also see the information further below).

▶ The PERFORM DEFECTS statement previously output an item line. Under Smart Forms, this takes place automatically, because the corresponding text nodes have been defined.

▶ After the loop is executed, the SAPscript main program generates the closing texts. Under Smart Forms, this takes place automatically, because the corresponding nodes have been defined.

▶ The PROTECT/ENDPROTECT function prevents page breaks between individual text elements. In Smart Forms, you can prevent page breaks by setting the corresponding parameter in the **Output Options** tab page of a text node.

Copying Program Coding

When data is changed within an output loop in SAPscript, the changes have to be modeled in Smart Forms with the suitable nodes. You created program node READ_CODE_TEXT above for this reason.

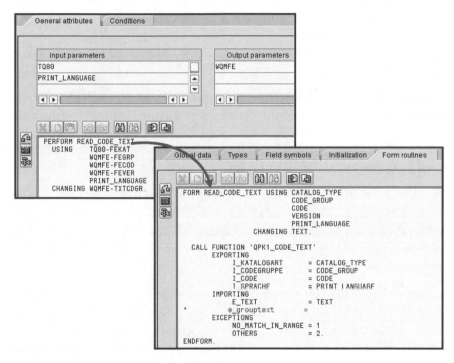

Figure 11.5 Program node and form routine

Figure 11.5 shows the contents of the program node. As in the original source text, only subroutine READ_CODE_TEXT is called. For this to work, however, this subroutine must be accessible under Smart Forms. This is why you defined it in the global definitions, under the **Form Routine** tab page.

Note another special feature: this subroutine also accesses the language indicator in PRINT_LANGUAGE. This was not a problem in the original source text, because this variable was defined globally. As a result, it was also available in subroutines, without being explicitly declared as a transfer parameter. The form routines in Smart Forms do not support global data in this sense. Therefore, you have to add the language to the subroutine call as an additional transfer parameter.

11.3.7 Standard Interface Parameters

So far, you have read about how you can migrate form contents from SAPscript to Smart Forms. You have not yet dealt with the functions for controlling the output itself. Of course, these parameters are present in both systems.

In Smart Forms, the main program has to specify additional interface parameters for this purpose. This was described in detail in Section 9.7, which divided the subject into the following areas:

▶ General output control
▶ Printer parameters
▶ Output by fax
▶ Output by e-mail

The corresponding parameters in the form interface are defined automatically when you create a new form, and can optionally be supplied with data by the main program.

Control Parameters Under SAPscript

SAPscript has a similar procedure for controlling the output. The required parameters are often supplied through a data retrieval segment, which, in turn, receives the information from output control, for example. Therefore, it makes sense to continue to use this information for the form interface in Smart Forms. This procedure is described below.

Each SAPscript form output is started with the OPEN_FORM function module. The parameters that are passed on in its interface are similar to those of the function module for the form under Smart Forms—which it is replacing, after all. Therefore, the parameters that are valid at this point can also be used for Smart Forms. Here is a typical call:

```
*&-------------------------------------------------------------&*
CALL FUNCTION 'OPEN_FORM'
     EXPORTING
*          APPLICATION          = 'TX'
           ARCHIVE_INDEX        = TOA_DARA          "TOA_DARA
           ARCHIVE_PARAMS       = ARC_PARAMS        "ARC_PARAMS
           DEVICE               = DEVICE
           DIALOG               = ' '
           FORM                 = TNAPR-FONAM
           LANGUAGE             = NAST-SPRAS
           OPTIONS              = ITCPO             "ITCPO
```

```
        MAIL_SENDER         = SENDER                "SWOTOBJID
        MAIL_RECIPIENT      = RECIPIENT             "SWOTOBJID
*       MAIL_APPL_OBJECT    = ' '                   "SWOTOBJID
*       RAW_DATA_INTERFACE  = '*'
*&- - - - - - - - - - - - - - - - - - - - - - - - - - - - - - - - - - - - - - - - - - - - - - - - - -&*
```

Listing 11.1 Listing 11.1 Opening form output under SAPscript

The names of the internal interface parameters are reminiscent of the parameters in the function module for the form under Smart Forms. The data types used to declare the components are named as comments. Some of these even have identical data types under Smart Forms. Therefore, you only have to assign the fields properly in order to continue to use the control function from the SAPscript main program.

Consider the following situations:

Parameters for General Output Control

The interface parameters CONTROL_PARAMETERS and OUTPUT_OPTIONS are responsible for preassigning output parameters, such as printer defaults. Under SAPscript, this was primarily an OPTIONS parameter, based on structure ITCPO in the ABAP Dictionary.

A list of possible assignments appears below. Because the parameters can have different names in different main programs, the names of the defined data types are used symbolically below:

```
*&- - - - - - - - - - - - - - - - - - - - - - - - - - - - - - - - - - - - - - - - - - - - - - - - -&*
*       transfer   Smart Forms  <<<  SAPscript
*       define user_settings
IF ITCPO-TDDEST <> '*' AND ITCPO-TDDEST <> ' '.
  USER_SETTINGS = ' '.
ENDIF
*- - - - - - Get CONTROL_PARAMETERS - - - - - - - - - - - - - - - - - - - - - - - - - - - - - - -*
* CONTROL_PARAMETERS-NO_OPEN    = .        " look for use of
* CONTROL_PARAMETERS-NO_CLOSE   = .        " function START_FORM
CONTROL_PARAMETERS-DEVICE      = DEVICE.
IF DIALOG = ' '.
  CONTROL_PARAMETERS-NO_DIALOG = 'X'.
ENDIF.
CONTROL_PARAMETERS-PREVIEW      = ITCPO-TDPREVIEW.
* CONTROL_PARAMETERS-PREVIEW    = US_SCREEN.      "Preview yes/no
CONTROL_PARAMETERS-GETOTF      = ITCPO-GETOTF.
```

```
*  CONTROL_PARAMETERS-LANGU     = NAST-SPRAS.
*------Get OUTPUT_OPTIONS---------------------------------------*
* MOVE-CORRESPONDING ITCPO TO OUTPUT_OPTIONS.
*------Fax options (SAPcomm)------------------------------------*
OUTPUT_OPTIONS-TDTELELAND   = ITCPO-TDTELELAND.
OUTPUT_OPTIONS-TDTELENUM    = ITCPO-TDTELENUM.
OUTPUT_OPTIONS-TDFAXUSER    = ITCPO-TDFAXUSER.
OUTPUT_OPTIONS-TDSCHEDULE   = ITCPO-TDSCHEDULE.
OUTPUT_OPTIONS-TDSENDDATE   = ITCPO-TDSENDDATE.
OUTPUT_OPTIONS-TDSENDTIME   = ITCPO-TDSENDTIME.
*------Archive options-----------------------------------------*
OUTPUT_OPTIONS-TDARMOD      = ITCPO-TDARMOD.    " Arch.Mod.
OUTPUT_OPTIONS-TDNOARMCH    = ITCPO-TDNOARMCH.  " Arch.Mod.
*------Output options------------------------------------------*
OUTPUT_OPTIONS-TDTITLE      = ITCPO-TDTITLE.
OUTPUT_OPTIONS-TDNOPREV     = ITCPO-TDNOPREV.   " No preview
OUTPUT_OPTIONS-TDNOPRINT    = ITCPO-TDNOPRINT.  " No prev.print
* OUTPUT_OPTIONS-TDNOARCH     = .
OUTPUT_OPTIONS-TDIEXIT      = ITCPO-TDIEXIT.
*------Text options--------------------------------------------*
OUTPUT_OPTIONS-TDDATASET    = ITCPO-TDDATASET.
OUTPUT_OPTIONS-TDSUFFIX1    = ITCPO-TDSUFFIX1.
OUTPUT_OPTIONS-TDSUFFIX2    = ITCPO-TDSUFFIX2.
OUTPUT_OPTIONS-TDCOVTITLE   = ITCPO-TDCOVTITLE. " title cover
*------Spool options-------------------------------------------*
OUTPUT_OPTIONS-TDDEST       = ITCPO-TDDEST.     " Output Device
OUTPUT_OPTIONS-TDPRINTER    = ITCPO-TDPRINTER.
OUTPUT_OPTIONS-TDNEWID      = ITCPO-TDNEWID.    " new spool entry
OUTPUT_OPTIONS-TDIMMED      = ITCPO-TDIMMED.    " immediately
OUTPUT_OPTIONS-TDDELETE     = ITCPO-TDDELETE.   " delete after
OUTPUT_OPTIONS-TDLIFETIME   = ITCPO-TDLIFETIME.
OUTPUT_OPTIONS-TDAUTORITY   = ITCPO-TDAUTORITY.
OUTPUT_OPTIONS-TDFINAL      = ITCPO-TDFINAL.
*------Cover options-------------------------------------------*
OUTPUT_OPTIONS-TDCOVER      = ITCPO-TDCOVER.    " cover page
OUTPUT_OPTIONS-TDRECEIVER   = ITCPO-TDRECEIVER. " report to
OUTPUT_OPTIONS-TDDIVISION   = ITCPO-TDDIVISION.
*------Page select---------------------------------------------*
OUTPUT_OPTIONS-TDCOPIES     = ITCPO-TDCOPIES.   " copies
OUTPUT_OPTIONS-TDPAGESLCT   = ITCPO-TDPAGESLCT.
```

```
*------XSF options---------------------------------------------------*
* OUTPUT_OPTIONS-XSFCMODE     = .
* OUTPUT_OPTIONS-XSF          = .
* OUTPUT_OPTIONS-XSFOUTMODE   = .
* OUTPUT_OPTIONS-XSFOUTDEV    = .
* OUTPUT_OPTIONS-XSFFORMAT    = .
*&-------------------------------------------------------------&*
```

Listing 11.2 Assignment of interface parameters to output control

If the main program did not explicitly specify an output device in SAPscript (in TDDEST), the user master record was automatically relevant. In the form interface under Smart Forms, in contrast, the USER_SETTINGS parameter—which you set in the above example—is responsible for this selection.

The lines in Listing 11.2 that do not have a direct assignment are dependent on the specific case. These values were either defined in the individual functions of the print program under SAPscript, or, like the parameters for XSF output, did not exist. Therefore, you should examine the previous program coding in detail.

> **Example:** The number of copies that were included in the same spool request was controlled by calls of function module START_FORM under SAPscript. Set the corresponding values for NO_OPEN and NO_CLOSE in the CONTROL_PARAMETERS under Smart Forms.

Because many fields in the ICPO structure have the same names as the entries in OUTPUT_OPTIONS, you could also use MOVE-CORRESPONDING for the assignment in the above example. It is more difficult to detect which parameters remain open in this case, however.

Archiving

The parameters have the same structure in both systems, and can therefore be copied directly to the form interface in Smart Forms.

```
*&-------------------------------------------------------------&*
* Transfer        Smart Forms <<< SAPscript
* ARCHIVE_PARAMETERS        = ' '.
MOVE-CORRESPONDING G_TOA_DARA_TAB   TO ARCHIVE_INDEX.
MOVE-CORRESPONDING G_ARC_PARAMS_TAB TO ARCHIVE_PARAMETERS.
*&-------------------------------------------------------------&*
```

Listing 11.3 Interface parameters for archiving

E-mail System

The parameters have the same structure in both systems, and can therefore be copied directly to the form interface in Smart Forms.

```
*&-------------------------------------------------------------&*
* Transfer       Smart Forms <<< SAPscript
* MAIL-PARAMETERS.
MOVE-CORRESPONDING SENDER    TO MAIL_SENDER.
MOVE-CORRESPONDING RECIPIENT TO MAIL_RECIPIENT.
MOVE-CORRESPONDING APPL_OBJ  TO MAIL_APPL_OBJ.
*&-------------------------------------------------------------&*
```

Listing 11.4 Interface parameters for e-mail system

12 New Features in Basis Release 6.10

12.1 Web Application Server 6.10

Smart Forms documents were introduced in Basis Release 4.6C, but development of the Smart Forms application did not end with this release. A wide range of enhancements has been implemented in the subsequent releases, Web Application Server 6.10 and 6.20. You may ask yourself: "Web Application Server 6.10— what is that? Do I have it?" Let's answer this question in detail.

What is Web Application Server 6.10?

Nowadays, the different SAP release numbers may seem completely random, or even illogical. For example, R/3 Enterprise Release 4.7 runs on Web Application Server 6.10. But there is a system behind this seeming chaos. In the past, there was only a single SAP product: the R/3 System, with release names like 3.1I, 4.0B, and 4.6C. In this context, Release 4.0B of the Basis technology runs with the 4.0B releases of FI, HR, MM, and SD, for example. In the last five years, however, SAP has expanded its product scope significantly, with new products such as the Business Information Warehouse (BW), the Advanced Planner and Optimizer (APO), Customer Relationship Management (CRM), and Strategic Enterprise Management (SEM).

Most SAP applications (R/3, BW, CRM, APO, and so on) use the same *technology stack* as their foundation. This technology stack received several major enhancements after Basis Release 4.6C, turning it into a full-fledged Web Application Server in version 6.10. Accordingly, SAP gave it a new name and an independent release number. The forms in Smart Forms are now a component of this technology stack; the applications themselves build on the same stack, using Smart Forms as a tool. The different SAP applications have their own release cycles and release numbers. As a result, CRM 3.0 runs on Web Application Server 6.10, for example, and R/3 Enterprise runs on Web AS 6.20. What does this mean for you? You only have to learn Smart Forms handling once for all these different SAP applications!

12.1.1 New Features in the Form Builder, Form Painter, and Table Painter

Undo/Redo

By default, the Form Builder stores any changes you made to the form since last saving it, independent of whether the changes occurred in the navigation tree, the Table Painter, the Form Painter, the PC editor, or input fields. You can undo these changes step by step. After undoing, you can also redo the changes.

For this function, the Form Builder must store intermediate states of the form. This happens whenever you press **Return** or call an application function. Under **Utilities · Settings** on the **General** tab, make sure the **Undo/Redo Form Changes** option is set (default setting).

Proceed as follows:

▶ To undo the last change, choose ⟲ in the application toolbar of the Form Builder. To undo previous changes, you can call this function again.

▶ To restore the form state before the last undo action, that is, to redo the last change, choose ⟳ in the application toolbar.

> **Note:** When you call one of these functions, Smart Forms collapses the nodes of the navigation tree. Otherwise, the Form Builder would have to store the exact state of the navigation tree after each action. This would result in an extensive loss of performance when working with the Form Builder.

> **Tip:** When very large form descriptions are involved, storing the intermediate states can adversely affect the runtime when working with the Form Builder. In this case, deactivate the undo/redo functions. In the Form Builder settings, deselect the option **Redo/Undo Form Changes**.

Uploading and Downloading Forms

You use this function to *download* and store an entire form or a subtree of it as an XML file on your local PC. Then you can *upload* the XML file into the same or a different form. This enables you to reuse a table output you created for one form, for example, in a different, related form.

> **Note:** You can also use the clipboard in the navigation tree to copy subtrees from one form to another.

When uploading subtrees of a form, it is your responsibility to make sure that the styles and fields of the downloaded subtree exist in the target form as well. If they don't, you have to create them yourself.

When uploading the subtrees of a Smart Form, Smart Forms writes the form data to the clipboard. This procedure deletes any data you may have stored there (with **Cut** or **Copy** in the context menu). Once again, the specific steps involved are:

- To download an entire form, choose **Utilities · Download Form**. When it saves the form in a directory you selected, Smart Forms automatically proposes the form name as the file name.
- To download a subtree of the form, double-click an inferior node of the **Pages and Windows** node in the navigation tree as root node of the form. Then choose **Utilities · Download Subtree** and save the subtree in a directory on your PC.
- To upload a file again, choose **Utilities · Upload**. Smart Forms automatically detects whether the file contains an entire form or a merely a subtree.
  - If the file contains an entire form, it overwrites the current form in the Form Builder. However, a warning message is displayed first.
  - If the file contains a subtree, Smart Forms copies the subtree into the clipboard. To paste the subtree, go to the position in the navigation tree where you want to insert the subtree, call the context menu, and choose **Paste**.
- Before uploading a subtree, you should check whether all fields and styles used in the subtree are known in the target form. If not, you have to create them.

12.1.2 New Table Output

The concept of table output in template and table nodes was revised in SAP Web Application Server 6.10. The new table node makes maintenance of output tables easier, thanks to the clearer navigation tree, since the individual table lines are explicitly displayed in the tree. In addition, the new table type automatically contains header, main, and footer areas so that you no longer need the **Events** tab page.

> **Note:** No new functions will be developed for the table type. It will be replaced completely by the new one. This means that you can no longer create nodes of the old table type, but you can still edit your old tables.

Several new functions are related to this change of the node type, and are described in brief below.

Line types
When you define line types for templates, what you now see in the Table Painter is what you get as output (without cell contents). You not only define the line types, you also specify directly how often—and in what sequence—they will be used. The context menu in the Form Painter features two new items for this task:

► Use the **Interval** menu to **Increase**, **Decrease**, or individually **Set** the interval in which you use a line type. Intervals correspond to the entries in the **From** and **To** columns of the Details settings.

► You can refer to an existing line type in the **Reference** menu.

Boxes and shading

You can now assign individual boxes and shading to each cell of an output table or template. This makes it much easier to perform tasks like outputting horizontal and vertical lines.

You can also group several cells together and draw a box around the defined group. This function is called the *Outer Frame* (in contrast to the *Inner Frame*, which you can also set for each cell). The shading function now features color selection. This means you can use differently colored backgrounds in different cells.

Calculations

When you output data in the new table node, you can not only read and output records from the internal table, but also perform calculations with this data at the same time. This permits you to calculate totals, averages, or the number of items, for example. The attributes of the automatic calculations are described in a new tab page, **Calculations**.

> **Note:** These automatic calculations are only possible only when the calculated value refers to a uniform unit or currency. To calculate values whose results refer to different units or currencies, you must include ABAP statements in the program node to perform these calculations manually.

The following steps are required to configure an automatic calculation:

1. First define an additional global field, the target field, which you will need to dIsplay the result of the operation.

2. Then choose the following items in the **Calculations** tab page, in the described order:

   ► An operation (total, average value, and so on)

   ► The field in the internal table for which the operation will be performed

   ► The events for initialization and calculation

3. Depending on whether the calculation is performed for all the records of the involved table or for the items in a sort level, output the target field either in the footer of the output table or at the beginning/end of a sort level, respectively.

12.1.3 Copies Window

You use the *copies window* to define an output area whose content you want to appear either only on the copy or only on the original. In earlier releases, you had to make extensive modifications to the main program to achieve this affect (see example in Section 9.6.4). You can now use the copies window to flag copies directly, for example.

> **Note:** You should use this window type only if you want to print copies of your form. You can set the value in the form interface or directly in the spool dialog screen (see Figure 13.29): set the number of copies accordingly.

You can determine where to print the inferior nodes of a copies window:

▶ Both on the original and on the copies (**Original and Copies**)

▶ Only on the original (**Only Original**)

▶ Only on the copies (**Only Copies**)

You can also use system field SFSY-COPYCOUNT or SFSY-COPYCOUNT0 to query whether a copy or the original is presently being output.

12.1.4 Final Window

You have surely encountered cases in which you want to query or output values in the first page of a form, but the results of the query are not known until later on in the processing flow. For example, you want to print the invoice total in the cover letter for an invoice. However, this amount is determined only after all the individual items have been listed. Likewise, how can you query the total number of pages within a condition on the first page?

The final window is the solution to these problems: all windows of this type are initially skipped during processing, until the end of the navigation tree is reached. Once this actual processing is finished, the final windows are processed in the order in which they appear in the tree, from top to bottom. As a result, all the information that is not available until the end of form processing is now available in this window type.

You can set this window type in Release 6.10 using a checkbox in the **General Attributes** tab page. You have to install a Support Package to implement this functionality in Release 4.6C or 4.6D. The window type is also chosen somewhat differently in these releases. It doesn't take many steps, however: simply create a window and set the window type using the **Window type** list box in the **General Attributes** tab page.

12.1.5 New System Fields

The new system fields are listed and described below:

Field name	Meaning
&SFSY-XSF&	Smart Forms sets this flag (SFSY-XSF = 'X') if you want to print the form in XSF or HTML format. You can set this field on the *Conditions* tab page for a node to suppress output that is intended only for these output formats, such as pushbuttons.
&SFSY-COPYCOUNT&	Queries whether the original is printed or which number the copy has. COPYCOUNT = 1: original, COPYCOUNT = 2: first copy; COPYCOUNT = 3: second copy, and so on.
&SFSY-COPYCOUNT0&	Queries whether the original is printed or which number the copy has. COPYCOUNT = 0: original, COPYCOUNT = 1: first copy; COPYCOUNT = 2: second copy, and so on.
SFSY-SUBRC	Return value that you can query in program lines nodes. This enables you to react dynamically to error situations during output. Up to now, this field can be used only for include texts and text modules: SFSY-SUBRC = 0: Text module or include text found and output SFSY-SUBRC = 4: Text module or include text not found
SFSY-USERNAME	Logon name of the user who prints the form.

12.2 Web Forms for Internet Applications

You can display the forms you use for your business process in the SAP System in the Web browser. Combined with other mySAP.com technologies, this enables you to implement Internet applications whose processes involve forms.

To improve your understanding of this subject, consider an example: instead of exchanging forms with business partners via ordinary mail, one of the partners, say a vendor, sends an e-mail to the customer that contains a link to a form. The customer clicks on the link, opening the Web browser, and logs on to the Internet application. A form with input fields now appears in the Web browser, which enables the customer to confirm the requested delivery and supply the vendor with additional information. When the customer submits the form, the input is passed to the vendor's application and evaluated there. This is an extremely efficient and time-saving way to model form-based business processes.

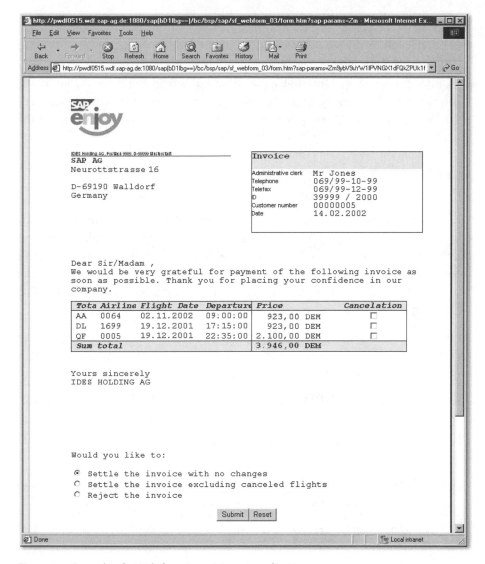

Figure 12.1 Example of a Web form in an Internet application

From the technical point of view, a Web form is an HTML form whose layout matches that of a Smart Form in the SAP System. Therefore, you define a form in the system or change an existing form, configure its Web attributes, and use the HTML output in Smart Forms as the output medium. You can embed the form in an Internet application with a BSP (Business Server Pages) application. This feature is described in detail later in this chapter.

The most important advantages for using Smart Forms as Web forms are:

▶ All the forms you currently use for printing can be used for Internet applications in the Web browser, after minimal modification.

▶ The Web form in the Internet application appears in the same layout as the printed form. Because users are familiar with the printed form—the input fields are in the same positions—they will find it easy to get around, improving the user acceptance of the Web solution.

12.2.1 HTML Output

To deploy forms as Web forms, Smart Forms transforms XSF output (see Section 10.3) to HTML. An XSLT program on the server performs this transformation by converting the XML tags of the XSF output into HTML tags. The XSLT program is executed on the server by an XSLT processor. The transformation result is called an *interactive Web form* or simply a *Web form*. Why "interactive Web form"? Simple: You can define active elements—such as text fields, radio buttons, pushbuttons with defined functions, and so on—in the form.

To format the Web form (fonts, spacing, and so on), Smart Forms uses the *Smart Styles* in the form to generate styles for a CSS style sheet. The CSS output is embedded in the HTML output.

There are several ways of integrating the HTML output into your business process. SAP recommends using a BSP application to integrate the form. BSP applications are Internet applications that can be implemented based on the Web Application Server.

> **Tip:** The jobs of form development and integration of a Web form in an Internet application (within a BSP application) are so far removed from one another that they can be performed by two different people without causing coordination problems.

12.2.2 Using a Web Form

To use a Web form—that is, to display and evaluate it—you have to integrate it in an Internet application using Web technologies. Flag the existing fields on the form as input elements or enhance the form with new input elements for Web use. Then evaluate the data entered in your Web form. This step is dependent on which Internet technologies are used.

> **Note:** In the form description, you can use the SFSY-XSF system field to hide any output that is only relevant only in the Web (for example, pushbuttons that you do not want to print). To do so, use this field in the condition Section of the output node to query whether XSF output was activated. If it was, the field is set.

12.2.3 Input Elements

Smart Forms automatically transforms the formatted contents of a form to HTML. If you want to allow input on the form, you can flag fields in text nodes as *Web input fields* by assigning an input type to selected fields of a text node. Users of the Web application can use these fields to enter values, which you can then evaluate in the SAP system.

You can flag Web input fields in text nodes on the *Web Attributes* tab page. If you specified a URL for evaluating the Web input fields, Smart Forms embeds the fields of the entire form into an HTML form when transforming it to HTML. The opening <FORM> tag then appears immediately after the <BODY> tag and the closing </FORM> tag appears immediately before the closing </BODY> tag. This implies that only one HTML form, which encloses all of the print pages, is possible for each form. For information on the values that are passed when the HTML form is transferred, see Section 12.2.4.

Simple Input Types

When you use simple input types, Smart Forms assigns the fields to HTML tag <INPUT>:

```
<input name="field name" type="(depending on input type)"
       size="field length" maxlength = "maximum length"
       value="(depending on field value)" readonly (if Display
Only is checked)>
```

> **Note:** The parameters **Field Length** and **Maximum Length** are valid only for input type **text**.

Input type	Corresponding type of the <INPUT> tag (attribute `type`)	HTML element
Checkbox	Checkbox	☐
Text	Text	[_____]

Input type	Corresponding type of the <INPUT> tag (attribute `type`)	HTML element
Submit	Submit	Submit Query
Reset	Reset	Submit Query
Hidden	Hidden	(Text field without output)

You use the **hidden** input type to pass data that you need to further evaluate the HTML form.

For example, you can supplement an invoice form that states flight bookings with a column that contains a checkbox for each line. To find out which lines the user checked, pass hidden Web fields in each table line, in which you store the key fields of the table line. When evaluating the checkboxes, this allows you to access the corresponding lines (see also: BSP application SF_WEBFORM_02).

Group Input Types

Input type	HTML element
Mapped on HTML tags	
List box	SAP ▾

```
<select name="field value of the field under Group Name">
   <option
      value="field name(1)"
      selected (if Default is marked for this field)> (field value for option)
      <option value="field name(2)"> (field value for option text)
   <option value="field name(3)"> (field value for option text)
...
   <option value="field name(N)"> (field value for option text)
</select>
```

Radiobutton	○

```
<input
   checked (if Default is marked for this field)
   name="field value of the field under Group Name"
   type="radio"
   value="field name(1)"> [text in text node]
<input name="Group Name" type="radio"
      value="Field name(2)"> [Text in text node]
...
<input name="Group Name" type="radio"
      value="field name(N)"> [Text in text node]
```

This example should also improve your understanding: define a GROUP field and assign value RADIO to it, before the text node containing the Web attributes. Then group the three fields OPTION1, OPTION2, and OPTION3 together in a list box by setting the input type **List Box** for them and entering GROUP under the group name. The user sees the field values of OPTION1, OPTION2, and OPTION3 on the Web form. If the user selects OPTION1, the browser passes the name/value pair RADIO=OPTION1. For radio buttons (input type **Radiobutton**), the browser would pass <field value of the group name>=<name of the field name for the radio button>.

Use the *Web Attributes* tab page of the text node to flag fields as ready for input. Then evaluate the entries the user makes on the form. The values of fields that have the input types **Submit**, **Reset**, and **List Box** are displayed as texts on the generated HTML page. To allow these texts to be translated, you must use text elements to define them before calling the Smart Form, and then pass them to the Smart Form in the form interface. For more information, refer to the BSP applications SF_WEBFORM_02 and SF_WEBFORM_03 as examples.

12.2.4 More Details on HTML Forms

This section provides more information on HTML formats, and is based on the fact that HTML skills are spreading. You can use your HTML skills to define custom Web forms. A variety of introductions to HTML and HTML forms are available in the Internet. The authors have found *www.w3schools.com* to be very helpful.

HTML forms usually contain a *submit button* to enable their evaluation. When a user clicks this button, the form data is sent to a target URL that you specify in the ACTION attribute. In the above example, the coding looks like this:

```
<FORM METHOD="POST" ACTION="GET_VALUES.HTM">
...
</FORM>
```

> **Note:** A URL does not necessarily have to be another HTML page. It can also be a CGI script or a Java servlet.

Smart Forms uses the POST method to pass the form data. Therefore, the name/value pairs for the input fields created by HTTP are not appended to the target URL, but instead are passed in the HTTP body. Besides, according to the HTML conventions, not all entries on the HTML form are passed as name/value pairs:

	HTML form		Name/value-pair according to HTML convention	
Input type	Field name	Value	Name	Value
Text	TEXTFIELD	Throughout SAP	TEXTFIELD	Throughout SAP
Checkbox	MYFLAG	(marked)	MYFLAG	
Reset	S_RESET	(clikked)	(no value)	(no value)
Hidden	S_HIDDEN	Throughout SAP	S_HIDDEN	Throughout SAP
Submit	S_BUTTON	OK	S_BUTTON	OK

Table 12.1 Examples of passing values with simple input elements

	HTML form		Name/value-pair according to HTML convention	
Input type	Groupname	Name of selected field	Name	Value
Radiobutton	RADIO	OPTION2	RADIO	OPTION2
List box	LIST	ENTRY1	LIST	ENTRY1

Table 12.2 Examples of passing values with complex input elements

Be sure to observe the following rules:

▶ The *Reset* button is used only to initialize input in the form; it is not passed.

▶ The fields are passed in the sequence in which they appear in the form.

▶ Several Web buttons with input type **Submit** are possible in one HTML form. Only the name and the value (corresponds to the pushbutton text) of the button that the user actually clicked are passed. For all others, neither a name nor a value is passed. Therefore, to find out which pushbutton was passed, it is sufficient to query the technical field name.

▶ If a checkbox is marked on a form, only the name of the field is passed, without any value. If a checkbox is not marked, neither name nor value are passed.

▶ For all fields of input types **Text** and **Hidden** in the HTML form, both the name and the value are passed.

▶ For complex input elements, the passed name corresponds to the group name and the value to the technical name of the selected field.

12.2.5 Calling a Web Form with a BSP Application

The architecture of the SAP Basis system received several major enhancements in Release 6.10. The application server in this architecture can act as a Web server and a Web client. The solution that is based on this new architecture is called *Web Application Server 6.10*.

BSP (Business Server Pages) applications are based on this new architecture. They allow you to develop Internet applications with server-side scripting in ABAP or JavaScript. Since BSP applications run directly on the Web Application Server, the developer can access all the resources of the R/3 application server, such as database accesses and function module calls. This makes it very easy to create an Internet application.

A discussion of BSP applications and the corresponding basics would exceed the scope of this book. For more information and instructions for building BSP applications, refer to the SAP online documentation.

Access to these resources is driven by events. A BSP application defines several standard events to trigger activities such as data selection, initialization, or input processing before or after displaying a Web page.

Note: You use the Web Application Builder (on the Web Application Server) to implement BSP applications. The Web Application Builder represents an enhancement to the familiar ABAP Workbench.

With the formatted XSF output, you can use the Web Application Server to send forms to the client via an HTTP response—that is, to display them in the Web browser:

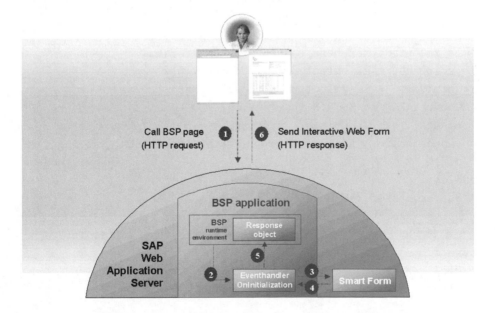

Figure 12.2 Calling a Web form with a BSP application

Examine the individual steps of the call in detail:

1. The BSP page is called by the user or by a preceding BSP page. The Web Application Server forwards the HTTP request to the *BSP runtime environment*.

2. The BSP runtime environment triggers the **Initialization** event. In the relevant event handler, **OnInitialization**, you can now select data for your form, which is usually based on the entries the user made on the previous BSP page.

3. To generate HTML with embedded CSS, specify the parameters of the Smart Forms function module and call it (see Section 12.2.4 for information on output in HTML format).

4. The function module returns HTML as a table in RAW format.

5. Of course, you can also encapsulate the last two steps in a method or in another function module.

6. To display the form in the browser, use the SET_DATA method to fill the response object provided by the BSP runtime environment. This method expects the data as XSTRING. Convert the XSF output appropriately and pass the string to the response object:

```
* Variables for formatted XSF and conversion
data: ls_xmloutput type ssfxmlout,
      lt_html_raw  type tsfixml.
data: l_xstring       type xstring,     "needed for HTTP response
      l_xlength       type i,
      l_html_xstring type xstring.
* ls_xmloutput has been returned by Smart Forms
ls_xmloutput = ls_output_data-xmloutput.
lt_html_raw  = ls_xmloutput-trfresult-content[].
* Convert RAW to XSTRING
loop at lt_html_raw into l_xstring.
   concatenate l_html_xstring l_xstring into l_html_xstring
                                                in byte mode.
endloop.
* Set header of response
response->set_header_field( name  = 'content-type'
                           value = ls_xmloutput-trfresult-
type ).
* Fill response object
l_xlength = xstrlen( l_html_xstring ).
```

```
response->set_data( data   = l_html_xstring
                    length = l_xlength ).
```
Listing 12.1 Sample coding for sending the Web form to a client

The Web Application Server sends the XSF output to the browser.

> **Note:** You can display three different forms that have not been specially
> adapted to Web use in BSP application SF_WEBFORM_01.

12.2.6 Evaluating Form Input

You can do more with Web forms than merely display them in a browser. You can
use the *Web Attributes* tab of text nodes to flag fields as input elements. Smart
Forms encloses all the input elements of a form within an HTML form. The procedure below describes how to use a BSP application to evaluate input in a Web
form.

You have already used Smart Forms to create a Web form in a BSP application. The
form contains at least one field, which is classified as the Submit button. You call
the Smart Form in event handler **OnInitialization** of your BSP page—in
FORM.HTM, for example.

To enable SAP Smart Forms to generate the target URL for the data input, within
the HTML output, you must specify this URL in the XSFACTION parameter. Before
calling the Smart Form, assign to this parameter the name of the BSP page that you
want to call as soon as the user presses the *Submit* button:

```
data: ls_output_options type ssfcompop.
ls_output_options-xsfaction = 'PAGE.HTM'.
```

> **Note:** If you do not fill the XSFACTION parameter, the browser loads the cur-
> rent page again (FORM.HTM) when the user clicks the Submit button.

Now retrieve the form input on the next page in event handler **OnInitialization**
(PAGE.HTM in this example). To do so, use method **get_form_fields** of the request
object:

```
data: http_fields type TIHTTPNVP.
call method request->get_form_fields
          changing fields = http_fields.
```

Evaluate table **http_fields** in your application. Each table line consists of the fields **Name** and **Value**—that is, a name/value pair. The input elements in the table are sorted by their appearance in the form.

> **Note:** Some HTML elements, such as the marked checkbox and clicked Submit button, are passed only if they are **active** (marked checkbox, clicked Submit button). Otherwise, they are not contained in table **http_fields**. For more information, see Section 12.2.4 or examine the BSP application SF_WEBFORM_02 as for an example in the system.

12.2.7 Maintaining Web Attributes in the Form Builder

You can maintain Web attributes directly in the Form Builder. You use the **Web Attributes** tab page of the text node to flag fields that you want to use as input elements in Web forms. The text node must have text type **Text Element** or **Text Module**.

Input Types

You can choose the following simple input types:

▶ Text input fields
▶ Hidden text input fields
▶ Checkboxes
▶ Reset and Submit buttons

The following grouping fields are available:

▶ List boxes
▶ Radio buttons

Copying Fields

To copy the field names of the fields you want to use as input elements in Web forms, either enter the field name(s) manually in the **Field Name** column or choose ⊞ to copy all the fields of the corresponding text node to the table.

> **Tip:** All the attributes of a field **abc**, which is specified here, apply to each occurrence of **abc** in the text node. If you do not want each occurrence of **abc** to have Web attributes, split the text into text nodes and output them consecutively.

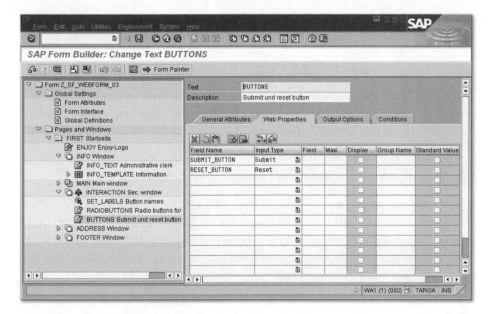

Figure 12.3 Example Web attributes of a form

12.2.8 Using Simple Input Types

The input types **Text**, **Checkbox**, **Reset**, **Hidden**, and **Submit** are simple input types. On a Web form, the user can assign a value to a field of this input type independent of other fields.

Flagging Fields

If you haven't done so already, add fields to the text element or text module that you want to use as simple input elements on a Web form. Then use a line of the table to specify the Web attributes for a field. For simple fields, the table fields **Group Name** and **Default** have no meanings. Refer to the online documentation (F1 help) for more information.

Assigning Texts to Pushbuttons

For the input types **Reset** and **Submit,** the value of a field is identical to the text of the pushbutton. This means that you must assign this text to the field before you can display the field.

> **Note:** You cannot create text elements within a form in Smart Forms. To allow texts of pushbuttons to be translated, you must create the text elements in the main program and pass the texts in the form interface.

In XSF output, Smart Forms now flags the fields you selected as input fields. In HTML output, these fields become HTML input fields.

12.2.9 Using Group Input Types

The input types **list box** and **radio button** combine two or more fields into a group. All fields with the same group name belong to a group and must have the same input type (list box or radio button).

On the Web form itself, the user can select only one option from each group. The text node must have text type **Text Element** or **Text Module**.

If you haven't done so already, add fields to the text element or text module that you want to use as simple input elements on a Web form. Copy the fields you want to group. Each field corresponds to one option in a list box or to one radio button, respectively. Then create a field in the form interface and assign a value to it. This value will be the group name of your group.

> **Tip:** You can also define the field in the global definitions. However, it is better to define it in the form interface because you can pass the group name directly to the BSP application from there.

Enter the field name from step 3 into the **Group Name** column for all fields of your group. The value of this field is used as the group name for the HTML element. This group name is valid not only within the text node, but also in the entire form. This allows you to use several text nodes for the fields of a group.

Mark one field of the group **Default**. This field will then be the default option within the group when the form is displayed.

> **Note:** If you want to use a list box or a group of radio buttons within a table, you must change the group name dynamically. For example, you can assign the index of a table line to the group name field. You can then access this information again within the BSP application.

Options Within the List Box

In a group of list box fields, the value of a field corresponds to the text of an option in the list box. This implies that you must assign this text to the field before you display the field.

In XSF output, Smart Forms flags the fields you selected as input fields. In HTML output, these fields become HTML input fields.

12.3 Web Application Server 6.20

Last, here are a few new features that have been announced for Web Application Server 6.20, even though development of the new release had not been completed when this book went to press.

12.3.1 Page Protection for Table Lines

The primary attribute of the main window is that output is automatically continued on the next page when space runs out on the current page. You can use the *Page Protection* (*No Breaks*) option to protect related information against these automatic page breaks. Previously, you could protect only individual table lines against page breaks, which prevented the table row from being interrupted when the cell contents ran over several lines. In Web Application Server 6.20 and later, you can also activate page protection for a number of table lines, by grouping all the lines you want to protect in a folder and setting page protection for that folder. Therefore, this enhancement to page protection for tables will prevent related table rows (in multiline tables, for example) from being output on different pages.

12.3.2 Uploading and Downloading Text Modules and Smart Styles

Until now, you could download only the form description to your local PC (or only a subtree thereof) as an XML file from the Form Builder, in order to upload it again later—for use in a different system, for example. You can now download and upload text modules and styles from the corresponding maintenance transactions as well.

12.3.3 Web Forms

HTML Input Type TEXTAREA

Until now, you could define the following input types in the Form Builder: text input fields, checkboxes, radio buttons, list boxes, hidden fields, and Reset and Submit buttons. Starting in Web Application Server 6.20, you can also generate an

HTML text area from a text node, to enable the input of longer texts in the Web form. To use this development in SAP Web Application Server 6.10, install the corresponding Support Package in your system (see SAPNet note number 434644).

Caching

The caching mechanism in the Web browser is now used for graphics and styles, which means they have to be loaded only once from the SAP system. This cuts loading times significantly for repeat visits.

Colored Boxes and Paragraph Numbering

Until now, it was not possible to display paragraph numbering or boxes in Web forms in color. This function is supported in Web Application Server 6.20.

URL Access to Smart Forms Objects

This is a development that does not involve the Web forms directly, but is relevant for Web applications. In Web Application Server 6.20 and later, you can use a URL to access the following Smart Forms objects in the SAP system and display them in the browser:

► Text modules
► SAPscript texts
► Graphics
► Styles
► The complete form description (corresponds to the XML format used to download from the Form Builder)

Use this URL, which contains the language, the system, and the format as parameters, to display an object in the browser. You can specify additional parameters in the URL to use automatic text replacement for fields (symbols) in text modules (SAPscript texts). These fields are replaced by the values specified in the URL before the screen is displayed.

13   Form Development Environment

13.1   Overview

During form development, you will occasionally encounter related SAP functions that do not directly involve form development, such as Customizing of output determination (sometimes also called *output determination*) and troubleshooting with the debugger in the ABAP development environment. You will find it advantageous to have some basic knowledge in these areas, in order to better develop and check your forms. This chapter provides the very information you need.

It covers the following topics:

▶ Transport and translation

▶ Text editing and storage in the SAP system

▶ Graphics administration

▶ Output determination and control

▶ Spool control (print/spool system)

▶ Development tools

These individual subjects are designed as a compendium, and are thus relatively independent of one another, like separate chapters. Therefore, you can skip around within this chapter as necessary when developing your forms. Each section contains a clear introduction for readers with no previous experience in the subject matter.

Please note that the information below is by no means complete, as this would exceed the scope of this book. Accordingly, the portrayed functions have been selected based on their relevance to form development. Nevertheless, you will also learn about some functions in great detail. But don't let this scare you off: if you have made it this far in the book, you are already familiar with all the basics of form development.

13.2   Transport and Translation

The forms and styles that are created in Smart Forms are client-independent. They are also managed as independent development objects in the Repository of the SAP system. As a result, all the functions that are provided for such development objects are available. In particular, forms, text modules and styles can be:

▶ Transported to other systems, using a transport request in the Transport Organizer

▶ Translated into other languages, using the central translation tool

13.2.1 Transport

You can include any form and any style in its entirety in a transport request. These overall objects are always assigned code R3TR as the program ID in the catalog of Repository objects (database table TADIR). The corresponding object types are:

▶ SSFO (SAP Smart Forms)
▶ SSST (SAP Smart Styles)

> **Note:** Because they are stored identically in the system, you will also find text modules and forms under object type SSFO.

When you develop a form or style and select a development class that is used for transports in the SAP system (that is, not temporary with $TMP), you are automatically prompted to enter a transport request the first time you save that form or style.

You can start the Transport Organizer to manage these requests, with SAP menu path **Tools · ABAP Workbench · Overview · Transport Organizer (transaction SE09 or SE10)**. A transport request with objects from Smart Forms will look like this in the Transport Organizer:

```
─☐ AE1K900394        ✓ USER02        Übergabe SSF an IDES per Transportauftrag

   └─☐ AE1K900395 ✓ USER02        Development/correction
      └─☐ Object list of request

         ├─☐ Comment entry: Released
         ├─☐ Program
         ├─☐ Logical information object for BDS: AEW ABAP tools
         ├─☐ Physical information object
         ├─☐ SAPscript Smart Form
         ├─☐ SAPscript Smart Style
         │
         │        ┌── ZBC470
         │        └── ZBC470_STYLS
         │
         └─☐ Table contents
```

Figure 13.1 Smart Forms and transport requests

The subordinate node, **SAPscript Smart Forms**, can contain forms and text modules. The transport request can also include other objects that are associated with form development, such as the relevant main program or graphics that are integrated in the form. They might be located in the **Program** or **Table Contents** nodes.

When you choose menu path **Request/Task · Object List · Display Object List**, the Transport Organizer displays a complete list of all the objects that are grouped together in a transport request or the corresponding task. The individual forms/ styles also appear here, with program ID and object type. If necessary, you can add to the list from here to perform tasks like transporting a finished form again.

13.2.2 Translating Texts

Forms that you create in Smart Forms are integrated in the translation process just like other development objects. Accordingly, transport object types SSFO and SSST are supported by the standard translation tools in the SAP system. When the translation of a form is involved, this primarily involves translating the contained texts. These can include:

▶ The descriptions of the individual nodes (that is, their meanings)

▶ The contents of text nodes (continuous/long texts)

Both cases are translated using the normal procedure for long texts.

To call the translation tool (transaction SE63), choose menu path **Tools · ABAP Workbench · Utilities · Translation**. The transaction initially displays a blank processing screen; the further procedure depends on which of the two above cases is involved.

Case 1: Translating the Node Descriptions

The node descriptions are considered to be short texts for logical objects. Therefore, you access them in the translation tool with menu path **Translation · Logical Objects · Logical Objects.** Then enter the following information in the input fields:

▶ The object type is SSFO for forms or SSST for styles.

▶ You can use the **F4** function key as value help for the text name, which gives you access to all forms, text modules, and styles (depending on the object type) in the system.

▶ Choose the original language of the selected form as the source language (default value).

▶ The target language indicates the languages into which the form will be translated. Please note that you can restrict the selection of target languages under the global settings in the form.

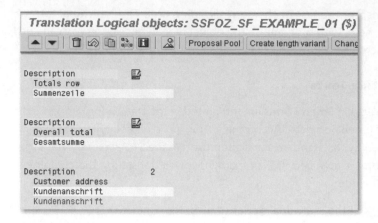

Figure 13.2 Translating node descriptions

When you click **Edit**, you will see a processing screen like the one shown in Figure 13.2.

The translation tool shows the entry in the source and target languages for each node, but only the contents in the target fields can be changed. Terms in the original language whose translation already exists in the proposal pool can optionally be translated automatically.

In general, however, you will only rarely translate node descriptions. You need to do so only if the form will subsequently be edited in the new language as well. In this case, you will also have to change the original language of the form (see Case 2).

Case 2: Translating the Contents of Text Nodes

The relevant texts for translation are those that will be output in the form. These texts are treated as long texts; therefore, choose menu path **Translation · Long Texts · SAPscript · Smart Forms** in the translation tool.

This direct access via the menu path eliminates the need for the object type query. Once again, enter the name of the form or text module (styles do not apply here), along with the source and target language. The following processing screen appears:

The translation tool has grouped the relevant nodes of the form together in a long text, where they can be processed in a long text editor. The upper half of the screen displays the individual texts in the source language, while the lower half contains the modifiable entries in the target language. You can use the options under menu path **Utilities · Default Settings** to customize several aspects of this processing screen.

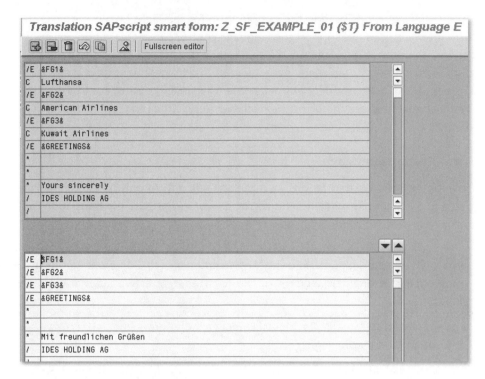

Fullscreen editor

```
/E  &FG1&
C   Lufthansa
/E  &FG2&
C   American Airlines
/E  &FG3&
C   Kuwait Airlines
/E  &GREETINGS&
*
*
*   Yours sincerely
/   IDES HOLDING AG
/
```

```
/E  &FG1&
/E  &FG2&
/E  &FG3&
/E  &GREETINGS&
*
*
*   Mit freundlichen Grüßen
/   IDES HOLDING AG
```

Figure 13.3 Translating texts in the form

You do not have to create a language-specific entry in the target language for every single text element. Text elements that do not have a separate translation in the target language are filled with the entries in the original language during output. In the above example, this was the case with the names of the airlines.

If text elements are already defined in the translation tool, they are automatically translated into the target language and inserted in the lower screen area, like the contents of GREETINGS in the example. If no proposals are available, you may find it helpful to copy the entire contents of the source language to the target language, and then overwrite the information there (menu path **Edit · Copy Source Text**). Save the translation. You can now output the form in the target language.

Tip: For a short test, log on to the SAP system again. This time, however, log on the language into which you just translated the form. Then call Z_SF_EXAMPLE_01 in reporting and enter the sample form as the parameter. The flight invoice is now output in your target language.

The logon language is used in the sample form for the flight invoice because the form interface does not support the language control parameter yet. In real applications, the output language for the text elements is specified by the main program (optionally with replacement languages). If a text element does not exist in the target language or a defined replacement language, output control uses the logon language instead. If no entry is available there, either, the form's original language is used.

Form Editing Language

Despite the previous translations, you can still edit a form only in its original language in the Smart Forms transactions. You always have to use the translation tool to maintain texts in other languages.

> **Note:** If a user calls up Smart Forms form maintenance in a different logon language than the original language of the form, there are two alternatives are possible:
>
> ► The form is displayed in its original language, as before—(that is, it is not displayed in the logon language).
>
> ► The original language of the form is changed to the logon language. Prerequisite: All the node texts of the form must already be available in the target language. An automatic check is performed for this purpose before the form is displayed; if necessary, the translation tool directly displays the remaining entries for processing as **logical objects**.

When you call a form in the Form Builder, all defined languages of the form are loaded, not just the original language. The form is not blocked for translation, however, which means both transactions can be active simultaneously in some cases. In this case, the contents of a target language in the translation transaction will be overwritten when the form is saved in the Form Builder.

13.3 Text Editing and Storage

13.3.1 Overview

One of the main activities involved in form creation under Smart Forms is the entry and formatting of texts. The correct placement of texts has already been described in detail in the context of windows, templates, and attributes of text nodes.

Smart Forms uses the *inline editor* for text entry in text nodes or text modules. This tool is also integrated in other applications of the SAP system in which users can input texts. Therefore, except for a few special functions, this is a standard application component that you should already know. Nonetheless, if you would like to learn more about the inline editor and the administration of texts in the SAP system, the most relevant information is summarized below.

You will also learn how texts are stored generally in the SAP system. This will enable you to integrate any texts in a form—even ones created outside of Smart Forms—in include text nodes.

13.3.2 Inline Editor

You use the inline editor to enter and format texts and fields. It is used both within text nodes and to create text modules.

You will now learn about the attributes of the text node based on the first node in the flight invoice form. Choose node INTRODUCTION in the FIRST page of the MAIN window.

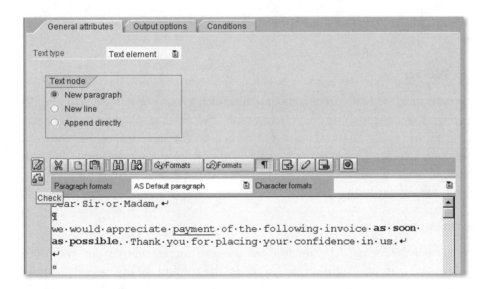

Figure 13.4 Editing text in the inline editor

The inline editor features simple word processing functions that you will be familiar with from most WYSIWYG editors. The display in the input area is largely identical to the later output—for example, with character formats like *Bold* and *Italic*, or with different font sizes.

The line breaks in the continuous text are inserted automatically, depending on the width of the superior window:

▶ A new paragraph is always characterized by a "hard" line break, which corresponds to the **Return** key. You can optionally assign a different paragraph format to the subsequent text.

▶ Press **Shift** + **Return** to create a "soft" line break. The texts share the same paragraph format in this case.

> **Note:** When you create a text within a template or output table and then assign it to a cell, the dimensions of the cell are unfortunately not used for text formatting. Somewhat annoyingly, the line breaks in the inline editor continue to be displayed according to the dimensions of the window, (although they are formatted to the cell margins correctly in the output).

You can select blocks of text with the mouse or by using the arrow keys on the keyboard, holding down **Shift** in the process. Selecting a block of text is a prerequisite for all the functions described below.

Several special editor functions are available in the application toolbar and format list.

Top Toolbar

Contains standard word processing functions such as cut, copy, paste, and find. To keep track of what is going on, you may find it helpful to display the control characters in the text (such as tabs and line breaks) on the screen; click the icon with the paragraph sign to toggle their display. Other icons serve to maintain fields in the text, and were already discussed in Section 6.2.2. Instructions for including hyperlinks appear further below.

Format List

The items in the format list, directly above the text, are selections of paragraph and character formats. The items in the list reflect the contents of the valid style in the node. You can define a uniform style for the entire form, which is defined in the form attributes. Alternatively, you can assign an individual style for each window, or you can assign an individual style directly to a text node (in the **Output Options** tab page). This entry overrides the corresponding definitions for the form.

The contents of the format list are:

▶ **Paragraph format**
When you create a new text node, Smart Forms automatically sets the default paragraph format (* = default), which is defined in the corresponding style.

Settings for the paragraph format always affect the entire paragraph in the current cursor location. Changes to the paragraph format are usually reflected immediately in the text formatting—when you change from *Left-Aligned* to *Centered*, for example, or when you change the font size or spacing.

▶ **Character format**
Before you can assign an individual character format, you have to select the text you want to format. This approach also enables you to assign multiple formats, such as *Bold* and *Italic*, to the selected text. Choose the **Display Formats** button to display a brief list of all character formats in the current cursor position.

A defined character format always overrides settings in the corresponding paragraph format. You can use the **Reset Formats** button to reset all the selected characters to the original settings in the paragraph format.

When complex character formatting is involved, you may want to change to the full-page line editor. All the defined control commands for formatting are displayed directly. You can also change them if necessary; see instructions further below.

> **Note:** In the initial versions of Smart Forms under 4.6C, the entries for the paragraph and character formats in the format line show the last selected formatting, not the formatting of the paragraph/character in the current cursor position. In this case, use the corresponding buttons in the toolbar (or install the necessary Support Package, see SAPNet note number 327636).

Left-Hand Toolbar

From here you can switch to the full-page editor, which you know as the *SAPscript editor*. You can also switch to the line editor here. This display form is especially helpful in some cases, because all control characters inserted in the text are displayed—and can be changed (see the detailed information in the next section).

The check function of the text node checks primarily whether the contained data fields are recorded with their correct names.

Inserting a Hyperlink (URL)

You can insert hyperlinks in a text—a link to your home page, for example, or to a page with additional service information. The system automatically underlines URLs in both the display and output media. Hyperlinks are especially useful in documents sent electronically (by e-mail, for example). The recipient can click the link to go directly to the information in the specified page, provided the page is accessible in the Web browser.

We suggest the following procedure for entering the URL:

▶ Enter the address directly as a text and select it.

▶ Click the icon to call the function to **insert a URL**.

▶ The selected text is automatically displayed in color and underlined.

> **Tip:** Alternatively, you can also choose the URL input mode before you enter the link. You can then press the **Reset Formats** button to return to the normal display. Therefore, you use the same method to flag hyperlinks as for other character formats.

Sample application

The hyperlink function is used in mySAP CRM in mailing lists, for example. The e-mail recipient can click the hyperlink to reach a Web page with additional information.

You can also define *tracking* for e-mail, for applications such as marketing campaigns. This function lets you track which of the e-mail recipients actually visited the specified page. To activate this function, you only have to enter two additional characters as the tracking symbol ("++" immediately following the URL) when composing your e-mail text.

When the e-mail is sent, the tracking symbol is replaced by a unique tracking ID that represents a combination of business partner and campaign. When your business partner visits the page, this ID can be read and used to greet him or her by name, for example.

To use the tracking function, the linked Web address must be able to call a suitable function module for interpreting the tracking ID (see the mySAP CRM documentation for more information).

13.3.3 SAPscript Editor (Page Layout)

You can use the toolbar on the left-hand side of the inline editor to call up the full SAPscript editor. This enables you to process the text in full-screen mode. The editor contains two modes:

▶ The text display in and operation of the *graphical PC editor* is similar to the inline editor, with the exception that the entire screen is available for input.

▶ The more "conventional" mode is the *line editor*, which is slightly less easy to use, but which provides other useful features.

You can toggle between the two modes with menu path **Goto · Change Editor** in the SAPscript editor; the **SAPscript** tab page contains the corresponding attribute **PC editor**. Please note that the configuration option for the "Form Painter" here does not affect Smart Forms. When you call the line editor, you see a screen similar to the one below:

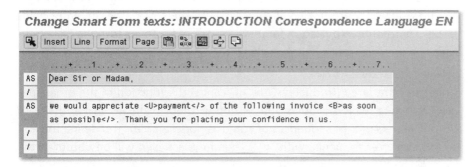

Figure 13.5 SAPscript editor in the line editor version

The text area in the line editor starts with a ruler. You can enter text in the subsequent lines.

The paragraph formats are displayed with their format keys to the left of the text lines, in a special two-character format column. Value help (F4) is available for this format column. It displays a list of the paragraph formats that are defined in the current style.

Additional, basic formats from SAPscript are also valid here. Smart Forms can process them even though you cannot assign them in the inline editor. For an overview, press **F1** in an input field in the format column. If you enter "/*" as the paragraph format, for example, the entered text is classified as a comment line. Such texts are displayed with a gray background in Smart Forms and are not output.

In the text area itself, all character formats are recognizable by the special characters that appear directly in the text. In Figure 13.5, for example, the words "as soon as possible" are marked in bold with character format <B>. The most important formatting commands are summarized below:

▶ **Character formats: <NN> ..</>**
All the characters following the character format key, <NN>, are output in the defined format. The end of the character format is indicated by </> (see "immediately" in the above example). You can also enter these format assign-

ments directly with the keyboard; when you return to the Smart Forms inline editor, the graphical screen display is updated automatically.

▶ **Tab signs: ,,**
Two standard commas in a row are converted to a tab stop in output formatting. If no tab position is defined in the paragraph format, the settings from the header information of the style apply.

▶ **Fields (symbols): &...&**
Fields are enclosed in ampersands (&) in the inline editor; unlike in the line editor, however, they are not highlighted in gray. Therefore, you can enter fields just like normal text (but don't forget the check of field names in the inline editor).

▶ **Special characters: <(·&<**
Characters that are introduced with "<(" cancel the function of the other special characters, which enables you to output them manually (if you need to output ampersands or sequences of commas, for example). You define the end of this character sequence with "<)". Therefore, a & sign will be output in the example here. You can also enter several consecutive characters of a string.

13.3.4 Text Administration

Texts are required to document objects in various places in the SAP system—for example, a material description, special conditions in a sales document, packing information in the delivery document, and so on. These explanatory texts are created within the application, using the SAPscript editor, and are stored in central database tables. The include text nodes in Smart Forms let you integrate these texts in your forms as well.

Whenever you create a new text, it is assigned a name, either entered by the user (for new standard texts, for example) or automatically by the system (within an application).

To ensure that each text is uniquely defined, despite the large number of texts in the SAP system, two other attributes in addition to the name serve to categorize the texts:

▶ **Text object**
A superior reference object must exist for each text. It indicates the global environment where the text is located. Here are just a few examples:

MATERIAL	Material master record
VBBK	Sales document header text

VBBP	Sales document item text
TEXT	SAPscript standard text

This code is determined by the object used to call the text editing function. When you create a basic material text in the transaction for material masters, for example, the system automatically creates a text with object entry MATERIAL in the background.

All texts that are created independently of a specific object are called SAPscript standard texts, which you maintain in the SAPscript initial screen, transaction SO10.

▶ Text ID

The text ID differentiates between different types of texts within a text object; this is sometimes also called the *text category*. Example for text object TEXT, the SAPscript standard texts:

ST	User-specific standard texts (custom texts)
ADRS	Address information defined as texts in organizational units such as sales organization, shipping point, and so on (text in address, header, footer, greeting)
SDTP	Terms of payment

All SAPscript texts are dependent on the client and language, which means the texts are also saved with values for these attributes.

You use transaction SE75 to maintain the **Text Object** and **Text ID** attributes. You can also display a list of text objects and text IDs in the system, with their names, by using the value help in either field directly in an include text node.

> **Note:** When editing texts in an object involved (in a sales document, for example), the objects are usually called *text types* instead of text IDs. Which text types can be used is defined by a text determination procedure in the corresponding object, (which only containsonly the text types with the code from the corresponding text object). You do not have to enter new texts each time; more often, you will create them as copies from existing documents (*text determination*). Access sequences control the automatic assignment of these text contents, and check the involved master record for possible contents (to perform tasks like copying texts from the material master record to a sales document, for example).

Document Texts in Smart Forms

When you edit a text in an application transaction, such as in the material master record, you normally use a short text editor such as the inline editor. To find out the name and attributes used to store this text in the system, proceed as follows:

▶ You can always switch to the SAPscript editor (full-page mode) from any entry screen.

▶ From there, switch to the line editor and choose menu item **Goto · Header.**

▶ An overview of the classification attributes for the text is displayed.

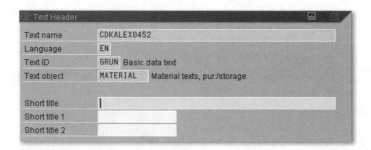

Figure 13.6 Attributes in the text header

Figure 13.6 shows the information for a basic data text in the material master. The material number was used as the text name. Specify this number, along with the text object, text ID, and language, to use this text in an include text node of a form in Smart Forms. Please note that the above diagram omits information that is not directly relevant, such as *Created by* and *Created on*.

Item Texts with Concatenated Names

The above example, with the basic text in the material master, involves text administration. This represents a comparatively simple case, because the text name is derived directly from the corresponding material (as object).

Of course, there are also more complex cases in which several parameters are responsible for forming the name, such as texts for document items. These parameters are concatenated to form the text name when you create a new text.

Object	Description	Elements in text name			
MATERIAL	Material master: Basic data text	MatNo(18)			
MATERIAL	Sales text	MatNo(18)	S.Org(4)	DChan(2)	

Table 13.1 Storage of texts in the system

Object	Description	Elements in text name			
	Vendor master:				
KNA1	Central texts	CstNo(10)			
KNA1	Sales texts	CstNo(10)	S.Org(4)	DChan(2)	Divis(2)
	Delivery document:				
VBBK	Header texts	DocNo(10)			
VBBP	Item texts	DocNo(10)	ItmNo(6)		
	Purchase order:				
EKPO	Item text	DocNo(10)	ItmNo(5)		

Table 13.1 Storage of texts in the system (continued)

Table 13.1 shows several examples. The number of characters that the respective elements contribute to the text name appears in parentheses.

Modeling the Concatenated Text Names

If you want to address a concatenated text name in Smart Forms, you have to model the text name equivalently in the form. Specifically, the variable that represents the text name in the include text node must be made up of the same elements. A similar example was described in Section 5.1.4 (see also Figure 5.5).

You have to use a previous program node to determine the variable contents. Here is an example of the procedure for a delivery item text:

```
*&----------------------------------------------------------------&*
* Get name of item text in delivery
CLEAR TEXT_NAME.
TEXT_NAME(10)   = GS_IT_GEN-DELIV_NUMB.      "Number of delivery
TEXT_NAME+10(6) = GS_IT_GEN-ITM_NUMBER.      "Item number
* Alternative using WRITE
* TEXT_NAME = GS_IT_GEN-DELIV_NUMB.
* WRITE GS_IT_GEN-ITM_NUMBER TO TEXT_NAME+10(6).
*&----------------------------------------------------------------&*
```

Listing 13.1 Determining the name of an item text

The input value for the program node is a field string that is supplied by the form interface, GS_IT_GEN, with general information on the position. It contains DELIV_NUMB as the delivery number and ITM_NUMBER as the number of the current item. The output parameter is the text variable, TEXT_NAME, which contains the text name when the form is output:

- The variable is reset in the first step. The delivery note number is then copied to TEXT_NAME with ten places, filled with leading zeros if necessary. The last line appends the text variable with the six-place item number. The offset "10" ensures that the item number is appended to the end of the field.
- An alternative approach that returns the same result is also listed in the source text above.
- Therefore, the text name from the program node has 16 characters. This corresponds to the formatting defined in the position text. Accordingly, the text is found when the form is output in the SAP system, and it can be used in the output document.

Database Tables in Text Storage

Texts in the SAP system are saved in the following centralized tables in the database:

STXH	Header information for the texts (SAPscript and external formats)
STXL	SAPscript text lines (compressed ITF format)
STXB	Text contents from external formats

The lines in STXL are not saved as they appear in the SAPscript editor, however, but instead are saved in larger blocks with binary format (field CLUSTD). When long texts are involved, the system creates several consecutively numbered blocks if necessary.

Because the text contents are encoded, you have to use suitable function modules to read and write them. Of course, such function modules are called automatically in include text nodes.

A function module is also available to search for texts with specific attributes (SELECT_TEXT). This selection can be helpful in a program node to see which texts already exist for the specified criteria, for example.

ITF text format

Texts that you create in the SAPscript editor are edited and saved in ITF (Interchange Text Format).

The ITF format is a human-readable format, which means it consists of only characters above the blank (by ASCII code) in the character set. It consists of two parts: the format field and the actual line contents. Certain elements of the format are fixed, such as paragraph format "/" for a new line or "/:" to flag the line contents as a control command. You define the other elements, such as the names of paragraph or character formats, during form/style maintenance.

When you output a form, the composer is responsible for converting the ITF text into a format that represents the print representation. This format is called *OTF (Output Text Format)* and contains all the information for line and page breaks.

External formats

The current SAP release also lets you edit texts on your frontend PC using an external word processing system, such as Microsoft Word. The SAP system assumes control of the local program in this case. The texts you create are also saved in the SAP database, but in the format of the respective text program (DOC, RTF, and so on). These documents are stored separately, in database table STXB.

The classification by text object and text ID is also used for such external formats. When you open a text for editing, SAPscript automatically starts the corresponding application program on your local PC.

Texts in external formats cannot be used in forms under Smart Forms. Although you can technically include them in a form (with include, like SAPscript texts), the output will consist of useless control characters, because the text contents are not interpreted correctly.

Form Texts in Smart Forms

Texts in forms and text modules for Smart Forms are independent of clients, in contrast to other SAPscript texts. They are saved by line in a separate database table, STXFTXT, with the node and form names as main attributes. These texts can be called only in the Smart Forms transactions.

13.4 Graphics Administration

In Basis Release 4.6C and later, graphics, such as company logos and images of materials, are managed in the SAP system using the *BDS (Business Document Service)*. This approach enables language- and client-independent storage.

Much like SAPscript texts, the storage structure is again characterized by the **object** and **ID attributes**. Please note, however, that the standard SAP system supports only GRAPHIC as object identifier and BMAP (bitmap graphics) as ID. You can create other, customer-specific attributes if necessary (see the information at the end of this section).

> **Background:** The individual graphics' administration information of the individual graphics is saved in database table STXBITMAPS, along with all the assigned classification attributes. The unique document ID used to access the document service is saved here.

Because the SAP system does not have a separate transaction for creating bitmap graphics, you have to import them from your local PC. Current supported formats include TIF (6.0) and BMP (without compression). Both formats are converted to an internal SAP bitmap format during import.

To call the graphics administration function (SE78) call SAP menu path **Tools · Form Printout · Administration · Graphic**.

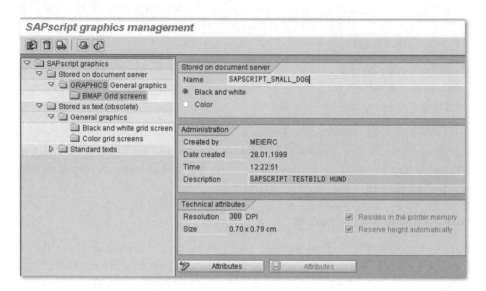

Figure 13.7 Graphic administration with screen information

In addition to the graphics for the BDS, the navigation tree shows the administration information for graphics that were saved as text in earlier releases. You can no longer include these graphics in a Smart Forms form (that is, not in an include text node).

Therefore, choose node **Store on Document Server** and the attributes GRAPHIC and BMAP. To help you find the available graphics, the same value help (with F4) is available in the name field as in the graphic node of the form. You can choose between two views, menu or toolbar, for the selected entry:

▶ **Graphic · Screen Information**
Corresponds to the display in the above diagram; you can change individual attributes of the graphic, such as the name, here.

▶ **Graphic · Print Preview**
Displays the contents of the graphic in their original size for inspection.

The screen information also contains several important technical attributes:

▶ The resolution and size are attributes of the original graphic. The system determines these values automatically when you import the graphic; they can no longer be changed. When you change the resolution in the graphics node of a form, this also changes the output size of the graphic; the system calculates this size automatically from the original size.

▶ The **Resident in Printer Memory** attribute controls the use of the internal printer buffer. We recommend setting this attribute for graphics that are repeated on every page of a form, such as your company logo. This considerably reduces the size of the print files created by the system, along with the print time required.

> **Note:** Please note that tThe printer memory is also limited. If you try to keep too many graphics resident in the printer memory, these graphics may be lost completely during printout.

▶ If you set the **Automatically Reserve Height** attribute, the graphic is taken into account when calculating page breaks in the form. In this case, the actual height of the graphic is reserved for the page break, which means the subsequent text begins below the graphic. Graphics can also trigger a page break in this case.

Importing a New Graphic

This function imports the graphic and stores it on the Business Document Server (BDS). You can now display it in a form. To create a new graphic, choose menu path **Graphic · Import**.

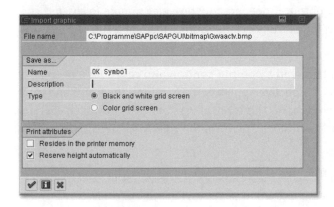

Figure 13.8 Importing a graphic

Select a path and file name on your local PC, as shown in Figure 13.8. Choose a unique name to save the object in the SAP system. If you choose an existing name, the existing object in the system is overwritten—intentionally or unintentionally.

Choose between black-and-white bitmap and color bitmap for the graphic type. If you want the graphic to be displayable in both **color** and **black-and-white** (depending on the selection in the form), you have to import the graphic once for each attribute, under the same name each time. The color information is interpreted during the import operation.

Transport

Use menu path **Graphic · Transport** to add a graphic directly to an SAP transport request (together with a new form, for example).

Classification of Graphics

In a standard installation, all bitmap graphics are classified with GRAPHIC as the object identifier and BMAP as ID.

If you require more complex graphics administration, you can create additional customer-specific values for these attributes. To do so, call transaction SE75 with SAP menu path **Tools · Form Printout · Administration · Settings**. Then choose the control tables for graphics objects and IDs. The new codes for object and ID must lie within the customer namespace (starting with Y or Z).

13.5 Output Determination and Control

13.5.1 Overview

Forms that you create in Smart Forms can be used in every application in the SAP system where form-based output is needed. SAP provides sample forms and corresponding main programs for a variety of applications, including HR, FI, SD, CRM, and EBP.

The output of the form is triggered by output control (also called *message control* in some applications) in the respective application. Therefore, the forms and main programs have to be declared there. This is not always the case, however, even for SAP's own sample forms. Accordingly, perform the following steps to activate a form in your system:

▶ Create a working copy from the sample.
▶ Revise the form (and main program, if necessary) in Smart Forms.
▶ Integrate the new form in output control.

Unfortunately, output control is structured differently in different applications. As a result, there is no single procedure for integrating forms. Keep this in mind when you read the model examples listed below. For information on integrating the SAP forms, see the corresponding SAPNet notes in the Appendix.

> **Note:** The names of existing SAPscript forms can have a maximum of 16 characters. The Customizing fields used to assign a form to a specific application are usually based on this length. Therefore, even though form names can be up to 30 characters long in Smart Forms, it might make sense to limit the names to 16 characters in your situation.

Depending on which output control method is used, you may have to perform another step: if no suitable main program is available, or if an existing main program has to be changed, you have to know how the respective output control forwards the involved information to the main program. This includes the object for the printout (with a document number, for example), the defined output device with the requested control parameters, and so on.

This information must be accessible for the main program to read the corresponding data from the database tables and supply it in the form. An example below illustrates this process from the output control side.

But first, start by integrating the forms.

13.5.2 Output Determination by Condition Technique

A number of applications in the Logistics area use the *condition technique* as the basis for output determination. This procedure has already proven its usefulness in many applications of the SAP system, such as pricing in SD or MM, text determination, and assessments in CO.

For example, message determination by condition technique is used in Materials Management (procurement) and in Sales and Distribution, where a wide variety of forms are output (delivery documents, billing documents, and so on).

When you create a document, output determination automatically finds proposals for the messages to be output in that document. This could involve a printout, for example, sending a fax form, or sending an e-mail to a customer or a co-worker in a different department. The condition technique for output determination enables you to output such individual texts automatically.

The most important components involved here are:

- ▶ Each document is automatically assigned a *output determination procedure*, which contains all the output types that can be output in that document.

- ▶ Each *output type* contains information about the form and main program used, as well as information regarding when and how to output a message (immediately upon saving, for example, or send at night).

- ▶ *Condition records* can be defined for each output type; they can contain a suitable output device, for example (fax, printer, and so on). These condition records are dependent on various attributes. For example, the shipping point is a logical attribute for a delivery, so the delivery note can be printed directly at the appropriate packing location.

- ▶ You can also define several condition records for each output type (if you want to use an alternative procedure for individual customers, for example). In this case, an *access sequence* ensures that only the highest-priority condition record is used. The access sequence is assigned directly to the output type.

This brief information is all you need to understand the basic process of the condition technique. If you want to learn more, please refer to the corresponding documentation, such as the SAP Library.

The next example shows how you can integrate a new form in output determination with the condition technique. Return to the delivery document. The two following steps are required, at a minimum:

- ▶ Maintain a output type with the form information.

- ▶ Include the output type in the appropriate output determination procedure, if it is not there already.

You configure these settings in Customizing. Other settings, such as condition records with suitable output devices, are required if you want the generated messages to be output automatically later on. Please note, however, that you should always output the delivery note manually here, for at least as long as the form is still under development.

Calling Customizing for Output Determination

You will now configure output determination by condition technique in Customizing for the respective application. For SD, for example, choose the following **IMG** activity: **Sales and Distribution · Basic Functions · Output Determination**.

You can also use transaction NACE, where the output determination settings for all applications are consolidated. The information in the following is based on transaction NACE, which does not have its own menu path in Customizing.

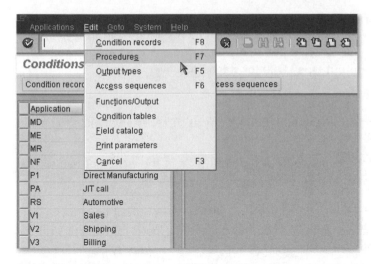

Figure 13.9 Customizing output determination with the condition technique

When you start transaction NACE, a list of all represented applications appears, as in Figure 13.9. From this initial screen, you can access all the individual processing screens for output determination from the **Edit** menu. First select the relevant application. For the delivery document, this is V2 = Shipping.

Step 1: Maintain the Output Type

When you open the processing screen for the output type from the menu in Figure 13.9, a list of all defined output types appears, as shown in Figure 13.10.

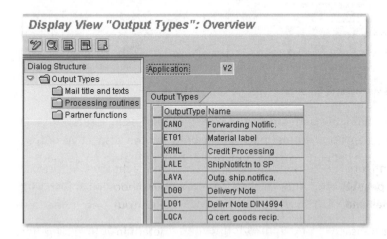

Figure 13.10 Output types

Copying output types

Assume that you want to use a new output type for the new form. Create it as a copy of an existing output type, preferably the same one used for output before. In this case, this is output type LD00 for standard delivery notes.

Proceed as follows:

▶ Create the copy with menu path **Edit · Copy as.** If necessary, switch to change mode first.

▶ Assign a code for the new output type (must lie in the customer namespace, starting with Y or Z) and enter an expressive name.

▶ Press **Return** to confirm your entries.

▶ You are prompted to choose whether or not to copy inferior table entries. Choose **Copy All**.

▶ Save the new output type. The system prompts you to enter a transport request; you can create a new one if necessary.

Assign the form

Now choose **Processing Routines** for the new output type, within the dialog structure on the left-hand side.

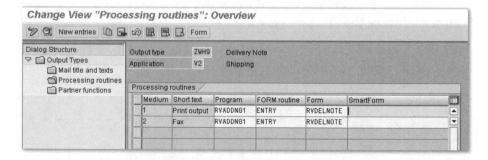

Figure 13.11 Processing routines for output type

The work area in the right-hand part of the screen appears as in Figure 13.11. It shows all the programs and forms that can be used for the respective output medium. If electronic data interchange is involved, no form has to be defined.

To configure print output to forms in Smart Forms, you have to change the entry in the corresponding line:

▶ The **Form** column contains references to previous SAPscript forms. This is followed by a column for the form in Smart Forms. Therefore, delete the entry in the **Form** column of the line with the **print output** and create a new entry in the **SmartForm** column. Use the value help (**F4**) function to avoid typographical errors. The standard form for deliveries under Smart Forms is called LE_SHP_DELNOTE.

▶ The **Program** column still contains the name of the main program for processing the SAPscript form; change this entry as well. The standard program for outputting the delivery note in Smart Forms is RLE_DELNOTE.

▶ Usually, the main program cannot be called directly; a corresponding subroutine is called instead. The associated interface is also used to exchange program parameters (see Section 9.2.2 for a description of this aspect from the perspective of the main program). The existing entry for this FORM routine, ENTRY, is also used by main program RLE_DELNOTE, and can therefore be left alone.

> **Tip:** It is sometimes difficult to find the right form and/or main program for an application. A complete list of all the standard forms provided by SAP is available (see the corresponding nodes in SAPNet and in the Appendix).

Output event

You should now check an additional attribute of the new output type:

▶ Double-click on the main entry, **Output Types**, in the dialog structure. This returns you to the main overview of output types.

▶ Double-click on your new output type to go to the corresponding detail screen.

▶ Choose the **Default Values** tab page and choose **Dispatch by Application Transaction** as the Send time. If you do not set this value, you will not be able to trigger output yourself when processing a delivery document.

> **Background:** The value for the **Send time** defines when a message for a given output type should be output: this can be immediately, when a document is saved, when triggered by the user, or automatically through a background process.

Save your entries and assign a transport request, if necessary. The overview of all the output types appears again. Press **F3** to return to the overview of all applications.

> **Tip:** The information in **Processing Routines** is saved in database table TNAPR. You can check the entries in this table (with transaction SE16, for example) to determine which applications already use a form or main program

Step 2: Integration in the Output Determination Procedure

A output determination procedure contains all the output types that can be selected in a document. Only one output determination procedure can be assigned to a given document. The system determines this procedure automatically, based on a defined sequence that is not described here.

> **Tip:** If you aren't sure which procedure is relevant for your settings, open a sample document in your application to test the output. The general information for the document frequently indicates which output determination procedure is used. For the delivery document, however, you can only find this entry only in the analysis of output determination.

In the next step, you will include the defined output type in the suitable output determination procedure. Perform the following steps to open this output determination procedure in Customizing for transaction NACE:

▶ Make sure that application V2 is still selected.

▶ Choose menu path **Edit · Procedures.**

▶ A list appears with all the output determination procedures used in the application. Choose "V10000" for the delivery document.

▶ Double-click on the **Control** entry in the dialog structure on the left. A processing screen like that in Figure 13.12 appears.

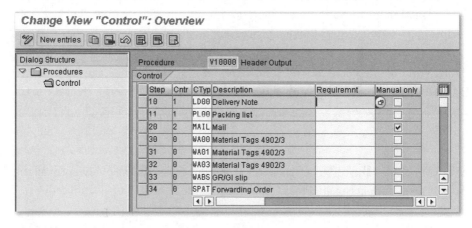

Figure 13.12 Output types in the output determination procedure

You will now see all the output types contained in the output determination procedure. However, this doesn't mean that all these messages will be output in a delivery. Other parameters, such as the execution conditions and the contents of the condition records, determine this. These parameters are not immediately relevant for your task of integrating the new output type, however.

Examine the existing numbering of the current output types. Be sure not to use any of the existing numbers for your new entry. Instead, choose a sufficiently large number, to ensure that your new entry will appear at the bottom of the list. Perform the following steps:

▶ Click the **New Entries** button to create a blank input line.

▶ Choose a new number and the new output type.

▶ Confirm your entries.

▶ Save your entries; if necessary, assign the transport request from the previous step.

The overview of all the output determination procedures appears again. Press **F3** to return to the overview of all applications.

Assigning Outputs in the Document

You have now configured the output determination in Customizing. As a result, a output type can now be found automatically (or assigned manually) for output as a specific message. Manual assignment is enough for your test purposes here; the procedure is described below. Once you define this assignment, you will be able to output the message for the first time.

Every application that uses output determination by condition technique has a unique path for maintaining the messages in a given document, in its respective editing transaction. Unfortunately, there is no uniform menu path that leads to this transaction. It is usually implemented in the **Goto** or **Extras** menu.

In this example of output determination, the editing transaction for the delivery document is VL02N, which is available in the SAP menu under **Sales and Distribution** and **Logistics Execution**. Choose any delivery as an example and press **Return**.

In the next processing screen that appears, choose menu path **Extras · Delivery Output · Header** to display the processing screen for messages as shown in Figure 13.13.

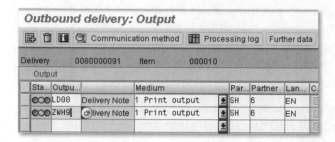

Figure 13.13 Output of the delivery document

You will see a list of all messages that have been created for the document. The traffic signal in the *Status* column indicates whether the messages are still pending for output or have already been processed:

Red	Error sending to spool; output cancelled. These messages usually also cause an entry in the message error log.
Yellow	Not sent to the spool yet; ready for output request.
Green	Sent to the spool successfully.

Therefore, you can start an output request only for messages that have a yellow light (see next section).

Adding Output

The output type you created does not appear in the list yet, because automatic assignment (*determination*) occurs only when a new delivery document is created. You can add such an output yourself, however: select the first blank line in the list and press **F4** to call the value help for the output type field. All the output types that appear now are contained in the current output determination procedure. Therefore, your new output type should also appear, unless a different output determination procedure is used (see above).

Copy the new output type to the input field and confirm your entry. The other fields are filled with default values automatically. The new entry is now set to yellow, which means it is ready for output.

Press the **Communication method** button to specify the output device. You can also save the new output settings directly; in this case, the system prompts you to enter an output device. Press **F3** to exit the processing screen for the delivery.

Triggering Output

You cannot start output directly from a processing screen for the delivery document. This ensures that all entries have been saved in the database first, since the form data is read there as well.

Instead, start the output in the initial screen for the delivery document (VL02N) with menu path **Delivery · Output Delivery.** A list of all the outputs set to yellow appears. Select your new output and press the **Print Preview** icon. The system may prompt you to enter an output device, but you will finally see your output form. From this window, you can forward the output to the spool for actual printout.

Note: You can preview an output as often as you want like without changing its status. When you actually output the document, however, the status of the output changes to red or green, depending on whether your attempt failed or succeeded. You cannot output that message again. If necessary, start the output processing screen again and enter the output type again, (or use the **Repeat** button to duplicate the existing entry).

Process Flow for Output Processing

You have now created a output type, created a suitable output in the delivery, and output this message. You will now learn how these processes are controlled in the SAP system. If you plan to include your own program in output processing, you will find this information especially relevant.

All the messages created for the document are saved uniformly, along with the current settings (such as printer, partners, and so on) in database table NAST (output status record). It is the central starting point for further processing; the main program for the delivery also receives its information from here.

When you create a new output, the send time in field NAST-VSZTP is taken from the output type. It determines when the system should execute this specific message (when saving the document, at a certain time, etc.). In production systems, NAST is usually evaluated by a report, such as RSNAST00, that selects all the messages pending for output and passes them on to the spool system (for example), using the corresponding output routines (program and form). You chose **Application-Specific Transaction** as the output time for the new output type. Therefore, the report ignores the outputs created for it, which means you have to trigger output manually.

The system can detect the output type from the entry in NAST and can therefore determine the corresponding processing routine from database table TNAPR. The current entries from both tables are also available to the main program for form output as global parameters. As a result, the program knows both the appropriate output parameters, such as the printer name, and the relevant form.

In return, the program reports whether the output attempt succeeded or failed; the interface parameter for the delivery document is RETURN_CODE. Its contents are updated in NAST, where they appear as the traffic light in the delivery document. The corresponding table field is NAST-VSTAT (i.e. 1 = processed); the processing date is contained in NAST-DATVR where applicable.

Any error messages that occur are also recorded and updated in two database tables: CMFK for header information and CMFP with the individual outputs as items. All outputs for a single output are identified through an internal log number in field CMFPNR.

> **Note:** Error messages are only created only for true output, (such as a printout.); Messages from the print preview are not saved in the database tables, and therefore cannot be evaluated in the manner described above.

You can display the contents of the error tables in the error log for the output.

13.5.3 Integrating Financials Forms

The output determination by the condition technique described above is already used in many of the Logistics modules. Different procedures have been defined in many other areas. To illustrate this, examine a new dunning form.

Integrating the main program
Standard form F150_DUNN_SF is provided in Smart Forms for the dunning letter. Create a copy of it for this example. In contrast to what you have seen previously, the main program that supplies this form with data is a function module itself, which is named FI_PRINT_DUNNING_NOTICE_SMARTF. Once again, the integration of this function module with the application is defined in Customizing:

▶ Choose **Financials · Basic Settings** and then the transaction for maintaining *business transaction events*. A blank processing screen appears.

▶ From there, choose menu path **Settings · PS Modules · Of SAP Appl** to display a list of business transaction events.

▶ Find the line with **Event 1720** and **Appl. FI-FI** and replace the existing SAPscript entry with the new function module for Smart Forms.

▶ Save the settings.

Integrating the form

Of course, the function module now has to know which form to use:

▶ Once again, you configure this setting in Customizing, this time in the **IMG: Financials · Accounts Receivable/Payable · Business Transactions · Dunning · Print**. Now choose **Assign Dunning Forms**.

▶ Select the requested procedure (such as **reminder, 14 days**) and then choose activity **Forms for regular legal proceedings** in the navigation tree on the left. The system prompts you to enter a company code.

▶ Enter the name of the form you created in Smart Forms in the *Form* field. Please note, however, that only SAPscript forms are displayed in the defined value help form. Because the internal check routine is also still configured for SAPscript forms, you will see a warning message (which you can ignore) when you save your settings.

13.5.4 Integrating QM Forms

In Chapter 10, you examined the complaint report from Quality Management as an example of the individual migration of forms. This form is used to document QM notifications. The complaint report belongs to the *shop floor papers* of the QM notifications.

In this section, you will learn how to retrieve the complaint report in the SAP system and configure it in Customizing. The original name of the form in SAPscript is QM_COMPLAIN; the main program is RQQMRB01. This combination has number 5999 in the shop floor papers in output processing.

Customizing

The output settings for the report are located in **IMG Customizing: Quality Management · Quality Notification · Output Processing · Print Control · ... Define Forms**.

To simplify things, assume that the call will continue to use shop floor paper 5999. Therefore, you will only replace the existing SAPscript form with the new version under Smart Forms. (Of course, during the development phase, you should start with copies of the original call.)

To integrate the new form under Smart Forms, choose the menu path named above.

▶ A dialog box appears. You can define (create or change) a shop floor paper here or assign a new shop floor paper to a notification type. Choose **Define Shop Floor Papers**.

- Answer the next prompt with "N" (= notifications).

- Double-click on shop floor paper 5999 (complaint report) to display its details.

- Change the entry for the output program to the new main program under Smart Forms. Because this program was migrated from the previous entry, the notation PRINT_PAPER must remain as a FORM routine.

- Change the entry for the form to the new name under Smart Forms. You have to enter the name directly, since the value help currently displays only SAP-script forms. This is also the reason for the subsequent warning "Form ... not found in language ...".

Save the changed entry. The entry is accepted despite the warning. You can now output the report with Smart Forms as well.

> **Note:** The standard complaint report is a shop floor paper assigned to notification types F2 and Q2 (defects and complaints against the vendor). This is relevant for selecting a suitable notification on the application side.

Outputting the Complaints Report

Start the application for managing quality notifications in the SAP menu with path **Logistics · Quality Management · Quality Notification**.

We assume that quality notifications have already been entered in your system. Therefore, choose **Display** (QM03). Then use the value help in the *Vendor* tab page to search for a notification with output type F2 or Q2, since the complaint report is assigned to these two areas by default.

Open the processing screen for the selected notification. Start the output using menu path **Notification · Print · Notification**. In the next dialog box, choose shop floor paper 5999. The print preview is once again available.

13.6   Print and Spool System

13.6.1 Overview

Even though electronic data transmission (fax, e-mail) is increasingly important as an output medium, the most prevalent method of form output is still the conventional printer. Consequently, printing the form correctly is of primary importance; moreover, vast differences between printers often require custom modifications in the SAP system.

> **Note:** Even though some of the settings described below are applicable to all output media, the terms associated with *printing* are used exclusively below to keep things simple.

Process Flow in the Spool System

The output generated in Smart Forms for printers or fax machines is forwarded to the central spool program in the SAP system. The contents of the output are managed there as a *spool request*. Such spool requests are stored temporarily before spool control forwards them to the specific output device as *output requests*. Depending on the information in the spool request, this can be as soon as possible, at a defined time, or when released by the user.

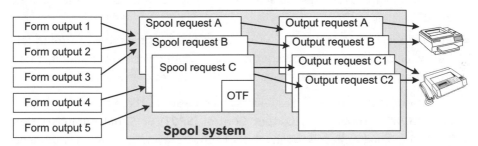

Figure 13.14 Spool control

To summarize these steps:

▶ You start the **output/print** function in any SAP application (referred to below as *print operation*). In this process, certain default parameters, such as the number of copies or the name of the output device, are passed on for the output.

▶ The SAP system then generates the *spool request*, which is equivalent to the *output request*, and sends it to *spool control*. The synonymous terms here are *print control* and *output control*. As Figure 13.14 shows, not every print operation results in a separate spool request. The spool request contains the results of the form output as an OTF intermediate document, as well as various administration information, such as the time of the planned transfer to the output device.

▶ Spool control forwards the spool request to the output device at the defined time. In particular, this involves converting the OTF document in the spool request to the specific format of the output device/printer. The document, which is generated in the format of the output device, is managed in an output request.

▶ A single spool request can also trigger several output requests. This is the case, for example, when the first attempt to send the job to a printer fails due to technical problems.

As long as a spool request is still waiting, the user can change several of its parameters. This can be especially helpful during the test phase of the form. Conversely, parameters in the form can also influence the spool control itself. For these reasons, it is important to know how spool control implements the print operation for a form—that is, how specific printer instructions are created.

Major Components

We differentiate between the following major components:

▶ The *spool control* processes the actual spool requests while they are in the wait queue.

▶ In *spool administration*, the SAP user defines the rules for spool control to follow when converting a spool request for an output device. If you modify these functions, you can take advantage of special features of the output devices.

The following path in the SAP Easy Access menu leads to these two components: **Tools · CCMS · Spool**, then **Output Control (SP01)** or **Spool Administration (SPAD)**. You can also reach spool control directly from any application with menu path **System · Services · Output Controller, or even more directly with System · Own Spool Requests.**

> Note: Because the term *output control* was already used in the context of form output (processing), *spool control* is always referred to here, (even though the menu items and screens mostly use terms with "Output..."). But then, the buffer involved is called the spool...

The Individual Steps

The transactions named above are referred to repeatedly in the next sections. First, however, a few comments on the spool dialog box, which may appear onscreen during a print operation. It enables the user to enter basic parameters for the print output. By necessity, many users get their first glance at the spool system functions in this dialog box.

The last section explains the basics of font and bar code management in the SAP system. This subject is especially relevant for form development, because direct access to the output device enables you to utilize its individual features, which also include individual fonts and bar codes.

13.6.2 Information in the Spool Dialog Box

When you generate output in the SAP system, often a dialog box appears that enables you to enter individual values for basic output parameters or to change the default values from the print program.

> **Note:** Whether or not the dialog box appears depends primarily on the setting in the active print program. This step is usually skipped during automatic output. But even in this case, the specified output device must actually be defined in the program. Otherwise, the dialog box is displayed no matter what.

The label for this dialog box is "Print". Because it specifies the general parameters for spool control, we call it by its regular description, *spool dialog box*, in this book. The dialog box can have a completely different structure for other output media, such as a fax machine, than during printing; see Figure 10.8. Figure 13.15 shows the standard structure for output via a printer.

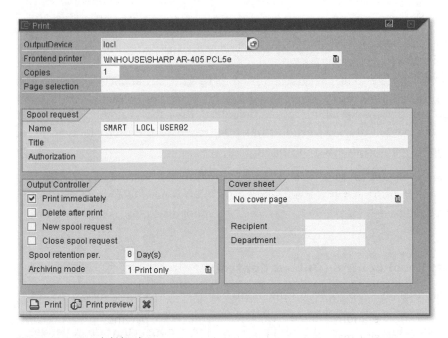

Figure 13.15 Spool dialog box

Most of the input fields are self-explanatory, or at least sufficiently documented with the **F1** help. General remarks:

▶ Normally, the name of a spool request is composed of three components. When a Smart Forms form is involved, it consists of a code (always SMART), the printer name, and the user ID. This is also the system proposal for the "title" of the corresponding spool request, if the user does not specify anything else in the input field. You can also have the entry proposed by the main program.

▶ You can preassign the parameters in the spool dialog screen individually in the form interface of Smart Forms. This option is described in detail in Section 9.7, Standard Parameters of the Form Interface.
If output is performed through output control, these parameters are preassigned by the conditions in the output type (see Section 9.2.2).

▶ Some of the settings apply to any type of output request (printer, fax, and so on), and can also be predefined as user defaults for the specific user—for example, the output device, plus the settings for **Immediate Print** and **Delete after Output**. You maintain these default settings in the system menu with path **User Defaults · My Data** (**Values** tab page).

> **Note:** Under Smart Forms, interface parameter USER_SETTINGS determines whether the user parameters will be used as default values or whether other values that are supplied by the main program will be used.

▶ The user can change all the system defaults in the spool dialog box. In the last stage—that is, after conversion to a spool request—the user can even make changes within spool administration.

During automated output without a user prompt, the individual parameters—basic information such as the output device—always have to be provided in the background (see Section 9.7). Otherwise, the spool dialog box is displayed in any case.

13.6.3 Spool Control (Output Control)

You can use transaction SP01 (or the menu path, see above) to display a list of the current items in the spool system; these items are selectable by criteria like creation date, output device, and author. You can also choose in the display between:

▶ Spool requests that were generated in the print operation

▶ Output requests that the spool control has already processed and forwarded

You can use the **System** menu in any application to call spool control directly from within any transaction. In this case, a second session is opened, so the currently processed background remains in the background. This menu path offers two alternatives:

▶ **System · Services · Output Controller** opens the spool control, with access to all spool and output requests (like transaction SP01).

▶ **System · Own Spool Requests** opens a list of the spool requests created for the specific user in spool administration. Because users are interested primarily in their own spool requests, this is often the best starting point (like transaction SP02).

Figure 13.16 shows the list of spool requests as in the second case above.

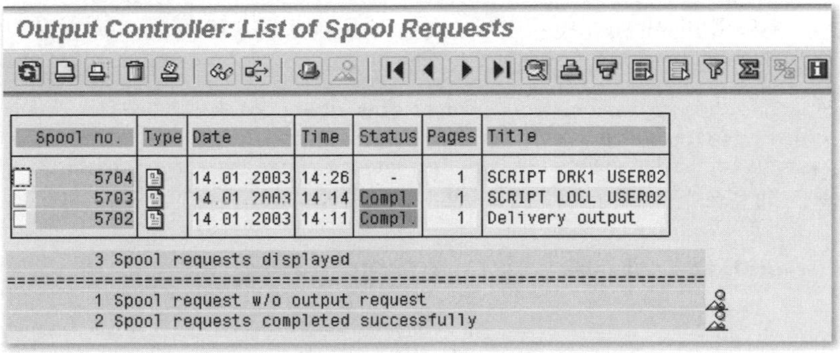

Figure 13.16 Spool control with display of spool requests

The list of spool requests is displayed with help of the ABAP List Viewer (ALV), which means you can configure the structure individually with display variants—menu path: **Settings · Display Variant · and so on**. The following basic information is available in the standard version of the list:

▶ Each spool request has a unique identification number.

▶ The type for form output is displayed as *SAPscript document* (OTF). Click the mouse on the corresponding symbol to open the graphical print preview under the default settings. You can also use menu path **Goto · Task List · Settings**, for example, to go to the direct display of the OTF data. This can be particularly helpful for tests.

▶ The values for date and time indicate the creation time.

▶ The entry for the title is composed by spool control from the three components: source, printer, and user name. You can also preassign the title parameters in OUTPUT_OPTIONS in the form interface for Smart Forms.

Status of the spool request

Of course, the primary measure of the processing progress for the spool request is the status. The most important indicators are described below:

Blank	No output request has been created yet for the spool request; therefore, the request has not been forwarded to the output device.
Waiting	An output request was created but has not been processed by the spool system yet. For example, the document has not been converted to the printer format.
In Proc.	The spool system is formatting the output request for printing, including conversion of the OTF document format to the printer output format.
Printing	The output request is currently being printed.
Compl.	The output request was printed properly.
F5	More than one output request was created, each with its own different status, but without a final processing status. Double-click on the status entry to display the individual information for each output request.
Error	A serious error, such as a network error, occurred during processing. See the output log for an exact description of the cause. Requests with errors remain in the spool system until they are deleted or until their retention period is reached. The user can also reactivate the spool request after an output error and send it to the output device again.
Time	The user has defined a specific time to output this request.

Of course, the processing status can change quickly when individual spool requests are being processed. If necessary, choose the appropriate icon to refresh the display.

You can also delete a spool request from the list at any time. Please note, however, that the corresponding output request will still exist in this case if it has already been sent to the output device or its upstream network spool.

> **Note:** If necessary, you can configure spool administration to generate an individual log for each output request that contains all the messages that occur during processing, not just the errors. You configure this option directly in the definition of the output device (with path **Goto · Test Tools**).

Attributes of the Spool Request

Choose menu path **Goto · Request Information** (or double-click the mouse) in the list of spool requests to display additional information for a given spool request. You may be able to change individual attributes, such as the output device, number of copies, or priority, depending on your system settings.

Grouping output requests

Although each printout of a form is processed in the spool, a new spool request is not created each time. Instead, spool control tries to group together print requests that have identical primary criteria, such as user, title, output device, number of copies, and so on. These attributes generally have nothing to do with the contents of the documents to be output. Whenever additional print operations are appended to a spool request, the total number of pages increases automatically.

You can also set attribute **Completed, No Further Appends Possible** in the request information to prevent new print operations from being appended to an existing spool request. In this case, a new spool request is created for the next similar print operation. When you create an output request that automatically converts the document into the printer language, this option is activated automatically.

> **Tip:** You can output the entire set of print operations that has been grouped in one spool request by setting the **Output Immediately** option for the last print operation.

The main program under Smart Forms can set the appropriate interface parameters to determine whether and when a spool request will be created.

> **Tip:** You can download the contents of any spool request to the local PC as pure text information (without control characters; menu path **Spool Request · Forward · Save as Text**). This can be very helpful for tests. The text is saved without a prior confirmation prompt in the local work directory of your SAP GUI (usually directory **SAPWorkdir** in the local user path).

TemSe file

Spool requests are temporary data that is deleted again at a given time—immediately after output, for example, or after a configurable retention period. This deletion avoids capacity problems that would otherwise result from the large number of spool requests created each day.

The SAP system uses a special type of storage to store such temporary objects: *TemSe data storage* (TemSe = temporary sequential objects). This type of data storage is also used to save background jobs, for example.

As a result, each spool request also has a unique TemSe entry (see the **TemSe** tab page within the **request information**).

Starting output

A frequently used function for form development is the direct trigger of output via spool control. This is required when the **Output Immediately** attribute was not set in the spool dialog screen of the application, or if errors occurred during the first output attempt.

To trigger the output of a spool request, in the list display for spool control, choose menu path **Spool Request · Print · Without Changes** or ... · **With Changed Parameters**. The cursor must be positioned on a spool request; multiple selection is supported. If you choose the menu path With **Changed Parameters**, you can change several of the settings that were configured in the printer dialog for the individual spool request—output device, number of copies, or even limiting to certain pages.

Output Request

To output a spool request on the destination device (printer, fax, and so on), spool control creates an output request either automatically or manually depending on the settings, as described above. The output request contains the document in the language of the output device; in this case, this means converting the OTF statements to printer sequences as defined in the corresponding printer driver.

In some cases, one spool request can result in several output requests, such as when an output has to be repeated after error messages from the output device. If necessary, from the spool request screen, choose menu path **Goto · Output Requests** (or the corresponding icon).

13.6.4 Spool Administration

In the previous section, you learned how individual print operations are temporarily stored in spool control and then forwarded to the output device in individual steps, including converting the OTF document format into the printer's control language.

You can configure the attributes of this conversion operation in spool administration. This involves adjusting the printer attributes to the requirements of the SAP system.

To reach the starting point for all activities in spool administration, choose menu path **Tools · CCMS · Spool Administration (transaction SPAD)**.

The corresponding processing screen (see Figure 13.17) features three administration modes:

► **Simple administration** for entering output devices and servers, as well as for managing spool requests

► **Extended administration**, with the additional **Output Management** tab page

► **Full administration** with all input options (including the device types, for example)

The information below relates primarily to the full administration mode.

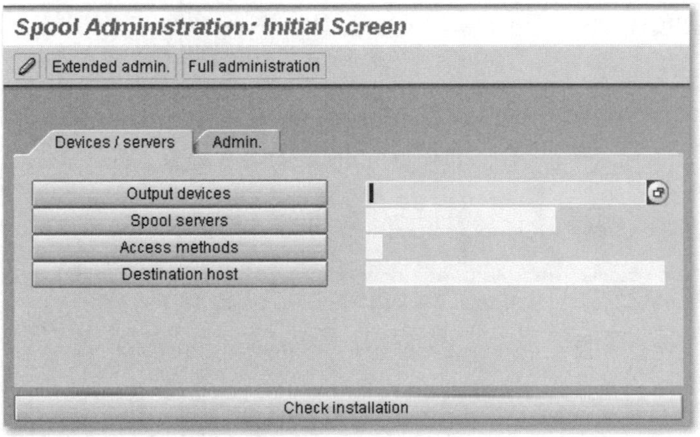

Figure 13.17 Spool administration

From the initial spool administration screen, you can switch to the individual processing functions. The procedure for calling an output device is described below briefly as an example:

► When you enter the name of an output device in the initial screen, pressing the **Output Devices** button takes you directly to the corresponding detailed screen.

► If you do not enter a name, a list of all output device devices in the system appears. Double-click on the required entry to display the detailed screen.

Printer driver

During form processing, the composer generates a document in OTF format, which is still independent of the actual output device. This document is passed on to spool control in the output request. In contrast, output from other programs/reports is temporarily saved in an ABAP list format.

It is up to the spool control to ensure that the received output documents in OTF format are converted to the appropriate, printer-specific commands, or into the commands of other output devices such as fax and e-mail. *Printer drivers* are defined in the system for this conversion.

As with the source documents, the system differentiates between two driver types:

▶ *OTF drivers* for output documents that were created from forms in Smart Forms (or SAPscript)

▶ *Print list drivers* for output from other programs

Table 13.2 lists several OTF drivers that are available in the standard system.

Driver	Application case
POST	PostScript printer
PRES	Kyocera printer (with PRESCRIBE printer language)
HPL2	HP-compatible laser printer (with printer language PCL-5 for all printer models HP LaserJet III and later)
STN2	Simple line printer (without proportional fonts, but with *Bold*, *Italic*)
SWIN	Conversion of local Windows printer drivers through the SAPLPD communications program. Enables you to address all Windows printers
TELE	Fax and telex transmission through the SAP communication server (only ASCII as output)
PDF1	Drivers for conversion to PDF format (in Basis Release 4.6D and later)

Table 13.2 Printer drivers in the SAP system

To output a form (or any other document), however, the user does not choose a printer driver, but instead a specific output device. This is a model of a physical printer, which the SAP system can address in the respective network. Its attributes contain the location of the device, the output of covers sheets, and default settings for the paper tray selection, including the paper format.

> **Tip:** You can also enter custom information for the margins of an output device in the **Output Attributes** tab page. The device can use this information for the printer. Define this information as horizontal and vertical offsets. You use these attributes, for example, when certain parts of a form are cut off when output to a specific printer. The defined offsets are then added to the left/upper margin of each output device in the form during printing.
>
> For example, enter a horizontal offset when contents on the left margin were cut off in the printout. Conversely, you can also enter a negative value if the output is cut off on the right. In this case, all the output areas in the form are shifted to the left during printout. Please note, however, that if the printer now cuts off output on the left margin, you will have to make changes to the form.

In turn, each output device is assigned to a device type that identifies the specific model of the printer or fax machine. The device type contains, among other things, the definition of which printer driver will be used for formatting. This results in three layers:

1. **Output device**
   Contains information on location, the output of cover sheets, default settings for the paper tray selection (including the paper format), and so on.

2. **Device type**
   Contains the name of the driver to be used (divided by SAPscript/Smart Forms and list printout). The device type also contains a list of all applicable print controls (see below).

3. **Printer / device driver**
   Specified by SAP, see Table 13.2.

A driver controls basic functions of the output device and ensures that the format information from the spool document is converted to the control sequences for the respective printer. To make this possible, a list of available formatting statements (print controls) is defined for each printer type. These statements consist primarily of a code and the suitable control commands (escape sequences) for the printer.

Examples of these print controls:

▶ CI010 (set character spacing to 10 characters per inch)

▶ COL2V (inverse type)

▶ TRY02 (feed paper from tray 2 on the printer)

You can also address print controls directly from a command node in the form (see Section 7.5). This is only rarely useful for standard print controls, however, since they are interpreted by the printer driver itself. You do, however, have the option of creating additional, individual print controls for a device type to address (for example) the specific functions of a printer. In this case, it makes sense to create a new device type and then enhance the functions.

13.6.5 Device Types (Print Controls)

The device type identifies the model of a printer or fax machine. The representation in the SAP system consists of header information and the various assigned components, such as print controls. To avoid having to create these components from scratch, you should always start with a copy of an existing device type that is similar to the new printer when you define a new device type. The following components of the device type are copied in this case:

▶ Device type definition

▶ Print controls (which can be extended later)

▶ Formatting types

▶ Font metrics

▶ Printer fonts and bar codes (for use in Smart Forms, for example)

Some individual attributes of these components are described further below.

The call of the copy function itself is concealed in the main processing screen for spool administration (SPAD), in menu path **Utilities · For Device Types · Copy Device Type**.

Select the source type and enter a name for the target device type. Also note the two other attributes for the copy process:

▶ **Use References**
The original device type is used as a reference type. This means that when new software versions are installed, the formatting functions in the source type are passed on to the copy. You should always activate this attribute when the original source device type was provided by SAP. Do not set this option if you have to implement comprehensive changes to the actions for device formatting in the new device type.

▶ **Adapt Includes to Source**
You can use *include coding* to add references to other functions/actions to a device type that were previously defined in that device type (and are sometimes used for formatting, for example). You should always set this attribute to ensure that the include coding is set to the functions of the new device type after the copy process.

Now return to the initial screen of spool administration in **full administration** mode.

Print Controls

The print controls contain all the control statements that a printer needs to implement a specific format. The codes of the print controls consist of five characters and have uniform naming conventions for the first letter.

Print controls were described in detail in the discussion of the command node in Section 7.5.2, at least from the form design perspective. Therefore, this section describes only issues that are related to the functions in spool administration.

Spool administration differentiates between two categories:

▶ **Standard print controls**

General items that are addressed directly by the printer driver. The **SAPscript** option is set for print controls that are addressed by SAPscript printer drivers. This largely involves print controls with S or T as their first letter. The *Printing Guide* in the SAP Library lists the print controls that are used in every SAPscript printer driver.

You can add customer-specific print controls (observe the customer namespace) for inclusion in a command node, for example.

Standard print controls should always have an entry in the device type; if necessary, as a blank statement, if no suitable escape sequence exists. Ootherwise, error messages are likely during output. The list of standard print controls is usually maintained directly by SAP.

To display a list of these print controls, choose the value help in the input field of a command node under Smart Forms.

▶ **Printer-specific (non-standard) print controls**

These print controls are not addressed by the printer directly, but instead through automatic functions that are defined there. When you change a font, for example, the printer font—and the defined print control—is derived from the system font.

Printer-specific print controls are not protected by a namespace, so you should enter them only for user-defined printer types, which are copied from SAP device types.

A list of all print controls for the respective output device appears in the **Print Controls** tab page in the processing window of the device type (see Figure 13.18).

To create a new print control, choose menu path **Edit · Insert Line or Edit · Insert via Print Control**.

You can optionally enter the control sequences in hexadecimal or text notation. The first variant is more common, since it corresponds to the information in most printer manuals. Set the corresponding attributes to choose the input format.

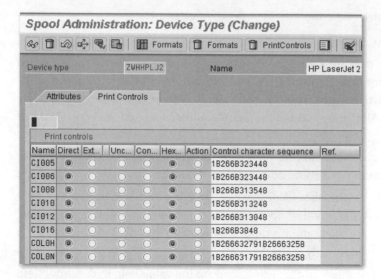

Figure 13.18 Device type with print controls

Example

The next section discusses the management of fonts in the SAP system in detail. Print controls are used to address the available fonts on a printer. The rough process is:

▶ The system interprets the style for a form to determine a system font for text formatting. This entry also appears in the intermediate document that the spool request manages (OTF format).

▶ The printer driver checks whether the selected system font is available on the printer; if so, it accepts the assigned print control from there and uses it to locate the escape sequence for selecting the font on the printer.

13.6.6 Fonts and Bar Codes in the SAP System

Based on the example in the last chapter, you can see that a font has to be defined in the SAP system for every font that a printer can output, including the appropriate information on character widths, heights, and so on, to ensure correct text formatting. You use this *system font* to format texts in a form in Smart Forms. Of course, this font also has to be assigned to a format in the style for the form.

You can consider *bar codes* to be a special type of font. Each transmitted character is converted to a sequence of bar codes. Due to this similarity, the same transaction is used to maintain bar codes in the SAP system. To simplify things, the term *font maintenance* is used exclusively below.

To reach the initial screen for SAP font maintenance, choose menu path **Tools · Form Printout · Administration · Font from the form printout screen**. Figure 13.19 shows the initial screen.

Figure 13.19 Initial screen for font maintenance

To maintain a font, perform the following steps:

▶ **Font families**
Enter the names of the fonts here (such as *Arial* or *Times*). The fonts are also separated into *proportional* and *non-proportional*. You can specify replacement fonts, in case the main font is not available on an output device.

▶ **System fonts**
Also called SAP fonts, these are composed of combinations of font family, font height (in tenths of a point), and the font attributes *Bold* and *Italic*. As a result, up to four system fonts may be defined for each font size. The font information in the formats under Smart Forms relies on this information.

▶ **Printer fonts**
Combinations of font family, font height, and the *Bold/Italic* attributes, which reflect the actual possibilities of an output device type. The fonts are always assigned and entered for the device type. An important attribute for the printer font is the definition of a print control that is required to address a font on the printer. The character width is the same for all characters in *non-proportional*

fonts (specified in CPI). This input field is not active for *proportional* fonts (set by default to AFM; see below).

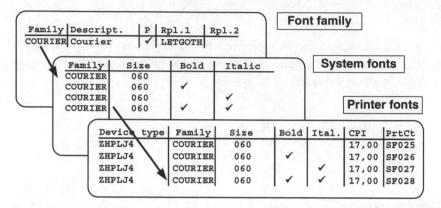

Figure 13.20 Controlling typefaces (fonts) in the SAP system

The following process flow is involved in form output via the printer driver (also see Figure 13.20):

▶ In the intermediate layer as OTF document, the required system font is determined first, with height information and so on.

▶ The driver then attempts to find an entry for this font in the printer fonts on the output device; if successful, it activates the corresponding print controls.

▶ If no suitable printer font is available, the system reads the entry for the font family to determine whether a replacement font has been defined. If so, the driver searches for the corresponding entry in the printer fonts, which must have the same attributes, such as *Height* and *Bold/Italic*.

Proportional Font

In earlier releases, each printer font had to be defined individually for each font size. Today many printer drivers also support scalable fonts (fonts that can be output in any size). In this case, the printer driver reads the necessary information for the height (and so on) from the *AFM information* (AFM = Adobe Font Metrics). A printer font that is flagged as "scalable" is automatically set to "000" for the font height.

Scalable fonts are usually also proportional, which means that the individual characters do not have a uniform width. Therefore, this information must be defined individually for each character. You enter this data under **Metrics Data** in the processing screen for the printer font. To simplify this step, you can also upload the data in standard AFM format from your local PC.

TrueType Fonts

Under the previous font management logic in the SAP system, it was assumed that the fonts were resident on the respective printer. Therefore, the SAP system fonts had to be synchronized with the printer fonts.

In recent years, however, a technology (*soft fonts*)has spread in the Windows environment for sending the fonts in a document to a printer individually before output is started. The standard format for these fonts is TTF (= TrueType Fonts).

You can use this technique to print on any graphics-capable printer; the print output program assumes full control of the print process. Due to the lower output speed, this technique is used primarily on laser printers. The major advantage here is that output will achieve the same result on all printers, because the formatting instructions are identical.

In Release 4.6C and later, some printer drivers in the SAP system are also capable of processing TrueType fonts. Because these fonts are independent of the respective device type, this simplifies administration enormously (see also the notes in the SAPNet and in the Appendix).

To use a TrueType font, you first have to import it to the SAP system by uploading it from a local PC. You call this function from the initial screen of font maintenance (SE73, see Figure 13.21) with the **Install TrueType Font** button.

Figure 13.21 Importing TrueType fonts

The first time you import a font, you always create a new font family. Therefore, the import process prompts you to enter a name for it (see Figure 13.21). During the *upload*, the SAP system copies all the information needed for font management, such as the width of the individual characters, and uses it to generate the proper entries for the system and printer fonts automatically. The fonts can be used immediately.

> **Note:** To print TrueType fonts, their use must be active for the respective device type. To activate itthem, go from the initial screen for font maintenance (SE73) to the processing of the printer fonts, then choose the device type and press the *TrueType Fonts* button to activate them.

TrueType fonts are infinitely scalable; the corresponding information in the **Printer Fonts** category is set automatically during the upload.

If several font styles (such as *Italic* and *Bold*) exist for a font family, you have to import the individual TrueType fonts into the new SAP font family individually. Be sure to set the suitable **font attribute BOLD/ITALIC** in the initial screen (see Figure 13.21).

> **Note:** This multiple import for an existing font family is not supported under Release 4.6C. The system responds with the message "Font family already exists". This is a program error that is corrected in Release 4.6D and later (see notes in SAPNet and in the Appendix).

Bar Codes

The handling of bar codes is similar to font management in many respects. The differentiation between information in the SAP system and the printer exists as well:

▶ **System bar codes**
These are the bar code entries that can be selected in the form or style. They contain basic attributes that are also required for formatting in the form, such as the number of characters, width, height, and degree of rotation for output. The specification of the **bar code type** is currently for informational purposes only. Customer-specific system bar codes are possible; observe the customer namespace.

▶ **Printer bar codes**
These are basically system bar codes that have been assigned to specific printers. The most important attribute here is the reference to a print control that serves to activate/deactivate the bar codes on the printer. Normally, these are the print controls with identifier SBPxx and SBSxx. When you output a form, the printer driver converts a system bar code to the specific entry defined for the printer in question. The characters that represent the contents of the bar code itself appear between the control commands to start/finish bar code output.

To print bar codes, you normally have to install an appropriate font cartridge in the printer (see the exception below). You can also output 2D barcodes in Release 4.6C and later (see notes in SAPNet and in the Appendix).

Local printout of bar codes
You can also output bar codes on a printer connected to a local Windows PC. The SAP system addresses such printers using output device LOCL. The printout uses a conversion program, SAPLPD, which also runs on the local work center PC.

Enhancements are available for SAPLPD that automatically convert bar code instructions in the data stream to graphics for printing. This enables you to output bar codes on any graphics-capable printer, even if no bar code module has been installed. To implement this enhancement, you have to install an additional DLL on the work center PC (from a third-party vendor; see the notes in SAPNet and in the Appendix).

13.7 Development Tools

13.7.1 Overview (Object Navigator)

In the previous sections, we frequently referred to tools that are part of the ABAP development environment. These tools include:

▶ The *Function Builder*, which you use to display the function module that the system generates from every form

▶ The *ABAP Editor*, which you use to write a suitable main program

▶ The *ABAP Dictionary*, where the data types—which you can use to define data in the form—are managed

Each of these tools has its own specific attributes, which are described in the sections below.

These tools have many similarities as well. Starting with the ABAP Editor, we will describe several of these shared functions, which you can apply directly to the other tools.

One of the most important similarities is the centralized management of the involved program objects (function modules, programs, and so on) in a central, shared directory: the *Repository*.

> **Background:** The contents of the Repository itself are saved in the tables of the main SAP database. Part of the Repository forms the *ABAP Dictionary*, which in particular describes the global data definitions for database tables and data types.

Consequently, almost any type of object in program development can be displayed and organized in this common user interface. The corresponding tool is called the *Object Navigator*. You call it in the SAP menu with path **Tools · ABAP Workbench · Overview · Object Navigator (SE80)**.

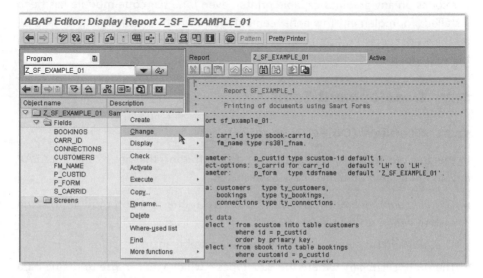

Figure 13.22 Main program in the Object Navigator with context menu

As Figure 13.22 shows, the Object Navigator also uses a tree display to represent the hierarchical structure of the programs and other development objects. Once again, use the sample form to find out about the most important functions:

▶ After starting the **Object Navigator**, select the type of object in the first drop down list. In this case, choose **Program**.

▶ Enter name SF_EXAMPLE_01 in the field below.

▶ Press **Return** to confirm your entries.

The selected program is displayed in the navigation tree, with all its variables and program blocks. In this example, only the information under **Fields** is relevant: it lists all the variables that the main program uses (and possibly passes on to the form).

Editing the Program

When you double-click on the first node in the navigation tree (program name), the ABAP Editor appears with the corresponding program coding in a work area to the right. When you double-click on a field in the navigation tree, you go directly to the corresponding definition line in the source text.

> **Note:** This is a standard function. Depending on which object type you select in the navigation tree, the suitable tool for displaying or maintaining that object appears in the right-hand work area.

Because you called the ABAP Editor through the selected program, the toolbar includes the most important functions for this tool. It may surprise you in the beginning that when you call a different program object in the toolbar, the entries in the navigation tree of the Object Navigator do not change. When you select an item in the navigation tree, this restores the former state.

Context Menu

The Object Navigator functions involve largely administrative functions for creating, deleting, and so on. The easiest way to reach these functions under Smart Forms is through the context menu.

> **Tip:** If you have a small monitor, you may find it helpful to completely close the Object Navigator and its navigation tree, so that only the corresponding editing tool remains. Of course, you can also go take the opposite path: choose menu path **Utilities · Display Object Window** within any processing tool to display the navigation tree again. All the functions of the Object Navigator are then available again.

13.7.2 ABAP Editor

The ABAP Editor is the common tool for writing executable programs. Several functions that are relevant for Smart Forms are described below, once again based on your sample program.

Open the tool in the SAP menu with path **Tools · ABAP Workbench · Development · ABAP Editor (SE38)** and choose sample program Z_SF_EXAMPLE_01, which you created in the *Getting Started* chapter. To modify the program coding, choose **Program · Change**. Of course, you can also call transaction SE80 directly, as described in the last section.

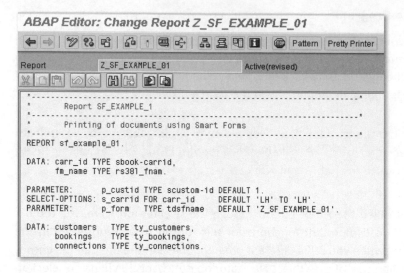

Figure 13.23 ABAP Editor

If the ABAP Editor in your installation appears differently than in Figure 13.23 above, the line editor is probably the default setting in your system. You can change this with menu path **Utilities · Settings.** Switch to the **Frontend Editor.**

Editor Functions

You should already be familiar with some ABAP Editor functions—such as the syntax check and the pattern function, which you can use to insert ABAP statements or entire function modules with the necessary statement patterns—from the program node in the form.

As in the form, you have to activate every ABAP program again after making changes in the system. If you do not activate the program, you can execute the changed source text only within the development environment. To activate the program, use function **Program · Test F8.**

The debugger provides another function: you can run through the program in single steps in order to monitor its proper execution. This important tool is described in Section 13.7.4 below.

Help Tools

You call the general help, as well as the keyword documentation, as described for the program node (see Section 8.2).

The *forward navigation* in the source text is another useful tool. It provides information on the definition of variables and subroutines. Simply double-click on a given term to reach the next level of detail. Press **F3** to return to the original location. Depending on which object you select, a different processing tool may be called, such as the Function Builder for function modules or the ABAP Dictionary for data types.

Once you have reached the definition of a variable, either directly or with forward navigation, you can double-click on it to open the *where-used list*. This list indicates all the places where the variable is addressed in the current program. Of course, you can also call this function directly, via menu path **Utilities · Where-Used List**.

You can also call the where-used list for other development objects, such as subroutines and function modules. The SAP system automatically records the use of all development objects in special database tables (the Repository). Therefore, the where-used list for a function module returns all the locations where that function module is called. Figure 13.24 shows a typical example, with a hit list.

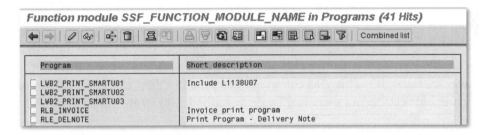

Figure 13.24 Hits in the where-used list

From the hit list, double-click the mouse in the right half of the screen to reach the actual found item. If you double-click on the left-hand side of the list, additional details are displayed.

> **Tip:** The where-used list is an excellent way to learn how modules are used in different positions.

Extended Search

The built-in full-text search is another useful navigation tool. Choose menu path **Edit · Find/Replace** to call the extended full-text search in the development environment. Don't bother using key combination **Ctrl + F**, since this only starts a reduced version. The initial screen for the full-text search should look something like Figure 13.25.

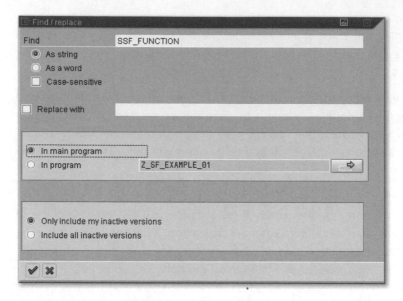

Figure 13.25 Full text search in development system

It is important that you set the **Global** option in the main program. It ensures that subordinate program components, such as include programs, are included in the search. The result is a list of all entries found for the specified text. Once again, you can double-click on an entry to go directly to the found location (and press **F3** to return to the list).

Worklist

You always work with more or less the same programs during a development project. The *Worklist* function is provided to give you faster access to these programs. You can use it to manage your access to such programs, as well as any other object in the Dictionary.

To add the current object to your worklist, choose menu path **Utilities · Worklist · Add Current Object**. Choose the same menu path with *Display* to display all the current programs/objects in your worklist. Double-click to call any entry in the list. The appropriate processing tool opens automatically.

Call Hierarchy

When you have to analyze complex program structures that contain nested subroutine calls, it helps to have an overview of which program blocks are called and, in turn, which subroutines are called from there. You can generate this type of overview with path **Utilities · Call Graph · Calls/Called by**. Figure 13.26 shows an example.

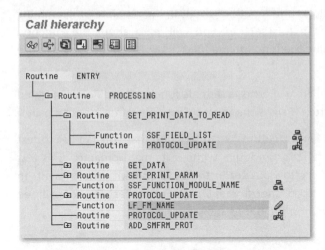

Figure 13.26 Call hierarchy in the ABAP Editor

Double-click on a name to display the source text of a subroutine. Each function module has its own subordinate navigation tree, which you can display with the corresponding icon.

13.7.3 Function Builder

As you already learned when you studied the interface between the main program and the form, all nodes in a form under Smart Forms are converted to a function module for execution. The form nodes can then be addressed by the main program.

Background: Function modules serve to encapsulate general functions, which can then be called by various ABAP programs. Function modules are maintained centrally in the SAP system and are available to all active modules. Function modules let you achieve a high reuse quota. The majority of current SAP program coding is implemented as function modules.

Calling the Function Builder from the form
Because of the wide variety of existing function modules, they are divided into function groups by subject. This division results in additional functions, such as shared data and subroutines, that only the modules of the respective group have. When you create a new function module, the corresponding function group must already be defined.

You maintain function modules and function groups in the separate programming tool, the Function Builder. In this section, you will learn about the Function Builder and the system behind the function modules to the extent necessary to use them in Smart Forms.

When you activate a form in Smart Forms, a suitable function module is generated in the background; the system assigns the function module name automatically.

The Form Builder in Smart Forms features a test function that you can use to test the basic functions of the function module, without its main program. This test function comes from the Function Builder in the development environment. In the Form Builder of Smart Forms, choose menu path **Form · Test F8**. You will see the initial screen of the Function Builder as shown in Figure 13.27.

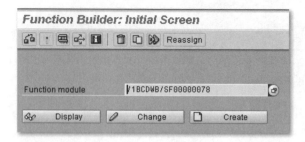

Figure 13.27 Initial screen of the Function Builder

The name of the function module for the form appears automatically. Its components include the code "SF" for Smart Forms and a sequence number. The further procedure for the individual test is described in Section 3.4.

> **Note:** The initial screen of the Function Builder also features a **Change** button. Changing the source text does not make sense in this case, however, because the program coding is generated automatically, and will be overwritten the next time you generate the form. (The change mode is subject to an authorization check anyway.)

In the first step, you will learn about the functions you use to work with function modules. Even though the maintenance of (changes to) function modules from Smart Forms does not make sense here, you may find the display formats helpful in certain situations. After all, sometimes it helps to simply know what is going on in the background.

Attributes of the Function Module

From the initial screen of the Function Builder (shown in Figure 13.27), press the **Display** button to switch to the maintenance functions for the function module. The main processing screen appears, as in Figure 13.28 below.

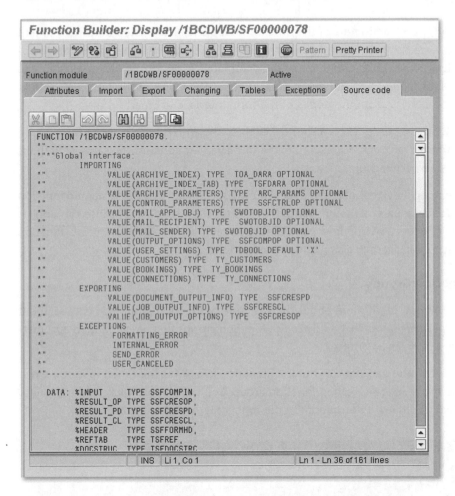

```
Function Builder: Display /1BCDWB/SF00000078

Function module      /1BCDWB/SF00000078            Active

  Attributes   Import   Export   Changing   Tables   Exceptions   Source code

FUNCTION /1BCDWB/SF00000078.
*"----------------------------------------------------------------------
*"*"Global interface:
*"      IMPORTING
*"             VALUE(ARCHIVE_INDEX) TYPE  TOA_DARA OPTIONAL
*"             VALUE(ARCHIVE_INDEX_TAB) TYPE  TSFDARA OPTIONAL
*"             VALUE(ARCHIVE_PARAMETERS) TYPE   ARC_PARAMS OPTIONAL
*"             VALUE(CONTROL_PARAMETERS) TYPE   SSFCTRLOP OPTIONAL
*"             VALUE(MAIL_APPL_OBJ) TYPE   SWOTOBJID OPTIONAL
*"             VALUE(MAIL_RECIPIENT) TYPE   SWOTOBJID OPTIONAL
*"             VALUE(MAIL_SENDER) TYPE   SWOTOBJID OPTIONAL
*"             VALUE(OUTPUT_OPTIONS) TYPE   SSFCOMPOP OPTIONAL
*"             VALUE(USER_SETTINGS) TYPE   TDBOOL DEFAULT 'X'
*"             VALUE(CUSTOMERS) TYPE   TY_CUSTOMERS
*"             VALUE(BOOKINGS) TYPE   TY_BOOKINGS
*"             VALUE(CONNECTIONS) TYPE   TY_CONNECTIONS
*"      EXPORTING
*"             VALUE(DOCUMENT_OUTPUT_INFO) TYPE   SSFCRESPD
*"             VALUE(JOB_OUTPUT_INFO) TYPE   SSFCRESCL
*"             VALUE(JOB_OUTPUT_OPTIONS) TYPE   SSFCRESOP
*"      EXCEPTIONS
*"             FORMATTING_ERROR
*"             INTERNAL_ERROR
*"             SEND_ERROR
*"             USER_CANCELED
*"----------------------------------------------------------------------

  DATA: %INPUT     TYPE SSFCOMPIN,
        %RESULT_OP TYPE SSFCRESOP,
        %RESULT_PD TYPE SSFCRESPD,
        %RESULT_CL TYPE SSFCRESCL,
        %HEADER    TYPE SSFFORMHD,
        %REFTAB    TYPE TSFREF,
        %DOCSTRUC  TYPE TSFDOCSTRC
```

`INS   Li 1, Co 1`   `Ln 1 - Ln 36 of 161 lines`

Figure 13.28 Function Builder: Maintenance functions for the function module

The maintenance functions consist of several tab pages; the tab page with the source text of the function module appears first. Despite the major functions available under Smart Forms, the generated source text is surprisingly short at first glance. Most of the processing functions are defined in subordinate function modules, however, and are not immediately apparent.

> **Tip:** You can set a breakpoint directly in this display of the source text if you want to monitor the form output process in the debugger. This approach, through the test function, is a good way of checking the data that is supplied by the main program (also see Section 13.7.4).

The interface parameters of the function module itself are listed only as comment lines, together with their type information. The system creates these lines automatically. The actual definition of the parameters is performed using separate tab pages, as in the Form Builder in Smart Forms. The labels of the tab pages should also be familiar from the nodes of the form interface in Smart Forms.

Likewise, the contents correspond exactly to the entries in the related form. Open the **Import** tab page, for example: the displayed list contains the same definitions as the respective form.

Now open the **Attributes** tab page. You will see that an identically named function group has apparently been created for the function module. Because this applies to every function module generated by Smart Forms, each of these function groups contains only a single function module.

Function Groups

You will now learn more about the structure of function groups, as well as about the special features that apply to the function groups that are generated automatically under Smart Forms.

The **Attributes** tab page of the maintenance screen for the function module displays the identically named function group. You can double-click on this entry to display additional information on the function group (see Figure 13.29).

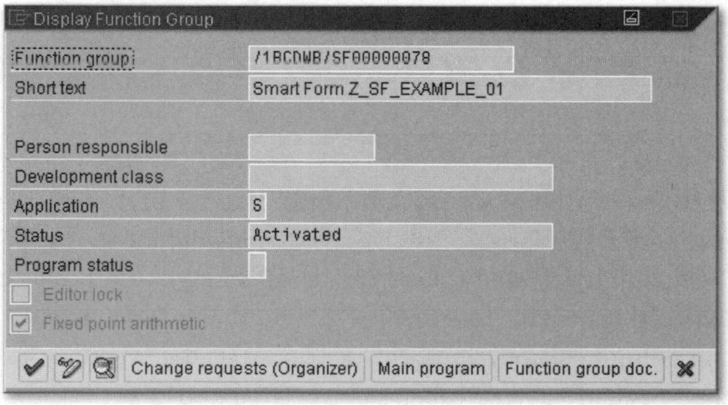

Figure 13.29 Information for the function group

This general information doesn't help you much. Therefore, press the **Main Program** button to display the contents of the function group as shown in Figure 13.30.

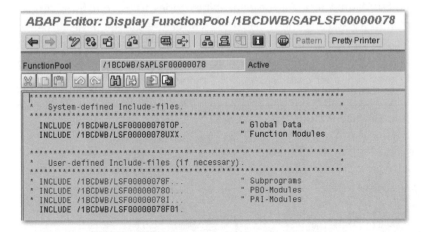

Figure 13.30 Source text for the function group

The system automatically starts the ABAP Editor. The source text for the main program of the function group is called a **function pool**. The main program of every function group operates according to the same system. It consists of:

▶ Global data definitions

▶ Assigned function modules

▶ Individual program routines that can be used as subroutines by all function modules in the function group

In the above example, the groups are also represented by three entries (as include modules, each of which contains references to the actual source text):

▶ **INCLUDE .../...TOP**
Contains all the global data definitions of the function group, especially those data definitions that you configured in the general definition node of the Form Builder in this case.

▶ **INCLUDE .../...UXX**
Contains a reference to the source text of the function module, which you also saw in the initial screen of the Function Builder.

▶ **INCLUDE .../...F01**
Contains individual subroutines for the form, which are called by the function module. This section contains, among other things, all the nodes that you created in the corresponding form.

Displaying the Contents of a Node

You can double-click on any of the include programs to display its contents. Try doing so with the last module. You will see the ABAP source text for a variety of subroutines (FORM routines). All the executable nodes from your form should also appear here. Try starting the full-text search for the graphic SMALL_DOG, which you included in the form in the *Getting Started* chapter (search for ENJOY if you did not perform the exercise). The corresponding ABAP coding for the graphic node should appear as in Figure 13.31 below.

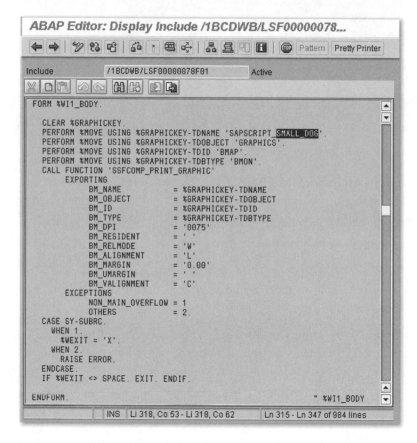

Figure 13.31 Subroutine for graphic node

Function module SSFCOM_PRINT_GRAPHIC is called from the system library to actually output the graphic. Double-click on this name to display its source text and the definitions of the transfer parameters. Subroutine %MOVE resets these transfer parameters to the values set in the form node.

Every other executable node of the form is also included here. You may find this method helpful for checking the program coding generated by the system (and for your own program nodes as well). Or you can set a suitable breakpoint for execution in the debugger (see the next section).

> **Note:** You cannot search for the contents of text elements (from text nodes), as since they are defined independently of the form and the function module (see Section 13.3.4, *Text Administration*). For the same reason, you cannot search for fields that are output in the text nodes.

After this brief introduction, exit the function group again and return to the initial screen of the Function Builder, as shown in Figure 13.31.

Other Functions

You have just learned about the main program and the definition of global data via the function group. You can also reach both program areas directly from the initial screen of the Function Builder or the maintenance screen via menu path **Goto · Global Data/Main Program**.

You can also display an overview of the structure within the function group in the object list, via menu path **Utilities · Display Object List**. This opens the Object Navigator (corresponding to transaction SE80).

13.7.4 ABAP Debugger

The correct retrieval of database information is frequently a primary requirement for the development of complex forms under Smart Forms. In this process, you will also have to write more complex program coding in the main program than was the case for the flight invoice. In some circumstances, complicated routines are also required in the program nodes of the form.

Usage Area

Assume that you are responsible for ensuring that the program coding is free of errors:

▶ The built-in syntax check is available for the formal check (correct input of statements, variable names, and so on).

▶ In addition, you can easily see the results of the program coding in the form output (as fields, for example).

If the contents meet your expectations, you can reasonably assume that the program coding is correct.

But even experienced programmers will admit that when complex program routines are involved, the results often fail to meet expectations on the first try, despite a formal check of the program coding. This can be due to a wide variety of causes, such as when the source variables are not set to the expected values, or when the developer interprets the options for the ABAP statements incorrectly.

Because the cause of an error is usually not immediately apparent—you could have avoided it in the first place, otherwise—localizing the source of the error can be a time-consuming process.

Overview of Debugger Functions

The ABAP development environment features a *debugger* to support program analysis. You can use this tool to perform any ABAP program in its individual steps—that is, program line by line. This means:

▶ When you call a program with active debugger, only the first program line is executed at first.

▶ The system then displays a special debugging screen that enables the program developer to monitor the state of the program environment (by displaying the contents of program variables, for example).

▶ You can then use the function keys to execute the next coding line, and so on.

Because a program can consist of thousands of lines of coding, a step-by-step check from the start of the program can quickly become arduous. For this reason, the debugger enables you to set the starting point in the program elsewhere than the start of the program, as a *breakpoint* in any program line.

You can also set more than one breakpoint. In this case, the debugger stops at each breakpoint in sequence. You can use this approach to compare the parameter values at the beginning and end of a program function, for example.

Because every form is converted to an ABAP program when it is activated, you can also use the debugger for troubleshooting. One major restriction applies, however: you cannot activate the full debugger directly from the Form Builder. Instead, use a statement in the program node if necessary (more on this below).

The path through the development environment is much easier. The brief introduction below demonstrates how Smart Forms developers—even those who have not had any programming experience—can benefit from this useful tool.

Step 1: Activate the Debugger

You will first learn how to activate the debugger for the source text in a program node of the form. Because the form is integrated as a function module in the calling main program, you will use the Function Builder—as the corresponding programming tool in the ABAP development environment—to call the debugger.

Choose menu path **Form · Test in the Form Builder to reach the initial screen** of the Function Builder. The name of the function module for the form appears automatically. Now press the **Display** button. The full Function Builder appears, with a display of the source text for the function module (see Figure 13.32).

In the first step, you will configure the program so that the main program interrupts execution immediately after the function module is called. To do so, set a breakpoint in the function module in the first executable line. Position the cursor on the first line of the program coding, which always starts with FUNCTION / 1BCDWB/....

Set a new breakpoint with menu path **Utilities · Breakpoints · Set/Clear** or with the STOP icon in the toolbar. You can use the same method to clear the point again later.

After a brief runtime, the system responds, but it does not highlight the first program line in the coding that you just selected. Instead, it highlights the first executable coding line. In this example, shown in Figure 13.32, this is the line with statement IF USER_SETTINGS <> SPACE.

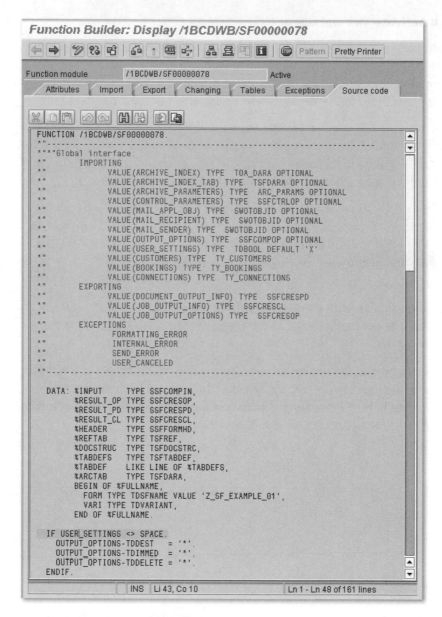

Figure 13.32 Function Builder with breakpoint

Obviously, the DATA statements for typing the data do not count as executable program coding.

Step 2: Call the Debugger

To call the debugger, you have to start the corresponding main program, either as a separate report or through an application with output determination, depending on the situation.

> **Tip:** The main program does not always detect immediately that a breakpoint has been set. If necessary, restart the transaction for the main program. That always helps!

As soon as the breakpoint is reached, the debugger window appears. Figure 13.33 shows the result from the example.

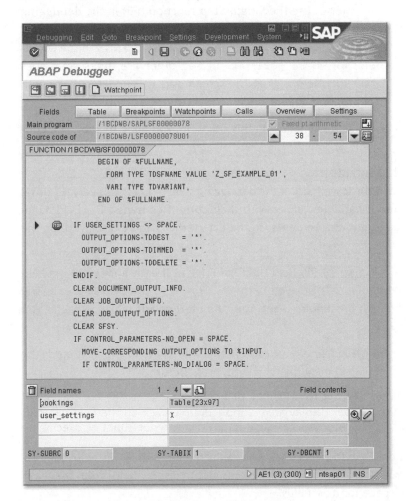

Figure 13.33 Debugger with breakpoint and field contents

The center section of the screen shows a program excerpt with the point where execution was interrupted.

> **Note:** You can scroll in the source text with **Screen**. Unfortunately, however, you cannot use the usual arrow keys to navigate forwards or and backwards. The full-text search is the most useful method for navigating to a specific point in the source text.

The breakpoint you already set is indicated by a STOP sign. The black arrow (*debugging cursor*) above it shows that program execution continued to this exact point, but the current statement has not been executed yet.

To execute this line, you can use the **Single Step** function (**F5**) in the **debugging menu**. The debugging cursor moves to the next executable line. In the example, an IF statement queries a condition for variable USER_SETTINGS. If the condition is met, the fields for OUTPUT_OPTIONS are set; otherwise, the system goes directly to the CLEAR DOCUMENT... line. The screen display is updated along with your progress in the program coding.

In order to tell which step will follow in this situation, you need to know the contents of variable USER_SETTING.

Displaying field contents

The display area in the lower part of the debugging screen serves this very purpose: it shows up to four variables, along with their current contents. The field name appears on the left and the contents (to the extent they can be displayed) on the right.

In the example in Figure 13.33, field USER_SETTINGS already appears in the field contents. Its contents are displayed with "X". However, the display area is still empty when the first breakpoint is set. You (the user) decide which variables you want to display:

▶ If you know the field name, you can enter it directly with the keyboard; the contents are displayed instantly when you press **Return**.

▶ It is even easier when the field name also appears in the excerpt of the program coding from the upper display area. Simply double-click on the field name to display it in the first free line of the lower list.

If you select more than four variables, you can scroll through the list with the corresponding arrow keys. The trash can deletes all the display fields from the view, freeing up the space for new fields.

Displaying contents of structured variables

This relatively simple procedure for fields is somewhat more difficult for internal tables. Nevertheless, you will have to check their contents frequently as well. The above example shows the internal BOOKINGS table, which the calling main program provides through the interface. When this data type is involved, the debugger lists only the number of entries (three in this case) and the width per line (maximum number of characters). However, you can double-click on a line to change the display to one like Figure 13.34.

Internal table		bookings				Type STANDARD	Format E	
1	CONNID FLDATE	BOOKID	CUSTOMID CUSTTYPE SMOKER LUGGWEIGHT			WUNIT INVOICE		
1	0400	|20010305|00000705|00000001|B	|X	|	12.3000 |KG	|X		
2	0400	|20010305|00000706|00000001|B	|	|	0.0000 |KG	|		
3	0400	|20010709|00000460|00000001|B	|	|	12.0000 |KG	|		
4	0400	|20010709|00000648|00000001|B	|	|	0.0000 |KG	|		

Figure 13.34 Debugger with table contents

You now see the contents of the first lines of the internal table (once again, up to four), with the index of the respective line in blue type to the left. You can display additional details from this point:

▶ Double-click on a cell to display additional information for that component.

▶ Double-click on the blue line index to open a detailed view of the data in the entire line, along with the display of all fields and their contents.

Press **F3**, as usual, to return to the previous view.

At this point, you have already learned about the most important functions for checking field contents in the program. You also saw a specific example of how to perform a check of the data that is transferred from the form to the form function module. Because you set the breakpoint to activate the debugger directly at the function module call, all the import fields of the form interface and their contents can be retrieved directly.

Note: You went through the function module to set the breakpoint in this example. You can also achieve the same result by going through the main program. In this case, simply set the breakpoint directly at the function module call.

Executing statements in steps

The program is still stopped at the same point where it was interrupted by the breakpoint (or several lines later if you have already tried the single step function). Of course, executing the remainder of the program in single steps from this point would be a very toilsome task. Instead, the *Debugging* menu and the toolbar offer additional useful navigation functions. The corresponding function keys are:

F5	Single step: Each statement is performed individually; subordinate function calls are also performed explicitly in single-step mode.
F6	Execute: Same navigation as with single step, however, calls of subroutines and functions are executed completely in a single step.
F7	Return: The debugger returns to the point where a calling program resumes control (at the end of a function call from the main program, for example).
F8	Continue (to cursor): The program coding is executed all at once ▶ To the current position of the cursor -or- ▶ To the next set breakpoint -or- ▶ Simply to the end of the program.

When you run through the program with **F8**, you will quickly see that choosing the appropriate breakpoints is essential to checking the program process. You already learned above how to set breakpoints before program execution. The debugger also enables you to set additional breakpoints directly in the debugging screen of the source text simply by double-clicking the mouse to the left of the respective line. Of course, this line should be located prior to the current debugging cursor. Double-click on an existing breakpoint to clear it.

An even easier way to continue is by positioning the cursor: when you set the cursor to a line before the current executable line, the program is only continued to this point when you press **F8**.

> **Note:** If you leave program execution in the debugger idle for several minutes, the SAP system cancels the entire transaction. The corresponding system session returns directly to the main SAP Easy Access menu. This safety mechanism exists primarily to safeguard system performance, as since an active debugger poses a significant drain on resources and may slow down other applications.

Please also note the following: breakpoints that you set in the program coding remain until the end of the current session. Therefore, remember to clear the breakpoints again before you exit (with the STOP icon in the toolbar of the ABAP Editor, Function Builder, and so on). You can also use menu path **Utilities · Breakpoints · Display** to display a list of all current breakpoints and clear them from there.

Step 3: Debugger in the Form

As mentioned above, you can also activate the debugger—with some restrictions—directly in the Form Builder of Smart Forms. The only entry point here is the program node. Although you also maintain the source text in the ABAP Editor here, the function for setting a breakpoint (with the STOP icon, for example) is not present in the user interface here.

Two options for setting a breakpoint are available:

▶ With an ABAP statement
▶ In the Function Builder after searching for the corresponding node

Breakpoint as ABAP statement
The first option is implemented as the ABAP keyword BREAK-POINT, which you can set in any source text line of a program node. The debugger then stops at the defined point.

This is the best method if you plan on using program nodes in form development. In this case, the fact that inserting the statement changes the source code, which requires you to reactivate the form, is something you can live with.

Setting a breakpoint in the node
If you choose the method with the Function Builder (option two above), you are independent of the node type. Therefore, you can also check the process flow during the processing of a text node, for example. Several tips for using this procedure appear below.

Every node in the form is implemented as an individual subroutine (FORM routine) in the generated function module, and each subroutine also contains the name of the corresponding node. In turn, all of these FORM routines can be grouped together in an include program.

> **Background:** The *include* term at this point has nothing to do with including SAPscript texts. In this context, it describes a specific program type that groups together the routines that will be included in other programs. Therefore, only the terminology is the same.

As with the corresponding function module, the name of the include program is assigned at random.

Example of node search
You can use the full-text search in the Function Builder to find the generated subroutine in a node. Assume that the node you are looking for is called INFO_TEXT:

▶ Select the function module via menu path **Form · Test** in the Form Builder and then open the Function Builder in display mode.

▶ Choose menu path **Edit · Search/Replace** to call the extended full-text search from the development environment (also see the notes in Section 13.7.2 on searching in the ABAP Editor). The **Global** attribute in the main program is important: it ensures that the assigned include programs are included in the search.

The result of this search operation is a list of all entries found for the defined text (but with only one found location). Double-click on an item to go directly to the corresponding point in the source text (see Listing 13.2).

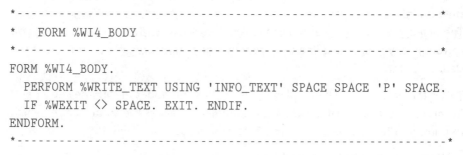

```
*----------------------------------------------------------------*
*    FORM %WI4_BODY
*----------------------------------------------------------------*
FORM %WI4_BODY.
  PERFORM %WRITE_TEXT USING 'INFO_TEXT' SPACE SPACE 'P' SPACE.
  IF %WEXIT <> SPACE. EXIT. ENDIF.
ENDFORM.
*----------------------------------------------------------------*
```

Listing 13.2 Text node in the function module for a form

Because a text node is involved in this case, the central FORM routine WRITE_TEXT is called. If you set a breakpoint here, you will be able to monitor the corresponding node functions directly.

It is more likely, however, that you will need to monitor program nodes in the debugger. To find the translated program coding, use the name of the node again as the search term.

When long coding sequences are involved, you may want to go directly to a specific point in the program node. In this case, choose a search term such as a local variable or the contents of a comment line, which you can also consider in the search. You can also add a unique comment to serve as a search term. Please note, however, that the function module for the form is not generated again until you activate it, which means that the corresponding search terms may not be contained in the function module until then.

Tip: Unfortunately, the breakpoint is not always set in the desired position in the function module when you find the location with the full-text search. Instead, error message "0000" is output, which is no help at all. In this case, set a temporary breakpoint in the first page of the function module, (even if you don't need it there), and then return to the original position in the program and set the breakpoint as required. The breakpoint should now work properly.

13.7.5 ABAP Dictionary

You already learned about the importance of the ABAP Dictionary and its data types in the discussion of typing variables. Typing enables you to define parameters with identical attributes for the form interface in the form and in the main program. To use this function when developing your own forms, it makes sense to create your own data types if a data type you need is not available.

The ABAP Dictionary is described in more detail here. Form development under Smart Forms involves two major issues:

▶ Which additional information can be retrieved through a data type?

▶ How can you create new data types and change existing ones?

Once again, a specific example is used below to illustrate these activities. In the process, you will take the existing transfer parameters of the form interface and group them together in a common structure.

Note: Of course, you can duplicate the exercise listed below in your own system. Please note, however, that the field names in the form and the main program will then be slightly different, which may cause confusion if you then return to earlier chapters of the book.

Starting the ABAP Dictionary

Start the ABAP Dictionary with menu path **Tools · ABAP Workbench · Development · Dictionary (SE11)**. Only two criteria in the initial screen are really relevant for Smart Forms users:

▶ **Database table**
Contains the descriptions of all transparent database tables in the system; the actual data is stored here.

▶ **Data type**
Contains all the entries in the Dictionary that you can use to define additional data.

Choose database table SBOOK as an example. It contains all the flight bookings that your sample flight invoice is based on. Because this is an original SAP database table, use the display mode; a screen like Figure 13.35 appears.

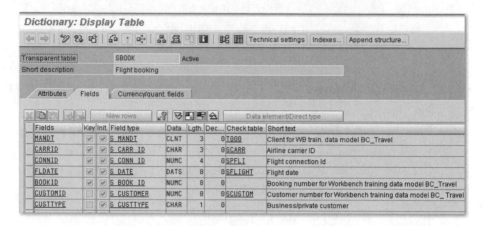

Figure 13.35 ABAP Dictionary processing screen

ABAP Dictionary Processing Screen

The center tab page shows the individual field definitions within database table SBOOK. You should already be familiar with the field names from previous exercises. Comments on the additional attributes:

▶ **Key**
The fields flagged here are key fields, and are therefore essential in uniquely identifying a data record.

▶ **Field type**
The attributes of fields in a database table are characterized using data types, just like in the definition of data in a program or a form. The assignment is defined when you define a new field, and contains a reference to any data type in the ABAP Dictionary. This can involve structures and table types, in addition to field types. When field types are involved, the subsequent fields indicate the length and, where applicable, the number of decimal places.

▶ **Check table**
Often, only certain values are allowed in a field, such as the codes of the defined airlines in your flight invoice. The SAP system monitors these entries automatically when you assign a corresponding check table here. The names of the fields must agree in this case.

You can double-click on an underlined attribute to display additional details for that entry. Now open the **Attributes** tab page. You will see that the current database table is contained in development class BC_DATAMODEL. This information is relevant when you need to find other tables in the flight data model, for example. You can enter the development class as a selection attribute for the value help in the initial screen of the ABAP Dictionary.

Utilities

Two functions are especially helpful for the further analysis of the database table. They are both located in the **Utilities** menu:

▶ **Graphic**
The links, especially those from the check tables, are displayed graphically. Double-click on the icon for a database table to display its structure. Double-click on a link branch to display the fields in the corresponding link.

▶ **Table Contents · Display**
Switches directly to transaction SE16 to display table contents. You can generally also maintain the table contents here.

> **Note:** You may find it helpful to enter test data directly in test maintenance for certain tables. In this case, use the *Create with Template* function of the *Table Entry* menu in the list display of the bookings. Change the fields to meet your requirements. Here, as well, the integrity of the data is ensured by comparing it with higher-level check tables. Please note, however, that a number of special programs that automatically generate a variety of bookings also exists for the flight data model.

Creating a New Data Type

Thus far, you have checked the attributes of an existing database table. You will now switch to the maintenance of data types and create a new one as an example. In this exercise, you will create a new table type that will contain all the individual tables in the existing form interface.

Choose option **Data Type** in the initial screen for the ABAP Dictionary and enter *ZSF_EXAMPLE* as the field contents. You have to observe the naming conventions for the data type. Choose **Create**; you are prompted to enter the subordinate type of the entry:

▶ A data element is the foundation for defining individual fields.

▶ A structure groups together any other data types; you can therefore use it to type field strings. In turn, each individual component of a structure can have any other data type, such as a table type in the example here.

▶ A table type serves as a template for defining database tables or internal tables. The form interface of the flight invoice uses table type TY_BOOKINGS, for example, to type the booking table. You can also display it directly from there.

Choose data type **Structure** in the dialog box to group together all the existing transfer tables; the ABAP Dictionary processing screen appears as in Figure 13.36 below.

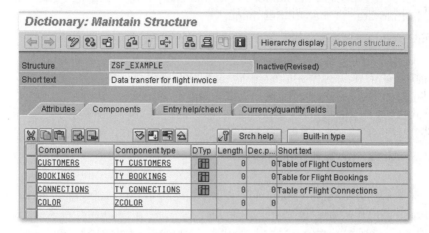

Figure 13.36 Creating a data type

Of course, the input area is still blank when you first create the object. Enter a name and define the three components used for data transfer in the form interface. The system automatically detects that table types are involved and displays the appropriate icons in column **DType**.

You have now implemented most of the requirements for redesigning the interface. Save and activate the new data type. Once again, the system prompts you to enter a development class (enter $TMP for local object).

You can then make other changes to the data type. You will do so to create an additional component, COLOR, below.

Sample Exercise with Individual Component Type

You will see a component in the last line of Figure 13.37, COLOR, which refers to data type ZCOLOR in the Dictionary. This component does not exist there yet. Therefore, the first time you enter this data type in the list, a warning message appears: "ZCOLOR does not exist in an active version".

You can create data type ZCOLOR directly at this point, without having to exit the current entry screen:

▶ Double-click to select the component type.

▶ If you have not done so already, the system saves your entries so far.

▶ You now have to decide, as you did for ZSF_EXAMPLE, which data type will apply to ZCOLOR: data element, structure, or table type. This means you can select a structure, etc., as the new data type.

This enables you to create nested data types of any complexity.

> **Note:** The contents of the later variables are identified by concatenating all these layers (joined with hyphens, like the two-layer data types described above). The mere length of the resulting field names should encourage you to keep the number of layers to a minimum, however.

Back to data type ZCOLOR: choose type **Data Element** in the initial screen. Because this elementary data type cannot contain any other components, a slightly different processing screen appears.

Choose the built-in data type CHAR with a length of four characters, as shown in Figure 13.37 below.

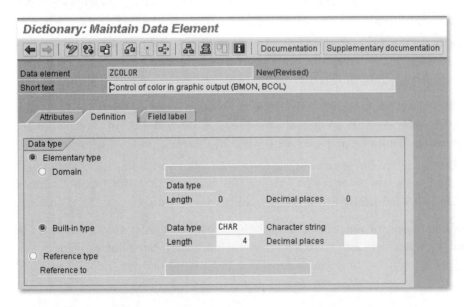

Figure 13.37 ABAP Dictionary: Create data element

> **Note:** The *built-in data types* in the Dictionary correspond to the basic types in the ABAP programming language, which you learned about in Section 6.3 on typing data. Their structures and corresponding codes differ, however (see the defined list in the **F4** help).

Maintain the labels of the field for applications under ABAP in the **Field Labels** tab page (simply enter "Color" in each field). Now save your entries and activate the new data type.

> **Note:** The new component is called COLOR because it is responsible for external color control in the graphics node. Once you have defined it in the form interface, you have to meet two additional prerequisites:
>
> ▶ Enter a variable in the corresponding graphic node of the form, to define the color dynamically.
> ▶ Set the contents to BCOL or BMON (depending on the printer, for example) in the main program.

Of course, the definition with a separate data type, ZCOLOR, was more elaborate than necessary. The entry screen in Figure 13.37 also contains the **Built-In Type** button. When you click this button, DTYPE and the following columns are ready for input, which means you can also set data type CHAR directly.

Effects on the form interface

If you want to use the new variable structure in the form interface, you still have to perform the following steps:

▶ Define a suitable structured variable in the form interface, such as SF_EXAM-PLE TYPE ZSF_EXAMPLE; the previous table definitions are no longer needed. Caution: You have to activate ZSF_EXAMPLE in the Dictionary first.
▶ Extend all the field names in the form with reference to the additional hierarchy level in the interface parameters; for example, CONNECTIONS becomes SF_EXAMPLE-CONNECTIONS.

Define an appropriately structured variable in the main program, supplement the form interface, and assign the data from the previous internal tables.

A Appendix

A.1 Notes in SAPNet (SAP Notes)

Here is a selection of useful notes that are available for Smart Forms (BC-SRV-SCR) in the SAP Service Marketplace. Many of them were already mentioned in the previous chapters.

SAP notes	Subject
430621 412293	Supplied print programs and form templates How do you proceed when no suitable form template is available?
352811	Note on the training example, SF_EXAMPLE_01
134810 359009	Postprocessing
359379	Entering attributes for a spool request
8928	List of current device types in the SAP system
201307 392030	Using TrueType fonts in the SAP system
197177 5196	Printing bar codes in the SAP system
323736 317851	PDF printout with the spool
363531 388271 392002	Language and translation of form texts

Table A.1 Recommended notes for Smart Forms in SAPNet

The SAP Service Marketplace also features a dedicated page with information on Smart Forms (*http://service.sap.com/smartforms*).

A.2 The SAP Flight Data Model

Most of the examples in this book use a sample flight invoice form that is based on the SAP flight data model.

The SAP flight data model is a special SAP module that is used exclusively for training courses and presentations. The flight data model, along with the corresponding database tables, is contained in every customer system. As a result, you can work out all the exercises directly in your own system (but be sure to use a test client, not your production system!).

Overview

The flight data model describes the flight operations of various airlines—with customers, flight schedules, bookings, and so on—in a simple way (see Figure A.1).

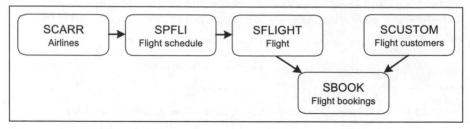

Figure A.1 Flight data model (Simplified)

This section contains information on the flight data model that you may find useful for working out the exercises in the book:

▶ Database table SCARR contains the codes and names of the airlines.

▶ The flight schedule for every airline, along with its flight connections, is saved in table SPFLI.

▶ The specific flight data for each connection—with day, departure time, and so on—is available in table SFLIGHT. This table is only rarely used in the flight invoice exercises.

▶ Bookings can exist for all the flights defined in table SFLIGHT; they are stored in database table SBOOK. The items in the flight invoice are based on these data records.

All the customer data—name, address, and so on—is saved in table SCUSTOM. The number of a customer who booked a flight is also saved in database table SBOOK.

Database Tables with Key Fields

As is usual for storage in database tables, each entry in the individual tables is uniquely identified by its key fields. The contents of these key fields must be known in order to read a specific data record. If all the key fields are not known, the database query returns a list of all the entries that correspond to the specified criteria.

Table A.2 lists the most important database tables and their key fields:

Database table	Description	Key fields
SCURX	Currencies	Currency key
SBUSPART	Business partners	Client, partner
STRAVELAG	Travel agents	Client, travel agent
SCUSTOM	Customers	Client, customer number
SCARR	Airlines	Client, airline
SCOUNTER	Points of sale	Client, airline, point of sale
SPFLI	Flight schedule	Client, airline, connection number
SFLIGHT	Flights	Client, airline, connection number, flight date
SBOOK	Flight bookings	Client, airline, connection number, flight date, booking number, customer number

Table A.2 Tables for the flight data model

Fields of the Database Tables

You can display the fields defined in any database table at any time in the ABAP Dictionary. An overview of the most important table fields that are used in the flight invoice appears below:

Field	Meaning	Remarks
Table: SCUSTOM = Customers		
MANDT	Client	
ID	Customer number	Unique when combined with client
NAME	Name of customer	Line 1 of address
FORM	Form of address for customer	Line 2 of address
STREET	Street of customer	
POSTBOX	PO box	
POSTCODE	ZIP (postal) code	
CITY	City	
COUNTRY	Country	
REGION	Region	

Table A.3 Contents of selected tables in the flight data model

Field	Meaning	Remarks
TELEPHONE	Phone number	
LANGU	Language key	
Table: SCARR = Airlines		
MANDT	Client	
CARRID	Airline code	Unique when combined with client
CARRNAME	Airline name	
CURRCODE	Currency code	
Table: SPFLI = Connections		
MANDT	Client	
CARRID	Airline code	
CONID	Connection code	Unique when combined with client
COUNTRYFR	Departure country code	
CITYFROM	Departure city	
AIRFROM	Departure airport	
COUNTRATO	Arrival country	
CITYTO	Arrival city	
AIRTO	Arrival airport	
FLTIME	Flight time	
DEPTIME	Departure time	
ARRTIME	Arrival time	
Table: SBOOK = Flight bookings		
MANDT	Client	
CARRID	Airline code	
CONNID	Connection code	
FLDATE	Flight date	
BOOKID	Booking number	
CUSTOMID	Customer number	
FORCURAM	Price of booking in foreign currency	Dependent on booking location
FORCURKEY	Foreign currency	

Table A.3 Contents of selected tables in the flight data model (continued)

Field	Meaning	Remarks
LOCCURAM	Price of booking in local currency	
LOCCURKEY	Local currency of the airline	
ORDER_DATE	Order date	

Table A.3 Contents of selected tables in the flight data model (continued)

The flight data model is defined as data model BC_TRAVEL in the SAP system. If necessary, you can display detailed information with the Data Modeler (transaction SD11) in your system.

> **Note:** Special programs that you can use to generate a variety of data records automatically are available for the flight data model. If necessary, contact your company's Basis administrator to start these programs.

A.3   Example Forms for the Flight Invoice

A.3.1   Supplied Sample Forms

The standard SAP installation of Basis Release 4.6C contains three sample forms for Smart Forms, including the corresponding main programs. The forms are all based on the flight data model, and their contents differ only slightly.

Program	Form	Contents
SF_EXAMPLE_01	SF_EXAMPLE_01	Course example
SF_EXAMPLE_02	SF_EXAMPLE_02	Also sorted by airline
SF_EXAMPLE_03	SF_EXAMPLE_03	Additional example from Web Application Server 6.10
SF_XSF_DEMO	SF_XSF_DEMO1	Example of XSF output; also illustrates how a form is controlled by the interface for the function module, and how the output contents are returned to the main program
Sample applications in Web Application Server 6.10 and later		
SF_WEBFORM_01 SF_WEBFORM_02 SF_WEBFORM_03	SF_WEBFORM_01 SF_WEBFORM_02 SF_WEBFORM_03	Examples of use as Web forms
SF_SUBTOTALS	SF_SUBTOTALS	Applies calculations to new table nodes

Table A.4 Sample forms for the flight data model in Smart Forms

A.3.2 Sample Printout for the Flight Invoice (SF_EXAMPLE_01)

The exercises in this book are based on sample form SF_EXAMPLE_01; Figure A.2 shows a printout of the original form.

[IDES Holding AG, Postfach 9998, D-99998 Musterstadt]

SAP AG
Neurottstr. 16
69190 Walldorf

Invoice	
Administrative clerk	Mr Jones
Telephon	(0 69 99) 99-10 99
Telefax	(0 69 99) 99-12 99
Signed	39999 / 1996
Customer number	00000001
Date	14.01.2003

Dear Sir or Madam,

we would appreciate payment of the following invoice as soon as possible. Thank you for placing your confidence in us.

Carr	Line	Flight date	Departure	Price	
AA	0017	03.03.2001	13:30:00	830.70	DEM
AA	0017	03.03.2001	13:30:00	830.70	DEM
AA	0017	20.10.2001	13:30:00	830.70	DEM
AA	0017	20.10.2001	13:30:00	830.70	DEM
AA	0017	12.01.2002	13:30:00	808,699	ITL
AA	0064	06.03.2001	09:00:00	830.70	DEM
AA	0064	10.07.2001	09:00:00	808,699	ITL
AA	0064	10.07.2001	09:00:00	830.70	DEM
AA	0064	15.01.2002	09:00:00	808,699	ITL
AA	0064	15.01.2002	09:00:00	830.70	DEM
Total sum				5,814.90	DEM
				2,426,097	ITL

Yours sincerely
IDES HOLDING AG

16 Travel Street; Foster City, CA 90123. Telephone : 1-800-fly-fast.
Board of Directors : Thomas Schmidt · Sharon Bishop · Chantal Willemin · Sigeruh Takahashi — Incorporated in Delaware.

Figure A.2 Sample printout of flight invoice SF_EXAMPLE_01

A.3.3 Source Texts for the Main Program (Original)

```
*-------------------------------------------------------------------*
* Report SF_EXAMPLE_1
*-------------------------------------------------------------------*
* Printing of documents using Smart Forms
*-------------------------------------------------------------------*
report sf_example_01
data: carr_id type sbook-carrid,
      fm_name type rs38l_fnam.
parameter:      p_custid type scustom-id default 1.
select-options: s_carrid for carr_id     default 'LH' to 'LH'.
parameter:      p_form   type tdsfname   default 'SF_EXAMPLE_
01'.
data: customers   type ty_customers,
      bookings    type ty_bookings,
      connections type ty_connections.
* get data
  select * from scustom into table customers
          where id = p_custid
          order by primary key.
  select * from sbook into table bookings
          where customid = p_custid
          and   carrid   in s_carrid
          order by primary key.
  select * from spfli into table connections
          for all entries in bookings
          where carrid = bookings-carrid
          and   connid = bookings-connid
          order by primary key.
* print data
  call function 'SSF_FUNCTION_MODULE_NAME'
       exporting  formname          = p_form
*                 variant           = ' '
*                 direct_call       = ' '
       importing  fm_name           = fm_name
       exceptions no_form           = 1
                  no_function_module = 2
                  others            = 3.
  if sy-subrc <> 0.
*   error handling
```

```
      message id sy-msgid type sy-msgty number sy-msgno
              with sy-msgv1 sy-msgv2 sy-msgv3 sy-msgv4.
     exit.
   endif.
* now call the generated function module
   call function fm_name
        exporting
*                 archive_index          =
*                 archive_parameters     =
*                 control_parameters     =
*                 mail_appl_obj          =
*                 mail_recipient         =
*                 mail_sender            =
*                 output_options         =
*                 user_settings          = 'X'
                  customers              = customers
                  bookings               = bookings
                  connections            = connections
*       importing document_output_info   =
*                 job_output_info        =
*                 job_output_options     =
        exceptions formatting_error      = 1
                   internal_error        = 2
                   send_error            = 3
                   user_canceled         = 4
                   others                = 5.
   if sy-subrc <> 0.
*    error handling
     message id sy-msgid type sy-msgty number sy-msgno
             with sy-msgv1 sy-msgv2 sy-msgv3 sy-msgv4.
   endif.
*------------------------------------------------------------------*
```

Listing A.1 Original program coding for the main program

A.3.4 Sample Printout of Flight Invoice After Changes

The book contains several exercises that you can work out, based on a copy of the sample form (Z_SF_EXAMPLE_01). Figure A.3 shows a sample printout that contains the most important changes.

** *Flying.Dog* **

Lufthansa	American Airlines	Kuwait Airlines

Mozartstr. 7	Fon(49)3333/4444-0
12345 Newtown	Fax(49)3333/4444-99

Flying Dog, Mozartstr. 7, 12345 Newtown

SAP AG
Neurottstr. 16
69190 Walldorf

Invoice	
Administrative clerk	Mr Jones
Telephon	(0 69 99) 99-10 99
Telefax	(0 69 99) 99-12 99
Signed	39999 / 1996
Customer number	00000001
Date	21.01.2003

Dear Sir or Madam,

we would appreciate payment of the following invoice **as soon as possible**. Thank you for placing your confidence in us.

Carr	Line	Date	Depart.	Price	USD
AA	0017	03.03.2001	13:30:00	830.70 DEM	462.32
AA	0017	03.03.2001	13:30:00	830.70 DEM	462.32
AA	0017	20.10.2001	13:30:00	830.70 DEM	462.32
AA	0017	20.10.2001	13:30:00	830.70 DEM	462.32
AA	0017	12.01.2002	13:30:00	808,699 ITL	462.32
AA	0064	06.03.2001	09:00:00	830.70 DEM	462.32
AA	0064	10.07.2001	09:00:00	808,699 ITL	462.32
AA	0064	10.07.2001	09:00:00	830.70 DEM	462.32
AA	0064	15.01.2002	09:00:00	808,699 ITL	462.32
AA	0064	15.01.2002	09:00:00	830.70 DEM	462.32
Total sum				5,814.90 DEM 2,426,097 ITL	4,623.20

Yours sincerely
Flying.Dog

Figure A.3 Flight invoice after changes in the book

The changes to the form include the table display in the form header. The printout also shows the enhancement for the local currency that you may have implemented in Section 8.6.

A.3.5 Source Text for the Flight Invoice After the Examples

The following source text shows the results of the most important changes that you implemented as a result of the exercises in this book. You made most of the changes in Chapter 9. The additions and changes to the individual lines in the listing each have a comment with a reference to the respective section.

Refer directly to the respective section for more information.

```
*--------------------------------------------------------------------*
*          Report Z_SF_EXAMPLE_1
*--------------------------------------------------------------------*
*          Printing documents using Smart Forms
*--------------------------------------------------------------------*
REPORT z_sf_example_01.
DATA: carr_id TYPE sbook-carrid,
      fm_name TYPE rs381_fnam.
DATA   cust_id            TYPE scustom-id.             "(Ch9.5)
DATA   exemplar           TYPE i.                      "(Ch9.6.4)
DATA   output_options     TYPE ssfcompop.             "(Ch9.6.4)
DATA   control_parameters TYPE ssfctrlop.             "(Ch9.7.3)
DATA   job_output_info    TYPE SSFCRESCL.             "(Ch9.7.5)
SELECT-OPTIONS: s_custid FOR cust_id  DEFAULT 1 TO 1.  "(Ch9.5)
SELECT-OPTIONS: s_carrid FOR carr_id     DEFAULT 'LH' TO 'LH'.
PARAMETER:  p_form   TYPE tdsfname DEFAULT 'Z_SF_EXAMPLE_01'.
PARAMETER:      p_exemp  TYPE i DEFAULT 1.
DATA: customers   TYPE ty_customers,
      bookings    TYPE ty_bookings,
      connections TYPE ty_connections.
* get data
* determine print data
DATA: fieldlist    TYPE tsffields.                     "(Ch9.6.1)
DATA: wa_fieldlist TYPE tdline.                        "(Ch9.6.1)
CALL FUNCTION 'SSF_FIELD_LIST'                         "(Ch9.6.1)
     EXPORTING      formname                 = p_form
     IMPORTING      fieldlist                = fieldlist
     EXCEPTIONS     no_form                  = 1
                    no_function_module       = 2
                    OTHERS                   = 3.
* now with more than one customer
SELECT * FROM scustom INTO TABLE customers             "(Ch9.5)
         WHERE id IN s_custid
```

```abap
              ORDER BY PRIMARY KEY.
SELECT * FROM sbook INTO TABLE bookings                  "(Ch9.5)
         WHERE customid IN s_custid
         AND    carrid   IN s_carrid
         ORDER BY PRIMARY KEY.
* select data only if needed
READ TABLE fieldlist INTO wa_fieldlist                   "(Ch9.6.2)
     WITH KEY table_line = 'CONNECTIONS'.
IF sy-subrc = 0.                                          "(Ch9.6.2)
   SELECT * FROM spfli INTO TABLE connections
            FOR ALL ENTRIES IN bookings
            WHERE carrid = bookings-carrid
            AND    connid = bookings-connid
            ORDER BY PRIMARY KEY.
ENDIF.                                                    "(Ch9.6.2)
* output_parameters
* output_options-tddest = 'LOCL'.                         "(Ch9.7.3)
* control_parameters-no_dialog   = 'X'.                   "(Ch9.7.3)
* control_parameters-preview      = 'X'.                  "(Ch9.7.3)
* control_parameters-getotf      = 'X'.                   "(Ch9.7.5)
* check whether "exemplar" is used in form
READ TABLE fieldlist INTO wa_fieldlist                   "(Ch9.6.4)
     WITH KEY table_line = 'EXEMPLAR'.
IF sy-subrc > 0.                                          "(Ch9.6.4)
   output_options-tdcopies = p_exemp.                    "(Ch9.6.4)
   p_exemp = 1.                                           "(Ch9.6.4)
ENDIF.                                                    "(Ch9.6.4)
* print data
CALL FUNCTION 'SSF_FUNCTION_MODULE_NAME'
     EXPORTING  formname           = p_form
*                variant            = ' '
*                direct_call        = ' '
     IMPORTING  fm_name            = fm_name
     EXCEPTIONS no_form            = 1
                no_function_module = 2
                OTHERS             = 3.
IF sy-subrc <> 0.
*    error handling
   MESSAGE ID sy-msgid TYPE sy-msgty NUMBER sy-msgno
           WITH sy-msgv1 sy-msgv2 sy-msgv3 sy-msgv4.
```

```
        ENDIF.
*       several customers
DATA wa_customer   TYPE scustom.                         "(Ch9.5)
LOOP AT customers INTO wa_customer.                      "(Ch9.5)
*       begin of loop in case copies are needed
        exemplar = 0.                                    "(Ch9.6.4)
        WHILE exemplar < p_exemp.                        "(Ch9.6.4)
*       make sure spool is not closed
        control_parameters-no_open    = 'X'.             "(Ch9.7.3)
        control_parameters-no_close   = 'X'.             "(Ch9.7.3)
        AT FIRST.                                        "(Ch9.7.3)
           control_parameters-no_open  = ' '.            "(Ch9.7.3)
        ENDAT.                                           "(Ch9.7.3)
        AT LAST.                                         "(Ch9.7.3)
           control_parameters-no_close = ' '.            "(Ch9.7.3)
        ENDAT.                                           "(Ch9.7.3)
*       now call the generated function module
           CALL FUNCTION fm_name
                EXPORTING
                     control_parameters = control_parameters  "(Ch9.7.3)
                     output_options     = output_options      "(Ch9.6.4)
                     user_settings      = ' '                 "(Ch9.6.4)
                     customers          = customers
                     bookings           = bookings
                     connections        = connections
                     wa_customer        = wa_customer         "(Ch9.5)
                     exemplar           = exemplar            "(Ch9.6.4)
                IMPORTING
                     job_output_info    = job_output_info     "(Ch9.7.5)
                EXCEPTIONS
                     formatting_error   = 1
                     internal_error     = 2
                     send_error         = 3
                     user_canceled      = 4
                     OTHERS             = 5.
        IF sy-subrc <> 0.
*          error handling
        MESSAGE ID sy-msgid TYPE sy-msgty NUMBER sy-msgno
                WITH sy-msgv1 sy-msgv2 sy-msgv3 sy-msgv4.
        ENDIF.
```

```
* next copy if more than one
    exemplar = exemplar + 1.                              "(Ch9.6.4)
  ENDWHILE.                                               "(Ch9.6.4)
ENDLOOP .                                                 "(Ch9.5)
*-------------------------------------------------------------*
```

Listing A.2 Main program with changes from exercises

A.4 Example of E-mail Dispatch via Smart Forms

A.4.1 Source Text

Section 10.1 contains an example that illustrates the dispatch of Smart Forms via e-mail. The source text for this exercise appears below. If you want to install the example in your system, you can use the existing sample programs in your system as a template. The following section describes the procedure.

```
*-------------------------------------------------------------*
* Call from the main program
Perform  mail_output
  USING  fm_name
         customers
         bookings
         connections .


*-------------------------------------------------------------*
*        FORM MAIL_OUTPUT                                      *
*-------------------------------------------------------------*
*                                                             *
*-------------------------------------------------------------*
FORM     mail_output
  USING  fm_name       TYPE rs381_fnam
         customers     TYPE ty_customers
         bookings      TYPE ty_bookings
         connections   TYPE ty_connections.
***************************************************************
*  Use of communication interface via Smart Forms:    *
*  This report uses a simple example to illustrate how
*  you can also use the functions of the new communication
*  interface in Smart Forms.
*  The example here involves the internal e-mail system.
***************************************************************
  TABLES: soud.
```

```
* PARAMETERS: land LIKE soxfx-rec_state DEFAULT 'DE' OBLIGATORY.
* PARAMETERS: number LIKE soxfx-rec_fax OBLIGATORY.
* Macros for access to BOR
  INCLUDE <cntn01>.
* Data declaration
* * (BOR)
  DATA: sender_id       LIKE swotobjid,
        appl_object_id LIKE swotobjid,
        recipient_id   LIKE swotobjid,
        recipient       TYPE swc_object,
        sender          TYPE swc_object,
        recipient_tab  TYPE swc_object OCCURS 0 WITH HEADER LINE,
        folder          TYPE swc_object,
        BEGIN OF sofmfol_key,
            foldertype   LIKE sofm-foltp,
            folderyear   LIKE sofm-folyr,
            foldernumber LIKE sofm-folno,
            type         LIKE sofm-doctp,
            year         LIKE sofm-docyr,
            number       LIKE sofm-docno,
            forwarder    LIKE soub-usrnam,
        END OF sofmfol_key,
        bor_key         LIKE swotobjid-objkey,
        address_string LIKE soxna-fullname.
* * (SAPscript)
  DATA: header LIKE thead,
        result LIKE itcpp,
        lines LIKE tline OCCURS 0 WITH HEADER LINE,
        otfdata LIKE itcoo OCCURS 0,
        options LIKE itcpo.
* Declaration of a container
  swc_container container.
* Smart Forms (new)
  DATA control_parameters TYPE SSFCTRLOP.
  control_parameters-device = 'MAIL'.
************************************************************************
*            Sender (BOR object ID)                                   *
************************************************************************
* Generate reference to a RECIPIENT object
  swc_create_object sender 'RECIPIENT' space.
```

```
* Clear container
  swc_clear_container container.
* Address (calling internal user)
  swc_set_element container 'AddressString' sy-uname.
* Address type (internal user)
  swc_set_element container 'TypeId' 'B'.
* Call of method RECIPIENT.FindAddress
  swc_call_method sender 'FindAddress' container.
* Output error message for exception
  IF sy-subrc NE 0.
    MESSAGE ID sy-msgid TYPE 'E' NUMBER sy-msgno.
  ENDIF.
* Determine BOR object ID
  swc_object_to_persistent sender sender_id.
**********************************************************************
*              Recipient (BOR object ID)                          *
**********************************************************************
*** 1.1 Create object reference to a RECIPIENT object
SWC_CREATE_OBJECT RECIPIENT 'RECIPIENT' SPACE.
*** 1.2 Write import parameters for method RECIPIENT.CreateAddres
s
***     to container
SWC_CLEAR_CONTAINER CONTAINER.
* Address (current internal user)
SWC_SET_ELEMENT CONTAINER 'AddressString' SY-UNAME.
* Address type (internal user)
SWC_SET_ELEMENT CONTAINER 'TypeId' 'B'.
*** 1.3 Call method RECIPIENT.CreateAddress
SWC_CALL_METHOD RECIPIENT 'CreateAddress' CONTAINER.
* Output error message for exception
IF SY-SUBRC NE 0.
  MESSAGE ID SY-MSGID TYPE 'E' NUMBER SY-MSGNO.
ENDIF.
*** 1.4 Set send attribute "Express" with RECIPIENT.SetExpress
*** 1.4.1 Write import parameters to container
SWC_CLEAR_CONTAINER CONTAINER.
* SendExpress flag
SWC_SET_ELEMENT CONTAINER 'SendExpress' 'X'.
*** 1.4.2 Method call
SWC_CALL_METHOD RECIPIENT 'SetExpress' CONTAINER.
```

```
IF SY-SUBRC NE 0.
* Output error message for exception
  MESSAGE ID SY-MSGID TYPE 'E' NUMBER SY-MSGNO
                 WITH SY-MSGV1 SY-MSGV2 SY-MSGV3 SY-MSGV4.
ENDIF.
**********************************************************************
*            Application object (BOR object ID)
*
**********************************************************************
* Parameter (MAIL_APPL_OBJECT) must be filled with the BOR
* object ID of the application object (i.e., invoice, purchase or
der) from
* which the send operation was initiated. The application object
is
* automatically linked with the document when sent.
* In this example, the BOR ID of the report caller's inbox is
* used as the application object ID.
* Read caller's inbox ID
  SELECT * FROM soud
         WHERE sapnam LIKE sy-uname AND deleted = ' '.
  ENDSELECT .
  IF sy-subrc NE 0.
* User does not have an office => Create it now
    CALL FUNCTION 'SO_USER_AUTOMATIC_INSERT'
         EXPORTING
              sapname       = sy-uname
         EXCEPTIONS
              no_insert     = 1
              sap_name_exist = 2
              x_error       = 3
              OTIIERS       - 4.
    IF sy-subrc NE 0.
*   Office not created: Inbox-ID = SPACE
      CLEAR soud.
    ELSE.
* * Try again: Read caller's inbox ID
  SELECT * FROM soud
         WHERE sapnam LIKE sy-uname AND deleted = ' '.
    ENDSELECT .
    ENDIF.
```

```
     ENDIF.
* Create an application object (here with type SOFMFOL)
   CLEAR sofmfol_key.
   sofmfol_key-type   = 'FOL'.
   sofmfol_key-year   = soud-inbyr.
   sofmfol_key-number = soud-inbno.
   bor_key = sofmfol_key.
   IF NOT bor_key IS INITIAL.
     swc_create_object folder 'SOFMFOL' bor_key.
     IF sy-subrc = 0.
* * Determine BOR object ID
       swc_object_to_persistent folder appl_object_id.
       IF sy-subrc NE 0.
         CLEAR appl_object_id.
       ENDIF.
     ENDIF.
   ELSE .
     CLEAR appl_object_id.
   ENDIF.
****************************************************************
*     Create the text modules, e.g., the text to be faxed  *
* intended for SAPscript, modify for mail under Smart Forms   *
****************************************************************
   REFRESH lines.
   CLEAR lines.
   lines-tdline = 'FAX via SAPscript with Device = MAIL,'.
   APPEND lines.
   CLEAR lines.
   lines-tdformat = '* '.
   lines-tdline = 'e.g. with the new communication interface.'.
   APPEND lines.
* Fill text header for SAPscript
   CLEAR header.
   header-tdobject = 'TEXT'.
   header-tdname   = 'Test fax'.
   header-tdid     = 'ST'.
   header-tdspras  = sy-langu.
   header-tdform   = 'SYSTEM'.
   CLEAR options.
   CONCATENATE 'Send via SAPscript' sy-datum sy-uzeit
```

```
                    INTO options-tdtitle SEPARATED BY space.
**********************************************************************
*     Call of form under Smart Forms                        *
**********************************************************************
* Break down recipient object into "flat" RECIPIENT objects
* using the EXPAND method.
* This breakdown is not really necessary in this example
* (RECIPIENT = exactly one e-mail address). This procedure
* is generally highly recommended, however, and is therefore
* illustrated in this example.
  swc_clear_container container.
  REFRESH recipient_tab.
  swc_call_method recipient 'Expand' container.
  IF sy-subrc NE 0.
    MESSAGE ID sy-msgid TYPE 'E' NUMBER sy-msgno.
  ENDIF.
* Read "Flat" RECIPIENT objects from container
  swc_get_table container 'ResultTable' recipient_tab.
  IF sy-subrc NE 0.
    REFRESH recipient_tab.
  ENDIF.
* Loop over "flat" RECIPIENT object.
  LOOP AT recipient_tab.
* * SAPscript call for each "flat" RECIPIENT object:
* * Determine BOR object ID of handle
    swc_object_to_persistent recipient_tab recipient_id.
* new: Call form under Smart Forms
    CALL FUNCTION fm_name
      EXPORTING
*                 archive_index      =
*                 archive_parameters  -
                  control_parameters  = control_parameters
                  mail_appl_obj       = appl_object_id
                  mail_recipient      = recipient_id
                  mail_sender         = sender_id
*                 output_options      = output_options
*                 user_settings       = space
                  customers           = customers
                  bookings            = bookings
                  connections         = connections
```

```
*        importing   document_output_info =
*                    job_output_info      =
*                    job_output_options   =
         EXCEPTIONS formatting_error      = 1
                    internal_error        = 2
                    send_error            = 3
                    user_canceled         = 4
                    test                  = 5
                    test1                 = 6.
   ENDLOOP.
ENDFORM.
*----------------------------------------------------------------*
```

Listing A.3 E-mail dispatch via Smart Forms

A.4.2 Creating Programs

If you follow the instructions in this section, you will be able to enter the source text with relatively little effort. The program is based on report RSSOKIF2, which uses an example to illustrate e-mail output in SAPscript, and is also available in your system. You can use this example for your requirements here.

Step 1: Copy the Source Code

▶ Use the ABAP Editor (transaction SE38) to open program RSSOKIF2 in display mode.

▶ Now open your existing main program for the flight invoice. Create a new subroutine, MAIL_OUTPUT, at the end of the source code (initially only as a structure; you will add the transfer parameters later).

▶ Copy the entire source text from RSSOKIF2 to your new subroutine. Then delete the first line with the REPORT statement, along with the two subsequent PARAMETERS statements. Use the Pretty Printer to clean up the display.

Step 2: Modify for E-mail Dispatch

When you look at your own source code, you will notice several discrepancies between it and the printout in Listing A.3. The original example in RSSOKIF2 is set up for fax dispatch. This default value is located in the definition of the recipient data. To switch to e-mail dispatch, you can now modify the existing lines for the recipient to the new version.

Help is also available here: another report that is set up for e-mail dispatch, RSSOKIF1, is also available in your system. The only disadvantage is that it doesn't run under SAPscript, which is why the first report is preferable. Perform the following steps:

▶ Because RSSOKIF1 uses the same variables as your previous copy, you can copy the statements for creating the recipient (between recipient and application object) from there. Mark the existing coding as commentary or simply delete it.

▶ Add the call with PERFORM MAIL_OUTPUT at the end of the main section of the existing main program.

▶ Now run an overall syntax check for the program. Make sure no errors are reported.

▶ Start the main program.

The previous Smart Forms form initially appears on the screen. In the next screen, you will see the output from the WRITE statements at the end of the new subroutine. These are still part of the fax output, and no longer belong, but you will remove them in the next step.

When you see this screen, you have already sent an internal e-mail to your own user ID. When you press **F3** to go back, you will see an express message like the one in Figure A.4. The labels here are not correct yet either.

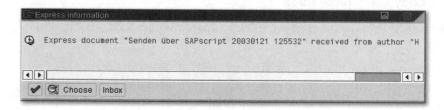

Figure A.4 Express message after first e-mail dispatch

Open your inbox to display the complete contents of the sent form.

Step 3: Call the Form for the Flight Invoice

The last major step is to modify the flight invoice for use under Smart Forms.

▶ First add the transfer parameters for the subroutine to both the program definition and the call.

▶ Change the previous output for the SAPscript form to comment lines, from the first call of OPEN_FORM to the last WRITE statement for log output.

▶ Instead, enter the function module for the form, as a copy from the previous call for print output.

If you test the output of the program now, you will see the same print preview twice in a row. Therefore, you still have to convert the second part to e-mail output.

Step 4: Convert to E-mail Dispatch

▶ Use data type SSFCTRLOP to define control structure CONTROL_PARAME-TERS in the subroutine.

▶ Assign the contents of MAIL to field DEVICE there.

▶ Supplement the form interface as indicated in the source text. Incidentally, the values for the e-mail parameters are contained in the OPEN_FORM call for the SAPscript form.

▶ When you test the form again, you should see only a print preview. Instead, you will see another note, like the one shown in Figure A.5, when you return.

The reference to the express document also contains the name of the function module for the form.

Figure A.5 Express document—received after sending from Smart Forms

A.5   Sample Forms for Automotive

A.5.1   Overview

This section contains three sample forms from the industry solution **Best Practices for mySAP Automotive**. They illustrate several possible design options under Smart Forms.

The forms for the delivery note and the freight order were developed from original forms in the standard SAP system. Therefore, you can compare the examples here with the original versions in your system. No changes were made to the main program, either; any additional data is retrieved directly in the form during output.

The forms contain a number of different output areas, each of which is modeled in windows. Most of the windows contain headings that are defined as text modules in the system. Because these forms already exist under SAPscript, the existing standard texts are used, which ensures that the maintained texts are equivalent under both technologies.

A.5.2 Material Tag in Accordance with VDA 4902 (ChLT Label)

This form was the result of a SAPscript migration. In particular, it illustrates the options for integrating bar codes in Smart Forms.

fehlt

Figure A.6 Box material tag in Best Practices for mySAP Automotive

A.5.3 Delivery Note in Accordance with DIN 4994/4992

The delivery note is characterized by a large number of small output areas. It is formatted using individual windows, along with some templates.

A special feature of this form is how the columns are portrayed in the main window: the corresponding vertical lines are printed in the full height of the main window. Therefore, their lengths are not dependent on the number of delivery items. As a result, you cannot generate these lines with the same output table that is responsible for formatting the items (or with a pattern, either).

The solution to this problem is an additional template that is overlaid upon the MAIN window. An appropriate pattern is defined in this template. This blank template and its margins are output on each new print page; no other text nodes for output have been assigned.

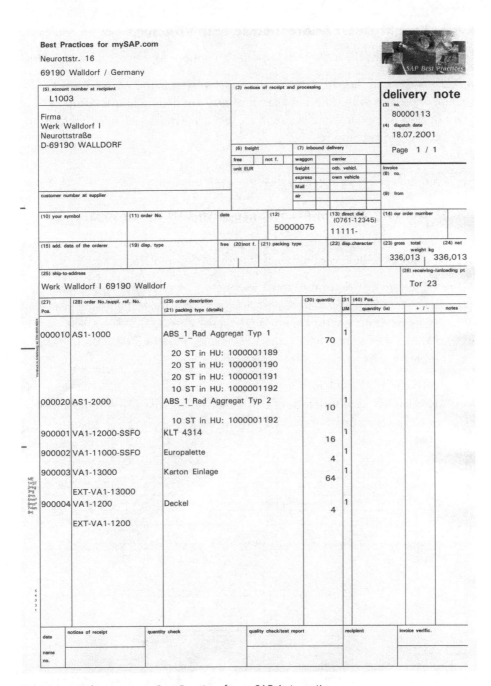

Figure A.7 Delivery note in Best Practices for mySAP Automotive

A.5.4 Freight Order in Accordance with VDA 4992

This form illustrates the individual form design options for boxes and shading that are available in Smart Forms.

Several wide lines with different shades of gray are defined in the form. Each of these borders is implemented in a separate window, which itself does not have any other content to be output.

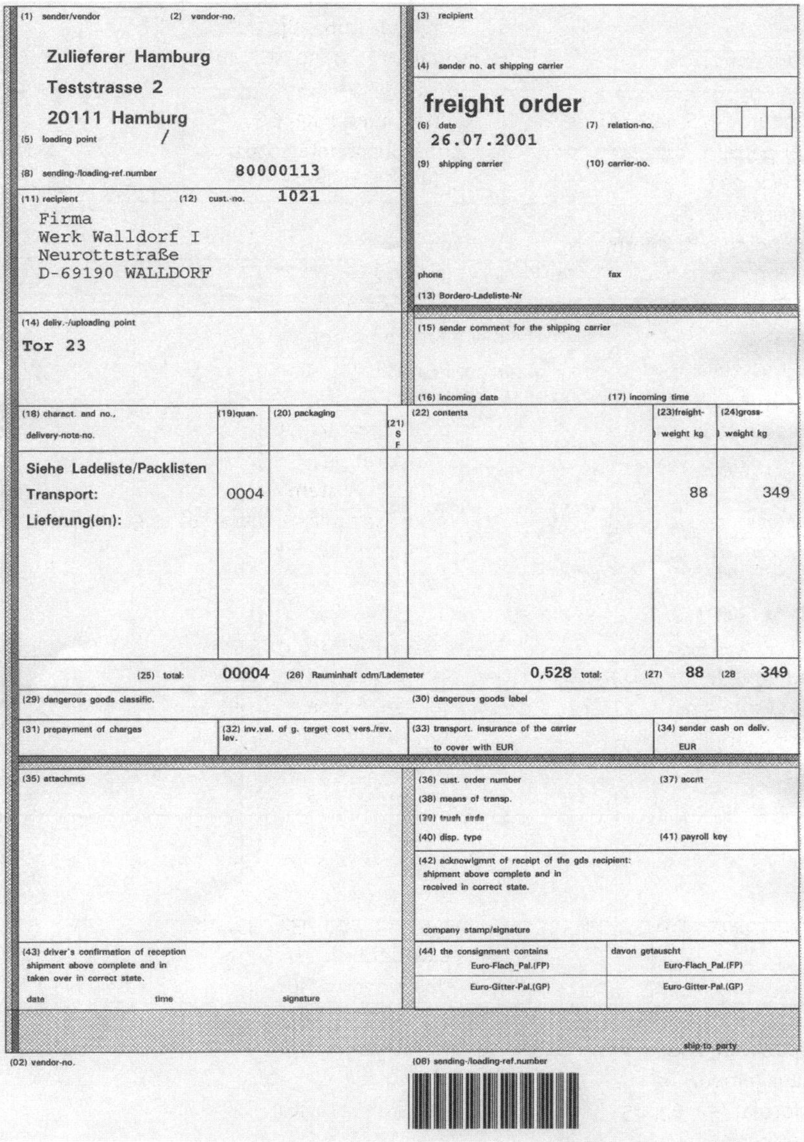
(1) sender/vendor (2) vendor-no.
Zulieferer Hamburg
Teststrasse 2
20111 Hamburg
(5) loading point /
(8) sending-/loading-ref.number 80000113
(11) recipient (12) cust.-no. 1021
Firma
Werk Walldorf I
Neurottstraße
D-69190 WALLDORF
(14) deliv.-/uploading point
Tor 23
(3) recipient
(4) sender no. at shipping carrier
freight order
(6) date (7) relation-no.
26.07.2001
(9) shipping carrier (10) carrier-no.
phone fax
(13) Bordero-Ladeliste-Nr
(15) sender comment for the shipping carrier
(16) incoming date (17) incoming time

(18) charact. and no., delivery-note-no.	(19)quan.	(20) packaging	(21) S F	(22) contents	(23)freight-weight kg	(24)gross-weight kg
Siehe Ladeliste/Packlisten Transport: Lieferung(en):	0004				88	349

(25) total: 00004 (26) Rauminhalt cdm/Lademeter 0,528 total: (27) 88 (28 349
(29) dangerous goods classific. (30) dangerous goods label
(31) prepayment of charges (32) inv.val. of g. target cost vers./rev. lev. (33) transport. insurance of the carrier to cover with EUR (34) sender cash on deliv. EUR
(35) attachmts
(36) cust. order number (37) accnt
(38) means of transp.
(39) trush sude
(40) disp. type (41) payroll key
(42) acknowlgmnt of receipt of the gds recipient: shipment above complete and in received in correct state.
company stamp/signature
(43) driver's confirmation of reception shipment above complete and in taken over in correct state.
date time signature
(44) the consignment contains Euro-Flach_Pal.(FP) Euro-Gitter-Pal.(GP) davon getauscht Euro-Flach_Pal.(FP) Euro-Gitter-Pal.(GP)
ship-to party
(02) vendor-no. (08) sending-/loading-ref.number

Figure A.8 Freight order in Best Practices for mySAP Automotive

Index

All-new edition–Thoroughly revised and significantly extended

Detailed descriptions of all ABAP language elements through Release 6.40

Includes SAP Web AS 6.20 test version on 3 CDs

1216 pp., 2. edition 2005, with 3 CDs, US$ 149,95
ISBN 1-59229-039-6

The Official ABAP Reference

www.sap-press.com

H. Keller

The Official ABAP Reference

Thoroughly revised and significantly extended, this all-new edition of our acclaimed reference, contains complete descriptions of all commands in ABAP and ABAP Objects, Release 6.40.

Not only will you find explanations and examples of all commands, you'll also be able to hit the ground running with key insights and complete reviews of all relevant usage contexts. Fully updated for the current Release 6.40, many topics in this new book have been revised completely. Plus, we've added full coverage of ABAP and XML, which are now described in detail for the very first time. The book comes complete with a test version of the latest Mini-SAP System 6.20!